A History of the Pakistan Army

A History of the Pakistan Army

Wars and Insurrections

Third Edition

Brian Cloughley

OXFORD
UNIVERSITY PRESS

OXFORD

UNIVERSITY PRESS

Great Clarendon Street, Oxford OX2 6DP

Oxford University Press is a department of the University of Oxford.
It furthers the University's objective of excellence in research, scholarship,
and education by publishing worldwide in

Oxford New York

Auckland Cape Town Dar es Salaam Hong Kong Karachi
Kuala Lumpur Madrid Melbourne Mexico City Nairobi
New Delhi Shanghai Taipei Toronto

with offices in

Argentina Austria Brazil Chile Czech Republic France Greece
Guatemala Hungary Italy Japan Poland Portugal Singapore
South Korea Switzerland Turkey Ukraine Vietnam

Oxford is a registered trade mark of Oxford University Press
in the UK and in certain other countries

ISBN 978-0-19-547334-6

Third Edition 2006

Second Impression 2008

Typeset in Times
Printed in Pakistan by
Pixel Grafix, Karachi.
Published by
Ameena Saiyid, Oxford University Press
No. 38, Sector 15, Korangi Industrial Area, PO Box 8214
Karachi-74900, Pakistan.

To
the memory of
HESKY BAIG
(1915–1998)
who was all that a soldier should be
also

To
the memory of
LIEUTENANT GENERAL SHAH RAFI ALAM
son-in-law of Hesky Baig
and

To
TAMEEZ BAIG ALAM
the daughter and wife of honourable men

Contents

List of Maps

Preface to the Third Edition

The third edition has been considerably revised in the light of comments and advice from experts whose opinions I much value. In one instance I had referred to General Zia as having 'left his country in better shape than he had found it eleven years before.' The distinguished academic, Dr Ian Talbot, told me I was talking rubbish. He was quite right, so I have omitted it from this edition, and after more research, altered some observations about Zia in the text.

The description of the 1971 war has been modified to include data and comments by the Hamoodur Rahman Committee whose report was declassified by the government in 2001, and disclosed information about people and incidents that, although suspected, had never been officially acknowledged. Other amendments of fact have been made in the light of correspondence with officers and officials who understandably do not wish to be identified, but want to contribute to accuracy.

The final chapter is entirely new, and covers the years from the coup in 1999 to late 2005. I have made some trenchant observations about the problems affecting the army, and criticized its attitude to civilian governance. There are many reasons for its distrust of politicians, given the chaotic decade between the advent of the Benazir Bhutto government after Zia's death and the coup against Nawaz Sharif, but the fact remains that democracy is preferable to military guidance, no matter how benign that may be. Of course, there are difficulties in moving the country towards democracy, but it is essential that it does move in that direction because, simply stated, soldiers should not rule countries.

The army is an outstanding institution with which I have been associated for over twenty-five years, and I greatly admire it. It is most competent in performing its duty of guarding the sovereignty of Pakistan, but is in danger of alienating the very people who support it because it has become so deeply and sometimes questionably involved in national affairs that are none of its business. As I write in the final chapter 'There is a virus attacking the army, and it is time it was dealt with. As with most viruses, the cure is a large dose of antibiotics, and in this case the best antibiotic would be a stiff dose of democracy mixed with an injection of accountability.'

1 The Beginnings

Pakistan and India have fought on three occasions since Partition in 1947. The first, undeclared, war began almost at once, when the Hindu Maharaja of the predominately Muslim region of Jammu and Kashmir decided his state should accede to India rather than Pakistan. The rights and wrongs of the Kashmir dispute are relevant to the development of the army of Pakistan, and will be mentioned in context. An excellent description of the disagreement is contained in *Kashmir: A Disputed Legacy*. Other references of great value are Manoj Joshi's *The Lost Rebellion*, and Victoria Schofield's *Kashmir in Conflict*.[1]

Division of the Indian Army between Pakistan and India had been planned before Independence, but could begin only a few weeks before sectarian killings increased and Partition gave rise to the problem of Kashmir. The War Department had been split on 19 July and many units had begun the task of moving components to one or other side of the border. Numbers involved were large: the British Indian Army was some 400,000 strong.* It was agreed that the new Indian Army should be allocated 260,000, with the balance going to Pakistan. Command at all levels of the new armies was a difficult matter as, in spite of a programme of 'Indianization' begun twenty-five years before, there were still 13,500 British officers in an officer corps of 22,000.[2]

---

* In 1945, before demobilisation, the Indian Army's strength was 2.5 million—all volunteers.

In spite of the capabilities of Indian (i.e. Indian and Pakistani) officers, they lacked expertise in logistics and the skills associated with managing (as distinct from leading) an army. These had in the main been provided by their British colleagues, although a major force on the civil side was Sir Chandulal Madhavlal Trivedi, Secretary of the War Department in the Government of India from 1942–6. Mountbatten described him as '...the only Indian who has any idea of high level defence organization'. Trivedi was to apply his energy to ensuring India retained large quantities of military *matériel* after Partition.

Pakistan received a fair share of officers, but not enough to fill all vacancies in establishment. The requirement was for about 4,000 of whom half were already serving. The shortfall was made up by retention of five hundred British officers who elected to remain (including the commander-in-chief and his deputy), and the commissioning of the balance from the ranks and, in some instances (in the technical corps), direct from civilian life. There were only fifty-six senior Pakistani officers, ranked from colonel to major-general. Although there were cases of over-rapid promotion and unsuitability, Pakistani and British officers worked hard to establish a basis for expansion, but problems came later when some officers, unwilling to accept the fact that promotion had to depend on competence rather than seniority—or connections and influence—indulged in intrigue.

The British Indian Army had twenty-nine infantry regiments, each having several battalions of up to a thousand men. Pakistan received eight regiments. A similar ratio of apportionment took place in the other fighting arms, with Pakistan being given six of the twenty armoured units and eight of the forty-eight artillery regiments. (Armoured and artillery units are called 'regiments' but do not have a multiplicity of units within the regiment, unlike the infantry with its battalions.) Division on the basis of religion meant that Pakistan received some 30 per cent of soldiers, but the mechanics of the split were complicated.

Many units were mixed in religions, ethnicity, and castes. In a battalion, for example, companies of about 140 men might be Muslim or Hindu or Sikh (see Annex A). A battalion ordered to join the army of Pakistan would retain only its Muslim company or companies and those headquarters' officers and men of the same religion. Naturally the 'Indian Indian' regiments—such as the ethnically defined Jat, Rajput, Sikh, and Dogra Regiments, went to India; and the Baluch and Frontier Force Regiments were allocated to Pakistan. The five regiments wearing the Punjab badge were divided between the countries (as was Punjab itself), with 1st, 8th, 14th, and 15th Punjabis, about twenty-six battalions, going to Pakistan.[3] The transfer was difficult and messy; it ended in sorrow and, in some cases, slaughter— although not of soldier by soldier.

In spite of regimental spirit and genuine emotion, the initial goodwill did not last long. Sikh soldiers leaving their regimental 'family' with tears in their eyes on the way to India from Pakistan were murdered by Pathan tribesmen. Groups of grieving Muslim soldiers were similarly treated by bands of Sikhs and Hindus. It is impossible to calculate the number of deaths at the time of Partition. There may have been half a million people killed, including thousands of disarmed soldiers who had expected—and been promised—safe passage to their homelands from either side of the new border. Creation of the new nations did not have an auspicious beginning. It is not surprising that the distrust engendered by mass slaughter has not entirely disappeared in spite of the passage of time. One example of appalling brutality will suffice to indicate the depth of hatred felt by each side for the other:

> In the flickering light from the bonfire, children, babies, lay on the ground like so many rag dolls, their heads smashed against the wall of a small culvert. For them the night of terror was over, but not for the remaining others...Knocked to the ground while others tore off their flimsy clothing, one after another the women were viciously assaulted...[4]

In the middle of chaos and terror the new armies had to grapple with the problems of creating balanced fighting forces. India received a high proportion of base installations (stores, depots and the like), because most of these were located within India itself. Wrangles took place concerning apportionment of equipment, and Pakistani officers complain to this day about the failure of the former Viceroy (then Governor-General of India), Lord Mountbatten, to ensure the fair division that had been agreed. 170,000 tons of equipment and stores for Pakistan were intended to be despatched in 300 trainloads from India; only three railway wagons arrived, and these contained either obsolete items or rubbish. General Gul Hassan recollects in his *Memoirs* that, 'Some crates even contained prophylactics left over from Early Treatment Centres set up during the Second World War in Burma. A benign gesture on the part of India...'

Allocation of equipment and stores to Pakistan was not the highest priority of the Indian government or of the Governor-General, and there is evidence that obstacles were placed in the way of those attempting resolution of the problem. It was not until 10 October 1947 that the Defence Committee in Delhi agreed that a standing committee should be set up to represent the Government of *India* (emphasis added) in the matter of allocating military assets. Following the meeting the private secretary to the Governor-General, Lt.-Col. (later Lt.-Gen.) Erskine-Crum, drafted a letter 'from yourself to the Supreme Commander [i.e. from Mountbatten to Auchinleck] on the division of moveable assets'. In his covering letter Erskine-Crum wrote, 'I don't think it would be appropriate, at the present stage, to inform the Supreme Commander of the full terms of reference of this Committee. I have therefore confined information as to its functions to 'liaison purposes'.' The letter was sent to Auchinleck without demur by Mountbatten, who therefore concurred that the Supreme Commander, the officer tasked to ensure that the new Dominions were given as good as possible a start in construction of their defence forces, should be told a lie concerning the function of a most important committee.

Negotiations about movement of stores westwards from India continued, but only a tiny fraction of the amount intended for Pakistan was received. Sir George Cunningham, Governor of the North-West Frontier Province, recorded in his diary on 6 October 1947 that '[Messervy, the Commander-in-Chief, Pakistan] told me that the Sikhs [the Sikh irregulars in East Punjab] are getting consignments of Belgian rifles by air and that the Pakistan army is so short of stores (all of them having been snaffled by India) that he is going home in 10 days to try to get more from HMG'. Messervy did fly to London and was successful in obtaining some war-surplus items, but in nothing like the quantities intended to be allocated to Pakistan from the holdings in India.

Field Marshal Auchinleck's protests fell on deaf ears in New Delhi.[5] When he complained directly to Whitehall, his approach was also ignored. The denial of equipment to Pakistan contributed to the rapid souring of relations.

Pakistan was fortunate in having the Army's Staff College in its territory, but there were no defence factories, major communications installations, or officer training establishments. The only technical school in Pakistan was in the West Wing, in Nowshera: the Army Service Corps School, responsible for instruction in the management of supplies and transport. The defence infrastructure in the west of the Indian Raj, in what became West Pakistan, had been based on a requirement to fight the 'little wars' of the British against the warlike tribes of the North-West Frontier (who also enthusiastically contributed soldiers to the Army of the Raj), while that in the east and south had been constructed to support the war against the Japanese.

Political and military leadership in Pakistan devolved upon Mohammad Ali Jinnah (the Quaid-i-Azam or Leader of the Nation), who became Governor-General; Liaquat Ali Khan, the prime minister (and defence minister); and the British commander-in-chief, General Sir Frank Messervy. Mountbatten had let it be known that he wished to serve as Governor-General of both countries, an ambition indicating his insensitivity to Muslim aspirations and his misunderstanding of how Jinnah saw the future. Mountbatten's lack of sympathy for the Muslim religion and personal dislike of Jinnah are well-documented in his own words. In spite of his charm and reputation as a man of the world, Mountbatten could be naïve when describing matters affecting his dignity. The Indians had insisted that independence be declared on an astrologically auspicious day and he was vulnerable on the subject:

> I sat between Miss Jinnah and Begum Liaquat Ali Khan. They both pulled my leg about the midnight ceremonial in Delhi, saying that it was astounding that a responsible government should be guided in such matters by astrologers. I refrained from retorting that the whole Karachi programme had had to change because Jinnah had forgotten that it was Ramazan [the Muslim month of fasting during the day] and he had to change the lunch party he had himself suggested to a dinner party.

This record (in the Viceroy's *Personal Report No. 17*, dated 17 August 1947) is revealing for its equation of superstition with the religion of Islam. But the overall tone had been set in *Personal Report No. 11* of the previous month, in which Mountbatten recounted his failure to convince Jinnah that the British white ensign should be flown by ships of the Pakistan Navy:

> ...and he [Jinnah] regretted he could not allow his ships to fly the white ensign... He was only saved from being struck [by Mountbatten] by the arrival of the other members of the Partition Council at the moment... the only adviser Jinnah listens to is Jinnah... He is suffering from megalomania in its worst form.

It is doubtful if even Mountbatten, a robust man, would have physically attacked the frail Jinnah, but the passage is remarkable for demonstrating his antipathy. His appointment as Governor-General of India made him even less popular in Pakistan than he had hitherto been. Pakistanis were suspicious of Mountbatten, not least because they believed that his activities resulted in the Kashmir problem. He had certainly made it clear that he wished India to be one country after Independence, and as late as 19 April 1947 wrote, 'I have the impression that Mr Liaquat Ali Khan intends to help me find a more reasonable solution than this mad Pakistan.'

Mr Liaquat Ali Khan had no such intention, in spite of being apprehensive about the possible results of Partition, but in any event was not the prime representative in negotiations. Jinnah was President of the Muslim League; Liaquat was General Secretary; neither was prepared to permit a Congress Party government to rule an undivided India. They were convinced this would spell disaster for Muslims. Partition was going to take place whether Mountbatten liked it or not, and eventually he had to accept the fact. His involvement with the commission appointed to determine the countries' borders, however, is somewhat mysterious. His actions following independence were perceived in Pakistan as blatantly pro-Indian.

On 3 June 1947, following his meeting with Indian and Pakistani leaders to present the plan for transfer of power, Mountbatten spoke on All-India Radio giving news of the decision for Partition. He explained that it had not been possible to obtain 'agreement...on any plan that would preserve the unity of India'. Had he left it at that there would not have been recriminations later, but he went on to say, 'there can be no question of coercing any large areas in which one community has a majority to live against their will under a government in which another community has a majority'. This is exactly what happened.

The Disputed Territories

Mountbatten's plan included the formation of two Boundary Commissions to determine the accession of areas of Punjab and Bengal to India and Pakistan. Both commissions were chaired by Sir Cyril Radcliffe, an eminent jurist with no previous experience of the subcontinent. His name had been proposed by Jinnah and was accepted by the Congress Party in spite of Nehru's misgivings.

Radcliffe arrived in New Delhi on 8 July and had five weeks to decide the new national borders. No man could have expected complete success. Being unable to attend meetings of both Commissions, many of which were concurrent, he decided to rely on daily examination of their deliberations in order to reach his conclusions. It was agreed by the Muslim League and the Congress that the decisions were to be final. There was to be no appeal.

Mountbatten used all his charm and eloquence to persuade the rulers of those of the some 500 independent Indian states (the 'Princely States') that after Partition were to lie within the borders of the new India to accede to India rather than attempting to remain independent or acceding to Pakistan. He succeeded, with three exceptions: Hyderabad, Junagadh, and Kashmir. The first two had Muslim rulers but a Hindu majority population; in the latter the situation was the reverse.

The Nawab of Junagadh, near Bombay, declared accession to Pakistan immediately after Partition. The population of his state was some 670,000, of whom only 20 per cent were Muslim, and although the principality was close to Pakistan's border, it was separated from it by Indian territory. Clearly, accession to Pakistan was neither practicable nor logical. The *dewan* or prime minister was Sir Shah Nawaz Bhutto (father of Zulfikar Ali Bhutto, later a leader of Pakistan), who, in consultation with Jinnah, 'had agreed that it was worth trying to wrest wealthy Junagadh from Indian control, especially because it was so close to Mahatma Gandhi's birthplace'.[6] On 8 November, after much negotiation, clouded by Pakistan's machinations, the Nawab fled to Pakistan and Sir Shah Nawaz requested the Indian government to take over the administration of Junagadh 'to save the state from complete administrative breakdown...' (Wolpert [1993]).

In February 1948, a plebiscite was held in the state, and of over 200,000 votes cast, only 99 favoured accession to Pakistan. The affair was minor in itself but is significant for the declaration by Pandit Nehru, India's prime minister, that:

We want an amicable settlement of this issue and we propose, therefore, that whenever there is a dispute in regard to any territory, the matter should be decided by a referendum or plebiscite of the people concerned. We shall accept the result of this referendum whatever it may be as it is our desire that a decision should be made in accordance with the wishes of the people concerned. We invite the Pakistan Government, therefore, to submit the Junagadh issue to a referendum of the people of Junagadh under impartial auspices.[7]

Nehru's tune was to change concerning plebiscites.

Mountbatten's account of the negotiations about the accession of Hyderabad was lengthy, but in essence the problem was that the state lay in the heart of India, and although ruled by a Muslim of ancient lineage, 86 per cent of its population of sixteen million was Hindu. At the time of Partition the Nizam, Osman Ali, decided to opt for neither India nor Pakistan, and it was agreed there should be a 'standstill' to last for a year from 29 November 1947. He was playing for time but there was no real hope that Pakistan would or could come to his aid. Negotiations foundered and Indian troops took over the state on 13 September 1948, two days after the death of Jinnah.

In two of the disputed territories there had been solutions; one involving a plebiscite, the other force of arms. India had succeeded in establishing governance over two areas which it considered, with good reason, to be vital to the integrity of the Union. The problem of Kashmir, although in many ways similar to those of Junagadh and Hyderabad, was not to be solved. It was to lead to war and to tension between the countries that continues to this day.

Kashmir

> *I have reason to believe that when Patel had tried to reason with Nehru [about Nehru's proposed visit to Kashmir] the night before our meeting, Nehru had broken down and wept, explaining that Kashmir meant more to him at the moment than anything else.*
>
> *Viceroy's Personal Report No. 15,* 1 August 1947

> *Who has not heard of the Vale of Cashmere,*
> *With its roses the brightest that earth ever gave,*
> *Its temples, and grottos, and fountains as clear*
> *As the love-lighted eyes that hang over their wave.*
>
> *'Lallah Rookh'* by Thomas Moore

In the 1990s, few roses were cultivated in the Kashmir Valley, in which a separatist uprising began in 1989. Such temples as were not destroyed were rarely used for worship. Grottos became weapons' stores for militants, and no fountains played. There was no love-light in the eyes of either the inhabitants or the Indian security forces; only distrust and even hatred. The lush valley, with its gardens, canals, rivers, and lakes, became a battleground.

India voiced much criticism of Pakistan for allegedly supporting the separatist guerrillas; Pakistan was equally censorious concerning human rights violations against Muslims by Indian soldiers and para-military troops. But the importance of Kashmir goes beyond the misery of its inhabitants: it is the greatest cause of discord and dissension between the two nations. The acrimony between them seems insoluble, in spite of genuine efforts on both sides in 2004–2005 to reach an accord, and they maintain enormous military forces, equipped with nuclear weapons, to counter what they perceive as threats to their sovereignty by the other. In the subcontinent there is a total of two million men prepared to wage war for which the catalyst would almost certainly be Kashmir.

There are two Kashmirs: in the east, the Indian-controlled area which was declared a State of the Union in 1950, and, to its west and north, *Azad* or 'Free' Kashmir, controlled by Pakistan but not treated as an integral province. Maps 1, 2, and 3 show the region divided by the Line of Control adopted following the 1971 war between India and Pakistan. This boundary was mutually agreed, replacing the Cease-fire Line established in 1949.

Outwardly, the dispute appears simple. Unlike Hyderabad, at the time of Partition Kashmir was ruled by a Hindu Maharaja, three-quarters of whose subjects were Muslim.[8] The region is not in the Indian heartland but is contiguous with both India and Pakistan. The state could have been divided between the countries (as was Punjab), but without ethnic or religious difficulties arising, had the Hindu area (Jammu) gone to India and the rest to Pakistan. There is a mountain divide between the regions, with the northern (Muslim) area being more easily accessible from Pakistan and the southern from India. (The only means of land access from India to Indian-administered Kashmir, even fifty years later, is a single-lane tunnel through the mountain range.)

But Maharaja Sir Hari Singh was a vacillator. He could not make up his mind whether to declare accession to India or Pakistan and simply wished to retain as much personal power as possible. He would have preferred his state to be independent (just as, unrealistically, some present-day separatists seek this option), but considered that power and a degree of independence might be more readily forthcoming from India than from Pakistan. In the words of Alastair Lamb, 'The Kashmir dispute... started life as a contest over rights to a *territory*, not the struggle to establish the wishes of a *people*.'

* * *

MAP 1   **PAKISTAN**

MAP 2 **NORTHERN PAKISTAN**

From approximately the line Mardan-Abbotabad-Uri-Srinagar the foothills of the Himalayas begin. The road from Rawalpindi to the north follows the Indus as far as the point where the river turns south, then wends its way to the Khunjerab Pass into China (Xinjiang Province). The road is named the Karakoram Highway, but has only two lanes and is frequently blocked by avalanches. The Khunjerab Pass is open, at most, for the summer six months.

In August 1947, the situation in the subcontinent was as confused militarily as it was politically. Pakistan would have liked nothing more than to have immediately occupied the area of Kashmir under the (loose) control of the Maharaja but was incapable of such action. It had no means of conveying forces to the region, and in any event the military reorganization then taking place made command and control difficult. Matters were complicated by the Commander-in-Chief of the Pakistan Army, General Sir Frank Messervy, being in London. The acting C.-in-C. was also a British officer, Lt.-Gen. Sir Douglas Gracey. Gracey was an honourable man and a fine soldier but, however much he empathized with Pakistan, his loyalties were perforce divided.

Within Kashmir several uprisings took place in the days following Partition. The Poonch District (Map 3) became ungovernable and there were raids across the 'border'—not yet a formal border, courtesy of the Maharaja's tactics of evasion. There were claims and counter-claims about 'invasions' of the region from the Pakistani side. What is certain is that there were numbers of tribesmen from Pakistan (and Afghanistan), motivated by religion, relaxation of the rule of law by the Raj, and intrinsic disposition for mayhem, who descended on the Valley of Kashmir intent on destruction, pillage, and rape.

In 1980, the author had a first-hand account from Sister Priscilla, a nun in Baramula, of the tribals' hideous behaviour thirty-three years before. Matter-of-factly, she told how she and the other seven nuns in St Joseph's Hospital were dealt with. Some were killed at once or died later following appalling indecencies. Sister Priscilla still prays for them—and for the tribals who committed the atrocities throughout the Vale.

> It is now like a dream, of course. I can't remember everything in detail. They were young and old; bearded, some of them, but others just boys. They destroyed all of the medicines, that was the worst part. The rape? I can't remember. I feel sorry for the men. I pray every day for them.

The tribesmen began to move towards Kashmir immediately after news of the Maharaja's indecision about accession became known. Forays were succeeded by invasion. Sir George Cunningham, newly-appointed Governor of the North-West Frontier Province, recorded in his diary[9] on 17 October 1947 that:

[A member of his staff] told me...that there is a real movement in Hazara [a region in north central Pakistan] for a jehad against Kashmir. They have been collecting rifles and making a definite plan of campaign, apparently for seizing the part of the main Jhelum valley above Domel [in western Kashmir]. I have warned everyone I could, including the Afridis and Mohmands, of the danger of taking part in anything like this, in case it leads to war between India and Pakistan. I am not quite sure whether it could be made a *casus belli* at present, as Kashmir has acceded to neither Dominion yet.

Cunningham's warnings were ignored by the tribes, whose blood was up. On 24 October he noted, in a somewhat partisan diary entry (for he was, after all, the servant of Pakistan and disapproved of the Maharaja's action in declaring for India):

The invasion of Kashmir seems to progress. Some of our tribesmen were reported at Garhi yesterday, and seem to be moving up in the Srinagar direction. I think we have about 2000 trans-border tribesmen, a mixed lot (who have gone through surreptitiously by night in small parties) and probably 2000 Hazarawals. There are many thousand more from West Punjab, but probably not so well armed.

Major incursions were reported to Mountbatten by Nehru on the evening of 24 October in New Delhi, causing the former Viceroy, now Governor-General of India, to call a meeting of the Defence Committee next day. Concurrently, in Pakistan, the Governor-General, Mohammad Ali Jinnah, ordered Sir Douglas Gracey to send troops to restore order in Kashmir. As head of state it was his right to do so, but Gracey demurred. He was acting C.-in-C. of Pakistan's forces and thus *de jure* owed loyalty to his Governor-General, but was also subordinate to the Supreme Commander of both countries' forces (Auchinleck, in New Delhi, who in turn was answerable to Mountbatten), and most reluctant to take any action that would range his soldiers against their erstwhile comrades.

There was a story circulating in Kashmir and, naturally, New Delhi, that three battalions of Pakistan's Frontier Force Regiment (the 'Piffers', regular troops) were operating within Kashmir in early October. This unfounded rumour, combined with the activities of the tribals and the Muslim soldiers of the Maharaja of Kashmir's army, who had joined them in killing Hindus and Sikhs, convinced Nehru and Mountbatten that as much of the Indian Army as could be

MAP 3   **NORTHERN AREAS,
KASHMIR AND AKSAI CHIN**

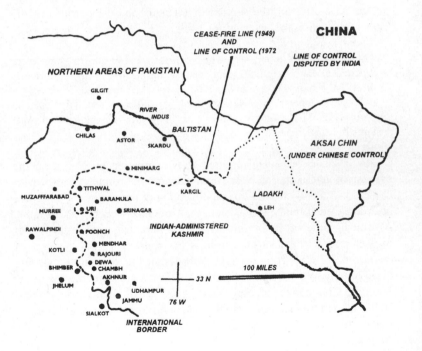

transported by air should be sent to the Valley. The decision was taken during a three-day meeting of the Defence Committee that began on 25 October, and was enforceable (and legal) on the 26th, when the Maharaja declared accession of his state to India. One development was the order to visit Kashmir issued to Mr V. P. Menon, the Secretary of the Ministry of States, on 26 October. He found the Maharaja in 'a state of panic' and returned to Delhi the following day to report that the tribesmen were within three days of arriving in Srinagar—and carrying the Maharaja's offer of accession. In the words of Mountbatten to the King in his *Personal Report* of 7 November: 'It was unquestionable that, if Srinagar was to be saved from pillage by the invading tribesmen, and if the couple of hundred British residents in Kashmir were not to be massacred, Indian troops would have to do the job.' Mountbatten was saying, in effect, that he did not trust Pakistani troops 'to do the job'. Had there been battalions of 'Piffers' in Kashmir, as apparently believed in India, these could easily have been ordered, by either Pakistan or by the Supreme Commander of both forces, to occupy Srinagar. Had they existed and done so, there is little doubt Kashmir would have become *de facto* Pakistani territory in spite of accession by the Maharaja. But Mountbatten had no intention of permitting Pakistani troops to move into the Valley.

Cunningham wrote in his diary on 7 November that 'Messervy came up from [Rawal]pindi for a talk; just back from England. He was in Delhi two days ago and was surprised to find Mountbatten directing the military operations in Kashmir.' The arrival of the Indian Army ended Pakistan's hope that the mainly Muslim territory would become part of Pakistan—unless, of course, a plebiscite was held.

Nehru's acknowledgement of the accession by the Maharaja of his state to India appears ambiguous. While he welcomed it, the wording of his reply to the Maharaja created problems for the future. He wrote that,

> ...my Government have decided to accept the accession of Kashmir State to the Dominion of India. Consistently with their policy that in the case of any State where the issue of accession has been the subject of dispute, the question of accession should be decided in *accordance with the wishes of the people of the State*, [emphasis added] it is my Government's wish that as soon as law and order have been restored in Kashmir and her soil cleared of the invader, the question of the State's accession should be settled by a reference to the people...

First, Nehru said he accepted accession by the Maharaja, but then stated that the wishes of the people should decide the question. No matter what he wrote or said about accession, however, Indian troops began to arrive in Srinagar on 27 October. The first conflict between India and Pakistan was about to begin.

The War of 1947–8

The 1st Battalion of the Sikh Regiment flew from Delhi to Srinagar throughout Monday, 27 October. The move was efficient, using as many civilian and Indian Air Force aircraft as could be obtained. Three companies of the battalion were deployed up the Valley, but the commanding officer, Lt.-Col. Ranjit Rai, was killed. The commander of 161 Brigade, which was to follow-up 1 Sikh, was wounded and the deputy director military intelligence, Colonel L. P. Sen[10] was promoted brigadier and took command. 1 Sikh established a blocking position north of Srinagar that prevented further advance by the tribesmen.

In Pakistan, there was resentment and a feeling of betrayal. Auchinleck flew from New Delhi on 28 October to tell Jinnah that if Pakistani troops were deployed to Kashmir there would be no question of British officers being involved. If there were any attempt to do so he would order their withdrawal from Pakistan's service. There was nothing for Jinnah to do but rescind his order that troops should be sent to defend the territory against Indian forces (which were commanded entirely by Indian officers). But there is a certain amount of disingenuousness detectable in Pakistan's contention that no regular troops were serving in Kashmir. Certainly, the invasion was conducted by tribesmen, but as time went on they were joined and indeed directed by Pakistani officers in civilian guise although referred to by military rank.[11] Many former servicemen who had settled in Kashmir joined in the fighting, as did more from West Pakistan itself. The forces were deemed to be those of *Azad* ('Free') Kashmir, the area of Kashmir in the west of the region that had declared independence from the Maharaja on 24 October. The territory of Azad Kashmir became an independent region under the tutelage of Pakistan but with its own president and government. The Azad Kashmir (AK) Regiment is now part of the Pakistan Army.

According to *Joint Planning Staff Paper (47) 2*, of 12 November 1947, Indian combat forces in the Kashmir valley amounted to eleven infantry battalions (each of about 1,000 soldiers), a light armoured regiment equipped with armoured cars, an artillery mountain regiment with twenty-four light guns, and an eight-gun field battery. Cunningham and others estimate the tribal *lashkars* to have had between fifteen and twenty thousand fighting men at any one time, although a point made by Sir Francis Mudie, Governor of Punjab, was that there were thousands of nomads, *powindahs*, travelling through the territory in the autumn and spring months, as they had done for uncountable years. These peoples, whose main interests were obtaining grazing for their flocks and avoiding confrontation with authority of any kind, were estimated by Mudie as about 50,000, which figure could account for New Delhi's assessment of the number of tribals in Kashmir.[12]

Fighting between the irregulars and the Indian army continued through the winter of 1947–8 with the Indians, reinforced in numbers and equipment, gradually establishing control over the Valley. The fighting was intense and ruthless. In the northern territory of Gilgit, the British commander of the Gilgit Scouts, the 24-year-old Major Brown, saved the Hindu population from slaughter and on 4 November declared accession to Pakistan. Sovereignty of the area had been in contention for many years and, as it was predominantly (Shia) Muslim and patently could not be controlled by the Maharaja or the Indian government, Brown acted to avoid bloodshed and took some personal risk in doing so. The rulers of the enclaves of Hunza and Nagar within the Gilgit Agency also declared accession to Pakistan.

In early 1948, Indian forces pressed west from the Valley. Jinnah's health was becoming worse and he knew his time was short. Kashmir was in the forefront of his mind, and in May he prevailed upon Gracey (who succeeded Messervy as Commander-in-Chief) to send regular troops to Kashmir. The army was by then in better shape and had settled in at the old Northern Command headquarters in Rawalpindi (where it remains to this day in a jumble of buildings, old and new). Although there had been no success in obtaining a fair share of military *matériel* from India, Pakistan managed to acquire supplies from Britain which, with a post-war surplus of equipment, was prepared to provide some to the Dominion.

Fighting between Pakistani regular and irregular forces and the Indian army took place in appalling conditions in difficult terrain. Even in spring, when the Indian army reorganized for the summer campaign, the melting snow created torrents impossible to cross. But in spite of reverses the Indians were gaining the upper hand. By May they had a

division of nine infantry battalions and supporting arms, totalling about
14,000 troops, but the commander, by then Maj.-Gen. Thimayya, asked
for three more brigades. His request was denied. Lt.-Gen. Sen states
that adequate justification was put forward for the extra troops, in that
the ground was mountainous and favoured defence; that it was
necessary to secure lines of communication between the Valley and the
south and within the Valley itself; and that 'the enemy had a numerical
superiority of nearly three to one'. This would put the strength of
Pakistan regular and irregular troops at about 40,000. The Pakistan side
places the figure much lower, but many Indian officials, including
Nehru, stated that there were over 100,000 tribesmen involved. If
Nehru really believed that figure, it is intriguing that he failed to order
reinforcement, as he was involved in all important decisions taken by
the Defence Committee. It may be of consequence that the Indian army
invaded Hyderabad State on 13 September 1948. The requirement to
earmark troops for this operation, together with other tasks, would have
made it difficult to despatch more soldiers to Kashmir. It is clear,
however, that Pakistan had three brigades in Kashmir by May 1948[13]
and that irregulars numbered some 10,000.

An initial approach by Pakistan to India in November 1947
proposing reference of the Kashmir dispute to the United Nations was
regarded with suspicion by Nehru[14] but, after further deliberation by
both sides, complaints and counter-charges were laid before the
Security Council on 1 January 1948.[15] Military developments in that
year made it clear that neither India nor Pakistan could force a
conclusion in Kashmir and that there was danger of full-scale conflict
between the two newly-independent nations. Britain regarded this
possibility with abhorrence and brought as much influence as it could
to bear on the Security Council, which on 3 June 1948 directed a
Commission of Mediation 'to proceed without delay to the areas of
dispute'.

This is not a history of the Kashmir dispute, although, as we shall
see, the problem was and is fundamental to development of the Army
of Pakistan (and that of India). Important as the topic is, it is sufficient
to record at this stage that negotiations throughout 1948 resulted in
agreement that there be a cease-fire on 1 January 1949. The United
Nations Commission for India and Pakistan (UNCIP) then brokered a
Cease-fire Line which existed, with minor amendment following the
1965 war, until the 1971 war, after which a 'Line of Control' was
established. As a result of the cease-fire the countries were placed in a

condition of uneasy peace, but mutual trust was lacking. There was to be no agreement concerning the terms of UN Security Council Resolutions establishing a Plebiscite Commissioner, or on any aspect of holding a plebiscite in Kashmir. The ill-will generated by bloodshed was compounded by exchanges of insults as well as accusations of bad faith. Accession to India of the Muslim state of Kashmir by a Hindu Maharaja created a festering sore in the subcontinent that affected all aspects of their relations and led to further conflict.

NOTES

1. Alastair Lamb, (1992), *Kashmir: A Disputed Legacy, 1846–1990*. Manoj Joshi, (1999), *The Lost Rebellion*. Victoria Schofield (2000), *Kashmir in Conflict*. See also Bibliography.
2. 'Indianization' had been gradual. In the 1920s, ten Indian cadets were selected to be sent to join each intake at the Royal Military Academy Sandhurst. Eight units were selected for Indianization at first, and in 1933 a further eight, plus many non-combat units.
3. Noor-ul-Haq (1993), an excellent Ph.D. thesis on the period.
4. E. W. Robinson-Horley, in Farwell (1989).
5. Auchinleck was a superb soldier who had commanded a battalion of the Punjab Regiment. When I visited the unit in Gilgit (Pakistan) in 1982 I was pleased to see his portrait in the office of the commanding officer.
6. Wolpert (1993).
7. Telegram of the Prime Minister of India, addressed to the Prime Minister of Pakistan, 10 November 1947, which included the statement that: '...We have pointed out to you previously that final decision should be made by means of referendum or plebiscite...'
8. The 1941 Census gave the population as 4,021,616, of which 3,101,247 were Muslims.
9. Cunningham (unpublished: in the Oriental and India Collection of the British Library).
10. A good description of Indian operations in Kashmir in 1947–8 is given in Sen (1969). 'Bogie' Sen was a gallant officer.
11. *Kashmiris Fight for Freedom* by Muhammad Yusuf Saraf (Ferozsons Ltd., Lahore, 1979) cannot be regarded as an unbiased version of events. It was described by Mountbatten in a letter to Saraf of 3 November 1978 as 'an exercise in aspersion and innuendo'. But Saraf makes it clear that Pakistani officers were in positions of command of the irregular forces when he states that, 'On 18th November ... Major (now Lt.-Col.) Khilji MC also arrived and was posted as deputy to Major Aslam.'
12. Mudie (unpublished; Oriental and India Collection) contains an Intelligence estimate dated 23 January 1948 of 'numbers of tribesmen known to have passed through North-West Frontier Province *en route* to Kashmir since October 1947'. The number given is 31,730 (including '3,500 from Afghanistan').

13. Statement of the Pakistan Foreign Minister, Sir Mohammad Zafrullah Khan, to the UNCIP on 8 July 1948.
14. Telegram of the Prime Minister of Pakistan to the Prime Minister of India of 19 November 1947, and reply of 21 November in Hasan (ed.) (1966).
15. Documentation of UN involvement in the Kashmir dispute up to the time of the 1965 war is contained in Lakhanpal (1965) and Hasan (ed.) (1966).

2 Ayub Khan—Adjutant-General to President

There was considerable speculation about the prospects of a Pakistani being appointed Commander-in-Chief at the end of Gracey's term. Gracey would have liked to continue, but the feeling was growing that the army should be commanded by a Pakistani.

Friends Not Masters—a Political Biography
Mohammad Ayub Khan

Friends Not Masters was published only eighteen months before Field Marshal Ayub Khan was deposed as president of Pakistan. He served his country well, but made many mistakes, not the least of which was to go to war with India in 1965. The book's title is not directed at the former colonial power, but was a riposte to President Johnson who, as was common with that volatile man, had at first overwhelmed Ayub with the full Texan treatment and then, when Pakistan appeared less than acquiescent concerning American foreign policy aims, especially regarding Vietnam and relations with China, cooled down to the point of frigidity. When Johnson entered the White House in November 1963, Ayub had been president for five years and was to remain so until March 1969. The story of the Pakistan army in the Fifties and Sixties is essentially that of Ayub Khan, as Commander-in-Chief and as President. His first phase spanned a period of tension with India, expansion of the army and improvement in training and administration, an attempted military *coup*, the war in Korea, Pakistan's involvement with SEATO and CENTO, diminution (but by no means eradication) of British influence, expansion of American ties especially concerning acquisition of defence equipment, and growth of internal corruption and political chicanery.

* * *

When conflict with India over Kashmir died down in late 1948 the Pakistan army had time to take stock of its order of battle and inventories. Much reorganization had taken place concurrent with the fighting, but there was lack of balance between the combat arms and the supporting services. There were many anomalies to be resolved.

Immediately after Partition the army's fighting arms consisted of six cavalry regiments, eight artillery regiments, and eight infantry regiments (Annex A). In 1948–50 two cavalry units were reactivated from the training role (Sam Browne's Cavalry [Frontier Force] and 15th Lancers), and four more multi-battalion infantry regiments were formed (The Bahawalpur Regiment, from that former Princely State; The Pathan Regiment [Frontier Force], recruited in the north-west; The East Bengal Regiment [in what is now Bangladesh]; and the Azad Kashmir Regiment, recruited in its eponymous area). Gradually, the army achieved a structure more appropriate to the conduct of modern war than that required to subdue dissident tribes—although the para-military Frontier Corps, led by officers seconded from the army, continued to keep order along the frontier with Afghanistan. But the main problem was training. There were neither the schools nor the personnel necessary to conduct centralized basic training of recruits, let alone initial and continuation training in technical skills. Almost all training was conducted within units and brigades which pooled their resources to achieve the best results they could in the circumstances. The results were fairly good, but the system was wasteful of experienced manpower at the very time when such men were most needed in units facing '...a powerful, truculent and unscrupulous neighbour'.[1] Bit by bit, school by school, the army built classrooms, gun sheds, tank parks, rifle ranges, kitchens, accommodation, all the plethora of the instructional centre.

The schools of armour and artillery were established at Nowshera on the Grand Trunk Road about thirty miles west of Rawalpindi, where GHQ was being expanded. Nowshera had been the site of the former Sikh Regimental Training Centre, which provided reasonable accommodation, and the large firing range nearby was a further factor in selecting the town. The Engineer School was housed at Risalpur, about five miles north, and the Pakistan Military Academy for the training of officers was built at Kakul near Abbottabad, fifty miles from Rawalpindi: 'Far enough,' as one commandant said to the author, 'to make it difficult for them to get here, but close enough for me to get to them if I really want to.'

Other schools and training establishments followed, year-by-year, but the one aspect of training in which Pakistan was from the start extremely fortunate was that of staff officers. The Staff College at Quetta in Balochistan opened in 1905, and many distinguished officers of the old Indian Army and from other countries attended the college in what was to become Pakistan.[2]

In spite of the hard work that was being done, it became obvious that training lacked standardization. It was easy enough for gunners or cavalrymen to apply their criteria in a uniform manner in technical skills, but quite another thing to apply consistent standards when armour and infantry (for example) had to work together. What was lacking was cohesion in both individual and collective training. It was essential that the army march to one tune and it was not doing so. What was needed was an overall training programme, but it was not until Ayub Khan became Commander-in-Chief in 1951 that this was achieved. Ayub can well be called the father of the Pakistan Army, for it was he who put it on course when it was suffering serious problems.

Mohammad Ayub Khan was born on 14 May 1907 in the village of Rehana, in North West Frontier Province, about fifty miles north of Rawalpindi. His father was a risaldar-major[3] of Hodson's Horse[4] in the British Indian Army but, in spite of this military background, wanted his son to choose a civilian profession. Ayub thought otherwise and opted for Sandhurst, where he went in 1926 with five other cadets from India. (He was selected for an interview with the Commissions Board by General Skeen, the Adjutant General, who visited Aligarh University, where Ayub was studying, on a talent-spotting tour.) He saw active service in Burma in 1945 and at the end of the war became president of the board selecting Indian officers for permanent commissions. During the period of Partition he was a member (as a brigadier) of the force intended to stabilize the border between Indian and Pakistani Punjab. The Boundary Force, as it was called, was a failure and had to be disbanded only two weeks after independence, but the effect on Ayub of serving in it was considerable. He had already made it clear that independence would 'mean freedom from both the British and the Hindus,' and the atrocities during Partition made him less than sympathetic to the new India.

Ayub demonstrated political awareness early in his time as a senior officer. When he was General Officer Commanding the army in the Eastern Wing (what is now Bangladesh) in 1948 he showed willingness to compromise when his authoritarian tendencies conflicted with the rabble-rousing instincts of politicians. After threatening Mohammad Ali Bogra (then in opposition, later a prime minister) with 'are you looking for a bullet?' when Mohammad Ali 'tried to work up the boys' to demonstrate against the government, Ayub made his peace with him when the Chief Minister said the government might fall if Mohammad Ali withdrew the five votes he controlled in the Assembly.[5] This practical approach to politics was to continue until the politicians themselves became incapable of either pragmatism or decision-making, but by that time Ayub was a master of political manoeuvring as well as being a popular and powerful national figure.

It was not only in politics that Ayub showed that he was calm and collected in thought as well as direct in action. He spent less than a year in East Pakistan before he was appointed Adjutant-General, the army's planner and manager of personnel, when he first began to exercise influence on the army's future. The AG is an important appointment in any army; in the newly-formed army of Pakistan it was a crucial one, and Ayub applied energy and some ruthlessness to control the most precious asset of any armed force: manpower.

The change from the well-regulated (perhaps over-regulated) British Indian Army (BIA) to the Army of Pakistan created problems in administration, not least because it was difficult to transform completely such things as the pay code. For one thing, Pakistan did not have the resources of the BIA in either funds or trained administrators. Further, the bureaucratic system created by the British, with its checks, balances, and counterchecks, played into the hands of those given to laziness or manipulation. Civilian bureaucrats seized upon the arts of procrastination and obfuscation and enthusiastically developed them to new levels that are, unfortunately, detectable even now. Ayub's 'arduous battle with the Ministry of Finance' over the pay codes took him seven years to win, but he had greater success in overcoming other problems that were purely military. Some units, according to Ayub, were 'still lacking in *esprit de corps*, thus adding to the general problem of indiscipline,' although it must be said that in such units as Probyn's Horse, commanded by the redoubtable Hesky Baig, neither was *esprit de corps* lacking nor discipline deficient.

Ayub wanted to target the officer corps, in which he detected many cases of indiscipline, but felt that Gracey, still Commander-in-Chief, would not wish to crack down as energetically as he considered necessary. Ayub considered it would be better to bide his time until a

Pakistani officer was appointed Commander-in-Chief before more direct action could be taken and sweeping changes made. He did not have long to wait.

* * *

While the army was struggling with its problems, the country as a whole was in similar circumstances. The prime minister, Liaquat Ali Khan, was a master politician—and an honest one—but was finding life difficult. Coping with the mercenary instincts of feudal landlords who found themselves in positions of national as distinct from local power was not easy. Sections of the bureaucracy were behaving irresponsibly, sometimes in league with the landlords and the growing business class, sometimes favouring one, sometimes the other, but usually with an eye on politicians who might become ascendant. It seemed that the training imparted by the old Indian Civil Service had been forgotten or ignored by some of the new breed. There were many who remained apolitical and gave of their best, but, although they were not in the minority—far from it—it appeared they did not wield as much influence as those who chose to follow the lures of money and the ephemeral esteem of politicians. Pakistan's difficulties were not confined to civil servants who had lost their way and politicians who knew only too well the paths they wanted to tread: in the Eastern Wing there was unrest which had been encouraged by the Indian deputy prime minister, Sardar Patel, in a speech in Calcutta on 14 January 1950. His intemperate urging of Bengali Hindus to 'seek more room for expansion'[6] fanned the flames that had not died down since the region was divided into East Pakistan and West Bengal. War hysteria spread throughout India, and in March units of the Indian army were deployed along the borders with both East and West Pakistan.[7] Pakistan did not want war, and Liaquat Ali, realizing how close hostilities were approaching, suggested to Jawaharlal Nehru, his Indian counterpart, that they meet to discuss the situation. In April, Nehru, courageously ignoring the wild men of Hindu extremism and a pro-war Press, invited Liaquat Ali to New Delhi where they succeeded in reducing tension by signing an agreement protecting the rights of minorities in each other's countries. After more meetings in Karachi and Delhi, it seemed that the new nations could act responsibly in concert to avoid over-dramatizing local disturbances and achieve not only dialogue but understanding and peace. But the goodwill was to last less than a year.

In mid-1951, India again moved forces to menace Lahore, at a time when the Pakistan army was facing problems in what became known as the Rawalpindi Conspiracy.

The subcontinent is well-known for conspiracies, genuine and imaginary, large and small, serious and ridiculous. The Rawalpindi Conspiracy was genuine, small, and serious. The leader of the plotters was a Maj.-Gen. Akbar Khan, a young and apparently popular officer but one who confused his sense of duty with his sense of importance (and who appears later in this story). He enlisted a handful of brigadiers and colonels, and some civilians (eleven officers and three civilians were charged), and the plot to overthrow the government was well advanced when an informant told the police some details, including several names. One of the conspirators was the 'unstable...emotional and impulsive' Brigadier Siddique Khan,[8] who was commanding a brigade at Bannu, south-west of Peshawar. Having denied involvement during an interview with Ayub, Siddique panicked and telephoned another plotter to alert him. The call was intercepted, as might have been expected by all but the most naïve conspirator, and the game was up. The trial was held in Hyderabad prison (as a 'Special Civil Tribunal,' not a court martial, because civilians were also involved) and those found guilty were sentenced to lengthy terms of imprisonment. The sentences were commuted by the government five years later, to the indignation of many officers who considered themselves sullied by the actions of a few disgruntled incompetents.

Ayub took over from Gracey as Commander-in-Chief on 17 January 1951 and was faced almost immediately by the drama of the plot. Although Gracey handed over a going concern, the army was not a cohesive body. It could hardly have been so, given that a proudly nationalist officer corps had a foreigner as Commander-in-Chief. A good foreigner, certainly, who spoke two regional languages and knew his subordinates well. Moreover he was loyal to Pakistan—but he was neither a Pakistani nor a Muslim. The latter deficiency was not too much of a problem: most of the educated and influential Pakistanis were westernised to a degree and inclined to secularism (although perfectly good Muslims), but not being a Pakistani as such had obvious drawbacks. Ayub was Pakistani through and through. He knew his countrymen inside out, including the erratic tribals, and although he was still learning about politics, he sensed what made men tick. He was the right man to sort out the legacy of the Rawalpindi Conspiracy in a way that Gracey, and perhaps some other Pakistani officers, could never have done.

Ayub was brutal. He examined the Military Secretary's records of every senior officer and, if in doubt about someone's competence, he sacked them. Well aware that a barrack-bound army could be a breeding-ground for malcontents, he increased the number of field training exercises, knowing not only that all ranks would benefit from learning and practising their responsibilities and being placed under pressure in their professional duties, but that they would be too busy to indulge in mischief-making. And there was the important matter of the Indian threat which might not, next time, be defused by high-level diplomacy. If India was intent on war, as it seemed, the army would have to be more efficient and better equipped to ensure the defence of Pakistan. The cavalry had six well-disciplined regiments—but only a handful of tanks to field against India's superiority in armour.[9] The Korean war began in June 1950 and Britain, coping with defence commitments there and elsewhere, could not provide much equipment to Pakistan. (It has been stated that Pakistan was prepared to send a brigade of troops to Korea and that the US had offered to equip it,[10] but it is strange that Ayub, then Adjutant-General, did not mention this in his autobiography.) Pakistan supported the UN military action in Korea while India did not (although India sent a Field Ambulance), and although Korea deflected much international attention from the crisis on the Pakistan/India border, the *Manchester Guardian* observed on 19 July 1951 that,

> India has made a deplorable impression by its troop movements against Pakistan, all the more so because of its denials. What has caused India's action? The world has not forgotten Hyderabad.* India complains of recent frontier incidents. But the principal United Nations observer has said these have not been as serious as others in the past. It complains that Sir Zafrullah Khan, the Pakistan Foreign Minister, made a menacing speech against India. But this speech could not by any conceivable interpretation be read as a threat of imminent action by Pakistan... the most plausible explanation is that India is putting itself in an advantageous position before the meeting of the Kashmir constituent assembly.

---

* It had, of course, but the editor was making a point.

Two days later Pakistan protested to the Security Council about Indian troop movements but, apart from the usual exhortations, the Council took no action. There were some 200,000 Indian troops facing about 70,000 Pakistani soldiers along the Punjab border, and two Indian destroyers were in the Gulf of Kutch, south of Karachi. Three brigades were moved from Calcutta and Assam to the frontier with East Pakistan. Indian deployment in the Amritsar area facing Lahore was completed on 11 July, and Pakistani troops began to move towards the border on the 15th. All of these military movements were observed and recorded by foreign correspondents including those of the *Manchester Guardian*, the *Daily Telegraph*, and the *Times*. These newspapers (and the *Observer* and the *New York Herald Tribune*) condemned India's actions. There was much correspondence between the prime ministers during the period of tension, the most noteworthy of which was Liaquat Ali's five-point peace plan of 26 July 1951. This was rejected by Nehru, but the London *Times* commented on 28 July that, 'Mr Liaquat Ali Khan has made a characteristically bold effort to stop the drift towards a collision between India and Pakistan,' and went on to state that the plan contained 'practical and constructive proposals for a comprehensive settlement between the two countries'. A fair endorsement, one might imagine—but not only did Nehru refuse to discuss the plan, he refused to withdraw troops from the border and stated that there were 'compelling reasons to continue precautions'. It seemed that India simply did not want to withdraw its troops, did not want a plebiscite in Kashmir (to which it had agreed), and was not prepared to renounce the use of force or declare it would not attack Pakistan. 'Practical and constructive' the proposals may have been; acceptable to India they were not.

Eventually the confrontation simmered down and the troops drove and paddled away in the September monsoon of 1951*—but the legacy was yet more distrust of India by Pakistan.

India gained confidence on the world stage in the Fifties and took advantage of its new prestige to snub efforts by international statesmen who proposed their 'good offices' to assist in a resolution of differences between the countries, especially over Kashmir. Sir Robert Menzies of Australia, for example, was given short shrift by Nehru, who was drawing closer to the Soviet Union and away from the western democracies whose political systems his country had adopted. Pakistan,

---

* Presumably there were no longer 'compelling reasons' for Indian troops to stay in position, but it has never been explained why they were there in the first place.

too, was a democracy (although more inclined than India to maintain close links with the West), but was about to suffer a harsh blow from which, it can be argued, it never recovered: the assassination of prime minister Liaquat Ali Khan on 16 October 1951.

* * *

Liaquat Ali was a strong man, as had been his mentor, Mohammad Ali Jinnah, whose death was extremely unfortunate for Pakistan. If Jinnah had lived a few more years, it is probable he would have put in place a system of governance that would have served Pakistan well. His ideas for a Constitution were sensible, but Liaquat Ali did not have enough time to hone them and then lay them before the parliament. His death in Rawalpindi halted the process until, after some false starts, a Constitution was eventually produced in March 1956. Not only did Liaquat Ali's murder (by an Afghan, motive unknown, who was killed by the crowd) interrupt the move towards regularizing governance of the country, it had the effect of bringing to prominence some politicians who otherwise would have remained in the background. In *Friends Not Masters* Ayub was scathing about the situation when he returned from London, where he had been at the time of the assassination:

> ...I met several members of the new Cabinet in Karachi—Prime Minister Khawaja Nazimuddin...and others. Not one of them mentioned Liaquat Ali's name, nor did I hear a word of sympathy or regret from any one of them. Governor-General Ghulam Mohammad seemed equally unaware of the fact that the country had lost an eminent and capable Prime Minister... I wondered at how callous, cold-blooded, and selfish people could be...It seemed that every one of them had got himself promoted...It was disgusting and revolting...I got the distinct impression that they were all feeling relieved that the only person who might have kept them under control had disappeared from the scene...

Ayub's political education was progressing. Although he may not have realized that the reactions of Karachi politicians to the death of a strong leader were no different to those that might be expected of politicians of any nationality, his opinion of them dropped even further than its previous low. But it appears he had no thoughts of interfering with civilian government. After all, he had stated as recently as January 1951 that the army should stay out of politics. He quit Karachi (which he had always disliked for its atmosphere of wheeling and dealing) and

returned to GHQ in Rawalpindi, where he embarked on his programme
of reform and reorganization of the army with energy and some
ferocity. He improved conditions of service for 'other ranks' (private
soldiers, non-commissioned officers, and warrant officers) and
introduced welfare benefits for ex-servicemen and their dependants, an
improvement which won him many plaudits. But he was not interested
in approval or disapproval; he wanted an efficient army and knew that
care of the soldiery was a main factor in achieving this. He knew the
importance of being able to maintain decent standards of living—not
only while serving but after retirement.

Ayub's preoccupation was training. He laid down policy, prescribed
an army training cycle, and set objectives to be met by every unit and
formation. He moved around the country visiting his army, especially
while units were conducting exercises. No element was safe from
inspection by the large figure who would descend on them with little
notice. He was firm but fair, as noted by General Gul Hassan Khan
(himself no mean critic of the second-rate):

> He exuded confidence and his presence was inspiring. He was professionally
> competent and consequently he could afford to be exacting in the demands
> he placed upon others. He never hesitated to remove commanders who
> proved inept. This had a salutary effect upon all of us, the more so on those
> who had been catapulted into vertiginous offices merely because of
> accumulation of service... Ayub Khan was never unjust, but he expected
> everyone to pull his weight and he himself possessed that unique quality of
> growing in his job.

Ayub realized that the army had to modernize in every way. The
idea that all army training centres should be able to carry out instruction
in every non-combat 'trade' in the army—cooks, drivers, clerks—was
not cost-effective. Each trade should have a central school, and this
Ayub achieved remarkably quickly. He also stepped into the minefield
of regimental tradition, which has blown up many a career, but Ayub,
although sensitive to regimental pride and tradition, was not prepared
to sacrifice efficiency for the sake of maintaining tradition for tradition's
sake. He wanted to enlarge the Baluch Regiment, reorganize the
plethora of Frontier units, and carry out other reforms, which he did,
gradually and with patience, expecting co-operation and usually
obtaining it. (The Baluch Regiment was expanded by absorbing
8 Punjab and the Bahawalpur Regiment into the existing regiment; the
new Frontier Force Regiment included the FF Rifles and the Pathan

Regiment; and 1,14,15, and 16 Punjabis formed the Punjab Regiment.) Another reorganization took place in 1956, and is described later, but the developments that were to change the direction of the Pakistan army—and of Pakistan—were the introduction of the United States' Military Assistance Program (MAP) in 1954, accession to the South East Asia Treaty Organization (SEATO) later that year, and joining the Baghdad Pact (later the Central Treaty Organization, CENTO) in 1955.

* * *

In May 1954, the United States and Pakistan signed a Mutual Defence Assistance Agreement that had been discussed for over a year. Pakistan's reasons for signing were clear: she wanted more—and more modern—equipment than Britain was prepared to provide, and was not averse to twisting India's tail by demonstrating an independent foreign policy she knew would be anathema to the left-leaning Nehru. But Nehru seized on the negotiations to try to justify his actions—or inaction—concerning Kashmir.

It seemed that the plebiscite agreed between Pakistan and India with the blessing of the United Nations Organization (that would permit the inhabitants of Kashmir to vote for accession to either India or Pakistan) could not be deferred much longer by India. On 20 August 1953, the two leaders (Mohammad Ali Bogra, Ayub's old enemy, was by then prime minister) issued a joint communiqué after a meeting in New Delhi stating that the Kashmir dispute '...should be settled in accordance with the wishes of the people of that State... The most feasible way of ascertaining the wishes of the people was by fair and impartial plebiscite'.[11] But Nehru, a Kashmiri Brahmin,[12] found a way out of his agreement to a plebiscite even before any formal arrangement had been completed between the US and Pakistan. On 21 December 1953, he wrote to Prime Minister Bogra that:

> We, in India, have endeavoured to follow a foreign policy which we feel is not only in the interests of world peace but is particularly indicated for the countries of Asia. That policy is an independent one and of non-alignment with any power bloc. It is clear that the policy which Pakistan intends to pursue is different. It means that Pakistan is tied up in a military sense with the USA and is aligned to that particular group of powers. This produces a qualitative change in the existing situation and, therefore, it affects India-Pakistan relations, and, more especially, the Kashmir problem.

A strange communication. If Pakistan, as a sovereign state, wished to pursue a different foreign policy to that of India it was Pakistan's right to do so. How Pakistan's relationship with the US could 'produce a qualitative change in the existing situation' is not explained, any more than the composition or relevance of 'that particular group of powers'. But Nehru, at least to his own satisfaction and that of his parliament, was off the hook about a plebiscite. Later letters and statements made it clear the issue was dead so far as India was concerned: Kashmir was regarded as Indian territory and would remain so. There were to be no further negotiations if India could help it.[13]

* * *

A team from the US Defense Department, headed by Brig.-Gen. Henry F. Myres, went to Pakistan in March 1954 to examine equipment and training requirements of the three services, and the American Military Assistance Advisory Group-Pakistan (USMAAG-P) arrived in Rawalpindi three months later. The army (and navy and air force) began to enjoy the many benefits of association with the US.

In the next four years the army created an armoured division of two brigades and a further independent armoured brigade, in addition to receiving enough *matériel* to equip seven infantry divisions. Airfields were improved to operate the new F-86 Sabre aircraft; the navy was given some priority, and the ports of Chittagong and Karachi were modernized. Pakistani officers went to the US for technical and staff courses, and there were regular exercises with other nations' forces, including Turkey, Iran, the UK, and the US.

Ayub visited Washington in October 1953 with the prime minister and the foreign minister. President Ghulam Mohammad followed in November, and relations became close at all levels, especially between Ayub and his counterpart. But there was a difficulty: precise interpretation of what was entailed by the military assistance agreement, and exactly what could be expected from the US in the way of political and military support as a result of Pakistan's joining CENTO and SEATO.

America was not a member of the Baghdad Pact/CENTO (although it had major influence on the group) but was a full member of SEATO and, naturally, exercised considerable leverage on its fellow members. The US considered both organizations to be bastions against Soviet expansionism and expected their members' total commitment in that regard. But Pakistan, although wary of the USSR's dabbling in west Asia, did not place the Soviet Union high on its list of security threats. It had only one threat of importance: India. Joining the Baghdad Pact and SEATO, concurrent with signing a military assistance agreement with the US, appeared to Pakistan to present three insurance policies against conflict with a neighbour that was becoming increasingly belligerent while claiming—to the approval of much of the world and especially the Soviet Union—that its intentions were peaceful and its international policy 'non-aligned'.

Pakistan wanted to use CENTO and SEATO as political allies against India, just as it wanted to use American military equipment against India if war broke out. The US had other ideas, and it was on this misunderstanding that the relationship began to founder.

In early 1952, Pakistan received US$10 million in direct economic aid and later that year was granted a US$15 million loan by the Export-Import Bank.[14] These funds were channelled through government committees whose expenditure details were subject to audit by fellow politicians assisted by selected civil servants. Ayub and the army—and the country as a whole—were unaware of what was going on in relation to disbursement of enormous sums. The peculation and corruption of the politicians had not yet intruded to a marked degree on the lives of ordinary citizens.

Pakistan faced possible famine in 1953, and the US acted in a generous fashion. When assistance was requested, President Eisenhower asked Congress to authorize a grant of over a million tons of wheat. The Bill went to Congress on 10 June 1953, and having been approved during two sessions, was signed by the President on the 25th, an amazingly short period in which to obtain Congressional accord. Within twenty-four hours of signature the wheat-laden ship *Anchorage Victory* left Baltimore for Karachi. Later, it was stated by Secretary of State Dulles at a Congressional hearing that: '[Pakistan and the USA are] very friendly to each other, that the people of Pakistan [are] very strong in their Islamic faith which is absolutely opposed, as our faith is, to the view of Soviet Communism which treats man as a mechanical thing to be dealt with on a purely materialistic basis.'

Small wonder Pakistan thought it could do little wrong in the eyes of its new-found supporter. Nehru was anathema to many members of the US Administration and Congress, and was distrusted to the point that President Truman directed his ambassador to India, Chester Bowles, to 'find out if that fellow Nehru is a communist at heart'.[15] But

Ayub and his fellow officers were straightforward, open, hearty—they might even be Americans. Pakistani politicians had good manners and were not about to rock the anti-Soviet boat. All was well between the US and Pakistan, for the moment.

In 1953, the government of Prime Minister Bogra, the erstwhile rabble-rouser of East Pakistan, attempted to introduce legislation to cut the size of the armed forces but reversed that policy under pressure from the country at large. Strangely, Ayub fails to mention this in his biography, but Mohammad Ali's statement to the effect that he was withdrawing the proposals was carried in the newspaper *Dawn* of 2 September 1953. Certainly it seemed that defence spending was a considerable drain on the country's economy, but Pakistan could not afford to drop its guard against the supposed threat from its large neighbour. American aid, through offset purchases, soft loans, direct grants, and general training assistance, went a considerable way to helping Pakistan to modernize its defence forces, but there was little effect on overall expenditure, as the Table shows:

Defence Expenditure 1947–59

YEAR (APRIL TO MARCH)	EXPENDITURE (MILLIONS OF RUPEES)	PERCENTAGE OF TOTAL GOVERNMENT EXPENDITURE
1947–8	236.0	65.16 (Aug-Mar)
1948–9	461.5	71.32
1949–50	625.4	73.06
1950–51	649.9	51.32
1951–2	792.4	54.96
1952–3	725.7	56.68
1953–4	633.2	58.70
1954–5	640.5	57.50
1955–6	917.5	64.00
1956–7	800.9	60.10
1957–8	854.2	56.10
1958–9	996.6	50.90 (9 months)

Source: Rizvi (ed.) (1986).

The army grew more confident and proficient as new equipment arrived and training doctrine evolved. Schools of instruction expanded and standards improved. Ayub's concentration on training paid dividends but there were some flies in the ointment. His personal approach to running the army meant that he took more interest than would be usual in officer appointments. Certainly, as Commander-in-

Chief he was required to approve or reject recommendations for officers considered for promotion and appointment to senior positions, but his attention to officers' characters and performance contributed to the placing of 'Ayub Men' in important appointments.

Ayub had three extensions as Commander-in-Chief and spent a total of almost eight years in the post. Eight years as Commander-in-Chief of a new army would be heady stuff for anyone, and although he worked wonders in reorganizing the army and creating an efficient fighting force, it was too long to spend at the helm.

Ayub's advice to his army to stay out of politics was appropriate but he did not abide by it himself. After dissolution of the parliament (the Constituent Assembly) on 24 October 1954, Ayub was asked by the Governor-General, Ghulam Mohammad, to be a member of the new cabinet. His political destiny, and that of Pakistan, was sealed by his acceptance. He justified his action in his biography by stating that, 'The one consideration that made me accept this offer was that I wanted to act as a buffer between the politicians and the armed forces,' but there was more to it than that. Ayub despised most politicians for their lack of dedication to Pakistan and their constant seeking after power for its own sake. He was becoming aware of some of the corruption that had been taking place and was also aware of—and worried by—the lack of direction demonstrated by the government, but Mohammad Ali was to continue as prime minister in the cabinet in which Ayub was prepared to serve. There were doubts about the mental condition of the Governor-General, whose behaviour had become erratic. Ghulam Mohammad's dismissal of the Constituent Assembly in 1954 was a blow to Pakistan's faltering democracy and created a crisis where probably none would have emerged but for his intemperate action. Ayub wanted to provide national direction as well as lead the army. It is open to question, however, if he should have remained Commander-in-Chief in addition to being a member of the cabinet as defence minister.

There was a peculiar ordinance in Pakistan known as the Public and Representative Offices (Disqualification) Act, or PRODA. Enacted in 1949 with the best of motives, PRODA provided for dismissal and disbarment from public office of anyone found guilty of misconduct while holding such office. It was an admirable Act in some ways, but it could be used by governors of a province or the Governor-General himself, without reference to parliament, to destroy anyone who failed to conduct themselves in a manner approved by them. Certainly, an alleged offence would be referred to a 'special tribunal' which, from the evidence of the seven cases referred to it in the five years of its existence, appears to have been fair—but the system was ripe for abuse, and abused it was, to the hilt, as charges could be brought against an individual by any five persons who were prepared to lodge 5,000 rupees with the tribunal. The inconvenience to an individual who had allegations made against him was immense; thus the threat of a PRODA charge was generally enough to make targets toe whatever, political line might be demanded by potential accusers. Ghulam Mohammad used it, as did the government itself, but in 1954 the government decided to rush a bill through the Constituent Assembly to repeal the Act and thus reduce the Governor-General's powers. It might be imagined that this was laudable, but the motives behind the move were far from honourable, although perhaps understandable. The government thought the Governor-General was about to act against it through PRODA and wanted to pre-empt him. But Ghulam Mohammad dissolved the Assembly before it could curtail his powers. The result of Ghulam Mohammad's action was an undeclared but effective suspension of the democratic system. He not only appointed the new cabinet but presided over its meetings—which behaviour prompted a commentator in the London *Times* to write that the arrangement reminded him of the Viceroy's Executive Council before Partition.[16] Ayub was appointed minister of defence, and a former member of the old Indian Civil Service, who had been defence secretary, then governor of East Pakistan, Iskander Mirza, was given the interior ministry. The military, serving and retired, were becoming involved in the governance of Pakistan, but it seemed there were few other reasonable choices: the politicians were almost to a man corrupt, and Ghulam Mohammad, teetering on the verge of instability as he was, had enough sense—or instinct for survival—to make use of those he considered loyal to Pakistan.

* * *

Ayub's reforms and introduction of modern procedures—and his sometimes swashbuckling attitude to rules and regulations—gradually forged a well-trained fighting force, but he did not object to the army being employed in support of the civilian administration. The military commanders in East Pakistan had permission to be generous with the army's time and resources when, as so often, the region was struck by cyclones and floods. In West Pakistan, the army contributed to the defeat of locust invasions, and was used to deal with food shortages and smuggling on several occasions. It was also called upon to put down riots in Karachi and Dhaka, but the most important instance of support was the actual conduct of civil administration in Punjab in 1953. The gap between providing assistance to the civil authorities in the course of natural emergencies and 'aid to the civil power' in a quasi-police role was being narrowed, and the Punjab religious emergency of 1953 involving the Ahmadiya sect and martial law was to have far-reaching consequences for the country.

* * *

It is the responsibility of the civil authorities to preserve and restore law and order. The role of the Armed Forces is essentially, and limited to, one of assistance.

Aid to the Civil Power
(UK Military Handbook in use in Pakistan)

The sect known as the Ahmadiya or Ahmadis (which eventually split into two: the Qadianis and the Lahorites) was formed in Punjab by Mirza Ghulam Ahmed in the late nineteenth century. Its founder is held to be an apostate by many conventional Muslims and its adherents have been (and continue to be) subjected to suspicion and sometimes persecution. Their unpopularity is in no way diminished by the fact that many members of the sect were and are successful in commerce and the professions.

In early 1953, mobs menaced the Ahmadis in Punjab and a grave internal security problem developed. Two main religious parties, the Ahrar-e-Islam and the Jama'at-i-Islami, demanded that Ahmadis be officially declared non-Muslims by the government, which refused. The ensuing riots in Lahore and elsewhere caused the deaths of at least 300 Ahmadis and the army had to be called out to restore order when the Punjab government displayed lack of will to deal with the problem. Martial Law was imposed in Lahore on 6 March and the local military commander, Maj.-Gen. Azam Khan, was appointed Chief Martial Law Administrator. He divided the city into six sectors, gave each sector commander powers to restore order, and brought the situation under control in a few hours. Those suspected of committing crimes were arrested, irrespective of religious adherence, and brought to trial swiftly. Lahore returned to normal in two days.

All would have been well had matters rested there. An awkward situation had been dealt with quickly and competently, and the army could have rested on its laurels and gone home within the week, confident that the mob had had a taste of what would happen if they tried it on again. Unfortunately—although from the best of motives— the army remained in control for over two months. Azam Khan considered he might as well make a thorough job of things while he was at it, and introduced the 'Cleaner Lahore Campaign', in which the city was given a face-lift of no mean proportions. Squads of labourers widened streets, picked up litter, cleaned drains, painted public buildings, and spruced up the parks. The army supervised them and got on with administrative tasks within and around the city, whose inhabitants were suitably grateful. The soldiers were withdrawn on 14 May, and two days later *Dawn* newspaper commented that, '...Memories of the army rule in Lahore will linger for a long time to come and the new look that Lahore has acquired and the sense of discipline among its people inculcated by the Army will bear eloquent testimony to the good work done by Maj.-Gen. Azam Khan and his men.' Dr Rizvi states in *The Military and Politics in Pakistan* that the performance of the duties of the civil government 'created an impression in the minds of the public that the army could restore peace and effective government when all other devices had failed'. This was true, but it was not only in the minds of the public that the thought of instant law and order was implanted. The army was becoming aware that many of the country's politicians were weak vacillators until it came to the important matters of amassing personal wealth and establishing a sycophantic power-base. Hard decisions were being avoided by the central government in Karachi just as they had been by Punjab's Provincial Government, and the soldiers took note of the ease with which they had solved Punjab's problems. If Punjab could be sorted out in a few days—why not the whole country if that were to be required?

The army had more to think about than running Pakistan, however, and Ayub's energy and innovations kept units and formations busy honing their skills while the schools produced better-qualified tank crews, artillerymen, platoon commanders, technicians, and tradesmen in ever-increasing numbers, year by year. It was a good time to be in the army: all ranks worked hard and played hard; in general, they had good equipment;[17] and their C.-in-C. was not only a fine leader and an inspiration, he was becoming a power in the land. The army had the respect of the population at large; it had a powerful ally (as it perceived) in the United States; and its words were given attention during conferences of CENTO and SEATO in Ankara and London and Bangkok and Melbourne and Paris. Above all, it had that one substantial, concrete, *raison d'être* envied by so many armies—an enemy.

* * *

India was building its defence forces, and at a greater rate than Pakistan. Its defence spending was from two to three times that of Pakistan in spite of being much less in terms of percentage of government expenditure and cost per head of population—both of which comparisons are employed to this day by some commentators to 'prove' that Pakistan spends more on defence than India. The facts, of course, speak for themselves, but the Pakistan Army was nonetheless not displeased that India presented itself aggressively. But Pakistan had defence problems elsewhere. The Afghan border was disturbed (the region had never been quiet), and the tribes indulged in mayhem whenever they thought they could get away with it. Worse still, the government of Afghanistan was strongly opposed to the inclusion of Pathan territory within Pakistan. It considered all Pathan peoples to be Afghan and was prepared to espouse the cause of those forced (as they considered it) to live in Pakistan.

The problem for Pakistan was not so much Afghanistan's statement* that US military aid to Pakistan would result in subjugation of the 'freedom-seeking people of Pakhtunistan' (the name given by Afghanistan to the border region in which most Pathan, or Pushtun, tribes live),[18] it was the visit to Kabul in December 1955 by Bulganin and Khrushchev, during which they declared that they sympathized 'with Afghanistan's policy on the Pushtunistan [Pakhtunistan] issue'. In the next five years the USSR gave over US$300 million in aid to Afghanistan, including construction of military airfields and other military assistance. This did not escape the notice of the US, which initiated even closer military co-operation with Pakistan because the country was being threatened (they thought), even at one remove, by the activities of Soviet Russia.[19]

---

* Made in Delhi, which was not entirely diplomatic.

So Pakistan had many problems, both external and internal, but the main worry was that governance was unsatisfactory and verging on the disastrous. Many senior politicians were incompetent and self-seeking, and matters were further complicated when the Governor-General, Ghulam Mohammad, had to be replaced when his peculiarities became impossible to ignore. Iskander Mirza succeeded to the position in September 1955, but government continued to be chaotic. 'The whole situation,' wrote Ayub in his autobiography, 'was becoming curiouser and curiouser.' The Constitution, produced eventually in 1956, was a mishmash of the 1935 India Act, some of the ideas of Mohammad Ali Jinnah (but without the lucidity of their originator), and a smattering of Islamic jurisprudence mixed with Westminster notions. The country ceased to be a Dominion and became 'The Islamic Republic of Pakistan'.

The Constitution was a disaster, confusing what should have been a precise chain of power and limiting the freedom of provincial governments. It was intended that there be a 300-member unicameral National Assembly divided equally between East and West Pakistan, but this depended on the holding of elections which did not take place. The 1955 Constituent Assembly was kept in being.

Prime minister followed prime minister, and the President (for such title was assumed instead of Governor-General in consequence of adoption of the Constitution) followed his private star of grandeur. The British High Commissioner wrote of Iskander Mirza in his memoir of Pakistan that:

> As well as brains and personality, Mirza possessed an impressive physique. As his second wife he had recently taken the beautiful divorced spouse of the Iranian Military Attaché in Karachi. The two of them made a magnificent couple as they stood, radiant and dignified, at the head of the grand staircase at the President's House in Karachi as the Pakistan National Anthem was played; when it was over they walked down to join their guests between the two files of Lancers of the Presidential Bodyguard...[20]

Mirza did not relish democracy. His instincts were far from egalitarian and he had no sympathy for the politicians and their business associates who managed their unsavoury affairs by the flattery and bribery which were becoming an open scandal. He had been unanimously elected President under the new Constitution and could have exercised enormous influence for good. Advice and persuasion— even coercion—could have been his weapons to place the politicians on the paths of decency (if not necessarily rectitude), but he took the easy way out by joining the game of placement, favouritism, and double-dealing, and the country suffered accordingly.

The ill-conceived 'One Unit' scheme of 1955, by which it was intended that West Pakistan should no longer have provincial governments but a central one located in Lahore, had failed; but in spite of the new Constitution the Provinces had little voice in their own administration. The central government provided no leadership, and it is almost impossible to explain the policies of any of the political parties in that period, simply because individuals changed parties—and therefore policies (such as they were)—at will and with amazing regularity. On one matter the politicians in the West Wing were agreed: there must be ascendance over East Pakistan, which had 54 per cent of the population of the country. The machinations involved in ensuring Western dominance were cynical and barely disguised. There is little wonder that the East Wing became thoroughly disenchanted. The politicians had few to blame but themselves for what happened as a result of their opportunism, deals, and intrigues in both parts of the nation.

* * *

The problem of Kashmir had not gone away while the army was building its strength and the politicians were feathering their nests. Some of the threat to Pakistan concerning Kashmir was presented by India, but some came from the failed Pakistan Muslim League. The party had been led first by Jinnah and then by Liaquat Ali, but no leader approaching their stature emerged after their deaths. A solid and respectable political party was hijacked by a coterie of feudal landlords, slick lawyers, third-rate politicians, and a few politicised ex-officers. It collapsed in 1956, but an awkward development was the creation of the so-called Muslim League National Guards, eventually some 60,000 strong, uniformed, armed with rifles, and led by Khan Abdul Qayyum Khan, who was anathema to both the Indian and the Pakistani governments. The Indian White Paper, *Pakistan's War Propaganda Against India*, noted that Abdul Qayyum had stated in the North-West Frontier Assembly that, 'If India was not agreeable to having a free plebiscite, there was no alternative except war and both the Provincial Government and the Pakistan Central Government shall have to respect the wishes of the people of Pakistan.' This was strong stuff and, in spite of being far from being official government policy, gave a fair indication of how some sections of the community felt about Kashmir. By 1958, Qayyum considered he could flex his muscles with impunity, and although Prime Minister Firoz Khan Noon banned the existence of para-military organizations on 20 September, Abdul Qayyum arrived in Karachi three days later to lead thousands of his supporters in defiance of the government. On 28 September, the Working Committee of the Muslim League (which, although fragmented and finished as a political force, retained much of its bureaucratic structure) adopted a Resolution that the government should be removed, 'if need be by extra-constitutional methods'. No government worthy of the name could be presented with such a challenge without meeting it—but the Government of Pakistan appeared incapable of action. Further, Ayub was worried about the pressure being put on some officers by disaffected politicians. The time had come for the Army to act.

* * *

A word for the disruptionists, political opportunists, smugglers, black marketeers, and other such social vermin, sharks, and leeches. The soldiers and the people are sick of the sight of you. So it will be good for yourself to turn a new leaf and begin to behave, otherwise retribution will be swift and sure.

From General Ayub Khan's broadcast to the nation,
8 October 1958.

The government was morally bankrupt and its legality questionable. While arrangements for the military take-over had to be discreet, there was little possibility of the *coup* being betrayed. The Army was entirely behind the actions of its Commander-in-Chief; the civilian population was more than prepared to have the soldiers move in; and those most directly affected in person—the corrupt, venal politicians and their adherents—were too engrossed in their own affairs to realize their time was about to end.

President Iskander Mirza informed the US Ambassador, James Langley, of the coup four days before it took place, and asked for assurance that there would be no problems over recognition of the new regime,[21] but Dennis Kux in his excellent book on US–Pakistan relations[22] notes that the State Department tried to 'head off the coup', although it must be said the terms of Langley's official protest were decidedly meek. The sentiment conveyed to Mirza was that the US hoped the 'interval of restricted rule would be as short as necessary to preserve democracy in Pakistan and to ensure [the] conditions under which free elections, already scheduled, may be held.' This was hardly a puissant threat or a swingeing condemnation.

Mirza said in his broadcast of 7 October 1958 that he had watched with 'deepest anxiety' the conduct of 'adventurers and exploiters'. He acknowledged that the Constitution was unworkable as, 'It is full of dangerous compromises so that Pakistan will disintegrate internally if the inherent malaise is not removed. To rectify them, the country must first be taken to sanity by a peaceful revolution.' So he abrogated the Constitution, abolished political parties, dissolved the National Parliament and Provincial Assemblies, and declared Martial Law:

> Until alternative arrangements are made, Pakistan will come under Martial Law. I hereby appoint General Mohammad Ayub Khan, Commander-in-Chief Pakistan Army, as Chief Martial Law Administrator and place all the Armed Forces of Pakistan under his command.

Mohammad Ayub Khan, the bluff and efficient soldier, Sandhurst graduate, gallant in combat, sagacious in dealing with men, and knowledgeable in his profession, was, at the age of forty-one, on the path to fame and eventual ruin. Had he chosen the harder road of re-establishing a political system that would work by virtue of a new Constitution rather than taking to himself the responsibility of governance, then the future of Pakistan might have been different. But when one considers the ability of Pakistani politicians, over the years, to confound the best intentions of those who sought and would seek to establish and nurture democracy, one wonders.

* * *

Mirza became duplicitous to the point that Ayub could no longer trust him. Although he had appointed Ayub Chief Martial Law Administrator, he did not fully understand what that meant. Or perhaps he did not understand what the CMLA himself was convinced it meant. There could be no meeting of minds. Mirza dabbled in the murky depths of politics and attempted to influence and even dismiss or arrest senior military officers—an offence that Ayub could not condone or forgive.

After he declared Martial Law, Mirza lasted three weeks as President, having, in a last desperate attempt to retain some semblance of power, appointed Ayub prime minister on 24 October. He had to go, but Ayub's justification was intriguing. The Army's legal experts said that as a CMLA had been appointed, the Constitution abrogated, and martial law declared, the position of President was redundant. This was nonsense and Ayub in his autobiography claims he rejected the notion. But Ayub's real reasons for getting rid of Mirza were that he had been an intriguer of mammoth proportions, was untrustworthy, and was unfit to be President of Pakistan. Ayub was right. Pakistan had to have new leadership and it appeared that Ayub was the only man to provide it. On 27 October 1958, General Ayub Khan assumed the Presidency. A new era was to begin for Pakistan. A decade of development, but also of war.

NOTES

1. *Secret Memorandum on India/Pakistan Relations*, 26 June 1949; Mudie (unpublished).
2. *See, Command and Staff College 1905–1980*, edited and compiled by the Command and Staff College, Quetta, Pakistan.
3. A risaldar-major in the British Indian Army was an important figure. His badge of rank was a crown worn on the shoulder, just as a British major, but he was junior to even the most junior British officer—very much in theory.
4. The origins of Hodson's Horse (4th Duke of Cambridge's Own Lancers) are lost in the mists of antiquity and military reorganization. Formed at the time of the Mutiny by William Hodson, the regiment survived amalgamation, expansion, contraction, and fragmentation. *See*, Gaylor (1992): 'Partition allotted Hodson's Horse to India. The Guides Cavalry, bound, logically, for Pakistan, handed over its Dogra Squadron in exchange for Hodson's Punjabi Mussulmans. This left Hodson's with two Dogra Squadrons so they passed on the Guides' Dogras to the Scinde Horse in exchange for the Sikh Squadron which the Scinde Horse had received from Probyn's Horse.' All correct, Sarn't Major?
5. In his masterly biography, *Ayub Khan* (1994), Altaf Gauhar suggests that 'That single incident was enough to convince Ayub that politicians could work on the emotions of the people but that they were utterly lacking in discipline and had no real principles.'
6. *The Annual Register*, London, 1951, p. 119.
7. *The Daily Telegraph*, London, 27 March 1950.
8. M.A. Khan (1967); Rizvi (ed.) (1986).
9. Ayub wrote (*Friends Not Masters*) that in mid-1951 Pakistan had 'only thirteen tanks with about 40-50 hours' engine life in them to face the Indian Army...'
10. Burke and Ziring (1990).
11. Joint Press Communiqué issued at the conclusion of the Indo-Pakistan Prime Ministers' Conference in New Delhi, 20 August 1953. Hasan (ed.) (1966).

12. Brecher (1959): 'He was born into the Kashmiri Brahmin community, one of the most aristocratic sub-castes in the Hindu social system.'
13. Hasan op. cit.
14. Brown (1963).
15. *New York Herald Tribune,* 19 April 1953.
16. Rizvi op. cit.
17. Gul Hassan Khan would disagree: 'The M24 tanks were well past their prime... Likewise the Patton Tanks (M47s), though of a later vintage, appeared far more menacing when arrayed in our tank parks than when taken out on exercises...'
18. *New York Times,* 23 December 1953.
19. The Soviet leaders' tour of India, Burma and Afghanistan in 1955 was described by their own foreign minister, Molotov, as 'adventurism' (William Taubman (2003), *Khrushchev*). At the time the situation along the Durand Line was even more sensitive than usual. In May the Afghan government had ordered mobilisation of its army and was warned by Ayub (as defence minister) that any action against Pakistan would result in forceful reaction, and the following month King Zahir, when opening the National Assembly, stated that Afghanistan supported the idea of an autonomous Pashtunistan. There was a lull in confrontational rhetoric, but in November, immediately before the Soviet duo arrived, several thousand armed Afghan tribesmen crossed the border into Pakistan in a demonstration of solidarity. It came to nothing, but the atmosphere was exceedingly tense when Khrushchev tried to make further mischief.
20. James (1993).
21. On 4 October Langley sent a cable to John Foster Dulles, the Secretary of State, informing him that Mirza had told him of his plan to 'take over the Government of Pakistan probably within a week and simultaneously proclaim martial law.' (Declassified, formerly Top Secret File: Karachi 775-790d.00/10-548, National Archives, Washington, DC)
22. *The United States and Pakistan 1947-2000,* Dennis Kux, Woodrow Wilson Center Press and Johns Hopkins University Press. Kux began his diplomatic career in Karachi in 1957. He states in his foreword that he hopes the book 'will prove useful' to those interested in the topic. For once he chose the wrong word. It should have been 'invaluable.'

3 Preparations for War

The armed forces were genuinely popular. Their past record of protecting Muslim lives and property during the post-Partition massacres and in Kashmir inspired confidence. In general, soldiers were exempted from the resentment which had crystallised against the deposed government. Their reputation for integrity was untainted. The Army, it was widely hoped, would be more responsive to popular aspirations and more effective in improving the standard of living.[1]

A few army units had been deployed in the days before Ayub assumed the presidency on but there was no requirement for them to intervene. Troops secured key buildings including airports, government offices, banks, and communications facilities, but not a shot was fired. The public, rather than objecting to their presence, thoroughly endorsed Ayub's actions, especially as he had been astute enough to keep armoured vehicles off the streets.

Martial Law was administered through the civil bureaucracy, most of whose members had resented imprecise instructions and irregular directives from corrupt politicians as to how to conduct affairs. Many civil servants openly welcomed the army's action, and the more efficient of them served well and had their careers advanced by acceptance of military rule.

World reaction to the take-over by Ayub was measured and reasonable. It had become apparent through diplomatic and press reporting from Pakistan that its government was inefficient and corrupt. Western governments—by and large not corrupt—considered that they should endorse the overthrow of an administration that was unsound and even noxious. Signals of approbation abounded. On 2 November, not a week after Ayub took over the presidency, Baghdad Pact navy manoeuvres (Exercise *Midlink*), began off Karachi, involving ships of Turkey, Iran, Pakistan, the UK, and the US, which demonstrated to the world at large that Ayub's actions met with the approval of their governments. Three days later Dr Erhard, the West German deputy prime minister, visited to offer investment for industrial development. Later, in November, the Canadian prime minister, John Diefenbaker, arrived, closely followed by his Norwegian counterpart, Einar Gerhardsen, who said he felt the new government 'had won the confidence of the people'. Ayub had reason to feel comfortable with his country's position in the world for even Nehru '...told the Lok Sabha in the course of a debate on foreign affairs that he considered the reports of border incidents between India and Pakistan to be greatly exaggerated. He also said that these disputes did not rise on the government level, but were a result of a local clash over petty matters'.[2] The road ahead for Pakistan appeared, if not completely smooth, certainly encouragingly free of major obstacles.

But there were to be problems for Ayub and the army—and for Pakistan. Ayub wanted to 'rehabilitate the civil and constitutional organs of the state,' which was a laudable goal, but he lost sight of his aim, a serious fault in any soldier. Then there was the desire to maintain good relations with America. Prime Minister Noon told the National Assembly on 8 March 1958 that western economic aid was funding India's military expansion and threatened to 'break all pacts in the world and shake hands with those whom we have made our enemies for the sake of others,[3] which went down badly in Washington. In an attempt to improve relations, in May Mirza despatched a team led by the finance minister, Amjad Ali (who had been ambassador to the US), to the US to 'undo the great damage' apparently effected by Noon. Ayub, as Commander-in-Chief, and the Chief of Air Staff, Air Chief Marshal Asghar Khan, were in the delegation.

Ayub received red-carpet treatment during his visit,[4] but his statement two years later that Pakistan could 'do business' with the USSR was regarded with suspicion in Washington, in spite of a July 1961 meeting with President Kennedy. The US–Pakistan relationship seemed to some in Pakistan to be uncertain, and US aid to India increased from its already high level. In his diary Ayub recorded on 3 September 1958 that there was 'Disquieting news of massive economic aid to India by America and other western countries... This will further release India's resources for a reckless military build-up against us thus making our position far more difficult.' (The problem with diaries quoted in autobiographies is that they can be amended in transposition, but it seems that Ayub was genuinely worried about India's agenda as he interpreted it.)

In 1959, however, there was a surge in US activity regarding
Pakistan. In March, identical bilateral defence agreements between the
US and Iran, Turkey and Pakistan were signed in Ankara, and although
it was made clear in the preamble that the treaty was entered into in
the context of 'the Pact of Mutual Cooperation signed at Baghdad on
February 24, 1955,' the wording of the document was such that it
would hearten any national leader who considered there might be an
external threat from whatever direction.[5] The next agreement to be
signed, on 5 March, was to have unforeseen international consequences.
It was innocently named 'The Pakistan–United States Communications
Unit Agreement', and in the coy words of a US public document,[6]
provided 'for the establishment and operation of a communications unit
at Peshawar [including] certain military rights and facilities and a status
of forces agreement.' The 'certain military rights' included use of
Peshawar airfield by U-2 aircraft to overfly the Soviet Union
illegally.

Pakistan wished to assert itself as a sovereign country, but first it
had to sort out the chaos in internal administration. Furthermore, Ayub
had to divorce himself from command of the Army, appoint a tough
successor who would continue his reforms, and become accustomed to
thinking and speaking as a persuader and advocate rather than as a
leader and commander.

He failed on most counts. Although Pakistan did become a player
on the world stage (and many internal problems were solved), and Ayub
relinquished the appointment of army chief, there was a lack of
understanding by Ayub of what made the world go round politically.
And he lost touch with the army.

On 28 October 1958, Ayub appointed General Mohammad Musa
Khan to be Commander-in-Chief of the Pakistan Army. Musa was a
good enough officer. He had never done anything wrong during his
career; yet he had never done anything out of the ordinary. According
to Lt.-Gen. Gul Hassan Khan, who served as Director Military
Operations to Musa for four years, he was 'humane, approachable and
considerate,' but was selected for 'dependability rather than merit'. His
period of command lasted until September 1966, another eight-year
stint; far too long for any officer to stay in such a position.

Ayub was not wholly to blame for Musa's lack of success as
Commander-in-Chief—but he was entirely responsible for his selection.
There was no one senior to Ayub on whom he could call for counsel,
and he was not inclined to accept advice on such matters from

subordinates (tactics, training, different). There were officers of higher calibre than Musa, but Ayub wanted someone who was uncomplicated, and above all, loyal to him. Ayub thought he would lead the army well and would not cause him any problems. In the event, he did not lead the army well, and although he did not cause Ayub any disquiet in the first few years, the build-up of problems stemming from uninspired leadership at the top resulted in failure in the higher direction of war.

* * *

It appears that one of Musa's defects was the desire to do something different just for the sake of it. He abolished the post of Chief of Staff, one of the most important appointments in a senior commander's headquarters. The COS acts as a high-powered filter (and has to be carefully selected lest he take unto himself too much power), and can be of almost inestimable value. Eradication of the position meant that Musa got involved in too much detail and became engrossed, then overwhelmed, by paperwork and minutiae that should never have reached his desk. Even when Lt.-Gen. Bakhtiar Rana became Deputy Commander-in-Chief and Chief of Staff, the value of the appointment had been diminished rather than enhanced.

Not all Musa's difficulties were of his own making. The British Training Advisory Staff had been withdrawn at the end of the period agreed for its loan. This organization had been invaluable to Ayub and his staff officers, who were still relatively inexperienced, especially in the planning of complicated manoeuvres. Being foreigners, the British had no axes to grind and no personal involvement in the army. They could advise and criticize without fear or favour, and they did. Further, they had assisted in the conduct of exercises involving a division's worth of troops and more (a full-strength division at that time had some 17,000 soldiers), and had been of immense value in creating the Directorate of Military Training which replaced it. It was essential that DMT be formed as it was inappropriate that the army should have to rely on foreigners for its training expertise—but the gap was felt, and DMT took a long time to shake out.

One thing DMT did do assiduously was to produce training directives. These were necessary, and, according to officers who served in the army in the early Sixties,[7] well written, cogent, and professionally applicable; the trouble was that the directives were 'fired and forgotten' by being despatched through the chain of command to units without further action by GHQ or other headquarters. There were few checks to ensure the directives were carried out, and the inevitable result was that only rarely were they put into practice in the manner intended by their originators. A malaise was entering the Pakistan army, which had expanded into a considerable force of one armoured and six infantry divisions, an armoured brigade, and two other independent brigades. There was still only a single corps headquarters, and considerable strain was placed on this HQ by the requirement to command such a number of widely-separated formations. Arguments in support of creation of a further corps HQ were put forward but failed to find high-level support. One problem was lack of money, but another factor was shortage of good officers.

The malaise stemmed largely from the fact that expansion had been rapid. The quality of officers had fallen steadily. When Martial Law required military direction of civil affairs, the number of above-average officers available for service in headquarters and units was reduced. The combination of poor quality and scarcity of officers meant dilution of standards, sometimes dramatically, as shown by Gul Hassan Khan's record that, 'In 1959 I was posted to command an infantry brigade at Sialkot. I was amazed that hardly any officer turned out for parades.'

Gul Hassan sorted things out in his inimitable way, but after only three months was posted to command the armoured brigade group at Kharian where, he relates in his *Memoirs,* he 'attended a tank regimental exercise without being preceded by the customary fanfare. My arrival...took everybody by surprise and in turn I was astounded by the chaos I witnessed. No one seemed to know what the hell was going on...' Again Gul Hassan put things to right, but unfortunately there were not enough officers like him. Many older officers whose sense of duty was paramount had resigned or retired (such as characters like Brigadier Hesky Baig, whose idea of fun as a commanding officer was to hurtle round the perimeter of the local airfield every morning with his officers panting behind him), and many of the senior officers remaining had been promoted too quickly and for the wrong reasons. Things were not good, but the country had taken on a new lease of life which produced a false sense of security verging on the euphoric. The public regarded the army highly because they had good reason to do so after the clean-up of Lahore, and in consequence the army had a high opinion of itself without having *done* very much except expand a bit and conduct some mediocre training with its new American equipment. As all military commanders know—or should know—there is a difference between pride engendered by measurable achievement and the self-satisfaction that grows, like slime, in the nourishing atmosphere of a mutual admiration society.

The army of Pakistan had an officer corps with potentially good raw material which, had it been pushed, stretched, and challenged, would have been amongst the finest in the world. The soldiery, and especially the NCOs and JCOs, *were* amongst the finest in the world, but the senior leadership was suspect and in some aspects inadequate.[8]

* * *

Ayub went ahead with his plans and wrote in his autobiography that: 'The civil organs of the administration were revived, the army went back to barracks. One by one the reforms were launched and we came to grips with the basic political problems of the country.' Well, not quite. Not all of the army went back to barracks immediately, because it was necessary to show that the new regime meant business. Further, the cabinet included three generals, and in any event martial law required participation by military officers.

Army *units* did go back to barracks after a few weeks during which some draconian action was taken by junior officers and JCOs on the orders of their superiors. Black marketeers, corrupt officials and politicians, and some businessmen who found it inconvenient to describe how their hoards of gold were obtained, were rounded-up and incarcerated. Military courts were severe in their judgments and sentencing, which met with approval amongst the population, but Ayub realized that he would have to take the army off the streets if it was not to be identified with repression. This he did in the second week of November, after contraband worth millions of Rupees had been seized. Prices of many commodities went down by as much as a quarter, and ordinary people found themselves able to buy such things as cooking oil, crockery, and cloth at reasonable prices.

Eight hundred and twenty-three civil servants were dismissed or made subject to compulsory retirement and a further eight hundred thirty-nine received minor punishments. Corrupt politicians were dealt with by special tribunals and the introduction of Presidential Orders covering disqualification from public office and elective bodies. As a result, several thousand individuals were disbarred from holding any political position. In the years 1958 to 1961, Ayub appointed twenty-three Commissions to report on such variegated matters as law reform, food and agriculture, land reform, and establishment of a new federal capital. (The last was headed by Maj.-Gen. A.M. Yahya Khan, who was to make his mark in other ways in later years.) There was considerable activity in all sorts of spheres. The Constitution Committee, for example, completed its work in just over a year, resulting in promulgation of the new Constitution in 1962. Ayub was indulging in the process that seems to have such attraction for dictators and for governments with apparently massive popular support: social engineering. He meant well, which is to damn him unfairly (and in hindsight) because he knew what was needed for his country—but he had no experience of governance. Another problem was that, although he tried to unite the country's disparate Wings, he could not see (or perhaps did not care) that government by a West Wing military elite would hardly appeal to Bengalis. In the words of Omar Noman:

> The Ayub Khan era is remembered for the regime's professional competence in its approach to economic management. There was a clarity of objectives and considerable efficiency in implementation. However the efficiency and clarity were marred by fundamental flaws in the choice of objectives....[9]

Noman goes on to state that Pakistan, as originally created, was 'an entirely artificial geographical enterprise,' which is of course correct—but it may be that, if the war of 1965 had not taken place, the Ayub regime might have succeeded in forging better relations between the Eastern and Western Wings of Pakistan in addition to creating a better climate for the introduction of democracy and, of equal importance, focusing with more expertise on the 'choice of objectives'.

India: The Goa Campaign and the 1962 War with China

The Pakistan army had problems in its officer corps but these existed, too, in the army of India, which the defence minister, V. K. Krishna Menon, had thoroughly upset by '...interfering in promotions, putting his own men into key positions and seeing those he particularly disliked passed over'.[10] This emasculated the army's leadership and created a climate of suspicion and servility, an appalling combination that led to panic and chaos when China attacked India on 20 October 1962. Unfortunately for the army and for Indian prestige, the invasion of the tiny Portuguese enclave of Goa the previous year had been greeted with euphoric approval by an Indian public which considered it to be a great feat of arms, which patently it was not.

During the period in which India's military take-over of Portuguese territory was being planned, China was planning its own venture against India. Nehru, contemptuously rejecting Ayub Khan's offer of a mutual defence agreement in 1959 ('Against whom?' he asked, mockingly; a reaction he doubtless did not care to be reminded of later), tried to forge good relations with China, which had a different agenda. Ayub also had a different agenda, and had no intention of joining India in anything resembling a defence pact but thought it a good idea to try to place India on the defensive, diplomatically. The energy with which India rejected his approach indicated fear in Delhi that the rest of the world might take his initiative seriously. Most countries ignored or failed to hear Ayub's suggestion—but Peking was about to show that, where territory was concerned, the Middle Kingdom took affairs very seriously indeed.

The Chinese had occupied the Aksai Chin plateau* in the western Himalayas for many years. So far as they were concerned the region belonged to them, and they built a major road through it to move troops from Xinjiang Province to Tibet. They also claimed other areas along the border between India and China, delineation of which had been settled in 1914. Disagreements grew between Delhi and Peking concerning boundaries, and Nehru, bolstered by his abrasive defence minister, who was in turn supported by incompetent generals of his own placement, decided to call the Chinese military bluff. But it wasn't bluff. It was Nehru's own generals who were bluffing.

Pakistan was not averse to witnessing a dispute between its two enormous neighbours and rather relished the rapidly deteriorating situation. Certainly, there were problems about Pakistan's cordial relations with China so far as the United States was concerned, but the general picture appeared clear to Pakistan's leadership: India was in trouble, and from that nothing but good could come for Pakistan. Wrong.

The Indian army was soundly defeated by the PLA, to the point of humiliation. China was no Portugal, and the easy occupation of sunny, sandy, coastal Goa bore no resemblance to real fighting in the

---

* Some 36,000 sq. km.; about the size of Belgium or Taiwan; half the size of South Carolina.

mountains against well-prepared and (fairly) well-led troops. The problem for Pakistan was that the Chinese victory was so complete that the rest of the ('Free') world panicked almost as much as Nehru. It should have been obvious that China had no intention of thundering south into India. But the world—especially America—saw 'Red China' on the move, and reacted accordingly. To the surprise and annoyance of Pakistan, it became apparent that Nehru's former critics around the world, hitherto so supportive of Pakistan, the open and loyal ally of the West, could happily drop Pakistan like a hot brick if India—which had so scorned the West—were to be threatened. Britain, France, America rushed to provide weapons. Nehru begged for fighter aircraft from the US, artillery from the UK, tanks from France, for support from anywhere against the supposed invader from the north. Nehru abased himself, turned turtle, ditched his 'non-aligned' principles in his desperation. Then China turned off the tap. It declared a cease-fire on 20 November. India had been defeated and humiliated, yet it was to experience rebirth, militarily. The Western world continued to rally to its aid. Pakistan was to see a huge effort by its former supporters, helped, ironically, by the USSR, to supply India with an enormous arsenal.

The Rann of Kutch Affair

In early 1965, fighting took place between Indian and Pakistani troops in the Rann of Kutch, a coastal border region between Bombay and Karachi (Map 1). Devoid of attraction, it is desolate, barren but for small areas of grazing, and covered in brackish water for much of the year. It is of no economic, social, or archaeological interest. On 4 April 1965, an Indian patrol overcame the Pakistani garrison of a fort at the euphonically-named outpost of Ding, on the Pakistani side of the border.[11] Pakistan moved reinforcements to the Rann (lit., marsh), and a minor war took place.

After only a small amount of fighting, the Pakistan army pushed the Indians back. It was a tight little campaign, won by superior tactics.[12] Such modern equipment as had been supplied to both countries by their supporters played little part in the mini-war. India had deployed almost all its new inventory in the northern border area against West Pakistan, but none in the south, and little against what had been the main, Chinese, threat in the north—for which it was intended by its donors.

A cease-fire was arranged between Pakistan and India on 30 June and took effect the following day. Later, an independent international commission was set up to adjudicate on the boundary.[13]

The significance of the Rann of Kutch affair was the false sense of optimism and superiority engendered within the Pakistan army concerning its ability to fight a war against India. The tiny affair was a Pakistani victory, but it created a mistaken euphoria for which payment was made in short order. There was little doubt that India was still spoiling for a war, but equally there is little doubt that Pakistan tweaked India's ultra-sensitive tail just a bit too much.

NOTES

1. Vorys (1965).
2. *Pakistan Horizon*, published by the Pakistan Institute of International Affairs, Vol. XI. No. 4.
3. Kux (2001).
4. '6 May – Addressed the House Foreign Affairs Committee in the Congress buildings... I... tried to dispel the illusion that India's arms build up was on account of the fear of China and that she had no aggressive intentions towards Pakistan' (*Friends Not Masters*).
5. Article 1 states 'The Government of Pakistan is determined to resist aggression. In the case of aggression against Pakistan the US Government, in accordance with the US Constitution, will take such appropriate action, including the use of armed forces as may be mutually agreed upon and as is envisaged in the Joint Resolution to Promote Peace and Stability in the Middle East, in order to assist the Government of Pakistan at its request.' The Joint Resolution (or Declaration) was issued on 28 July 1958 at a meeting of the Baghdad Pact's Joint Ministerial Council, and did not go much further in emplacing the notion that the US would sit on its hands if Pakistan were attacked from the east. Ambassador Langley, who was no diplomat, but no fool either, had already warned Washington that 'We cannot afford to participate or close our eyes to an arms race between India and Pakistan'.
6. *Area Handbook for Pakistan*, US Government Printing Office, Washington, DC, 1965.
7. Conversations with, amongst others, Major Generals Wajahat Hussein and Shah Rafi Alam.
8. The columnist Hamid Hussain, writing in Pakistan's *Defence Journal* of January 2003, is withering about Ayub's selection of officers. He wrote that commanders 'have relied mainly on enticement and selective patronage to deal with even the potential rivals. Few examples will amply clarify this point. Ayub Khan, when got suspicious of Major General Sher Ali Khan Patudi [Pataudi], retired him and sent him as High Commissioner to Malaysia. When ambitious Lt General Habibullah Khan Khattack was perceived as a threat, he was retired but Ayub married his son to Khattack's daughter.'

9. Noman (1990).
10. Maxwell (1970). A superb examination of the 1962 war. For an account of the Indian defence minister, *see, My Days with Krishna Menon* in *Not a Nice Man to Know* by Khushwant Singh, Penguin, 1993.
11. Z. A. Khan (1988). A good description of the Ding engagement and the Rann of Kutch in general in an enjoyable book of reminiscences.
12. Ahmad (1973). See also, *In the Desert* by Brigadier Muhammad Taj, SJ, in *Defence Journal*, Karachi, April 1988, and Z. A. Khan (1988) in the March issue.
13. The Rann of Kutch conflict was ended by British intercession and the dispute was solved when both countries agreed to appointment of the *Indo-Pakistan Western Boundary Case Tribunal* by the UN Secretary General. The Tribunal presented its report on 19 February 1968. It awarded Pakistan a mere 300 square miles out of a claim for 3,500 and upheld almost all the Indian claim. This was an excellent example of how international 'Good Offices' and mediation, followed by independent analysis and arbitration, can result in lasting solutions to territorial disputes.

4 1965 Phase One— Kashmir

On 28 August 1965 Pakistan troops crossed the cease-fire line in Kashmir which had been established and kept under UN supervision since January 1949. A second attack was launched on 1 September. The Pakistani air force conducted some successful operations but the crucial land attacks were held by the Indian army and on 6 September India retaliated by invading Pakistan itself. Thereafter the fighting rapidly came to a stalemate.[1]

T his description of the 1965 war between India and Pakistan is as concise and accurate as a brief word picture can be. But the origins of the war, its conduct, and its consequences are quite complex. Most books covering the period deal in the main with the outcome of the war rather than the reasons for it. This is understandable given that there appears to have been no national aim on the part of Pakistan for going to war in the first place.

In 1965, the war aim of Pakistan was neither enunciated nor apparent. 'Survival' is not an aim, it is a pious desire, and although Pakistan's armed forces fought well during the 1965 war, they lacked the openly-declared Clausewitzian objective that they should fight to overcome the enemy, invest his territory, and ensure his total defeat. India's forces fought extremely well—and had no inhibitions. They invaded Pakistan on 6 September with the aim of crushing it. Destruction of Pakistan was essential, according to India's leaders, if India was to be confident of supremacy in the subcontinent.

But who began the war? And why?

* * *

Following India's defeat at the hands of China in 1962, the Pakistan Army considered its potential opponent to be ineffective and incompetent—which in 1962 it was. GHQ analysts in Rawalpindi conducted their annual assessments of the Indian Army's capabilities in 1963 and 1964 and concluded that little had changed. They were wrong, and their reading of the Rann of Kutch engagements led them further down the road of complacency.

After the Rann of Kutch the army was cocky, even truculent. Indeed, the whole of Pakistan was self-confident and resented Indian procrastination concerning a plebiscite in Kashmir where New Delhi was establishing its rule. In 1964, Pakistan's foreign minister, Zulfikar Ali Bhutto, wrote to the President of the Security Council that:

> It is clear...that the Government of India is deliberately set on defying the Security Council and on 'integrating' the Indian-occupied part of Jammu and Kashmir with the Indian Union. This is being done in flagrant repudiation of India's commitment to the principles contained in the two resolutions of the United Nations Commission for India and Pakistan, which enjoin that the question of accession of the State to India or Pakistan will be decided through the democratic method of a free and impartial plebiscite, conducted under the auspices of the United Nations.[2]

Bhutto's contention that India was bent on integrating Kashmir within the Union was correct. It was and it did. Pakistan felt that Muslims in the Indian-controlled area would vote to accede to Pakistan rather than India (if only because the 'Hindu Raj' treated them as second-class citizens, just as they had been during the rule of the Maharajas).[3] The Indian government feared such an outcome and was uncompromising in its intention to thwart UN resolutions, indigenous hopes, and—indubitably—Pakistani machinations. There could be no meeting of minds between Pakistan and India about Kashmir, and there was not—and is not, to this day—any intention on the part of India to consider self-determination by the Kashmiri peoples a reasonable aspiration.

Whether Indian intransigence concerning the status of Kashmir was sufficient reason for Pakistan's aggressive stance and actions in 1965 is open to question. The UN, after all, had declared that there should be a plebiscite in Kashmir and had adjured both sides to refrain from conflict. But India's decision that there would never be a plebiscite caused Pakistan to foment discord in Indian-controlled Kashmir. On the night of 5/6 August 1965, hundreds of armed men crossed the cease-fire line from Pakistan-controlled Kashmir to the Indian side to start Operation *Gibraltar*.[4] The incursions took place in the areas of

Akhnur, Rajouri, Gulmarg, Uri, and Mendhar (Map 3). The war was about to begin.

* * *

Disposition and Strength of Opposing Forces

Following the engagements in the Rann of Kutch, the Indian army, which moved several formations to the south-west in the early months of 1965, conducted a major redeployment. Formations sent to the border with Pakistan and along the cease-fire line were:

FORMATION	FROM	TO
1 Armoured Division	Jhansi	Amritsar
15 Infantry Division (newly-raised)	Dehra Dun	Amritsar
4 Mountain Division	Ambala	Ferozepur
6 Mountain Division	Bareilly	Jullundur
2 Armoured Brigade	Patiala	Amritsar
116 Mountain Brigade	South India	Ferozepur
10 Infantry Division	Bangalore	Kashmir
7 Infantry Division	South Border	Ferozepur

Redeployment of six divisions by any army, at any time, is a significant operation. The number of troops moved to the eastern border by the Indian army in mid-1965 was about 125,000 which involved an enormous quantity of road and rail transport, and the move was impressive in scale and efficiency. (This expertise is still evident in the Indian logistics and railway systems. When India mobilised against Pakistan in early 2002, following a terrorist attack on the Lok Sabha on 13 December 2001, similar numbers of troops were moved to the east, and the smoothness of the operation was in no small measure due to the efficiency of the railways and GHQ planning.)

The three infantry divisions (19, 25, 26) already along the Cease-fire Line (CFL) in Indian-administered Kashmir remained in the area, along with three independent brigades under command of 15 Corps HQ at Udhampur. 30 Infantry Brigade moved from the north-east of India to southern Rajasthan, the only redeployment from that region, under command of the newly-designated 11 Infantry Division (formerly 11 Mountain Division).

A major problem for (West) Pakistan was and is its lack of depth. The country is only 200 miles wide along the line Peshawar–Rawalpindi, and little wider in the Lahore area further south. A compensation is that only minor redeployment is required from peacetime to wartime positions. 10 Division at Lahore and 15 Division at Sialkot (both of four infantry brigades) did not have to move far, and neither did 1st Armoured Division from its base at Kharian to a position in depth around Sargodha, where it was joined by 7 Infantry Division from Peshawar. Along the CFL the Pakistanis had 12 Infantry Division, whose HQ was at Murree, which had one regular brigade and 18 Azad Kashmir battalions of locally-enlisted soldiers.[5]

According to Gul Hassan, all was not well in the Pakistan army in spite of (perhaps because of) the Rann of Kutch success. He relates that there was '...a prevalent attitude of complacency that pervaded the decision-making echelons of the Army,' and his account of planning processes is unflattering to the army's senior leadership.

In reserve, India had two divisions in the centre of the country and eight in the east. Pakistan had no properly constituted reserve, save the *ad hoc* 6 Armoured 'Division' (the old 100 Armoured Brigade, renamed), which was not in a condition to fight as a formation but was despatched to the eastern front soon after battle was joined.

The main personalities of the Pakistan army at the beginning of operations were:

1. Commander-in-Chief, General Mohammad Musa
2. Chief of the General Staff, Maj.-Gen. Malik Sher Bahadur
3. Director of Military Operations, Maj.-Gen. Sahibzada Mohammad Yaqub Khan[6]
4. Commander I Corps, Lt.-Gen. Bakhtiar Rana

Divisional Commanders:

1	Armd. Div.	Maj.-Gen. Nasir Ahmed Khan
6	Armd. 'Div.'	Maj.-Gen. Abrar Hussein
		(2 tank regiments)
7	Inf. Div.	Maj.-Gen. A. M. Yahya Khan
10	Inf. Div.	Maj.-Gen. Sarfaraz Khan
11	Inf. Div.	Maj.-Gen. Abdul Hamid Khan
12	Inf. Div.	Maj.-Gen. Akhtar Hussein Malik
15	Inf. Div.	Brig. Sardar M. Ismail Khan

(8 Inf. Div, commanded by Maj.-Gen. Tikka Khan, consisting of 51 and 52 Brigades, was in the Rann of Kutch area and saw no engagements during the 1965 war.)

The Indian Army had eleven divisions and three independent brigades. Senior Indian officers were:

Chief of Army Staff   General J. N. Chaudhuri

Commanders:

Western Command	Lt.-Gen. Harbaksh Singh
I Corps	Lt.-Gen. P. O. Dunn
XI Corps	Lt.-Gen. J. S. Dhillon
XV Corps	Lt.-Gen. K. S. Katoch

Divisional and Brigade Commanders:

Srinagar Operations ('V' Sector)	Maj.-Gen. Umrao Singh
1 Armd. Div.	Maj.-Gen. Rajinder Singh
4 Mtn. Div.	Maj.-Gen. Gurbaksh Singh
6 Mtn. Div.	Maj.-Gen. S. K. Korla[7]
7 Inf. Div.	Maj.-Gen. H. K. Sibal
10 Inf. Div.	Maj.-Gen. D. B. Chopra
11 Inf. Div.	Maj.-Gen. N. C. Rawlley
14 Inf. Div.	Maj.-Gen. R. K. Ranjit Singh
15 Inf. Div.	Maj.-Gen. Mohindar Singh
19 Inf. Div.	Maj.-Gen. S. K. Kalaan
25 Inf. Div.	Maj.-Gen. Amreek Singh
26 Inf. Div.	Maj.-Gen. M. L. Thapan
2 Independent Armd. Bde.	Brig. T. K. Theogaraj
68 Ind. Inf. Bde.	Brig. Z. C. Bakshi
121 Ind. Inf. Bde.	Brig. V. K. Ghai

In the air and at sea Pakistan was also outnumbered, having, for example, only 60 fighter/ground attack aircraft as against 340, and 7 main surface combatants against 12.

* * *

Chronology of the War

5/6 August: *Infiltration from Pakistan across the Cease-fire Line (CFL).* Training of groups for infiltration on Operation *Gibraltar* began in May/June 1965 when instructors in 'irregular warfare' from the Special Services Group,[8] based at Attock and Cherat, were moved to Pakistan-controlled Kashmir and attached to Azad Kashmir battalions of 12 Division. Locally-recruited *mujahids*[9] were administered by the AK units but their training (about which the Indians obtained details from POWs) appears to have been poor. Six raiding forces were formed, each consisting of about three companies of sixty-six *mujahids* and some forty AK and regular soldiers, including the company commanders. Orders to the *mujahid* forces were imprecise and reflected the woolliness with which the entire confrontation with India was conjured up. The groups were despatched into enemy territory following inadequate training and with only the haziest notion of what they were to undertake other than general sabotage and encouragement of the Muslim population to rise against the Indian government. They were in poor physical condition and unfit to engage in protracted guerrilla warfare. It was little wonder that they revealed much information to their Indian captors when, as was inevitable, most of their efforts failed. Pakistan's planners failed to realize that the inhabitants of the Kashmir Valley had no interest in taking up arms against their Hindu masters. It was to take thirty-five years of vote-rigging and general misrule before the Muslims of Indian-administered Kashmir revolted against the Delhi government. In 1965 their interests lay more in tourists, woodcrafts, and papier mâché than in aspiring to political freedom.

    7 August: *Pakistani raid in the Kargil area. (see,* Map 3). This was reported to UN HQ New York by UN observers in Kashmir. It was intended by Pakistan that Indian road links between Srinagar[10] and Ladakh be cut. This would have given little impetus to Pakistan's war aims, such as they were, but India had to react to the attacks because the road was its only ground access to Aksai Chin, where China continued to occupy territory claimed by India.

    12–16 August: *Pakistani attack on Indian Army post at Kargil; Pakistan shelling in the Chhambh sector; 121 Independent Inf. Bde. takes posts near Kargil occupied by Pakistani troops. The Indians are persuaded to withdraw by UN observers but later reoccupy the positions.* As noted, the Indians could not permit interruption of their lines of communication to Ladakh. There was little locally-produced food available, and air supply was expensive. Further, the Indians were becoming wary of Pakistani intentions to the west and south along the CFL and seized the opportunity to move towards the Uri salient in preparation for an attack there in order, in turn, to disrupt Pakistani communications and supply routes to the north of the Line. War was now becoming inevitable as both sides committed regular troops to combat. There were statements in the respective parliaments, letters to the UN, and briefings of international media, but there was a sense of buying time. On the Pakistan side, it was still hoped that the actions of the *mujahids* would persuade the population of the valley to rise up, whereafter Pakistani regular troops could be deployed with a semblance of legality. The Indians were not averse to escalation of the conflict as it would, in their view, provide an opportunity to make up for the humiliation in the Rann of Kutch and settle things once and for all with their recalcitrant neighbour. They wanted to 'get at and smash the Pak war machine'.[11]

18–31 August: *Heavy exchanges of shellfire across the CFL; regular forces of both sides engage in conflict in the Chhambh sector; increased exchanges of small arms and artillery fire across the CFL. Indian troops capture posts near Tithwal. Indian attacks near Uri and Poonch resulting in capture of the Haji Pir Pass. Pakistani brigade attacks in the Bhimber/Chhambh area.* On 21 August, the Indians began to react forcefully against the infiltrators in the Valley. The *mujahideen* had been brave enough and had tried hard, but 15 Corps (HQ Srinagar) killed or captured most of them by the end of the month.

The last ten days of August saw a gradual growth in the scale of conflict, and incidents abounded. Sometimes trifling in themselves, they contributed to an increase in tension that both sides were prepared to give as justification to their citizens for increased preparations for all-out war.

* * *

Annexure G to GHQ Letter No 4050/5/MO-1 dated 29 August 1965. Directive from President Ayub Khan to General Mohammad Musa, Commander-in-Chief Pakistan Army.[12]

Political Aim for Struggle in Kashmir

...to take such action as will defreeze Kashmir problem, weaken India's
resolve and bring her to a conference table without provoking a general war.
However the element of escalation is always present in such struggles. So,
whilst confining our action to the Kashmir area we must not be unmindful
that India may in desperation involve us in a general war or violate Pakistan
territory where we are weak. We must therefore be prepared for such
contingency.

2. To expect quick results in this struggle, when India has much larger
forces than us, would be unrealistic. Therefore our action should be such
that can be sustained over a long period.

3. As a general rule Hindu morale would not stand more than a couple
of hard blows delivered at the right time and place. Such opportunities
should therefore be sought and exploited.

This is an intriguing document, and, it might be thought, a poor
directive to be issued by the leader of any country. The comment about
Hindus was crass. The extraordinary thing is that the person giving the
direction was himself a soldier who should have known that India
would react violently to assaults on what she regarded as her territory.
And the President should have been aware that 'our action should be
such that can be sustained over a long period' is tantamount to
advocating a policy of attrition, and that his acknowledgement that
India had 'larger forces' is a direct negation of attrition as a political
tool.

31 August–6 September:

During the last week in August President Ayub was absent from Rawalpindi
on a visit to Swat and early in that week public official responses to India's
crossings of the CFL near Tithwal on 24 August and near Uri on the night
of 25/26 August were muted. When a briefing due to be held at noon on
26 August was cancelled it was explained that the Foreign Minister, Zulfikar
Ali Bhutto, would make a statement that evening; none was made...[13]

While the PAF [Pakistan Air Force] increased its combat posture from day
to day, the...country's leadership, incredibly, continued to languish in the
shade of the Foreign Office's assurances concerning escalation. According
to Air Commodore Aziz Ahmed...of the India desk of the Inter-Services
Intelligence Directorate, he sent a signal on 30 August...that an Indian
attack outside Kashmir was 'imminent'...Mr Aziz Ahmed, the Foreign

Secretary, kept pooh-poohing the...signal and the army top brass present seemed to share his lack of concern.[14]

It has been difficult to determine a military aim for the Pakistani attack at Chhamb on 31 August. GHQ in Rawalpindi subsequently explained the move as being necessary to neutralize Indian guns which had been firing on Pakistani positions, and because the area was believed to be occupied by a strong force whose destruction would convince the Indians that further activity would be futile. This does not stand up to scrutiny. The artillery fire was of nuisance value but no more—and the area was defended only by a battalion of para-military police strung along the CFL, with depth provided by 191 Infantry Brigade supported by a normal allocation of artillery and a squadron (plus) of French AMX tanks. This was a fair-sized force but hardly 'strong' in any military sense. (Pakistan Intelligence did not know that the Indian Army had failed to plan for deployment of Centurion tanks in the area. When this became necessary it was discovered that none of the bridges could carry them.)

The most likely explanation, according to Lt.-Gen. Gul Hassan Khan, who of all people should have known, is that Operation *Grand Slam* was intended to capture Akhnur in order to 'sever the only road link between India and Kashmir'. This is a plausible aim, but one still wonders why it was disclaimed by GHQ.

The Pakistanis attacked from the area of Bhimber at first light on 1 September following an artillery bombardment of ninety minutes that began at 0300.[15] The infantry component comprised 102 Infantry Brigade (Brig. Zafar Ali Khan), 4 AK Brigade (Brig. Abdul Hameed Khan), 10 Infantry Brigade (Brig. Hayat) and two companies of 12th Frontier Force Regiment; seven battalions in all. Two armoured regiments, 11th Cavalry and 13th Lancers,[16] moved with the infantry, and fire support was provided by 4 Corps Artillery of some 40 field, 40 medium, and eight 8-inch guns—a formidable punch that was used to considerable effect by forward observers.

By mid-afternoon the Pakistanis had advanced as far as Chhamb and Dewa (Map 4). The situation was becoming critical for the Indians and, for the first time in a conflict between India and Pakistan, combat air support was involved. The Indian Air Force (IAF) carried out strikes using about thirty aircraft, of which at least two were shot down by PAF fighters. These were elderly Vampires which had been committed to ground attack before air superiority had been obtained: a costly

MAP 4   CHHAMB AND AKHNUR

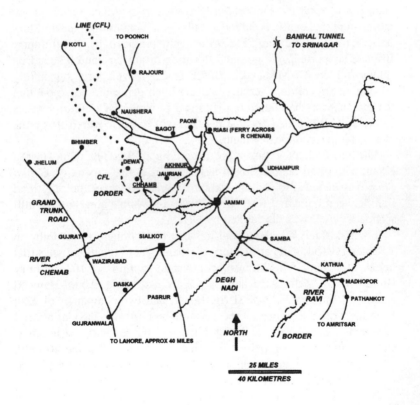

mistake. The IAF did not again employ Vampires in combat, but the strikes disrupted the Pakistani advance, destroying, according to the *Times of India* and other Indian sources, thirteen tanks and thirty to forty soft-skinned vehicles.

An objective Indian description of the battle is given in *Battle Honours of the Indian Army*:[17]

> The enemy opened the attack with a massive artillery bombardment from 0345 to 0630 hrs (Indian Time) 1 September and followed it up at 0830 hrs with a three-pronged attack. Headquarters 10 Division was told to assume immediate responsibility and 41 Mountain Brigade en route for Jammu was placed under it. By nightfall, 191 Brigade defences were crumbling and it withdrew for defence of Akhnur during [the] night of 1/2 September.

The Indians broke contact on the line of the Munnawar Tawi River in the evening of 1 September, and the Pakistanis regrouped. It is claimed in many accounts of the Chhamb battles written by Pakistanis that Phase 1 of the operation was then over and that Phase 2 was to begin after 102 Brigade had achieved its objective, presumably the river line. There appears to be no justification for this claim, and the next advance seems to have been decided separately. This is not to deny the success of 102 Brigade in driving back an almost equal force a considerable distance, but it must be stated that the Munnawar Tawi was not the most formidable natural obstacle and that regrouping could have been effected quickly in order to maintain momentum. As it was, the advance did not continue until 1730 on 2 September, when 10 Brigade (6 Bn. Frontier Force Regiment, 14 Punjab, and 13 Lancers) crossed the river and created a bridgehead for a breakout and follow-up of the Indian forces. The news of the crossing of the Munnawar Tawi was greeted with consternation in Delhi as it was confused with the *other* river Tawi that flows through Jammu and is bridged by the main supply route from southern India to Kashmir and Ladakh. So far as can be determined, there is no evidence that this misappreciation led to an earlier Indian attack in Punjab than had been planned, but for obvious reasons it is likely that this was the case.

Gulzar Ahmed states that 'HQ 7 Inf. Div. had arrived in the area and it was felt that the command of this sector would be exercised more expeditiously if 7 Div., commanded by Maj.-Gen. Mohammad Yahya Khan [later President], controlled the operations. 12 Div. HQ was too far from the area...' This statement raises some questions. Why did HQ

7 Div. 'arrive', and *was* HQ 12 Div. permitted to become 'too far from the area'? The concept of the forward, or tactical, HQ was hardly unknown, and the radios of the time did not have anything like the range to be able to establish a voice link between Murree and the brigades eighty miles away. In fact, a tac HQ was functioning, albeit based on the artillery headquarters of the nascent HQ 4 Corps. Why, then, the 'justification' that HQ 12 Div. was too far away? And why was Maj.-Gen. Akhtar Hussein Malik relieved of command? He had produced as good a plan as possible, given lack of an overall aim and the guidance that should have been provided to an officer of his rank and responsibilities, and had performed well. Brigadier Z.A. Khan says only that 'General Musa, visiting Major General Akhtar Malik's headquarters and finding the prevailing conditions unsatisfactory, ordered Major General Yahya Khan to assume command of operations.'[18] What went on? Even Gul Hassan was confused by what took place and states, 'It is apparent that there is much more to it than meets the eye, and I do not think we shall ever learn the truth.' Probably; but Dr Wright thinks a possible explanation of General Malik's dismissal is that he argued against the advance to Akhnur because he considered the operation would stretch the army too far. While reasonable, this would indicate that Malik was unaware that the plan for *Grand Slam* supposedly hinged on cutting the Jammu–Rajouri road at Akhnur as a vital Phase 2 to the entire operation. This appears not to have been the case, as Malik told Gul Hassan that, 'it would take him no longer than seventy-two hours to seize Akhnur'.

The Indians were no doubt as confused as anyone else when they examined the battle after the war but were under no illusion as to the advantage conferred upon them by what took place: 'The comparative lull on 2 September which gave 24 valuable hours to the defenders was due to the fact that the enemy's Headquarters 12 Division was being replaced by that of 7 Division....'[19]

* * *

Units of India's 41 Mountain Brigade took up an intermediate defensive position at Jaurian during 2 September and promptly came under attack led by 14 Punjab of 10 Infantry brigade. 41 Brigade held on until the 4th but was then forced to withdraw to 191 Brigade's secure perimeter round Akhnur that night when 6 FF Battalion joined the assault. Jaurian fell following a final Pakistani attack that went in at 0700 on

5 September, but the advance came to nothing because next day the Indians 'launched a full-fledged offensive aimed at Lahore and Sialkot to take the pressure off the Chhamb sector. Within a few hours [Pakistani] troops started thinning out. However, efforts between 6 to 10 September to regain the lost territory failed....'[20]

It appears the Pakistan Army's foray into the Chhamb sector was successful as far as it went. But overall it must be judged a failure—if the aim was to cut the road to the north expeditiously, and neither India nor Pakistan appears certain on this main point. The thrust caught the Indians on the hop and went far and fast—at least initially—but this was micro-battle, just as the Rann of Kutch had been. Infantry brigades on foot; cavalry regiments, pennants flying, advancing to meet the enemy over good tank country; the soldiers' war, the opportunity for demonstrations of daring and courage, presented itself to both sides. And both sides showed great gallantry.

One problem for Pakistan was that the army seemed to think in brigades, not divisions, and certainly not corps. After all, there was only one real corps headquarters—1 Corps—as 4 Corps HQ was still in the process of formation. Application of overwhelming force was taught as a principle of war, but, according to such as Gul Hassan, not practised on exercises. Further,

> the decision to launch *Grand Slam* was inordinately delayed...Secondly, command...should have been given to GOC 7 Division from the start or there should have been no change of command in the middle. To let things happen as they did is mind boggling and contributed immensely to our failure.

Perhaps the best summary of *Grand Slam* is in a British Intelligence Appreciation of 1966:

> Had the [Pakistani] attacks been pressed home with a greater determination and sense of urgency it is difficult to see how they could have failed to capture Akhnur. Whether they would have held it after the Indians took the inevitable step of further escalation is very doubtful. The problem did not have to be put to the test.

The war proper then began.

NOTES

1. Peter Calvocoressi, *World Politics Since 1945*, Longmans, 1968. *See also*, Z. A. Khan (1988) for a most readable account of Operation Grand Slam.

2. Letter of the Minister of Foreign Affairs of Pakistan, Zulfikar Ali Bhutto, to the President of the Security Council, 16 January 1964 (S/5517) in Hasan (op. cit.).

3. Kashmir was indubitably within the overall embrace of the British Indian Empire but considerable autonomy was exercised by the ruler. Unfortunately he was a maharaja whose feudal proclivities, dissipation and laziness were remarkable, and it could not be said that his interests lay entirely with the peoples over which he had dominance. It is hardly surprising that when he was required to make a decision about accession to Pakistan or India he did not even consider consulting his subjects. They existed for the good of the maharaja, not the other way round.

4. There is a good description of Operation *Gibraltar* in Z. A. Khan (1988), and in memoirs by officers who served at the time.

5. A battalion level 1965 ORBAT is available from www.orbat.com, compiled by Babar Mahmud. This is an excellent site, run by Ravi Rikhye. Brigadier Zahir Khan's, *The Way it Was* gives first-rate detailed descriptions of the war and much else besides. The book is hard to get, and I am most grateful to his brother, Lt.-Gen. Javed Alam Khan (commanding 1 Corps in 2005), for giving me a copy when he was commander 37 Division. Z.A. Khan was the eldest of a remarkable family of eminent military brothers.

6. Sahibzada (Prince) Yaqub Khan is one of the most outstanding figures in Pakistan's history. His distinguished army career began before the Second World War (in which he was awarded the Military Cross for gallantry in North Africa). His later contributions in public life, especially as foreign minister, were notable for his unswerving devotion to principle and his sometimes severely-strained loyalty.

7. General Korla had the DSO and the MC. Generals Rawlley and Mohinder Singh had the MC.

8. The Special Services Group (SSG) was raised from 17 Baluch in 1956 by (then) Lt.-Col. A.O. Mitha. His record of this task, in cooperation with US advisers, is in his biography *Unlikely Beginnings*, (OUP 2003), which is excellent reading. His observations on his six years of association 'with the Americans in Cherat' while in command are pithy and pointed. Major General Mitha was prematurely retired by Z.A. Bhutto and his persecution thereafter included non-release of his (miserable) pension for seven years, withdrawal of a well-earned decoration, and a multitude of other indignities. When he died on 4 December 1999 the SSG were true to their salt, and provided the ceremonial at his funeral.

9. Literally, soldier of the *jihad* or Holy war. According to *The Concise Encyclopaedia of Islam* (Stacey International, 1989), 'an important precondition of jihad is a reasonable prospect of success, failing which a jihad should not be undertaken.'

10. Indian-administered Kashmir has two centres: Srinagar in the Valley and Jammu in the south. The former is used during summer and the latter from October to April.

11. An Indian senior officer quoted in a British intelligence document of the period.

12. Wolpert (1993). The paper is given a GHQ number rather than a Presidential one. Furthermore, the order is an Annexure. This seems to indicate that the actual directive emanated from the Presidency some time before being included in a GHQ letter.

13. Wright (1972). Dr Wright's understanding of military affairs is prodigious. The author does not agree with some quoted facts and figures or some of the conclusions, having access to sources not available to Dr Wright over thirty years ago, but the original work must stand as one of the most distinguished of its type.
14. Pakistan Air Force (1988).
15. Gulzar Ahmed (1986).
16. According to Riza (1980), two of 11 Cavalry's squadrons were each equipped with fourteen M48s, comparatively modern tanks, but the third had fourteen ancient M36 B2s which lacked power traverse for their turrets.
17. Sarbans Singh (1993). A highly-readable account of Battle Honours awarded to Indian Army units from 1757 to 1971.
18. Z.A. Khan (1998).
19. Sarbans Singh.
20. Ibid.

5 The September War

Pakistan had miscalculated. The Indians were not prepared to treat the conflict in Kashmir as an issue divorced from Indo–Pakistan relations in the wider sphere. In any event, the Indian army was prepared to give battle and the politicians in New Delhi were in no mood to restrain their forces, although there is some evidence of hesitancy following attempted intervention by the UN.[1] India's leaders saw India's integrity as being under threat and were determined to wrest the initiative from Pakistan, which they did.

The Indians launched a major attack on September 6 across the international border towards Lahore, the fabled city of religion and history, lying fifteen miles from India. A second offensive began next day against Sialkot, an important railway and road centre, fifty miles to the north.

...neither side was capable of fully exploiting a major offensive while simultaneously resisting the outflanking attacks of the opponent. In the Akhnur area and on the Lahore front this situation apparently resulted in a military draw.

There are indications that the Indians were stopped at Sialkot by rugged Pakistani defences which were assembled with relative speed. Some observers believe the Indians failed to achieve their objectives in this battle area because their offensive began twenty-four hours too late—a delay apparently imposed by the inadequate organisation of the attacking force—yet at this point the Indians were in a far better overall military position than the Pakistanis. There is also evidence that Indian military authorities

came under increasing control from political leaders who were responding
to fresh UN appeals for peace.

Brines (1968)

The Pakistanis captured the hamlet of Jaurian and penetrated four
miles from Akhnur on 5 September, at which time their advance
ceased. On the same day General Musa issued an Order of the Day to
his troops with the message that, 'You have got your teeth into him
[the enemy]. Bite deeper and deeper until he is destroyed. And destroy
him you will, God willing.' It would have been more to the point to
issue clear orders to his commanders than rhetoric to the soldiers
because the previous day GHQ Rawalpindi had received reports of
Indian movement towards the border in Punjab.

On 3 September, the UN Secretary-General, U Thant, reported to
the Security Council that he had not,

> obtained from the Government of Pakistan any assurance that the Cease-
> Fire and the CFL will be respected henceforth or that efforts would be
> exerted to restore conditions to normal along that line. I did receive
> assurance...that India would act with restraint to any retaliatory acts and
> will respect the Cease-Fire Agreement and the CFL if Pakistan does
> likewise,

but next day the Indian representative at the UN told the Security
Council that a cease-fire could come only after Pakistan had been
'condemned as an aggressor'. Mr Lal Bahadur Shastri, Prime Minister
of India, then raised the stakes by declaring that a cease-fire could be
effective only if Pakistan withdrew 'not only its armed forces but also
the infiltrators' from Indian-occupied Kashmir. India knew it was
impossible for Pakistan to withdraw the infiltrators—but of course had
right on its side in insisting they leave disputed territory.

India was aroused and angry, and whether right or wrong about its
actions over the years in and about Kashmir, was ready to go to war.
It was apparent to much of the world that Mr Bhutto's claim on 3
September that India had launched an 'undeclared war' across the
Cease-fire Line was nonsense and that the so-called 'Revolutionary
Council of Kashmir' was neither based in Indian-held Kashmir nor
representative of its peoples. As Ayub's foreign minister, Bhutto was
the ultimate hawk. He had 'assured his president that India would not
attack in Punjab,'[2] but after the attack began could only grasp at straws

to explain his misunderstanding of the situation. He advised Ayub to condemn the US for supporting India and went so far as to state that,

> if the United States should succeed in its designs against Pakistan it would mean the isolation of our leadership not only from the mainstream of African-Asian trends, but it would also serve the purpose of isolating them from their own people. The next inevitable step will be in the direction of liquidating our national leadership which would then find itself in no position to offer effective resistance.[3]

This was hysterical gibberish, but Bhutto had convinced himself that America was an enemy—for, after all, there had to be *some* external reason for the Indian attack, because he, Bhutto, could not be wrong. This was to have the effect of colouring Bhutto's perceptions of the US during the following years in which America was to figure large on Pakistan's horizon. For the moment, in September 1965, it was enough for Bhutto to find someone to blame—but the soldiers had to continue fighting.

* * *

India's priority was the Akhnur area. It was essential to relieve Pakistani pressure in that sector. If the Pakistanis had cut the road leading to Indian-administered Kashmir and established a defensive position of even modest dimensions, it would have been difficult to dislodge them. Had the Pakistanis managed to advance only another ten miles, matters might have been critical for India. The Indians, however, had contingency plans for an attack in Punjab 'based on the hypothesis that Pakistan would have the initiative in launching an attack in Kashmir with possible diversionary attacks in other sectors'.

This 1949 plan, approved by the Indian Cabinet, was prescient. It continued:

> ...In the event of such actions Indian troops in Kashmir would seek to contain the opposing forces while the main Indian field army made a determined and rapid advance towards Lahore and Sialkot, with a possible diversionary action towards Rawalpindi or Karachi to prevent a concentration of Pakistani forces in the major operational theatre in the West Punjab. The primary aim of this strategy was to inflict a decisive defeat on Pakistan's field army at the earliest possible time and, along with the

possible occupation of Lahore, to compel the Pakistan government to seek peace.[4]

Although India's immediate concern was to prevent Pakistan severing the link with the north, the aim of their advance into 'West' Punjab was clear: to defeat the Pakistani army. On 6 September at 0530 their forces crossed the border towards Lahore; on the night of 7/8 September the advance began in the Sialkot sector. The main battlefields were to the south and east of these cities.

The Indian XI Corps mounted an offensive about fifty miles wide on the Lahore front along three main axes (Maps 5, 6, and 7):

- 15 Division from Amritsar astride the Grand Trunk Road leading to the heart of Lahore;
- 7 Division north-west on an axis leading from the Patti area to Lahore via Burki; and
- 4 Mountain Division north-west from the Harike area towards Bedian/Rohiwal (near Kasur) with the Ferozepur-Kasur Road leading to Lahore approximately on the left flank.

Headquarters I Corps moved from Delhi only on 3 September to command the operation in the Sialkot sector, which involved 1 Armoured Division, 6 Mountain Division, and 26 Infantry Division. 14 Division was brought from Saugor in central India but had been attacked by the PAF *en route* and had received severe blows that rendered it temporarily off-balance. The axes were:

- 26 Division striking south-west astride the Jammu-Sialkot road; and
- 6 Division and 1 Armoured Division (the latter the main threat to Pakistan) moving further south of 26 Division from the Jammu area towards Chawinda.

The battles are described below, but it is well to bear in mind that Dr Wright's observations that:

An initial difficulty in discussing both the Lahore offensive and the later one against Sialkot is the disputed nature of India's overall objectives. There can be no doubt that India's immediate objective was to relieve the pressure on Akhnur and that it decided to achieve this by mounting operations against the territory of West Pakistan. It is the territorial goals within West

MAP 5   **SIALKOT AND LAHORE**

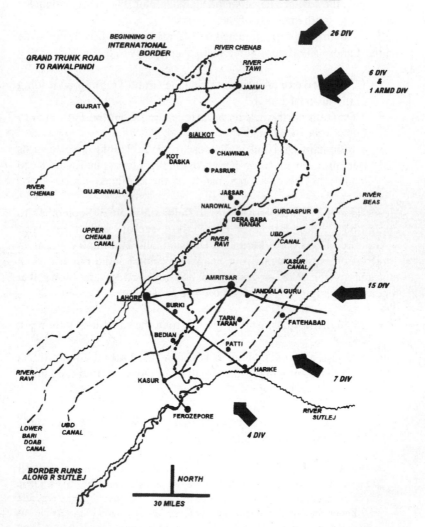

Pakistan of these operations that the belligerents dispute. Indian and Pakistani accounts not only contradict each other but are sometimes also internally inconsistent; neither government has published nor assisted in the publication of a balanced study of the war. Instead, semi-official, selective accounts have been put out which play up successes and gloss over failures.

* * *

Terrain is always important to both attacker and defender but the nature of the country around Lahore was especially significant, there being a major obstacle in the shape of the Ichogil Canal (also known as the Bambanwala-Ravi-Bedian-Dibalpur [BRBD] Canal), east of Lahore, which runs north-south for some sixty-five miles from the Upper Chenab Canal to the River Sutlej, passing underneath the River Ravi (Map 6). This, and the many other irrigation canals in the area that had been constructed in the time of the Raj and later, assisted and hindered both sides, but overall the Ichogil was an asset to the defenders—which it had been designed to be when built in the years immediately after Partition. It was a medium-sized obstacle, being steep-walled to about 4 metres in height, about 3 metres deep (depending on width), and from 25 to 40 metres wide. There were ten bridges and two other possible crossing points formed where the canal narrows to pass under rivers. To the layman, a formidable barrier; to well-trained troops, an obstacle demanding care and good equipment to establish a series of crossing points if attempts at rushing bridges failed. Not a pushover, especially if facing well-established defences, but not an obstacle on the scale of the Jhelum or the Ravi.

The first Pakistani elements to detect the attack were parties of Rangers (para-military border troops), who were quickly overrun by the Indians who also ran into parts of 10 Division's screen, which was not fully deployed. (Major Arif Jan and his thirty soldiers from various units held their position around Wagah to, literally, the last man.) That the screen was not where it should have been when it should have been was the fault of GHQ, not the commander of the division. Orders for 10 Div. to move out of barracks were not received until the afternoon of 5 September.

Deployment began shortly after midnight, just as the Indians were preparing to move. By dawn on 6 September, according to a report written in 1966 by a neutral country's intelligence agency, when the forward elements of the Pakistan Army were concentrating behind the [BRBD] canal preparatory to taking up defensive positions they found with astonishment that the Indian Army forward elements were on the opposite bank. Frantic efforts were then made to blow the bridges, some of which had been prepared for demolition. All were eventually blown except for that carrying the Grand Trunk Road, where the proximity of the Indians prevented further engineer effort. There then followed a tactical operation which possibly changed the course of the battle. The GOC 10 Pakistan Division appreciated the urgency of demolishing the bridge and accordingly ordered a counter-attack in broad daylight across the canal using the bridge to the north where the siphon carried the canal under the River Ravi. This move was carried out by 17 Baluch with a squadron of tanks in support and though some losses were suffered, the Indians, threatened in their flank, withdrew and the bridge was blown.

The 15 Indian Division advance towards Lahore from Amritsar was led by 54 Brigade, made up of 3 Jat, 15 Dogra, and 13 Punjab infantry battalions. The advance was slowed by intense Pakistani artillery fire directed by forward observers whose accuracy was assisted by prominent concrete pillars along the border. These had been positioned over the years by survey units for just this eventuality. 3 Jat pushed ahead and crossed the bridge over the BRBD Canal at about 1000 PST on 6 September but were repulsed by 3 Baluch in fierce fighting around the Bata shoe factory and withdrew to the area of Dograi on the east bank, followed up by 3 Baluch which had about fifty men trapped on the west of the canal when Pakistani sappers blew up the bridge (and most others) during the night of 6/7. Throughout the day the PAF conducted ground attack missions on elements of 15 Division with considerable effect, thus lessening the pressure on 10 Div.'s forward localities.

India's 50 Para Brigade moved up on 7 September to relieve 54 Brigade which had shot its bolt. Its forward troops had been permitted to advance beyond artillery range and suffered more casualties than would otherwise have been the case. It is amazing that 3 Jat were allowed to cross the main obstacle and, apparently, establish a bridgehead, without armour and artillery as far forward as possible. It can be assumed only that either no orders were given to CO 3 Jat concerning his limit of exploitation, which is so unlikely as to be discounted; or that he advanced without orders to do so, which indicates a breakdown of command, which there was not; or—most likely—there was a nonsense regarding artillery and armour

MAP 6   # THE LAHORE FRONT

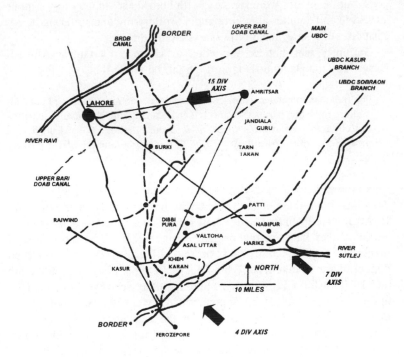

co-operation with the infantry. It appears that artillery fire could be brought down as far west as the canal line but that no gun positions had been made available closer to the front line. Whatever the cause, the battles on the line of the canal were savage. 50 Brigade attacked the isolated group of 3 Baluch on 7 and 8 September but failed to dislodge them. The commander of 15 (Indian) Division was replaced (as was his counterpart in 15 [Pakistan] Division in the Sialkot sector), for failure to reinforce success in crossing the canal and for withdrawing under pressure. 'Under a new GOC,' says a neutral intelligence report, 'the Indian forces on this axis probed and counter-attacked continuously up to 23 September, but made no headway.' This is correct as far as it goes, but the battles were see-saw, with both sides' infantry and armour attacking and counter-attacking under artillery fire and suffering heavy casualties whose evacuation was extremely difficult.

Gallantry was not as one-sided as claimed by Gulzar Ahmed. Describing the Batapur–Dograi dogfight, he wrote that,

> The Indian commander...now calculated the economics of killing Pakistani soldiers in terms of rupees...and felt that considering the family pensions and children's allowances to be paid to the families of the dead it was cheaper to confine to artillery shelling. It was also a safer method of passing the day...

This type of diatribe does not befit a gentleman and is regrettable as it demeans the soldiers of both sides, who fought bravely and with skill. It is true that an Indian writer states that, 'in a series of actions up to 18 September, battalion and brigade commanders in 15 Division sector displayed a conspicuous lack of the killer instinct and a marked disinclination to take risks,'[5] but attacks were put in against 16 Punjab and 18 Baluch on 12 September and again between the 14th and 16th and on the night of 21/22 September. All were repulsed, but 3 Jat's attack of 22 September, just before the cease-fire, got through to Dograi. Risk-taking succeeded in the end—but over five hundred men (about 250 from each side) died for the sake of a few square miles of ground.

* * *

The Indian Central Axis (Map 7)

The central axis in the Lahore sector was directed north-west towards Lahore and was intended to cross the BRBD canal near Burki, a hamlet about 400 metres on the eastern side of the Canal defended by a company of 17 Punjab, part of the two-company covering force of 13 Infantry Brigade. The company commander, Major Aziz Bhatti, thoroughly deserved the award of the *Nishan-i-Haider* (the highest gallantry award) and his men, too, fought bravely. But there is a question as to why they were left alone to fight bravely for so long.

Claims that the area of Burki and Nurpur/Hudiara (half-way between the border and the BRBD Canal) was strongly defended appear incorrect. If an examination is made of units available to the Pakistan Army on 6–10 September, and where they were in other sectors according to Indian and independent sources, it can be calculated that the Burki–Nurpur area was not well-defended—to the point, indeed, of indicating poor planning. There were, however, about a dozen pill-boxes camouflaged to resemble huts, each occupied by three-man heavy machine-gun teams, and the area was mined.

Perhaps it should have been obvious that the three main roads leading to Lahore from India would be important to an advance because the bridges crossing the BRBD Canal along these routes would be of a higher load-carrying capability than any others in the area. Militarily, it was not exactly brilliant to choose them as axes because, if an advance is aligned to a straight-line road (thus making it easier for planners and logisticians to calculate times past points and all the arcana of movement and resupply), once it is detected by the opposition it can work to the advantage of the defender rather than the attacker. This did not appear to be realized in HQ 1 Corps Pakistan Army, although it certainly was by the PAF, whose attacks were devastating.

* * *

The battle of Burki shall ever remain an epic story of intense heroism, cool courage and dauntless spirit of a handful of men opposing immensely larger forces.

Gulzar Ahmed (1986)

MAP 7 **THE AXES TO LAHORE FROM
KHALRA AND ATARI**

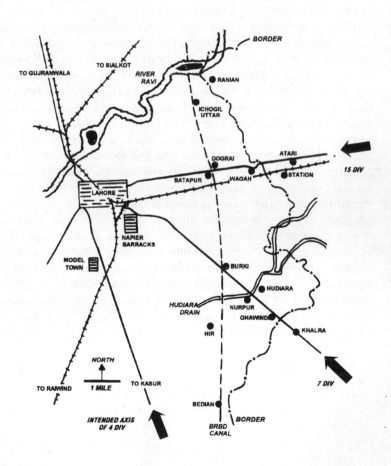

Little was heard of the rate of advance on the central axis. The Indians appear to have reached the village of BARKI (sic), but to have been driven back from the canal.

Foreign Country Intelligence Report, 1966

In one of the key battles, Indian forces captured the village of Burki on September 10, after a full day's battle. The objective of the central advancing column, Burki was situated in a dominating position on the east bank of the canal and had been made into a major fortified position...

Brines (1968)

It appears that the advance towards Lahore via Burki was indeed slowed by Pakistani troops and Rangers in the Nurpur–Hudiara area and along the axis to the canal at Burki, but that their numbers were not as large as claimed by some commentators, although there was a strong Pakistani artillery presence in the shape of two regiments, one each of field and medium guns, and a battery of 8-inch heavy guns.[6] Nurpur–Hudiara could be seen from specially-constructed observation posts in Burki, and artillery observers directed fire on the advance to the rear and flanks. The reason for the advance being slow is probably that forward troops were hesitant about pressing on through or around the opposition, not realizing that the area was so lightly defended. In difficult country with poor observation, as in the flatlands around Burki, it is not possible to assess immediately what size of force might be blocking an advance. A quick platoon attack might flush out an infantry section placed specifically to delay an advance, and after having done so another platoon can press on without the momentum of the advance having been interrupted for any appreciable time—or the intended 'quick' platoon attack might run into a battalion, in which case there is always a muddle in trying to extricate the unfortunate platoon whose commander was simply bearing in mind Slim's dictum that the first duty of an advance guard is to advance.

The Indians did not advance quickly and could not take Burki on the run. The Pakistanis failed to reinforce the company in Burki and relied on artillery to break up the attacks, which it did for the first three days. 'Enemy artillery,' says one Indian commentator, 'fired more than 2000 shells in 30 minutes,' but at 2000 on 10 September the Indians put in a brigade attack (4 Sikh and 16 Punjab) which succeeded in driving the Pakistanis out of Burki. The bridge across the canal had been blown and, in spite of drawing up to the canal, the Indians could not force a crossing. There was stalemate on the central axis, as on the northern.

The Southern Axis of the Indian Attack

Pakistan's 11 Inf. Div. was allocated a front defending Lahore and centred on Kasur, about eighteen miles south, extending 'from Bedian in the north to excluding Suleimanki to the south-west'—about fifty miles in a straight line, but almost double that when the configuration and terrain of the border are taken into account. This was too great a frontage for a division of seven battalions (in three brigades), although it was well balanced and had a normal allocation of armour and artillery.

1st Armoured Div. was intended to pass through the line secured by 11 Div. and exploit forward using its own infantry and such of 11 Div. as might be allocated. The main problem with the operation was lack of a Corps HQ to command it. Confusion was caused by conflicting orders. This might have been ameliorated had the divisional commanders chosen to confer with each other, but even the most pliable divisional commander (and, by definition, divisional commanders are not pliable souls) would find it hard to accept that one of his peers should be placed over him. This is especially the case when the abilities of commanders—and hence their reputations—are about to be tested in battle.

1st Armd. Div.'s concentration area was in the Kasur area, through which the Indian southern axis was drawn. It was here that Pakistan had planned as long ago as May to mount its counter-offensive, but plans were altered. Lt.-Gen. Gul Hassan gives the revised mission* for the operation as being:

- To seal off the Beas-Sutlej corridor by seizing the bridge over the Beas River to cut off Indian forces threatening Lahore; and
- To thwart the enemy's advance through Kasur to Lahore.

Manekar[7] reproduces a captured Pakistani operation order dated 8 September. The paper is considered to be genuine. It was originated by HQ 4 Armoured Brigade and addressed to its infantry unit, 10 Battalion

---

* The mission was revised because 7 Div. had to remain in Akhnur.

Frontier Force Regiment. The order gave details of 4 Brigade's tasks and outlined those of 1 Armoured Division's other two formations, 3 and 5 Brigades. The order is consistent with Lt.-Gen. Gul's outline above, and even with Brigadier Gulzar Ahmed's version, although it is not mentioned by either. Manekar attempts to make it appear that Pakistan intended to thrust at Delhi, and goes so far as to say that, '...the Grand Trunk Road lay open, practically undefended, with all our forces on the other side of the Beas—thus bringing within an ace of realisation Ayub's dream of 'strolling up' to Delhi.' The Grand Trunk Road was hardly undefended, there being three corps in Western Command, between Delhi and the border, comprising an armoured division and eleven infantry divisions. The use of quotation marks around 'strolling up' gives the impression that the phrase had been used by a figure of authority in Pakistan. Even Prime Minister Shastri said on 26 September that, 'President Ayub had been talking a great deal about the tanks and other military equipment Pakistan had acquired and had on many occasions boasted that if they decided to march on Delhi, it would be a walk-over.'[8] Although Brines claims that Ayub had 'taunted' Shastri, Dr Wright points out that, 'Ayub's public utterances do not contain a single example of such a boast'. He adds, a trifle sarcastically, 'Perhaps Shastri was directly or indirectly privy, 'on many occasions' to his private conversation.'

In spite of later attempts to alter facts to fit convictions, the situation was grave enough for India. The captured operation order stated that 1 Armoured Division was to move against the Grand Trunk Road from the Kasur area as follows (Maps 6 and 8):

- 3 Armd. Bde. astride the Upper Bari Doab Canal (UBDC) to secure Jandiala Guru, eighteen miles south-east of Jammu;
- 5 Armd. Bde. astride the straight road from Khem Karan to Amritsar; and
- 4 Armd. Bde. across the grain of the country north-east to Valtoha then south-east to Nabipur.

(There were to be two further sets of orders, on 7 and 8 September, and matters were to be complicated by Commander 11 Div., as 'co-ordinator' of the two-division force, issuing orders to the armoured division and its individual formations.)

The operation was to be conducted in three phases:

- assembly, and marrying-up between armour and infantry units;
- advance to and securing of the line Tarn Taran—Fatehabad; and
- securing of the bridge across the Beas River.

Initially, 11 Infantry Division was ordered to blunt the Indian offensive, which it did in spite of having only five infantry battalions at the beginning of the battles instead of a normal divisional complement of nine. (21 Brigade, of two battalions, had been withdrawn on 5 September to reinforce in the north but returned to the division on 7 September.) If the situation developed favourably, 11 Div. was intended to secure a bridgehead through which the armoured division would advance together with elements of 11 Div.'s infantry.

Command of the two-division force was assumed by GHQ Rawalpindi. As observed by Lt.-Gen. Gul Hassan: 'This was far from ideal but there was just no alternative.' This is true, but not only was it far from ideal, it was verging on the disastrous because GHQ had much more to deal with than the direct command of two divisions, no matter how important the engagement in which they were involved.

According to a foreign intelligence document of the period,

...the attacking force, comprising probably a brigade of the Indian 7 Infantry Division with armoured support, moved along the FEROZEPUR road and succeeded in reaching KASUR. The brigade commander however seems to have had some premonition that he was moving into a trap and withdrew about four miles to the west bank of the River Sutlej.

This incursion is mentioned by Brines as coming from Khem Karan, which is unlikely, but it is possible that some elements of 7 Div. (perhaps reconnaissance patrols) managed to advance close to Kasur and gave the impression that a deeper penetration had been made than actually obtained. If the brigade had moved forward it would not have been caught in a trap because the Pakistani counter-offensive was about to begin and there were no troops available to deal with an entire brigade group let loose behind the main Pakistani force.

The Pakistani thrust was reasonably well-planned but the machinery and expertise of higher command were not effective enough for it to be successful. In his examination of the operation in his *Memoirs*,

Lt.-Gen. Gul Hassan explains not only, 'Why the Counter-Offensive Failed,' but states that, 'The tale of the [1st] Armoured Division was decidedly heart-rending... After the 1965 War I met many officers who expressed disappointment that this division had let the side down. The allegation could not be denied but there must have been cogent reasons for its atrocious performance.' *The History of Pakistan Artillery* states that, 'The brigade and regimental commanders [of 1 Armd. Div.] were good professional men. But with Nasir as GOC they did not have a chance.' (Riza [1980].)

* * *

At 0430 on 6 September India's 4 Mountain Division advanced into Pakistan on a front of about sixteen miles stretching from Bedian to Rohiwal (Map 8). The offensive was stopped. 13 Dogra Battalion captured Bedian but were driven out by 7 Punjab's counter-attack next day. 11 Division stood against the attack and, according to plan, acted as a firm base for the passage through of the armoured division to which 11 Div. was to allocate infantry. In an efficient operation, engineers bridged the Rohi *nala* under sporadic Indian attack, and a battalion group of 1st Battalion Frontier Force Regiment (minus one company) and a squadron of 6th Lancers moved east and forced their way to Khem Karan, which they reached at last light on 7 September, by which time Pakistan's 1st Armoured Division was well on the move from Raiwind to the Kasur area to attempt a counter-thrust towards Amritsar.

The 1FF/6L operation was admirable. Some 450 infantry soldiers and a dozen tanks conducted a text-book advance against stiff opposition and established a secure base for 5 Armd. Bde. and 21 Inf. Bde. to deploy to the area of Khem Karan, from where it was intended that they and the rest of the Armoured Division would debouch to the confusion of the advancing Indians. In spite of the élan and determination shown by the armoured regiments and infantry battalions, there was no comparable display of drive and energy on the part of some of their senior commanders, especially the commander of 5 Armoured Brigade and his superior, the GOC 1st Armoured Division.

Maj.-Gen. Nasir had been given orders by GHQ that were then conveyed to his brigade commanders by his staff. Latitude had been given to junior commanders to seize such opportunities as they could by exploiting weaknesses detected in the enemy's dispositions. Such

MAP 8   **KHEM KARAN AND KASUR**

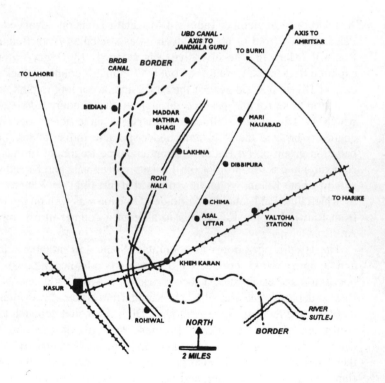

flexibility requires that the senior commander keep an eye on developments because junior officers—usually—are anxious to press on and win glory. Sometimes they fail to consider external circumstances when they are on a winning streak, which is why commanders, knowing the bigger picture, can either rein them in, let them be, or encourage their dash. It helps if the personalities of those involved are compatible, as they will be if a commander has been allowed to have a say in the selection of his subordinates and follows this up with careful, but discreet, monitoring. It probably did not assist matters that the brigade commanders had not been permitted to visit one another in the concentration area and that none of them was on good terms with their GOC. The latter is not unknown, if a trifle unusual, but should have been detected and corrected at a higher level. But the next higher level was GHQ, not a corps HQ, and monitoring of this sort of situation is almost impossible by a headquarters that is not structured for it.

According to the *War Diaries* of 1 and 11 Divs. the following orders were issued by their commanders on 7 September (Map 6):[9]

11 Div.:

- 21 Bde. with 5 Frontier Force to move into bridgehead after last light 7 September.
- 1 Armd. Div. to build up in bridgehead and be poised for breakout.

1 Armd. Div.:

- 3 Armd. Bde. with 6 Lancers ex 11 Div. to advance along Sobraon branch [canal] and secure Beas bridge [at Harike].
- 4 Armd. Bde. to advance along Kasur branch [canal] and cut Grand Trunk Road in area Jandiala Guru.
- 12 Cav. to follow 4 Armd. Bde. and secure class 50/60 bridges over Kasur branch [canal].
- 5 Armd. Bde. revert to under command [from 11 Div.] and come in reserve.

* * *

6 Lancers (formerly the Duke of Connaught's Own Lancers [Watson's Horse] in the time of the Raj) once again showed that regimental tradition and pride, together with the high standard of training that will be produced by good leadership, are important factors in winning battles. But there is another requirement: inspired leadership from above.

The Lancers rolled forward seven miles from Khem Kharan to take the hamlet and railway station at Valtoha on the evening of 8 September, while 24 Cavalry (another fine unit) reached the village of Asal Uttar. The presence of two enemy armoured units in Indian territory on the Lahore Front disturbed the Indians, who imagined that reports of armour in the Sialkot sector indicated that *all* Pakistani armour, in the shape of 1st Armoured Division, was much further north. According to Manekar, quoted by Wright, Indian intelligence had not detected the creation of 6 Armd. Div. and assumed that only a single armoured formation existed. Manekar states that failure to identify 6 Armd. Div. 'was a vital omission from the Army's viewpoint and cost us a lot in the Khem Kharan sector'. This does not stand up to examination as a reason for Indian losses. As we have seen, 6 Armd. Div. was 'no more than the old 100 Independent Armoured Brigade Group,' a fact which must have been on the Indian intelligence's Order of Battle of the Pakistan Army. When reports about the identity and locations of enemy units and formations were examined by Indian intelligence officers, the failure to locate 100 Armd. Brig. should have sounded alarms. That it was not located did not mean that 1 Armd. Div. was the only armoured formation opposing the Indian advance. Whatever the inadequacies of Indian intelligence, the fact is that the Pakistani counter-strike was successful. 4 Mountain Division took some hard blows and presented an opportunity for 5 Armd. Bde. to continue advancing against a withdrawing and inevitably demoralized force. But the commanders of 1 Armd. Div. and 5 Armd. Bde. failed to follow up the advantage won by their forward units.

One Indian account of battles in the area, taken from *Battle Honours of the Indian Army*, is:

...On the 7th enemy armour broke through at Palanwala and by 1200 hrs the situation was desperate. Of the six infantry battalions 2½ had abandoned their positions and the rest were in penny packets and under heavy pressure. The Corps Commander sent a frantic hand written message to the Army Commander requesting, inter alia, for replacement of 4 Division and disbandment [?] of four battalions. In the meantime, by 8th morning the Division had hastily occupied a defended sector in area Asal Uttar to deny the Amritsar and Patti axes to the enemy. The gap south east of Valtoha was flooded and some anti-tank mines laid along the main approaches.

Which is, by any standards, an objective description of the unfortunate vicissitudes of one's own side.

On the night of 8 September the commander of 5 Armd. Bde. ordered 6L and 24 Cav. to return to Khem Karan to laager for the night. Even Gulzar Ahmed states that, 'to fall back without adequate reason is never acceptable to a soldier,' which is obvious, but one must consider the viewpoint of the commander at the time, who, with sketchy intelligence and doubtless worried about whether his two tired regiments would be able to withstand a counter-attack at dawn, decided to withdraw them. The other side of the coin is that the two units had their tails up, were ready to go forward after a night's rest and re-supply, and would suffer from being withdrawn. As it was, the units motored back to Khem Karan, obtained ammunition, fuel, and rations, tightened their tanks' tracks, and caught a bit of sleep before moving out again on 9 September to cover the same ground. By this time 4 Mtn. Div. had had a chance to regroup, dig in, and have a hard look at the situation. Further, the Indian 2 Independent Armoured Brigade arrived in the area that day, and there are few things more cheering to a tired, depressed infantry soldier than hearing the squeaking, creaking, grinding, and roaring of his own tanks moving forward.

During 8 September GHQ Pakistan Army gave orders to 1 Armd. Div. to 'Overrun maximum enemy territory' on breaking out. Maj.-Gen. Nasir gave amended orders as follows:

- 4 Armd. Bde. to advance along Sobraon branch [canal] and *destroy* bridge at Harike (emphasis added).
- 5 Armd. Bde. to advance on the road Khem Karan-Amritsar and secure bridges *en route*.
- 12 Cavalry to advance along the Kasur branch [canal] and secure bridges *en route*.
- 3 Armd. Bde. in reserve.

This turn-round in orders might go some way to explaining why Commander 5 Brigade withdrew his units on 8 September (unless that was coincidental—and one is drawn to assume this), but the difference to the orders given at 1800 the previous day is so great as to make one wonder whether the originator was thinking clearly at the time. Orders have to be distributed, examined, and if required, explained further by the originator or his (well-briefed) subordinates. It is essential they be conveyed down to the last soldier. Given the requirement for translation of higher-level plans into more detailed orders at brigade, unit, and sub-unit level, and the conducting of 'O(rders') Groups' down to infantry platoon and tank troop level, it would have taken a minimum of three hours to inform all concerned—if everything went to plan; if every unit and sub-unit commander was available immediately for briefing and then instantly conducted his own O Group—and if there were no questions requiring clarification further up the chain. A movement plan, to take account of altered axes, would have to be compiled concurrently—not impossible for a well-trained staff, but a needless imposition nevertheless—and of much importance, gun areas would have to be reconnoitred and guns moved to them before the advance began. 'The confusion of orders between [the divisions] tried the tempers of artillery commanders... In order to support [the] advance, field guns had to be repositioned...' says *The History of Pakistan Artillery*. The whole thing was, there is no kinder word for it, a shambles.

On the night of 9 September both 6L and 24 Cav. were *again* withdrawn to Khem Karan. (*Battle Honours of the Indian Army* claims there was an assault on the Indian positions at 2100 but there is no evidence of this. There may have been a lost tank or two rolling forward causing confusion. The picture can be imagined—the roaring noise of tracked vehicles in the night followed by a few bursts of machine-gun fire; then illumination by Very lights or mortars; moving shadows; more gunfire—any soldier knows what night-time can do to nerves.) They had been allowed to do a Duke of York while the Indians recovered from the mauling they had received. The two regiments should have been encouraged to press forward on 8/9 September until they met opposition, while concurrently being reinforced, especially with infantry, to make a quick attack while the enemy was still relatively off balance. Re-supply could have taken place when contact with the enemy was broken, and intermediate ground secured by a reinforcing unit, be that tank or infantry. The fact that the artillery supporting the advance on 9 September fired only thirteen rounds per gun is indicative of the comparatively light resistance met by 5 Brigade.

The commanders of 1 Armd. Div. and 5 Armd. Bde. lost their chance of fame, and indeed, should have been replaced when the timid decision to laager at Khem Karan on 8 September was reported to GHQ. The advance that began on 10 September moved towards positions that had been well-constructed. 4 and 5 Armoured Brigades went forward to disaster against 4 Mountain Division and 2 Independent Armoured Brigade.

The Indian formations' flanks were secured by two *nalas* (watercourses, in many places steep-sided), the Rohi and the Nikasu. Pakistani attempts to penetrate the *nalas* by an outflanking movement would have been detected by the tanks placed at each crossing-point and would have drawn speedy counter-attacks in country of the Indians' choosing. The Indians had put their thirty-six-hour respite to good use by creating well dug-in positions, with minefields covered by observed artillery fire. The defenders' Centurion tanks were sited in camouflaged positions in high crop to draw the Pakistan Pattons close, in order to minimize effects of the latter's better gun range. Tank-killing teams of jeep-mounted 106 mm recoilless launchers could be moved quickly to areas of most threat. The defensive position in the area of Asal Uttar (Map 9) was shaped as a horseshoe, the classic killing ground, with fire being directed at the sides of tanks, where armour is thinner. The defenders breached the banks of the Rohi Nala to create a bog into which many of the Pattons sank. Centurion squadrons were positioned ready to move quickly when the opportunity arose to counter-attack. The divisional artillery was closed up and protected from flank assault by minefields. It is not said by any commentator whether Pakistani reconnaissance patrols were sent out on the nights of 8/9 or 9/10 September, but it must be concluded that they were not, because any patrol could hardly have failed to detect the preparations being made. Obviously, tactical air reconnaissance was not employed. The Pakistanis went forward blind into a well-constructed trap.

5 Armd. Bde., with supporting infantry, advanced at first light on 9 September from Khem Karan to attack the main Asal Uttar positions and attempted a right flanking movement. It was brought to a halt by early afternoon. Dr Wright states that the Divisional Commander, Maj.-Gen. Nasir Ahmed Khan, was mortally wounded in the village of Chima while rallying his men, but it appears he is mistaken, and that the senior officer's death he describes was that of the commander of 11 Div. artillery, Brigadier Ahsan Rashid Shami, a 'character' of some note, whose loss was deeply felt. Major Sarbans Singh states that, 'In

MAP 9

ASAL UTTAR

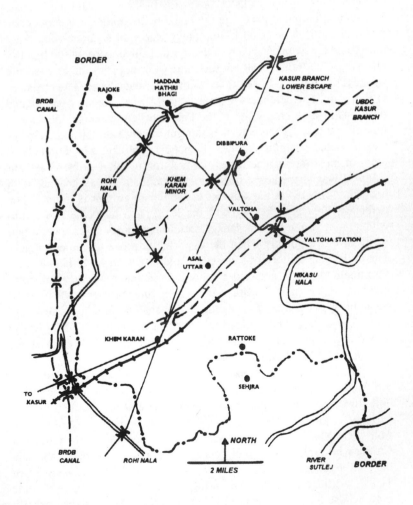

desperation the enemy commander collected his Reconnaissance Group
[Singh probably means O Gp] which was caught by our artillery fire
as a result of a radio intercept. The enemy Divisional Commander was
seriously wounded and his Commander Artillery killed.'

3 Armd. Bde., which originally had been intended to advance to the
Beas-Sutlej junction on a separate axis, and was then ordered to remain
in reserve, was given the task of following up 4 and 5 Bdes. but did
not get the chance to do so.

It had been planned that 4 Armd. Bde. outflank the Indians' position
from the north-west and cut them off in the rear. 4 Cav. led the advance
but lost its way and, after being placed on the right axis by the
Divisional Commander, who had seen their mistake from his helicopter,
soon outran its infantry. The Indian tank-hunters took a heavy toll and
the flooded area of the Rohi Nala prevented many of the heavy Pattons
moving forward. Tank commanders, true to the traditions of their
regiments and the spirit of cavalry and armour, did not move 'closed-
down', but exposed their heads and shoulders above the turrets of their
tanks. Many, of course, were killed.

4 Cavalry ceased to exist. They lost radio contact with HQ 4 Bde.
about 1400 on 10 September, just after the CO reported his own
position as being 1000 yards from the 32 milestone on the main Kasur-
Amritsar road. They had outrun not only their infantry but also their
re-supply vehicles, most of which were wheeled. Altogether some forty
Pakistani tanks were destroyed that day. There was no possibility that
the Pakistanis could mount a further attack in the area. They were
placed on the defensive throughout the war zone and, on the night of
10 September, had to move 1 Armd. Div., minus 5 Bde. (i.e., 3 Armd.
Bde. and the remnants of 4 Armd. Bde.) to the Sialkot sector, where
another Indian attack was under way. 3 Bde. received these orders at
1400, just as 4 Cavalry went off the air and it was becoming obvious
that both brigades' attacks were stalled. According to *The History of
the Pakistan Artillery*, the withdrawal of 3 Bde. was 'by no means a
reassuring sight'. (The *History* also states that artillery support for the
operations of 4 and 5 Armd. Bdes. consisted of 72 field guns, 30
mediums, and 12 heavy guns—a large and potentially devastating
grouping but one that lacked effectiveness because there was no HQ
to co-ordinate fire.)

The Indians, scenting victory, quickly regrouped after the battle
(having themselves lost about thirty tanks) and mounted an attack on
Khem Karan on 12 September with an infantry brigade and an

armoured regiment (the Deccan Horse). The attack failed, as did another shortly afterwards. Fighting continued over the following week but Indian forces made no territorial gains. 11 Div. managed to reorganize its defences but had only seven battalions and a handful of armour, although it retained 36 field guns, 30 mediums, and 8 heavy guns as divisional artillery. These were invaluable in breaking-up Indian attacks. On the nights of 21/22 and 22/23 September, just before the cease-fire was due to take effect, the Indians again attempted to capture Khem Karan but all efforts failed and the Pakistanis were left holding about fifty square miles of Indian territory. It is noted by the author of *Battle Honours of the Indian Army* that, '...this [4th] Division tarnished its name again when a divisional attack on 21/22 September to capture Khem Karan failed miserably,' which is a forthright and honourable admission of defeat.

If the Pakistanis had maintained the offensive on 9 and 10 September, it is likely they would have covered the twenty miles to Amritsar by the night of the 10th and got behind the Indian 15 Div. at a time when it was in disarray. Even the newly-arrived Indian 2 Armd. Bde. would probably not have presented a decisive threat to their right flank as it would have been forced to move north to counter-attack— which could have been met by 3 Armd. Bde. if it had followed up the advance. Whether the Pakistanis could have held on to what they might have gained is, however, another matter. The Indians had considerable reserves, and, in spite of the PAF's qualitative ascendancy over the IAF, it did not have the numbers of aircraft necessary to achieve air superiority while concurrently giving close support to troops.

Whatever the ifs and might-have-beens about the Lahore sector battles, there were some lessons learned the hard way. It was obvious that outstanding leadership at the junior level as well as gallantry and good equipment (the Patton was superior to the Centurion, even if there were not enough of them), excellent artillery support, and high morale do not compensate for inadequate reconnaissance, lack of press-on spirit in commanders (in only two cases—but very important ones), poor communications, shockingly bad command at the highest levels, and indifferent logistical planning. Tactics were a mixture of (mainly) good at unit level and fair to bad at brigade and above.

* * *

Suleimanki and Munabao

To the south of the main areas of conflict around Lahore and Sialkot, the Pakistani 105 Infantry Brigade (4 and 10 Punjab) advanced into Indian territory near Fazilka, ninety miles south-west of Lahore, on 6 September. Further south, about 120 miles due east of Hyderabad, an Indian force moved across the border but was repulsed by 51 Infantry Brigade, which then struck back and advanced to Munabao railway station on the Indian side. Both brigades did well and their commanders, Brigadiers Mohammad Akbar of 151 and Azhar Khan of 51, became lieutenant-generals in later years, but although their victories in the deserts of Sindh were welcome, they did not alter the course of the war. It is tempting to contemplate, however, what might have happened had either of them been commander of 5 Armoured Brigade or even 1 Armoured Division. (In November 1996 the author, visiting Pakistan, had as his driver a former soldier who had hoisted the Pakistani flag on the railway station building. His recollection was that the advance happened so fast that he never actually saw any Indian troops.) 105 Brigade tied down almost the whole of the Indian 11 Infantry Division, although it must be said that that formation did not include, with the exception of 1 Garhwal Rifles, representation from the best units in the Indian Army.

Dera Baba Nanak (Map 5)

In the Punjab, a little to the west of the town of Dera Baba Nanak which is 55 miles north-east of Lahore and 36 miles by road north of Amritsar, a road and rail bridge capable of carrying a locomotive and train and most probably therefore Centurion and Patton Tanks, crosses the [river] Ravi. As its eastern end is located in a Pakistani salient on the left bank of [the] river, the bridge is situated wholly within Pakistani territory. However there is an Indian salient [abutting the western end] of the bridge...[the village of] Jassar stands three miles from the bridge on the Narowal road.

Wright (1972)

The confusion reached its peak on the night of 6/7 September when the enemy attacked Jassar bridge. The border between Pakistan and India near Jassar follows a course that can be aptly described as 'cockeyed'. We had inherited a small enclave on the Indian side of the Ravi river while they

had one on our bank...On 7 September I received a report that HQ 1 Corps
had ordered 15 Division to restore the situation at Jassar...

G.H. Khan (1993)

The significance of the battles around Jassar and Dera Baba Nanak is
that, had either side been able to secure the bridge and bring up anti-
aircraft guns to neutralize air attacks, it would have been possible to
induct a comparatively large force (perhaps an armoured brigade
group) into the territory of the other. This might have affected the
battles around Lahore and Sialkot by encouraging withdrawal of troops
to counter a thrust, but it is unlikely there would have been any great
difference to the outcome of the war. An Indian commentator claimed
that the Pakistani advance was intended 'at striking at Gurdaspur and
the vital road and rail centre of Pathankot,'[10] while Gulzar Ahmed
states the advance was a feint to draw Indian troops away from more
important areas. It seems the Indians attacked simply because capture
of the bridge would have been a bonus, permitting a wider front and
keeping the Pakistanis off-balance, and the Pakistanis responded in the
best fashion possible at the time. For the Pakistan army the action was
important in that it highlighted deficiencies in command and control.

   The Indians attacked on the night of 5/6 September and achieved a
lodgement in the Pakistani salient on the east bank of the Ravi at about
first light on the 6th. Concurrently, 4FF drove out Indian troops
occupying the western salient. Accounts of the battle thereafter are
conflicting but it appears that, following Indian occupation of the west
end of the bridge on 6 September, the Pakistanis thrust east across the
bridge on the 7th. This caused a withdrawal of Indian troops that might
have become a rout but for the courage and leadership of Lt.-Col.
Chajju Ram, who rallied his men to counter-attack, forcing back the
Pakistanis who then demolished the western span of the bridge, leaving
some hundreds of troops on the far bank of the river. Ram was awarded
the *Vir Chakra*, the highest Indian medal for gallantry. The commander
of 15 (Pakistani) Division was replaced at midday on 7 September, and
it was rumoured that an Indian general (perhaps the commander of 26th
Inf. Div.) was court-martialled.

   It would be incorrect to claim that Pakistani command and control
arrangements broke down during the operations at Dera Baba Nanak;
it is more to the point to state that their imprecision was such that no
commander should have been expected to live with them. Gul Hassan
notes that although there was confusion at HQ 15 Division, it was

'exacerbated by HQ I Corps which exercised overall command in this Sector,' and that the divisional commander was a Service Corps officer who should not have been expected to command a fighting formation. He states that HQ I Corps should have exercised closer supervision of the GOC 15 Div., but the crux of the matter is that he should never have been appointed in the first place. It appears that commander I Corps exercised direct command down to brigade level when it was possible to do so, and otherwise relied on HQ 15 Div. to relay orders or originate them when necessary. A strong divisional commander would have insisted on orders defining responsibilities—or simply taken command, which is what leadership is all about. But no officer should ever be placed in such a situation. Definition of the chain of command is the responsibility of the highest headquarters, which in this case was GHQ in Rawalpindi.

The battle of Jassar-Dera Baba Nanak appears to have been poorly handled by both sides. The Pakistani 115 Infantry Brigade (2 battalions, a battery of 6 field guns, and a troop of tanks from the divisional tank regiment) which defended Jassar was well-commanded by Brigadier Muzaffar-ud-Din, but had to cover a three-kilometre front in country that did not permit mutual support unless sub-units were close together. Had an accurate appreciation of the situation been made by HQ 15 Div., the brigade would have been reinforced by 24 Brigade on 6 rather than 7 September, but the opportunity was lost. Similarly, the Indians hesitated and failed to grasp the moment to strike hard. Understandably, they considered the area around the bridge would be defended by larger forces than they encountered, but aggressive patrolling would have shown the true state of affairs.

Jassar-Dera Baba Nanak was hardly a side-show, but perhaps its main effects were to release an Indian armoured regiment for use in the attack on Asal Uttar-Valtoha on 8/9 September, and bottle-up 115 Brigade and prevent its employment in direct defence of Sialkot. It soon became apparent from the ferocity of the fighting that neither side was going to be a pushover. Although the Indian forces were more numerous, they were not sufficient to overcome the opposition. Equally, although the Pakistanis were arguably better led at the lower levels and had better (if fewer) tanks, they could not advance in sufficient numbers to exploit successes. Stalemate looked inevitable to outside observers and the UN became more deeply involved.

* * *

Diplomacy and Politics

The UN Secretary-General, U Thant, visited India and Pakistan from 9–15 September but failed to persuade the leaders of either country to declare an unconditional cease-fire. He went first to Pakistan but was obviously poorly briefed. If he expected the Pakistanis to accept any sort of compromise on 11 September (he flew to Delhi on the 12th), the death anniversary of the Quaid-i-Azam, Mohammad Ali Jinnah, he was mistaken. In reply to U Thant's request, Ayub insisted that an agreement for a cease-fire must include an arrangement for settlement of the Kashmir dispute. In his turn Prime Minister Shastri replied that India, 'shall not agree to any disposition which will leave the door open for further infiltrations,' which, as he must have known, was an impossible condition—just as Ayub could hardly have counted on India agreeing to discussion of Kashmir.[11] Negotiations continued in New York, as the Soviets, Americans, French, and British were apprehensive about China entering the war. On 16 September, the Chinese sent the Indians a belligerent Note indicating, among other things, support for Pakistan. It contained the ominous statement that,

> ...non-involvement absolutely does not mean failure to distinguish between right and wrong; it absolutely does not mean that China can approve of depriving the Kashmiri people of their right of self-determination or that she can approve of Indian aggression against Pakistan on the pretext of the Kashmir issue.12

Burke and Ziring (1990) suggest that intervention by China 'would bring in the USA on India's side,' which may be going a bit far, but it was disquieting that China was making bellicose noises and it was in the interests of all concerned that the waters be muddied no further. Ayub and Bhutto paid a visit to Beijing on 20 September and met with Zhou Enlai and his defence minister, but obtained nothing of moment. Apparently the Chinese advice was consistent with what Chinese strategy would be in such circumstances as were obtaining in Pakistan: let the Indian army advance and conduct a 'people's war' which would overcome the enemy—in the long term. This was unsatisfactory and only contributed to Ayub's sense of failure.

US bilateral diplomacy was effective in alienating both countries. The cut-off of military aid was vexing to Pakistan, which had thought (naively) that the US would stand by the 1958/9 Agreement to 'assist the Government of Pakistan at its request' if there were a threat to its 'national independence and integrity'. Although this Accord was specifically aimed at containing Communist aggression, the preamble stated, grandiosely, that, 'The US regards as vital to its national interest and to world peace the preservation of the independence and integrity of Pakistan.'

Ayub did not for a moment think that the skies would be filled by United States Air Force Sabres shooting down Indian MiGs, Hunters, and Mysteres, but he did hope that the US would intervene to stop India's invasion across the international border. India, more sophisticated in its approach to international diplomacy, and attuned to the give and take of wheeling-dealing democracy, understood the US stance. Of course it postured and protested, but quietly it reinforced its ties with Moscow and got on with the business of ensuring that the flow of war *matériel* from the Soviet Union and France continued.

Pakistan, relying almost entirely on the US and Britain for weapons and ammunition, was in a poor position. The Air Force had but two weeks supply, at wartime rates, of starter cartridges for the engines of its Sabre aircraft, the mainstay of the fighter force. There was no alternative supplier. The PAF faced the Indian Air Force knowing that its air effort would come quickly to a halt. Similarly, GHQ knew that supplies of ammunition were finite, as were spares and replacements for American and British equipment. The squeeze applied by the US and Britain had considerable adverse effect on the defence forces of Pakistan. The Security Council of the UN knew and cared little about such matters. Initially there was no agreement in New York concerning the conflict, for the several reasons of its members. But their positions coalesced as they came to realize that the war served few of their direct interests. Out of cynicism and self-serving nationalism came compromise and direction. Meantime, as negotiations, deliberations, and obfuscation continued around the conference tables of New York and world capitals, the war, too, went on.

The Sialkot Sector (Maps 5 and 10)

Sialkot is closer to Indian territory than Lahore, being only six miles from the border. It is not in 'good tank country' as there is little room for mass manoeuvre because the extensive canal systems interlock with the main rivers. Further, the Chenab and Jhelum rivers would be major obstacles to movement north-westwards towards Pakistan's capital, Islamabad. Fifteen miles west of Sialkot is the Grand Trunk Road linking Lahore with the capital and northern Pakistan. Across the border to the north-east, only twenty-five miles away, is the winter capital of old Kashmir, Jammu (now an administrative centre for the Indian-controlled region of Kashmir).

There are differing accounts of the reasons for the Indian advance towards Sialkot. It may be that the objectives were imprecise at the time of orders being issued, which is unlikely given long-standing plans for war in the west, or that they were concealed afterwards in the interests of avoiding criticism of the failure to attain them. One incontrovertible fact is that a captured Indian army order indicated the intention to cut the Grand Trunk Road and railway at Gujranwala, but this was probably a local tactical objective.[13] The overall plan was and remains undefined, but reasonable conjecture may be made concerning its details based on examination of Indian, Pakistani, and neutral sources. Notwithstanding any territorial imperatives, it is apparent that the Indian aim was to defeat the Pakistan Army in the field, and according to Dr Wright, their accounts concerning the advance in the Sialkot sector had 'a cluster of general objectives' aiming to:

- pre-empt a Pakistani advance on Jammu planned for 10 September;
- draw off Pakistani forces from the Chhamb sector,
- prevent Pakistan reinforcing on the Lahore front; and
- draw into battle, then destroy, Pakistani armour.

There does not appear to be evidence that a Pakistani plan existed to attack Jammu on 10 September. Their advance on Akhnur, twenty miles north of Jammu, had been halted five days previously and it was obvious that they could go no further without substantial reinforcement in the Chhamb area. It may well be that there was an Indian plan to draw away Pakistani forces from Chhamb and Lahore but, if so, it is open to question why they should have committed an entire corps of more than three divisions, including the premier armoured formation, to an area in which a feint would have been enough to achieve these objectives. The possibility that one objective was the destruction of Pakistan's armour is difficult to substantiate as existing *before* the advance, although it might have become an aim after the Pakistani armour was committed. The Indians admit they were unaware of the existence of 6th Armoured Division, which was south-west of Sialkot. Even had its location and identity been known, the defeat of two tank units would hardly have represented 'destruction of Pakistani armour'. The argument that the thrust would draw in all other Pakistani armour from elsewhere to meet with destruction does not stand up, because there could be no guarantee that all other armour would move into the Sialkot sector, and even were there a desire to do so, Indian pressure on Lahore would militate against complete withdrawal of Pakistani tanks from that area. As it happened, three more armoured regiments *were* brought in, but even this was hardly the concentration that would meet an objective of annihilation.

Accounts differ as to how many tanks were put out of action by both sides, but if it was India's intention to win a battle of attrition this did not succeed. The advance was blunted and the Pakistanis were able to hold their positions and prevent penetration of the vital ground between Sialkot and Lahore. It appears that the Indian aim was simply to attack where it considered the enemy was weak and to gain as much ground as possible while endeavouring to keep the enemy off balance. Exploitation would come later, when either the Lahore or the Sialkot offensive was successful. This is a perfectly understandable aim, and one that might just have been achieved had it not been for the stubborn resistance of numerically inferior Pakistani formations. That it was not achieved is no reason for criticism of Indian soldiers, who fought bravely.

The Indian invasion of Pakistan in the Sialkot sector began on the night of 7/8 September on two axes: the Jammu-Sialkot road, and a parallel route some twelve miles to the south-east. I (Indian) Corps was commanded by a steady and experienced officer, Lt.-Gen. P.O. Dunn, who had been given only a few days to move his HQ from Delhi to Jammu, where he arrived on 3 September. His corps consisted of:

- 26 Infantry Division, which advanced on the axis of the Jammu-Sialkot road via the Indian border village of Suchetgarh. Gulzar Ahmed claims that the division had four infantry brigades and two armoured regiments, rather than the conventional three plus one, and it appears from other sources that this was so in at least the early stages of the advance. It is likely that the extra brigade and armoured regiment were corps' assets allocated for a specific phase of the operation—but whatever the arrangements, there was a powerful punch on this axis.

- 6 Mountain Division, on the southern axis, crossed the border near the Pakistani village of Charwa. It is claimed by Johri that this formation and 1st Armoured Division were understrength, but no yardstick is given. A mountain division, by definition, does not have an integral armoured regiment. Johri may have mistaken the division's order of battle at the beginning of conflict with the organization that applied on 10/11 September, when one of its brigades came temporarily under command of the armoured division.

- 1 Armoured Division joined the advance at first light on 8 September, crossing the border near Charwa and moving south-west towards Chawinda. It had two armoured brigades each of two tank regiments and a lorried infantry battalion; and a lorried infantry brigade of two battalions. Its artillery included medium and heavy guns. It was a well-balanced formation, but the division had exchanged one, and possibly two, of its Centurion-equipped regiments with Sherman regiments of 2 Independent Armoured brigade, thus reducing its clout.

- Elements of 14 Infantry Division were in the area but there are conflicting accounts of its role. Wright states that it, '7 Mountain Division' (see below), and 1 Armoured Division advanced 'on a front stretching from exclusive of Bajra Garhi to just east of the Degh Nadi, apparently with the initial task of cutting the Sialkot-Narowal-Lahore railway'. Gulzar Ahmed claims it 'rolled down across the wide stretch Charwah-Bajra Garhi...' But it appears that the division was not complete in the area of operations until some days after the initial Indian assault, and even then that it had the task of covering the left flank of 1 Armd. and 6 Inf. Divs., and the right flank of 15 Corps, which was attacking on the Lahore front. During its move to the Jammu sector from Saugor (in central India) it had apparently 'received a pasting from the PAF' and was, as a result, 'in poor shape.'[14]

- '7 Mountain Division' is mentioned by Dr Wright but, so far as can be determined, by nobody else who has written about the war. 7 Infantry Division fought on the Lahore front, but it is possible that a misidentification occurred, resulting in confusion of 7 Mtn. Div. with a brigade of the same number that belonged to 6 Mountain Division.

* * *

In the opening stages of the battles, Pakistan's I Corps covered the Sialkot sector with 15th Infantry Division consisting of seven battalions in four brigades (24, 101, 104, and 115), with 25 Cavalry as its armoured regiment, and a good allocation of artillery. But there were problems, not the least of which was that 115 Brigade was fighting in the Jassar area, where it was required to remain for the rest of the war. 101 Brigade (19 Punjab and 13 FF) was the only formation directly defending Sialkot, and was located astride the main road to Jammu where it faced the onslaught of the Indian 26 Division. 24 Brigade (2 Punjab and 3 FF, plus 25 Cav. under command) was between the border and Chawinda, which lies due east of an almost right-angled bend in the Sialkot-Lahore railway (Map 10). 104 Brigade, which consisted of a single battalion, 9 Baluch, was in reserve in the area of Uggoke/Raipur, about four miles west of Sialkot. It seemed that in the Jammu/Sialkot sector the Indian Army might be able to bring sufficient force to bear to carry the day and even win the war. India's I Corps advanced with two infantry divisions and an armoured division against a Pakistani armoured brigade and a single infantry division that had fragmented and understrength fighting units, no cohesive defensive plan, and some leaders of dubious quality who were already under considerable pressure. India's 1st Armoured Division was ready to exploit the advantage won by the infantry force preceding it. The way to the west seemed open.

* * *

6 Armoured 'Division', consisting of the Guides Cavalry, 22nd Cavalry, 1st (SP) Regiment of 25 pounder guns on tracked chassis, and 4th Battalion Frontier Force Regiment (in fact no more than a brigade of eighty tanks, 12 guns, and 700 infantry in lorries), was in leaguer around Kot Daska, fifteen miles south-west of Sialkot and thirty miles west of the border. Chawinda, where it was to win its spurs, was twenty miles away. The units moved quickly when it became apparent that the Indian invasion was taking place.

* * *

MAP 10   **THE SIALKOT FRONT**

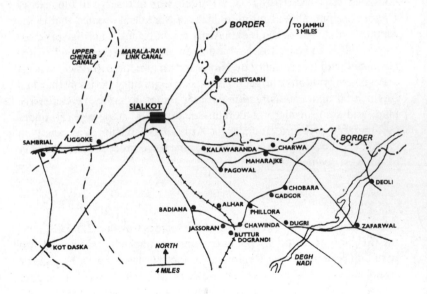

The Indian Thrust along the main Sialkot Road

In the north, two battalions of India's 26 Division crossed the border astride the Jammu-Sialkot road at about midnight on 7 September. They quickly overcame the outposts of the Sutlej Rangers (light scouting forces) but were brought to a halt by 101 Brigade and the weight of Pakistan's artillery. According to Manekar (1967) and Johri, the approaches to Sialkot 'bristled with pill-boxes, bunkers and gun emplacements,' the latter including 'three field and one medium artillery regiments, one heavy battery and one heavy mortar regiment'. A concentration of this number of guns and mortars would cover an area of about 500 metres by 150 metres in which the weight of shells and mortar bombs from one round of fire from each equipment would be approximately two tons.[15] Not only this, but the artillery was well-handled and 'some senior Indian army officers who had served in World War II likened the scale of Pakistani artillery fire to heavy concentrations in the latter stages of that war. While this is not borne out by inspection of battlefields it does indicate that Pakistan artillery fire was substantial and effective.'[16]

* * *

26 Division managed to reach the village of Kalarawanda, about three miles west of the border, by the time of the cease-fire on 23 September. There was a massive effort on the part of the Indian Army on the northern axis of the Sialkot front, but an advance of only three miles cannot be called satisfactory when one considers the numerical superiority of 26 Division. The defence of Sialkot by 19 Punjab and 13 FF and their supporting gunners was more dogged than glamorous, and indefatigable than dramatic. But however effective—and perhaps decisive—their actions were, their tenacity and courage were overshadowed by what happened at Chawinda.

The Chawinda Battles[17]

Also at about midnight on 7 September, two brigades of India's 6 Mountain Division crossed the border south of the 26 Div. axis and occupied the villages of Maharajke and Charwa just inside Pakistan. The battalions in the assault were 4 Rajputana Rifles and 2/5 Gurkha

Rifles. They secured the firm base for the advance of 1 Armoured Division at first light, about 0600 Pakistan Time. In fact, although the armour came through as planned, the immediate border area was not secure for several days because Pakistani stay-behind parties wreaked havoc by sniping and ambushing. The Division's 1 Armoured Brigade reached the village of Phillora and the line of the Sialkot-Lahore railway by 0900 but its right flank was exposed by the failure of 43 Infantry Brigade to move quickly enough to keep up. Explanations vary as to the reasons for this: Johri claims there was a downpour which bogged their vehicles; Verghese states the armoured simply outran the brigade's wheeled vehicles, which sounds reasonable; but whatever happened, the armoured brigade had no flank protection. In fact this was largely irrelevant, as Pakistan's hastily-assembled *ad hoc* force, under direct command of HQ 1 Corps located at Gujranwala, moved east quickly and struck on 8 September. It forced the Indians back to the border, where they remained for two days before advancing again.

The Pakistanis had three armoured regiments and three infantry battalions—a mixture of units from 1 Armoured Division and 24 Infantry Brigade. India had two armoured brigades each of two tank regiments and an infantry battalion. Forces of about equal strength had met in battle, and one had been made to retreat. Unfortunately for Pakistan, it had insufficient armour immediately available to strike a quick blow that would have destroyed the Indian armour which was, naturally, in some disarray. Even Indian commentators acknowledge that 1 Armoured Brigade was 'hit...hard in the ribs' because it 'dashed forward somewhat rashly...' (Verghese).

Both sides used the comparative lull to regroup. The Indians rapidly regained balance and probed forward, while the Pakistanis brought up as many reinforcements as they could to match the preponderance of Indian armour, which was also being augmented. It was a desperate time for the Pakistanis. They well knew that India had large resources on which to call, while almost every unit on the Pakistani Order of Battle was already committed to the fight. 11 Cavalry arrived from Chhamb along with 10 Infantry Brigade (14 Punjab and 6FF) not a minute too early to join in defending the area against the Indian assault that began at first light on 11 September.

The Indians advanced on two axes, Charwa-Chawinda and Kaloi-Pagowal. The battalion group advancing on the latter route was repulsed and forced to fall back to the Kaloi area. On the Chawinda axis, the Indians reached Phillora after a series of head-on tank and infantry battles in which the two sides slugged it out until dusk when 5 Jat (which suffered 100 killed), 5/9 Gurkha Rifles, elements of the Poona Horse, and 4 Horse (Hodson's Horse) took and held the village. Battles raged over the area until the cease-fire twelve days later. The Indians knew it was essential for them to take Chawinda; the Pakistanis knew that if they did, the ground between Lahore and Sialkot would open up for their further advance as there were no forces available for defence further west. On 12 September the Pakistanis tried without success to retake Phillora and next day the Indians attempted to outflank Chawinda from the east but, in an impressive display of flexibility, the Pakistanis moved 19 and 20 Lancers and 1 FF (of 1 Armd. Div.) to its defence and the Indian advance was halted after fierce fighting. Even Gulzar Ahmed acknowledges that, 'It must be said to the credit of the Indian Army that they fought with commendable courage and determination on this day'—a well-deserved tribute. An attack against Chawinda was planned for the 14th but, in a classic employment of good intelligence and efficient artillery, the Pakistanis located the forming-up place of the Garhwali battalion that was to lead the assault and brought fire down on it. The battalion was forced to withdraw and the attack did not take place.

On the night of 15/16 September the Indians again tried to outflank the main Pakistani force, this time by pressing west to Jassoran, three miles due west of Chawinda, across the railway line, then south to cut off Chawinda from the rear. Once the village was isolated, the Indians considered it would fall. At first the advance went well, with Jassoran being occupied at about 1100 on the 16th by 8 Garhwal Rifles supported by a squadron of 2nd Poona Horse. The infantry then turned south and managed to take the village of Buttar Dograndi, but their armour was engaged so heavily by Pakistani anti-tank weapons that it could not advance further. The battalion held out until 17 September, when it was forced to withdraw to Jassoran. It had been impossible to reinforce the unit in order to continue the advance, but neither could the Pakistanis bring in enough force to mount a counter-attack. Furthermore, the Pakistani artillery was running short of ammunition. By mid-September the daily allocation of 155mm ammunition was five rounds per gun, about ninety seconds' fire at the 'intense' rate. Ammunition for the Pattons was also limited. The US embargo on supply of military *matériel* to its SEATO ally was taking effect, but in spite of this the Pakistanis fought magnificently in the Chawinda battles. This is not to denigrate the bravery of the Indians; but the Pakistanis were heavily outnumbered, short of ammunition, and subject to increasing international pressure that it found more difficult to counter than the Indians, who were more skilful in selling their point of view to the international media.

In spite of ammunition shortages and tank casualties, the Pakistanis regrouped yet again, and on 18/19 September cleared the area west of Chawinda, around the railway line, but did not manage to fully retake the station at Alhar, the north side of which remained in Indian hands until the cease-fire. The Pakistanis planned Operation *Wind Up* for 19/20 September with the aim of outflanking the Indians and penetrating west to cut them off. Weather forced postponement to 21/22 September, but the operation was then cancelled.[18]

The war ended on 23 September. Both countries' economies were badly affected and their defence forces had suffered severe blows. There was no winner, but important military lessons had been learned.

NOTES

1. The Secretary General, U Thant, had 'urged a halt in hostilities' (Dennis Kux, *The United States and Pakistan 1947-2000*, OUP 2001, an elegantly written *tour de force* of immense value). Informal approaches were also made, and U Thant actually visited both countries. See Note 10.
2. Wolpert (1993).
3. Ibid.
4. Quoted in Wright (1972).
5. Sarbans Singh (1993).
6. In 1965 field guns were 25 pounders, named for the weight of shell, or American 105mm howitzers with 32lb shells. Medium guns were 5.5 inch calibre and fired 80 pound shells. 155mm guns were regarded as heavy equipments although their shells weighed only 90 lbs. The shells of 8 inch (203mm) heavy guns weighed 200 lbs. There were eight 25 pounders in a battery, 24 in a regiment, as with 5.5 inch guns. A heavy regiment usually consisted of three batteries each of four guns, two batteries being 155mm and one 8-inch.
7. Wright (1972) draws on Manekar (1967).
8. Lal Bahadur Shastri, *When Freedom is Menaced*, New Delhi, 1965.
9. There is a good description of *The Battle for Ravi-Sutlej Corridor 1965* by A.H. Amin in the Pakistan *Defence Journal* of December 2001. Excellent maps.
10. B.G. Verghese, *India Answers Pakistan*, Bombay, 1966.
11. 'During U Thant's visit on September 13th, a cabinet meeting was in progress, in which Lal Bahadur Shastri recommended the acceptance of the UN Resolution for

the cease-fire. This was opposed by General J.N. Chaudhuri, who suggested avoiding the acceptance of the cease-fire.

The Army, he said was on the verge of inflicting a great defeat on the Pakistanis and it should be allowed to exercise maximum damage on Pakistani war machine. The Indian military circles were in favour of prolonging the war to enable them to reduce Pakistani armour and other to reduce threat of future attacks. In this line the Defence Minister Chavan too supported the Army's stand.' *The 1965 India Pakistan Air War Project*—Bharat Rakshak http://www.bharat-rakshak.com/IAF/History/ 1965War

12. *Documents on the Foreign Relations of Pakistan: China, India, Pakistan*, Pakistan Institute of International Affairs, Karachi 1966.
13. NCID.
14. NCID.
15. The author is grateful to Colonel J.C. Longfield, MBE, Commandant Royal School of Artillery, Larkhill, in 1989, for providing technical advice.
16. NCID.
17. An excellent personal account of part of the battles is given by Major Shamshad Ali Khan in the Defence Journal (Karachi) of March and April 1988.
18. See Musa (1987), who claims that US pressure precluded further activity. A full account was provided to the author by Brigadier Muhamad Hayat, SJ, in May 1998, for which he is most grateful.

6 The Last Years of Ayub

Aftermath of the War

The army was shaken by the result of the 1965 war, but not as much as the population at large, which Pakistan's government-controlled media had led to believe that India would be defeated. Disillusionment created internal problems which, fed by adverse economic conditions, led to the emergence of Z.A. Bhutto as a national figure and the eclipse of President Ayub Khan. The reputation of the fighting forces did not suffer greatly, and they continued to be regarded as the mainstay of probity in the country. Pakistan's relationship with the US was seriously affected, while China and the eastern bloc began to assume greater importance in diplomacy and as suppliers of military equipment. The country was not so much leaderless as punch-drunk. The army licked its wounds and made efforts to improve its force structure, administration, training, equipment, every aspect of military potentiality—but it needed firm direction, a sense of purpose and, not least, money. All three were to be in short supply.

Lessons of the War

There were many mistakes made by both sides before and during the war. Some lessons were learned. Unfortunately, there was a tendency in the army to ignore unpleasant reality and excuse poor performance by placing blame on inadequate weapons, insufficient ammunition, and lack of US support. To be sure, some of the equipment was far from modern, there was a shortage of several important natures of ammunition, and the US displayed a singular lack of loyalty to an ally.* But it was apparent that there had been inadequate training at all but unit level, misguided selection of officers for some higher command appointments, appalling command and control arrangements, poor intelligence gathering, and almost unbelievably bad intelligence procedures, in that measures for collation and dissemination were at times confused or even non-existent. In short, the Pakistan Army was not ready to fight *any* war in 1965, never mind a war against an enemy smarting from previous defeats, anxious for revenge, well-equipped, and with enormous reserves of equipment, ammunition, and manpower. Further, the Indians had a command structure in the higher echelons that was more sophisticated, larger (naturally, but therefore providing a better base for selection), and less parochial than that of Pakistan. The fact that Pakistan's army managed to fight the Indians to a standstill is amazing—and much credit should be given to the Pakistan Air Force for its part in countering its much larger Indian opponent and supporting the ground forces. The PAF was 'well-handled and controlled by the Commander-in-Chief, Nur Khan... A tremendous sense of purpose was displayed and attacks were carried out with considerable determination... It is also clear there was excellent cooperation between the army and the air force at all levels, in contrast to poor Indian inter-service liaison.'[1]

The Pakistan army, in spite of self-inflicted limitations and many errors, conducted itself honourably and with gallantry in battle (as did that of India). It deserved better senior commanders than it possessed, and these might have been available had the army not been so politicized. Only eighteen years after its creation, the army was suffering from a defect that was to become acute in later years—the appointment of senior commanders and staff officers on grounds of loyalty to presidents.

* * *

---

* See letter from the US Ambassador in Iran to Washington of 2 January 1978. Ambassador McConnaughey in Islamabad, pre-1965, was allegedly 'authorised to inform Pakistan that even if... attack... came from... India, the US would consider itself bound by the bilateral [agreement]. (Ibid. [1986]).

Command

So far as tactics were concerned, the army could congratulate itself on spirit and élan at the lower levels. Gallantry was apparent, and even prevalent, but on occasion overrode the basic rules in the textbooks— which is no bad thing if wise senior commanders can induce or discourage the enthusiasm of junior leaders as might be required.* Unfortunately, there were few such commanders. It had been thought and even intended that GHQ would have been able to take to the field in wartime, to be closer to the battlefront, but this did not eventuate and it is unlikely that it would have improved matters if it had. It was not the location that was at fault: it was the system, or lack of it.

Operation *Gibraltar* had been planned for four months (at least) and, in spite of the Foreign Office claim that the Indians would not attack across the border, it should have been obvious in GHQ that wider conflict would result from that unfortunate foray. Even were it not obvious, the army had had adequate time to constitute another corps HQ and should have done so. IV Corps HQ was in nucleus, but with a total of six divisions and two semi-divisions (6 Armd. and 8 Inf.) in existence, it should have been clear that the span of command was far too wide for a single Corps HQ to cope effectively. According to General Gul, it was stated later by the Commander-in-Chief, General Musa, that he had not had time to select a commander and staff in spite of the fact that authority had been given to raise the HQ. Whatever the excuses, it was unfortunate that the army put over six divisions into the field with only one corps headquarters. Musa, furthermore, wrote that,

> the new doctrine [of defence, apparently introduced by his predecessor]... envisaged employment of minimum essential force using firepower which was greatly enhanced by us...for holding ground thus allowing greater resources for offensive purposes. The concept enabled us to use our limited means for deployment of our troops on the wide frontages on which they had to operate in an emergency, and in great depths.[2]

This, sadly for the reputation of an honourable and decent man, is hardly the stuff of which great generalship is made.

---

* History does repeat itself, sometimes.

Pre-war training at formation level had been neither testing nor lengthy, in spite of what was claimed by General Musa. Had there been extended exercises, the shortcomings of such as the commander 1st Armd. Div. should have become apparent to the degree that he would have been replaced. Maj.-Gen. Nasir was committed to a war 'for which he had [not] trained his command,' says General Gul—but what had GHQ done about it? The buck must stop somewhere, and it certainly does not stop at the level of major-general, no matter how ineffectual he may be. Someone put him there and someone kept him there in spite of it being widely-known he was not up to the job. One of Nasir's key subordinates, the commander of 5 Armd. Bde., displayed critical lack of judgement in withdrawing his tanks to leaguer on 8 September—but nothing happened. He was not dismissed. The war went on. To be sure, the army was not greatly flush with senior officers who could be brought in to command a brigade (or a division, for that matter) at a moment's notice, but there were *some* officers available who could have been swiftly promoted and transferred to the vital slots. The fact that this was not done was the fault of GHQ and finally, that of the Commander-in-Chief, General Mohammad Musa Khan, whose name has not appeared as often as that of an army chief should in a narrative of this nature. He had been Commander-in-Chief for over seven years: far too long in such an important appointment. (On his eventual retirement in September 1966, he was made governor of East Pakistan where, according to Altaf Gauhar, he 'proved singularly inept and ineffective'[3] in a period when the Eastern Wing of the country badly needed a governor who would empathize with the Bengalis and counter the condescending manner of the many Punjabi officials, politicians, and military officers who considered the East to be a poor and backward adjunct to the go-ahead West.)

Intelligence

The tactical intelligence gained by forward troops was reasonable. Some instances of failure to send out patrols into the right areas occurred, as did mistakes in passing information to higher formations. This is understandable in war and will always happen. What is inexcusable is that higher-level intelligence was so poor. The Foreign Office, in the person of its minister, Z. A. Bhutto, claimed until the last moment that India would not invade across the international border. In spite of indications to the contrary, GHQ appeared to accept this position, at least in so far as failing to order defensive measures was concerned. The Inter-Services Intelligence Directorate (ISI) had fallen down on the job, perhaps because it was required to devote much time to the distasteful task of conducting surveillance on military officers following the Rawalpindi Conspiracy. Further, Wolpert (1993) states that the Director-General of ISI, when taken to task by Ayub on 7 September for being unable to identify the location of India's 1st Armoured Division, is said by Zulfikar Ali Bhutto to have replied that, '...from June 1964 Military Intelligence has been given political assignments on elections and post-election repercussions'. This raises questions: was it Army Intelligence that Riaz referred to, or was it the ISI? And were *all* intelligence resources devoted to political matters? Bhutto's version must be treated with caution, but it does appear that neither ISI nor MI was able to inform the country's leaders where the main threat to its security was located.

Armour

The armoured battles were the more spectacular features of the war and led to conflicting claims by both sides. On the Lahore front 1 Pakistan Armoured Division advanced rapidly having outdistanced its infantry support and ran into a trap laid by the Indians, suffering heavy losses to its Pattons. This was a classic example of unsound tactics, tanks operating bunched close together on narrow roads between fields of standing sugar cane, masking each others fire and losing the ability to manoeuvre. In the SIALKOT sector where the major tank battles were fought the two forces were drawn into a straight-forward slogging match in which the tactical handling of armour was conspicuous only by its absence. Both sides suffered heavy tank casualties but, although the Pakistan Army was severely mauled, the main defensive line had not been breached by the Indians when the cease fire came into effect.

Foreign Country Intelligence Document, 1966

The above description is fair enough but does not take into account the flair and gallantry of individuals and units in the armoured corps of Pakistan which, heavily outnumbered, contributed greatly to stopping the Indian army from invading their country. The report stated, however, that,

The Four Chiefs of the Army Staff after General Zia

General Aslam Beg*

General Asif Nawaz*

General Abdul Waheed*

General Jehangir Karamat*

* courtesy ISPR

The 1965 War

During the advance to the River Tawi (courtesy ISPR)

Capture of Munabao (courtesy ISPR)

The author calls on General Ziaul Haq, September 1985 (courtesy ISPR)

The author calls on President General Musharraf.

The Army in Siachen

A patrol returns to base (courtesy ISPR)

Gunners at the roof of the world (courtesy ISPR)

Passing-out parade at the Pakistan Military Academy (courtesy ISPR)

The first generation of army missiles—the HATF1

Multi-barrel rocket launchers on parade

Type 59 Tanks rehearsing for the National Day parade

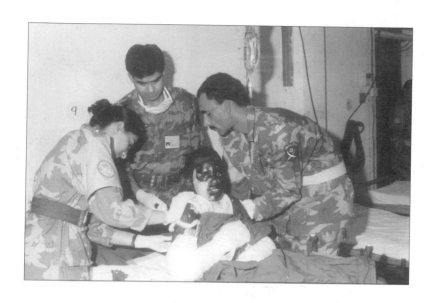

*Aid for the sick and injured: Pakistan Army medical assistance in Somalia (above) and
Bosnia (below)* (courtesy ISPR)

A detachment of the special services group. Joint Services Pakistan Day Parade, 23 March 1998 at Islamabad (courtesy ISPR)

visual evidence of tanks which had been engaged... clearly shows that the 20-pounder gun mounted in the Centurion and the 75mm gun in the AMX 13 [both Indian tanks, of British and French origin, respectively] do penetrate the armour of the Patton [Pakistani/US], and at various angles; that the Centurion will take considerable punishment and still afford protection to its crew.

There is no point in attempting examination of claims by both sides concerning numbers of tanks damaged, destroyed, or captured. The Indian official claim is that they suffered only 80 tanks lost and 123 damaged. Accounts of the battles (including those of Indian commentators) show that these figures cannot be correct, but Pakistani figures are equally suspect. The fact is that both sides lost many more tanks than they ought to have because of poor tactics.

Mention has been made of the Commander-in-Chief, General Musa, and it is relevant in a discussion of armour to state that his grasp of affairs did not appear to be entirely satisfactory. In Chapter 5 it is recounted that 6th Armoured Division was no more than a two-regiment brigade; that it had been formed from the old 100 Independent Armoured Brigade; and that it was moved to counter the enemy's main armoured thrust when that became apparent. General Musa has written[4] that, 'Long·before the war broke out, the 6th Armoured Division, which came into being as a result of reorganisation, was positioned in the area to deal with the enemy's armoured threat' — which was patently not the case.

Communications

In spite of many difficulties, it appears that most units and headquarters were able to maintain communication for much of the time. This is, however, more a comment on good signal training at the individual level, and effective use of line, than prudent procurement of radios and good communications plans. But, in spite of technical efficiency, the constant use of relay made intercept by the Indians much easier. Both sides' communications security was extremely poor, especially at officer level. Codes were compromised and individual idiosyncrasies were detected, resulting in simplification of unit identification and location. This enabled interdiction by artillery fire.

The Need for New Alliances

Pakistan had to rely on overseas suppliers for weaponry. At Partition there were many ordnance factories, but none was in Pakistan, and investment in a national arms industry was not attractive: there were higher priorities. The Pakistan Ordnance Factory at Wah, near Rawalpindi, was in its infancy and capable of manufacturing only minor items. During the war Pakistan sought supplies of arms and ammunition, but time was too short for these to arrive in significant quantities. There were no alternatives to the US and the UK for re-supply of equipment obtained from these countries, and both had cut off supplies (as they had to India—but India possessed vastly greater reserves). It was essential to engage more reliable suppliers and to diversify sources—but diversification has its own problems. Acquisition of a number of different systems imposes strain on, among other things, logistics, technical support from base workshops to battlefield, availability of spares, training (technical and operational), and interoperability. Better, sometimes, to stick with a single supplier for an item such as a main battle tank and ensure that spares can be manufactured or obtained on the open market, rather than have three types of tank each requiring different means of support.

Reliance on foreign powers for armaments was more complex than simply identifying what was needed and then despatching purchasing missions to the country of manufacture. For Pakistan the main points were quality, cost, and guarantee of support. The US and the UK made most of the best systems, but had proved to be unreliable suppliers. Not only that, their military support of India in the period 1962–5 had been energetic and extensive to the point that it had probably been crucial to India's decision to invade Pakistan in September. At a meeting in Nassau on 29 September 1962, President Kennedy and Prime Minister Macmillan agreed provision to India of military aid valued at $120 million—an enormous sum in the Sixties. A British-American-Canadian military mission was sent to assess requirements. (The US also sent a separate, independent, mission, for reasons of its own.) Six months later it was agreed by the US and the UK that a further $60 million should be granted. Further, the US and India agreed, bilaterally, that India would receive military aid of $100 million a year for five years.[5] Of some significance, although not known outside the innermost circle of government in India (which does not mean it was not known by Pakistan), the US was permitted to place instruments in

Indian territory in the Himalayas to record 'Chinese atomic tests and missile firings'.[6] Concurrently, India received large quantities of military aid from the Soviet Union, which had its own agenda in the subcontinent.

Pakistan regarded the quantities and quality of equipment being poured into India as a threat to its existence. Tanks supplied by the US, France, and Britain, it considered, were not much use in the Himalayas but were intended for operations in the plains, against Pakistan. Nor could heavy artillery be used against China, or even transported to Ladakh or the North-East Frontier Area of the border. Frigates transferred by Britain to India were not intended to counter the Chinese navy. Pakistan was not only wary of the western powers: it considered it had reason to distrust them.

* * *

President Ayub went to Washington in December 1965 to talk with President Johnson, who made it 'clear to the Pakistani ruler that the alliance between the United States and Pakistan was now over'.[7] The American President also emphasized that the relationship 'would hinge to a great extent on Pakistan's willingness to curtail its ties to China'. This was asking more—much more—than Pakistan could give.[8]

Pakistan was not prepared to sunder the link with China that was of such potential benefit. On 7 September 1965 China said, amongst other things, that, 'the Indian Government's armed attack on Pakistan is an act of naked aggression,' and agreed to supply tanks and aircraft, in addition to granting a soft loan of US$ 60 million. No other country showed such support. It is difficult to see how Johnson and his advisers could have imagined that Pakistan, betrayed (as it thought, and had some reason to think) by the US and the west in general, would be prepared to break or even diminish its contacts with China for the sake of approval by the US, a flawed and inconstant senior partner. The US promised nothing, had given much to an enemy, demanded betrayal of a friend, and sought almost unconditional allegiance. It is little wonder Pakistan looked elsewhere for a dependable ally—and its relations with China were to prove beneficial for the US when a new president changed the country's policy. But that, although only six years away, was almost unthinkable in 1965, when the US was implacable in its hostility to the PRC.

In addition to China, the only countries that openly supported Pakistan in the 1965 war were Indonesia, Iran, Turkey, Jordan, and Saudi Arabia. None of these had a modern arms' industry, and all had problems. Indonesia was waging an undeclared war against Malaysia and had grave internal schisms. Iran was beholden to the US, as was Jordan, and the crowns of their monarchs depended on American goodwill. Turkey was in NATO and dependant on the US for arms and, indeed, stability. Saudi Arabia, in spite of burgeoning wealth, at that time counted for little in world affairs. Pakistan was rejected by the west and its allies were incapable of providing much military equipment as most items in their inventories were of US or UK origin. (Turkey did send some ammunition, and Iran provided aviation fuel, but not much else could be done.) There is little wonder that Pakistan turned elsewhere than the US and UK for equipment as well as political support.

In 1965, Washington and Moscow had a coincidental view: China must be kept out of the Indo–Pakistan war. On 12 September, the Soviet Union went further in its seeming desire to defuse the conflict when Secretary Brezhnev stated: 'We want to develop good neighbourly relations with Pakistan as well [as India]. We consider that such relations are in the interests of the peoples of both countries and we have noted with satisfaction that this effort on our part has met understanding on the part of the Pakistani government.'[9] This was a shock to India, which considered the USSR a supporter, but India, too, learned that super-power friendship is rarely unconditional. The Thatcher doctrine of 'an ally is an ally'[10] would have seemed as quaint to Johnson and Brezhnev as it does to contemporary world leaders. Moscow's interest in the subcontinent still centred on neutralizing Pakistan's links with the US (which were waning, anyway) while encouraging India to stay out of the western camp. But following the Sino–Soviet split of 1960 a new imperative arose: to counter Chinese influence wherever it might make itself apparent—even in Vietnam, where both countries aided the North. The 'good offices' of the USSR led to the Tashkent talks from 4–10 January 1966 at which Premier Kosygin obtained agreement from President Ayub and Prime Minister Shastri to withdraw from territory occupied after August 1965 and to other measures designed to reduce tension. Unfortunately Shastri died on the 11th and his successor, Mrs Gandhi, was a more aggressive leader whose view of India was that of supremacist rather than partner. There was little chance of lasting *rapprochement*.

Internally, the Tashkent accord was greeted with dismay, mainly because there was no mention of Kashmir, about which at least some sort of settlement had been expected. In fact, the omission of Kashmir was caused by Bhutto, who had agreed at preliminary meetings that the subject need not be included, but it was Ayub who signed the document and, in spite of making it clear, later, that Bhutto had been with him all the way, the blame for the less-than-satisfactory accord was laid firmly at Ayub's door. There were student riots, leading to wider violence, and Bhutto used these for his own political purposes.

New Equipment and Defence Expenditure

Only two months after the Tashkent meeting, China demonstrated its close links with Pakistan by having President Liu Shao-chi and Foreign Minister Chen Yi visit the country in March. Arrangements had been made at the time of the war to provide Pakistan with defence equipment, including forty F-6 fighters and about 100 Type-59 tanks. F-6 pilot training began immediately after the war, with the first PAF squadron being formed by the end of the year, and the aircraft and tanks first appeared officially at the National Day parade on 23 March 1966, three days before the Chinese President's visit. Considerable quantities of vehicles, small arms, and ancillary items—enough to equip three infantry divisions—were also supplied. In return, Pakistan was to press China's case for entry to the United Nations Organization. (The Soviet Union, too, provided economic and even some military assistance. The air force chief visited Moscow in June 1966 and one result was provision of military helicopters and some transport aircraft, supplied on the same basis as to India, which annoyed India and did not please the US.) The Chinese visit had a politically significant concomitant: Liu went to Lahore accompanied by Bhutto, not Ayub, whose biographer, Altaf Gauhar, wrote that,

> By giving Bhutto the opportunity to appear as a hero in Lahore in the company of the Chinese Chairman Ayub had handed over the political initiative to Bhutto. It was a tumultuous reception... The people lifted the car in which Bhutto was travelling and carried it on their shoulders. Bhutto had won their hearts. In retrospect it would appear as if Ayub had himself launched Bhutto on his political career.[11]

This may not be entirely correct, as Bhutto had already decided to go his own way as soon as possible in an independent political career and would doubtless have succeeded without Ayub's gaffe in failing to go to Lahore with Liu, but it shows how naïve Ayub was, politically, to trust Bhutto in any way.

Later in 1966 the US and the UK had second thoughts about Pakistan's military situation in the light of Chinese guarantees and Soviet overtures. In June the US restarted economic aid programmes to India and Pakistan, and gradually extended this to include supply of defence equipment, but the countries of the west had lost any reputation they might have had as constant friends—not just in Pakistan but elsewhere.

Ayub's lack of support for the US in its embroilment in Vietnam frustrated Johnson, who seemed to consider all world leaders to be either for or against him based on how they felt about Vietnam[2]—but the Chinese imperative loomed large in the US mind. When US defence assistance began again in 1966, it was hesitant and confined to 'non-lethal' items. The following year the embargo was relaxed to permit provision of spare parts for existing American equipment (some of which had by that time been obtained through Turkey). It appeared to China, however, that Pakistan might be tilting away from the PRC, one reason for this perception being the dismissal by Ayub of the pro-Chinese Bhutto. The real reason for the dismissal was that Ayub had at last realized that Bhutto was disloyal and devious, but Zhou Enlai himself paid a visit to Pakistan in July and was assured by Ayub that Sino–Pakistani friendship was 'not based on expediency but on principles and will continue to flourish over the years'.[12] Next to go from Ayub's cabinet was the finance minister, Shoaib,* who was thought to be pro-US, thus re-establishing the fact that Pakistan was not again veering westwards.

In spite of some equipment from China, the US, and UK being provided gratis, with soft loans, or on easy terms, it was necessary to acquire much *matériel* on a barter basis (as with China) or with hard cash (France and other European countries). Defence spending increased during the 1960s. As shown below, the percentage of total government expenditure rose in 1965–7 but then stabilized at around its former figure, which was, it can be argued, still far too high.

---

* To the World Bank, like so many high-grade Pakistanis.

Defence Expenditure 1959/60–1969/70[13]

YEAR	EXPENDITURE (Rs MILLIONS)	AS PERCENTAGE OF TOTAL BUDGET
1959–60	1043.5	56.10
1960–61	1112.4	58.73
1961–2	1108.6	55.80
1962–3	954.3	53.16
1963–4	1156.5	49.49
1964–5	1262.3	46.07
1965–6	2855.0	53.67
1966–7	2293.5	60.92
1967–8	2186.5	53.63
1968–9	2426.8	55.62
1969–70	2749.1	53.35

Over the period the rupee-dollar exchange rate was about 4.5:1.
Financial Year 1 April to 31 March.

The figures do not take into account equipment provided in gift or barter but give an indication of the emphasis placed on improving defence capabilities.

East Pakistan

There had been no conflict other than sporadic exchanges of fire and some minor aerial activity in East Pakistan during the 1965 war. Claims by both sides of provocation must be discounted as there are no reliable witnesses to the skirmishes that took place. Military reasons for there being no eruption of fighting include the falling of the monsoon in September, which rendered the area difficult for movement, and, perhaps of more importance, reluctance on India's part to engage in hostilities that might have demanded commitment of forces from the Sino–Indian border. China's position was far from clear in regard to the degree of support it was prepared or preparing to give to Pakistan, and it would have been imprudent of India to take action that might have resulted in further reduction of troops in the north, as three divisions had already been moved to the eastern front. Pakistan was not anxious to open another military front, but neither was India.

Terminology plays a part in the sad story of what was East Pakistan and is now Bangladesh. Reference was made by West Pakistan to the 'garrison' in the East. Nobody ever referred to troops in the West as a 'garrison', and this exclusive use of the word was inappropriate and, understandably, resented by many in the Eastern Wing of the country.

The Bengali did not consider himself soldier material. At Partition there were only 155 Bengali officers in the army, and the situation did not improve much over the years. There are few military heroes in their history or mythology, and the soldier was not the respected figure he was in North-West Frontier Province or the Punjab. Little attempt was made by the Western Wing to encourage recruitment of Bengalis until after the 1965 war, and by that time it was too late to try to instil unity in an army that was patently split asunder, to the extent that recruitment simply laid the basis for the revolt of a rather more efficient East Pakistan Army against the Western Wing in 1971.

On 8 September 1965, the Indian Defence Minister, Y.B. Chavan, said in the Lok Sabha that Pakistan,

...has attempted to escalate the war in the Eastern sector. We have no quarrel with East Pakistan and while our troops have taken up positions within our territory in order to meet any threat of aggression by Pakistan, at the present moment I do not visualise our taking any action to escalate the war in that field except to the extent Pakistan's action compels us to do so.[14]

Pakistan had certainly not attempted to escalate the war in the East. To try to do so, with one division of troops (14 Infantry Division, Maj.-Gen. Fazal Muqeem Khan) against eleven infantry/mountain divisions in India's Eastern Command, would have been foolhardy and would have resulted, monsoon or not, in retaliatory action by the redoubtable Lt.-Gen. Sam Manekshaw, the commander in the region. The PAF's 15 Sabre jets would have been no match for the IAF's 32 Hunters and 48 Ouragans based in Eastern Command. But, rhetoric aside, the important part of the statement (that should have been noted for future reference by West Pakistan as it undoubtedly was in the East), was that 'We have no quarrel with East Pakistan'. If ever a country was trying to exploit tensions existing in the peoples of its enemy (and quite legitimately, in time of war), it was India in September 1965. As became apparent in the 'Agartala Conspiracy Case' of 1968, there was little doubt that India was dabbling in Pakistani affairs to the extent of supporting dissidents in the Eastern Wing, just as they were to do before and during the 1971 war.

At the time of the 1965 war there were some 13,000 Bengalis in the Pakistan Army,[15] mainly in the East Bengal Regiment which had been formed just after Partition. The Regimental Centre was in Chittagong, and its tenth battalion was 'somewhat optimistically raised in 1971...,'[16] but it appeared that nobody, least of all the Bengalis, considered the Regiment to be truly integrated into the Pakistan Army. Ayub himself was contemptuous of Bengalis and knew that the Eastern Wing would not stay part of the greater Pakistan for much longer. He told Altaf Gauhar that he had given the Bengalis the second capital (Dhaka) 'because they are going to need it one day. They are not going to remain with us.'[17] Perhaps he based this prediction on the Agartala case, which obviously perturbed him.

Conspiracy Again—The Agartala Case

In late 1967 and early 1968 President Ayub was suffering from the effects of a pulmonary embolism and came close to death. His vitality was diminishing and he seemed to lack the will to go on. During his illness Sheikh Mujibur Rahman, the Bengali separatist leader (and first president of Bangladesh), was charged with conspiring with the Government of India to encompass the secession of East Pakistan, of which he was almost certainly guilty in the round, although it is hardly likely he could have indulged in conspiracy from the prison cell where he had spent some months under tight security.

Agartala is the capital of the Indian State of Tripura, lying 200 kilometres east of Dhaka, the capital of East Pakistan (now Bangladesh). It was alleged that a first secretary of the Indian Deputy High Commission in Dhaka, P.N. Ojha, had met some senior civil servants (Ruhul Quddus, Fazlur Rahman, and Shamsur Rahman) and a naval commander (Muazzim Hussain) in Dhaka and that they visited Agartala regularly to discuss secessionist matters with two Indian army officers, Lt.-Col. Misra and Major Menon. This appears to be true. Ojha was probably not a member of Indian Intelligence,[18] but he did meet with Pakistanis who were less than enthusiastic about the East Wing remaining part of Pakistan. It is the job of diplomats to meet, discreetly, with dissidents in order to be able to inform their government of current matters and forecast what is likely to happen in the country to which they are accredited. Ojha perhaps overstepped his remit by arranging meetings in Agartala, but the level of 'conspiracy' was low, involving only junior officials and officers. Inevitably, however, Mujib was brought in (and a total of thirty-five alleged conspirators charged by the end of May 1968), but the case was dropped, first against Mujib, in 1968, then against the rest in February 1969. The affair was badly handled, not least by East Pakistan's Governor, Monem Khan, Musa's replacement, and the resentment created in East Pakistan fuelled the flames of secession.

In 1968 an East Pakistani Member of the National Assembly (MNA) stated that '...our defence forces must reflect the population of the country and be representative of different areas that constitute Pakistan...the defence services must be manned in proportion to the population of different areas so that it may give a national character...' This quotation has been included to give some idea of the frustration felt in East Pakistan—but also because it reflects, predictively, present-day 'politically-correct' theories of positive discrimination. The riposte, by Hasan Askari Rizvi in the mid-seventies, could have been written today:

The military is a particular type of organisation with distinctive features and special responsibilities. It is so different from the other institutions of the state that the pure and simple theories of democracy cannot be applied to its internal structure. Democratisation of the military in the manner suggested above [by the MNA] could result in the loss of these qualities. The military would cease to be an effective fighting force.

Dr Rizvi had never been a soldier, but he knew that clever sociological theories had and have no part in the development of military organizations as effective fighting forces. There are no perfect armies, or other fighting services, and there will doubtless be problems in all of them for all time to come. But there will be even more problems for them to cope with if social experiments continue to be conducted on the energetic basis supported by so many academics and politicians who have no idea what discipline and Service entail.

The government in Karachi tried to satisfy the East Pakistanis who complained of inadequate representation by Bengalis in the defence forces, but it was difficult to encourage the Bengalis to the recruiting office. They were physically smaller, so restrictions on height were relaxed, but to no avail. There was simply no tradition of military service. In the Second World War there were over two million volunteers for service with the British Indian Army (a figure that few in India care to acknowledge because the myth of the all-embracing fight for independence must be kept alive), but the figure for Bengal is relevant to its later development: it contributed 170,000 recruits, while Punjab and the North-West Frontier Province provided over four times as many (712,952), from a much smaller population. Few Bengalis served in combat arms.

The Eclipse of Ayub

Ayub had been a healthy man of temperate habits and regular physical exercise. His unexpected illness presaged spells of 'inertia and indifference' and indications that he was living in the past and dwelling on such successes as the land reforms. He was becoming increasingly vulnerable to pressure—and pressures were growing, externally and from within. In November 1968, a Bhutto supporter was shot by police during a violent demonstration in Rawalpindi. That served Bhutto well, and, even better than that, he was arrested on 13 November following further demonstrations. The fact that an assassination attempt on Ayub a few days before had not sparked public protest was indicative that sympathy for the president was dwindling or even non-existent. Support for Bhutto, who had been assiduous in moving around the provinces, was growing. He had made skilful speeches ever since his dismissal in June 1966, but at first was careful to avoid outright confrontation with Ayub who, he thought, might strike out if he overstepped the mark. As Bhutto sensed Ayub's diminishing grip on power he became less circumspect: 'Ayub Khan Sahib,' he shouted during one speech, 'I am not a coward, I cannot be browbeaten... I am not scared of your guns...Come on, take up your guns; I have the power of the people with me...'[19] Bhutto was striking back at the man who had offended his pride in 1962. Bhutto, a master philanderer, had thrown his wife, Nusrat, out of the family house after a dispute and Ayub, scandalized by such behaviour, gave him the option of taking his wife back or leaving the Cabinet. There was no question as to what Bhutto would do when faced with such a choice. But Bhutto's arrest was a mistake by Ayub and made Bhutto even more determined to take revenge. Bhutto wanted power at almost any price; when accession to power could be combined with humiliation of an enemy, that would be sweet indeed. He had formed the Pakistan People's Party in November

1967 and was not prepared to wait indefinitely to take over the government of Pakistan.

In January 1968, Ayub handed over the presidency in all but name to the Army's Commander-in-Chief, General Yahya Khan. On 25 March the following year, his poor health exacerbated by social and political difficulties he was unable to understand or solve (including atrocities in East Pakistan, which was verging on anarchy), Ayub resigned in favour of Yahya, who proclaimed martial law and dissolved the National and Provincial assemblies. Yahya assumed the presidency on 31 March. The Ayub years were over.

NOTES

1. NCID.
2. Musa (1987).
3. Gauhar (1993).
4. Musa op. cit.
5. G.W. Choudhry, *Pakistan's Relations with India 1947–1996*, London, Pall Mall Press 1968.
6. Daniel Patrick Moynihan, *A Dangerous Place*, London, Secker & Warburg, 1979.
7. *Lyndon Johnson Confronts the World—American Foreign Policy 1963–1968*, edited by Warren I. Cohen and Nancy Bernkopf Tucker, Cambridge University Press, 1994.
8. The situation is described by Dennis Kux in *The United States and Pakistan 1947-2000*, in the Section aptly titled 'Johnson: The Alliance Unravels'.
9. *Soviet News*, London, 13 September 1965.
10. For example, Thatcher disliked Zia ul Haq as a person, but after Zia refused Argentina's request to sell it Exocet missiles during Britain's campaign in the Falklands, she sided with him ever after, no matter what the UK may have said publicly. (Private information from a very senior British diplomat.)
11. Gauhar op. cit.
12. Quoted in Burke and Ziring op. cit.
13. Rizvi, op. cit.
14. *Foreign Affairs Record* (New Delhi) XI:9, p. 256, September 1965.
15. Statement of the Parliamentary Secretary, Defence, reported in *Dawn*, 20 July 1965, Quoted in Rizvi op. cit.
16. Gaylor (1992).
17. Wolpert op. cit.
18. Private information.
19. Wolpert op. cit.

7 Yahya Khan and the Inevitability of the 1971 War

General Yahya Khan was a different person from his predecessor. He was liked by more people than was Ayub because of his sociability, and was more approachable and informal, although he could stand on his dignity when he considered it appropriate. Sir Morrice James records in *Pakistan Chronicle* that when he was Yahya's guest in an officers' mess on one occasion, 'Yahya in a mood of good-humoured tomfoolery took over the regimental bandmaster's hat and baton and for some time conducted the music. For Ayub to have unbent in this way would have been unthinkable.' But Yahya, although not as cerebral, principled, or puritan as the man who had appointed him Commander-in-Chief, was no fool.

In September 1966 he had succeeded General Musa and concentrated on improving leadership and training. Unfortunately, two years later he was drawn into political affairs and then appeared more intent on preparing to take over from Ayub than devoting energy to enhancing the army's standards. This was not in character. He had had a successful career and was well-regarded in Pakistan and by foreign officers who met him over the years. After graduating from the Military Academy at Dehra Dun he served with the British Army in the Middle East and Italy, where he had been captured but escaped. He had done well since Independence, climbing rapidly up the ladder (brigadier at 34, major-general at 40, lieutenant-general at 49), and had commanded his division as skilfully as circumstances allowed in the 1965 War. But power, or the prospect of greater power, seems to have had an adverse

affect on him, and it is now apparent he was the wrong man to be
president of a country that needed political skills as well as honesty.
He could provide the latter but few of the former, which were important
to counter the ambition of Zulfikar Ali Bhutto (who 'knew Yahya, who
had hunted with him in Larkana and drunk with him before and after
each shooting'[1]) and the equally marked ambition and political acuity
of Sheikh Mujibur Rahman of East Pakistan.

Bhutto had been in prison since November 1968 but Ayub released
him on 17 February 1969 when ending the state of emergency declared
the previous year. This was regarded as a major victory by Bhutto's
supporters, and even by some of those who were suspicious of Bhutto
but who had had enough of an autocratic presidency. Others of his
critics considered he was a rabble-rouser who was intent on bringing
the country to chaos and then emerging as its saviour.[2] Bhutto regarded
his release as an act of weakness on the part of Ayub and went in for
the kill by making rabble rousing speeches to his 'adoring Sindhis'.[3]
Concurrently, Sheikh Mujib had been set free in East Pakistan, where
he continued his agitation for a separate state.

The situation was precarious, but a harsher imposition of martial
law was not the way to achieve understanding, compromise, or stability
in either Wing of the country. Tact, flexibility, and political *savoir faire*
were needed. A dash of deviousness might have helped, too, in defusing
or at least placating the touchy Bengalis. It is probable, however, that
nothing would have been effective in countering Bhutto, whose
intrigues and political artfulness were becoming even more
remarkable.

At the 'working level'—in the headquarters and units outside
Rawalpindi—the army continued to re-equip and train in its normal
peacetime fashion. Nothing of great consequence was achieved and
there was no pressure to prepare for further conflict. Both sides were
licking their wounds and wondering where they had gone wrong in a
messy war that brought little kudos to the high command of either
nation. No matter how much the Indians maintained that they would
have totally defeated Pakistan had it not been for the influence of other
nations, and no matter how violently the Pakistanis refuted the claim,
the fact remains that at other than the level of individual gallantry, the
armies did not cover themselves in glory. But in the late 1960s another
conflict appeared unlikely, if only because there were too many internal
and other problems to be resolved by New Delhi, Dhaka, and Islamabad
(by then the national capital).

Mrs Gandhi complained to the Soviet Union concerning the supply of weapons to Pakistan, and stated in parliament on 22 July 1968 that India 'cannot but view with concern this further accretion of armed strength to Pakistan'—which was overstatement and perhaps demonstrated more dissatisfaction with India's ally than real apprehension about the addition of twelve Mi-8 helicopters to Pakistan's inventory. But there were other irritants. On 19 February 1969 agreement was announced by an international tribunal concerning the Rann of Kutch dispute, but the award was regarded by India as unsatisfactory—in spite of the ratio of land apportionment being 90 per cent to India and 10 per cent to Pakistan. Mrs Gandhi had to accept the tribunal's ruling, and representatives of the countries met in Islamabad on 4 July to sign an accord ending the affair. This was greeted with enthusiasm by much of the rest of the world. It was considered evidence that there could be understanding and peace in the subcontinent, but this was more optimistic than realistic.

India considered it had further cause to complain in 1970 when the US decided to provide military equipment to Pakistan 'to replace equipment previously supplied'.[4] This included F-104 fighters, B-57 light bombers, and M-113 armoured personnel carriers. In fact, the US had supplied little equipment in the previous five years. Its military mission left Pakistan in July 1967 and, although permission had been given (in the same month) for purchase of spares for the inventory of (predominantly) American weapons, all requests were treated on a case-by-case basis.

Yahya had established a rapport with Richard Nixon, who became US president in 1969. Nixon had visited Pakistan in 1953, when he was Eisenhower's vice-president ('The least friendly leader I met on this trip was Nehru')[5]; then in 1964 as a private citizen continuing his campaign to be president and thus wishing to keep up his foreign policy credentials ('...I saw my old friend President Ayub Khan...'); and last on his presidential round-the-world trip which was an adjunct to the success of the moon-lander Apollo XI that splashed-down on 24 July 1969. It was during this visit that he met Yahya for the first time and decided he preferred him to Mrs Gandhi. In fact, Nixon preferred almost anyone to Mrs Gandhi. References to her in his *Memoirs* are complimentary, but Dr Kissinger leaves us in no doubt concerning his true feelings, which were 'not always printable'.[6] Nixon was pro-Pakistan and anti-India, which, after all, was a supporter of Godless communism in the shape of the Soviet Union. The fact that China was also communist was passed over. Nixon was about to achieve a diplomatic success in which Yahya was to play an important part: *rapprochement* between the US and the People's Republic of China. Pakistan was to be affected by Nixon's aversion to the clever and condescending Kashmiri Brahmin and his attraction to the hospitable, convivial Yahya Khan.

The defence budget of Pakistan for the financial year 1971–2 rose by $109 million to $114 million, about 3.8 per cent of GNP. Re-equipment was taking place but, as Gul Hassan states, there were considerable problems in organization and leadership. He wrote that, 'I do not think GHQ had ever been so ineffective as it was in the months prior to the outbreak of the war with India in 1971. Events buffeted us mercilessly owing to absence of direction and a sense of cohesion in the nerve-centre of the army.' He gives accounts of sub-standard officers being promoted and of indecision in planning. A retired senior officer who was serving in a regiment at the time recollects that, although the units trained effectively enough, and of course welcomed the new equipment, 'there seemed to be no good orders coming down. Perhaps it was us, but I don't think so. I think it was probably that a lot of people [officers] had shot up quickly and although we had plenty of good fellows lower down [in units] we didn't see much of our senior officers.' Gul Hassan puts the lack of direction down to the involvement of GHQ (and presumably other officers further down) with the administration of martial law, and this is probably the explanation. For military officers to take part in running a country, especially involving petty detail in settling land disputes, lawsuits, and so forth, debilitates the martial ethos and leads to inefficiency. It also leads to officers being tempted to become involved in politics and local affairs. This is the path to corruption.

General Gul's story of how, in 1970, two officers were promoted major-general in spite of having received poor reports makes distressing reading. His succinct tale emphasizes that, 'at that fateful Selection Board General Yahya Khan was very much present and was aware that the two officers were promoted in total disregard of the recognised procedures'. This is damning stuff, and one cannot but agree with him that the army was heading in a dangerous direction if 'promotions, demotions and dismissals were [to be] dictated by the whims and fancies of rulers....'

The military capabilities of India and Pakistan in 1970–71 were marked by disparities in almost every aspect, from strength of forces to quantities, sources, and quality of equipment. In the armies the main figures were:

EQUIPMENT	INDIA (ARMY STRENGTH 860,000)	PAKISTAN (ARMY STRENGTH 365,000)
Main Battle Tanks	200 Centurion (UK) 250 Sherman (US) 450 T54/55 (USSR)	200 M47/M48 (US) 150 T54/55 (PRC)
Medium and Light Tanks	300 Vijayanta (UK) 150 PT-76 (USSR) 100 AMX-13 (France)	225 T-59 (PRC) 200 M024 (US) 75 M-41 (US)
Field Artillery Guns	2500	800
Medium Artillery Guns	400	300

Based on *Strategic Balance 1971/72*, The International Institute for Strategic Studies.

These figures indicate approximate numbers of equipments. As with all quantitative tables, they cannot convey information concerning comparison of one weapon with another of a like nature. Nor can they indicate serviceability under battle conditions, levels of individual or collective training, or such matters as efficiency of fuel and ammunition re-supply. But the raw figures provide some understanding of the relative strengths of two armies that were about to go to war again.

* * *

'Mrs Gandhi, you know the accusation that it was you Indians who provoked this [1971] war and attacked first. What do you say to that?'

'I'd answer by admitting that, if you want to go way back, we helped the Mukti Bahini. So, if you consider it all as beginning with that aid and from that moment, yes—we were the ones to start it.'[7]

We faced a dilemma. The United States could not condone a brutal military oppression in which thousands of civilians were killed [in East Pakistan] and from which millions fled to India for safety. There was no doubt about the strong arm tactics of the Pakistani military. But Pakistan was our sole channel to China; once it was closed off it would take months to make alternative arrangements.[8]

The facts are unpalatable, but it must be stated that the army of Pakistan did not distinguish itself by other than brutality in its suppression of Bengali nationalists in the Eastern Wing in 1971. The atrocities—by both sides—beggar belief; their details confound description. It is amazing that a disciplined army could act in such a fashion. But act it did, and with cruel efficiency, in carrying out the orders of Yahya Khan to crush the insurgency in East Pakistan. Dr Kissinger states that 'thousands' of civilians were killed. He erred. Several hundreds of thousands of Bengalis were killed. Why did Yahya 'with his patrician manner and his military background' (wrote Kissinger) permit—order—the slaughter of civilians? Why did his Governor in East Pakistan, General Tikka Khan, and the military commander, General Niazi, encourage their soldiers to kill without discrimination? Why did soldiers obey and even relish their orders?

* * *

When British India was partitioned into India and Pakistan, the latter country consisted of two disparate wings separated by over a thousand miles of Indian territory. There was little overland travel between them. Some took place, but procedures were laborious and often disrupted by officious or corrupt border officials. Air travel was expensive. Sea sufficed for the small amount of commerce between the two regions. From the beginning there were difficulties. The founder of the nation, Mohammad Ali Jinnah, was a West Pakistani and could not be expected to give more attention to the East than to his birthplace. While he might have managed to keep things on an even keel had he lived long enough, none of his political successors in the West saw reason to pay more than lip-service to the aspirations of the East Wing.

West Pakistan, from which area had come so many of the warriors of the British Raj, had nothing in common with the East other than religion and, amongst the educated, the English language—and these were no basis for cohesion or even understanding. Bengalis were regarded as inferior by those proud Pathans and swaggering Punjabis who had met them, and nowhere was this more marked than in the military. It became apparent to the educated classes in East Pakistan that discrimination on the part of their western colleagues was to be entrenched. The Bengalis of East Pakistan had lost colonial masters who had cared nothing for creed or caste as a basis for justice, only to have them replaced by a regime whose administration of the law, they considered, was capricious and usually biased against them. The voluble, argumentative, and energetically litigious Bengali came up against the taciturn, dogmatic, and (comparatively) law-accepting Punjabi and the equally taciturn but endemically lawless Pathan—and could understand neither. Civil servants posted from one Wing to another rarely met on other than official occasions. There was no meeting of minds. In this cauldron of resentment stirred Sheikh Mujibur Rahman, the main political force of East Pakistan.

Mujibur Rahman had been a secessionist for many years but seized his chance, as leader of the Awami League party in East Pakistan in 1966, to publish his Six Point Plan which 'distilled the various Bengali claims and frustrations over East Pakistan's perceived mistreatment in economic and national affairs'.[9] The Points were vague, perhaps by intention. Some are difficult to understand in practical terms; but the Sixth Point was well understood and could not be accepted by West Pakistan—as Mujib well knew:

The government of the federating units shall be empowered to maintain a militia or para-military force in order to contribute effectively towards national security.

What everyone knew was that the *original* Sixth Point was:

The setting up of a militia or para-military force for East Pakistan.

Armies do not relish the creation of para-military forces. They consider them dangerous. If they are foisted upon them they want to exercise control. The Frontier Corps in Pakistan, which looks after the border areas in the west, is an example of this: the Inspector-Generals of the FC in Quetta and Peshawar answer to the Interior Ministry in Islamabad but are serving major-generals, and all other officers are seconded from the army for a specified tour of duty. The Pakistan Rangers, who police the border with India, are another example of firm army interest and similar control, as is their Indian counterpart, the Border Security Force—as were the East Pakistan Rifles, pre-1971. But the notion of a 'militia or para-military force' being controlled by the 'federating units' (read the Awami League) was anathema to the army. Defence against external threats was the army's responsibility. Were it desired by anyone that other armed elements should be established to 'contribute effectively to national security', it would have meant that the army was not doing its job. Manifestly it was. So what reason could there be for wishing to create this element? Only, the army thought, darkly, to act as the private militia of the leader of whatever federated unit took it into its head to form such a body.[10]

The army's fears were to be justified. In Bangladesh the Mukti Bahini guerrilla movement, formed by supporters of Mujibur Rahman (and funded and trained by India), was to rise to harass the Pakistan army in the East and contribute to its defeat by the Indian force which invaded the country. The Mukti Bahini were exactly what Mujib had in mind when formulating the Six Points. What was created in 1970, as a compromise pleasing nobody, was the 'East Pakistan Civil Armed Force,' commanded by a West Pakistani major-general. The force was trusted by Bengalis as much as it was respected by West Pakistani soldiers.

There was never going to be compromise about the future of East Pakistan so far as Mujibur Rahman was concerned. Mujib knew the level of his popularity and the depth of feeling amongst Bengalis. He was a founder member of the Awami League in 1949 and became its leader in 1954. The League's policy was that there should be autonomy for the East—and that was that, no matter how they may have wrapped up their aspirations when dealing with politicians and generals in the Western Wing. Similarly, there was no question that West Pakistan would accept the loss of half the country by permitting the East to secede.

East Pakistan's complaints were many. For example, in 1970 there were only 6,668 hospital beds in the East (population 70 million) and over 26,000 in the West (55 million). Per capita income was 313 rupees in the East compared with 463 in West Pakistan. But East Pakistan had a lot to offer economically to the country as a whole. The two most important products were jute and tea. In pre-Partition days these products of the eastern part of Bengal were sent to the west of the state to be processed for onward trade with the rest of the world. In return, manufactured goods were imported through the west, via Calcutta. It was dependence by one section of the state on another, but no resentment was felt on that score: resentment was reserved for the British. But when Pakistan was created, the East Wing was formed from the eastern part of the state and the western part became the Indian State of West Bengal. Mountbatten refused to countenance the inclusion of Calcutta in East Pakistan, which continued to grow jute (80 per cent of world production) and tea (and many other primary products). But foreign exchange earnings from their export were centralized in West Pakistan. One colonial master—as Pakistan's Bengalis saw matters—had been replaced by another. There was no doubt that East Pakistanis had every right to take exception to domination from Karachi and Islamabad. There *was* domination—and arrogance, as well. This was too much for a proud and volatile people to live with. There was bound to be bloodshed, but it came in a manner and with a ferocity that astonished the Bengalis and the rest of the world.

On 28 November 1969, President Yahya Khan announced that elections were to be held throughout Pakistan a year later on the basis of universal suffrage. This rather took the wind out of the sails of the Bengalis as it was exactly what they wanted. The results would almost certainly mean ascendancy of the Awami League in the national parliament. Surely Yahya did not intend this to happen?

Many explanations have been put forward for Yahya's decision, but the most likely appears to be that he thought the politicians would make such a mess of things (again) that the army—and of course President Yahya Khan—would remain in control. Or perhaps he thought the Pakistan People's Party might win the greatest number of seats and that he could continue as President with the blessing of its leader, Zulfikar Ali Bhutto, who would become prime minister. Whatever his rationale—and one must not discount the possibility that it just might have been a genuinely democratic decision at the time—Yahya followed through in March 1970 by publishing the Legal Framework Order (LFO) defining a new Constitution. Amongst other things, Pakistan was to be a federally organized nation with some 'provincial autonomy'. There was to be a National Assembly of 313 seats (13 reserved for women) with 169 seats allocated to East Pakistan and 144 to the West.

The apportionment was generous on Yahya's part. There was, after all, a likely majority of twenty-five seats for the East Pakistanis and no stipulation that there should be a (say) two-thirds majority for the passage of laws affecting the Constitution. In terms of straight majority voting, the Awami League would be able to dictate to the whole of Pakistan unless there were significant gains by other parties in the east.

In April, Yahya flew to Dhaka to discuss the LFO with Mujib and other Bengali leaders. To his dismay and apparent shock, he heard Mujib, in a tape recording made by Military Intelligence, state that his aim was to establish the independent nation of Bangladesh and that he would 'tear the LFO into pieces as soon as the elections are over. Who could challenge me once the elections are over?' After this, Yahya could not trust Mujib—but then Mujib had not trusted Yahya or anyone else, although at that time he had no grounds for not placing faith in the president. Nor did his equally devious political rival, Z. A. Bhutto, whose machinations were legion. Mujib distrusted Bhutto most of all, especially following the latter's visit to Dhaka in January 1971, when he assured Mujib that he would be content with appointment as 'deputy prime minister or even foreign minister'—following which he allegedly threatened Mujib with 'dire consequences' if an understanding between them could not be reached.[11] The thought of Bhutto, at this stage in his career, even considering playing second fiddle to anyone—especially Sheikh Mujibur Rahman, the quintessential political rival—strains the imagination.

* * *

The members of the Martial Law Administration, which lasted until Yahya appointed a civilian cabinet in 1969, were of course hand-picked by the President. Yahya's principal staff officer (PSO—an appointment of considerable importance) was Lt.-Gen. Peerzada, who had been Adjutant-General and then Military Secretary under Ayub. Peerzada was, says Wolpert, 'a man of sharp intellect and political ambition, self-effacing, patient, able to achieve under a less-than-sagacious Yahya Khan the position he had aspired to, but was obliged to resign from, by Ayub at the first sign of his physical frailty'. Peerzada had had a heart attack while he was serving Ayub who, entirely in character and looking after his subordinates in the old-fashioned way, dispensed with his services in the man's own best interests, but apparently Peerzada 'could never forget' his dismissal. In fact, Peerzada was a politician *manqué* who preferred the cut-and-thrust of political manoeuvring to that of the battlefield. He was of the type that rises in the military by being an efficient courtier and a source of balm to his superiors while demonstrating boundless energy in promoting their interests in addition to his own. This type of officer treats subordinates poorly and is usually disliked and feared by his peers. They tend to fail when a crisis arises.

A Commander-in-Chief's Committee was formed, consisting of Yahya and the heads of the armed forces. It was responsible for major defence decision-making and was the link between Yahya and the Services. These continued to provide the nuts and bolts of martial law but were no longer concerned with policy, which was the responsibility of the Headquarters of the Chief Martial Law Administrator (the President), of which the head was the ubiquitous Peerzada. The service chiefs exercised civil authority through their membership of the Council on Administration headed by Yahya, who also oversaw the portfolios of foreign affairs and defence. The Chief of Staff of the Army, Lt.-Gen. Abdul Hamid Khan, had the ministries of Interior and Kashmir Affairs; Vice-Admiral S.M. Ahsan was responsible for Planning, Finance, Industries, Commerce, and Food and Agriculture; and Air Marshal Nur Khan had the ministries of Education, Health, Social Welfare, and Labour. The responsibilities were not quite as onerous as might at first appear, because the professionals in the ministries were encouraged to get on with their tasks without interference, but some important decisions were taken. Nur Khan, for example, introduced a new labour policy with the blessing of Yahya. It restored the rights to strike and of collective bargaining. Among other actions, union office bearers were given legal protection, and a minimum wage for unskilled workers was set at Rs 140 per month. Ahsan introduced anti-trust legislation and a code of fair trading. Autonomy was restored to universities, and a National Literacy Corps was established to work in rural areas. These were remarkable reforms for a martial law regime and complemented pursuit of corrupt officials, 303 of whom were suspended in December 1969. Generals Peerzada and Hamid disliked Nur Khan and Ahsan, perhaps because of their very effectiveness and popularity, and persuaded Yahya to appoint them Governors of West and East Pakistan respectively in August 1969.

The Council on Administration met weekly but ceased to exist in August 1969, when Yahya appointed a civilian cabinet. There also existed a National Security Council (chaired by Yahya) whose membership included the Director-General Inter-Services Intelligence (DGISI, General Akbar Khan), the Director of the (civilian) Intelligence Bureau, the Home Minister, and Maj.-Gen. Ghulam Umar, the National Security Adviser, who was close to Hamid. None of these organizations was co-ordinated with another. Their work was important and generally effective, but fragmented. Nobody quite knew everything that went on except, perhaps, General Peerzada.

It was in this atmosphere that important decisions were taken affecting the Eastern Wing, and it is little wonder Yahya failed to

construct safeguards in the new electoral arrangements or to understand
the likely consequences of his apportionment of National Assembly
seats. There was no committee or cabinet member experienced enough
in politics to proffer advice. Even had there been, the system of
governance was not structured in a manner that would have given
Yahya access to sage counsel. And Zulfikar Ali Bhutto was not going
to make recommendations to the man he schemed to replace.

One of the worst natural disasters ever recorded struck East Pakistan
on 12/13 November 1970, just before elections were to take place. The
Ganges Delta was hit by a cyclone that caused immense tidal waves.
Over 400,000 people died. Countless were made homeless, perhaps
millions. The situation was appalling but the martial law administration
coped as well as any government in any country could have in similar
circumstances. Overseas aid was requested, and provided and promised
on a large scale. The World Bank offered a massive loan. None of these
generous actions could produce instant solutions to the disruption that
had been caused. Aid was largely intended for the longer-term: to
rebuild roads and villages; to assist in re-establishing primary
production and cottage industries; and to restore the infrastructure of
local administration. Instant relief was impossible, just as it is in
disasters that occur in highly-developed countries in an age of speedier
communications. But of course the Awami League, skilled Bengali
politicians to a man, took the opportunity to castigate the central
government in emotional terms for the perceived lack of sympathy and
immediate action. The depth of feeling was made clear by one
writer:

> For ages to come Bengalis will remember bitterly that while more than a
> million people perished and thousands were made homeless by the terrible
> cyclone accompanied by tidal waves as high as 30 feet, no help, not even
> a word of consolation, came from the leaders of West Pakistan...no help
> was sent or even promised from West Pakistan. The naval...ships, the army
> and air force helicopters and transport planes were not used to help the
> cyclone affected people in the offshore islands and the coastal areas where
> no other mode of transport was available at that time...Many Bengalis even
> felt that their sufferings were relished by the ruling junta in Pakistan.[12]

The emotion of Bengalis is understandable. A disaster had occurred
whose size was beyond the comprehension of most people. The whole
of East Pakistan was stunned. There was no instant relief. Who to
blame other than the government? Where was the government? In the

West. Therefore the West was not only culpable for inaction but had wilfully ignored the entire terrible circumstances in which the East Wing found itself. Elections were to be held throughout the country and, no matter how damaged and desperate was East Pakistan, the people—the voters—were made aware by their politicians that a vote for any representative of a political party based in the West was a vote against the East Wing; against Bengal; against 'Bangladesh'.

But the election was duly held and the result was overwhelmingly in favour of the Awami League. It was then that the real problems began.

The results of the elections held in Pakistan on 7 and 17 December 1970 gave East Pakistan 162 seats and the West 138, voting being almost entirely on ethnic lines. West Pakistan could not accept supremacy on the part of the East. What was to be done? And by whom?

NOTES

1. Wolpert op. cit.
2. Discussions with some such critics in Pakistan, November 1996.
3. Wolpert op. cit.
4. Department of State News Briefing, 8 October 1970.
5. *The Memoirs of Richard Nixon*, Vol. 1, New York, Warner Books, 1978.
6. Kissinger op. cit.
7. Oriana Fallaci, *Interview with History*, Houghton Mifflin Company, Boston, 1976.
8. Kissinger op. cit.
9. Sisson and Rose (1992).
10. Information from a retired senior Pakistani officer, November 1966.
11. G.H. Khan op. cit.
12. Islam (1974).

8 Civil War and the Indian Invasion[1]

It is a sad commentary on the efficiency of our Army leadership which appears to have landed us in a major war with a powerful neighbour without any psychological preparation or coordinated planning. This was a war in which everything went wrong for the Pakistan Armed forces. They were not only out-numbered but also out-weaponed and out-generalled. Our planning was unrealistic, strategy unsuit[able], decisions untimely and execution faulty. The ignominy [of surrender] [lay in] the lack of leadership from the higher command.

The Hamoodur Rehman Commission, Chapter 25: Conclusions, paragraph 16.

It is unlikely that the crisis that took place in East Pakistan (Map 11) in 1971 could have been avoided, given the standpoints of leaders in the East and West Wings and the depth of feeling on the part of Bengalis about the manner in which they perceived they were being treated. What might have been reduced was the enormous loss of life. Many would have died, no matter how events unfolded, because there could be no curtailment of Bengali aspirations for independence, but the size of the tragedy and the brutality associated with it might have been less had there been goodwill on the part of political leaders, West and East. Manifestly there was not. Mujib was riding the galloping horse of insurrection. Had he checked, he would have fallen. At first it mattered little to him that many of his supporters would die on the streets. Indeed, it suited his purpose. Later, when events had gone beyond his control and the killings became more numerous, he was appalled at the state of affairs, but there was nothing to be done by that stage to halt the civil war or the slaughter.

The West Pakistanis—Yahya and his immediate group of advisers—were doomed by their lack of understanding of the situation. They had no sympathy for Bengalis and came to regard them as revolutionary rabble. They considered Mujib's inflexibility in the matter of the Six Points to be the root of the crisis but failed to realize how crucial they were to him, the Awami League, and the people of East Pakistan. Yahya was worried about the course of affairs, but his seeming lack of concern

MAP 11

EAST PAKISTAN
(BANGLADESH)

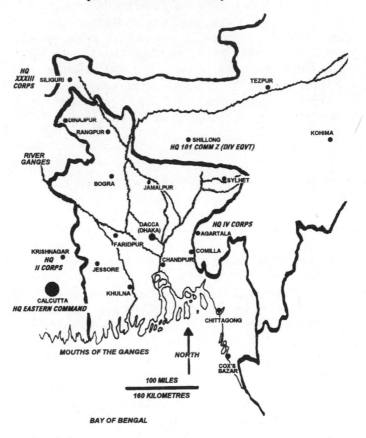

HQ
XXXIII
CORPS   SILIGURI ●   TEZPUR ●

●DINAJPUR
RANGPUR ●   ● SHILLONG   KOHIMA ●
                                       HQ 101 COMM Z (DIV EQVT)

RIVER
GANGES
                        BOGRA ●   JAMALPUR   ● SYLHET

                                    DACCA   HQ IV CORPS
                                    (DHAKA)   ● AGARTALA
                        FARIDPUR ●
KRISHNAGAR   COMILLA
HQ   ● JESSORE   CHANDPUR
II CORPS

                        KHULNA ●
● CALCUTTA
HQ EASTERN COMMAND   CHITTAGONG

MOUTHS OF THE GANGES   NORTH

                                                    COX'S
                                                    BAZAR
                        100 MILES
                        160 KILOMETRES

        BAY OF BENGAL

about India's likely reaction to events in the period perhaps stemmed from his emergence as a statesman.

On 25 October 1970, during a state visit to Washington, Yahya was taken into President Nixon's confidence and asked if he would assist in plans for the US to normalize relations with China. Next month he visited Peking, carrying a letter from Nixon 'which formally raised the question of a presidential visit, to be preceded by a visit from Kissinger...'[2] Chairman Mao himself received Yahya, who also had meetings with Zhou Enlai, apparently discussing the Nixon initiative. Yahya was a head of state, to be sure, and a significant person in his own right, but to be treated as a valued ally by the president of the United States as well as the legendary Mao and the brilliant Zhou placed him in an altogether different and more important league. There was little wonder he was sure of himself. Other international occurrences contributed to that feeling over the next few months— although he was to be shaken by Mujib.

* * *

When the results of the December elections were made public Z.A. Bhutto congratulated the Awami League on its victory— but with a sting in the tail of his felicitations. He made it clear that although the PPP 'respected the majority...both Punjab and Sind are centres of power. We may or may not be able to form a government at the Centre but the keys of the Punjab Assembly Chambers are in my pocket...' In the other pocket, he said, 'lie the keys of the Sind Assembly and...no central government can run without our co-operation. If the People's Party does not support it, no government will be able to work, nor will the Constitution be framed...'[3] These were curious statements on the part of a politician within a democratic system. A political leader who claims that a legally elected government with a distinct majority cannot conduct its business without his co-operation is hardly a respecter of a majority decision. He was rebuked by the General Secretary of the Awami League, Tajuddin Ahmed, but Mujib himself cared little for his defeated political opponent or his unveiled threats. He had won, and leadership of the government of Pakistan was his. The President had referred to him, after all, as the 'next prime minister',[4] so why should he not take the reins of office?

On 3 January, 417 Awami League politicians took an oath at a rally in Dhaka. The gauntlet was thrown down to the West when they swore:

In the name of Allah, the Merciful, the Almighty;
In the name of the brave martyrs and fighters who heralded our initial victory by laying down their lives and undergoing the utmost hardship and repression;
In the name of the peasants, workers, students, toiling masses and the people of all classes of this country:
We, the newly elected members of the National and Provincial Assemblies, do hereby take oath that we shall remain wholeheartedly faithful to the People's mandate on the Six Points and the eleven-point programme.

Yahya flew to Dhaka on 12 January with his PSO, Lt.-Gen. Peerzada. The Governor, Admiral Ahsan (he of the liberal reforms when a senior Martial Law Administrator), was summoned by Peerzada to a meeting with Yahya and Mujib at which Yahya hoped to reach a 'thorough understanding' of the Six Points—as if there was any more to discuss. Ahsan, who knew this well, described to Siddiq Salik[5] what took place at the meeting. According to Ahsan, Mujib described the Six Points and answered questions, after which Yahya said that he accepted the Points, 'But there are strong feelings against them in West Pakistan. You should carry West Pakistan with you.' Mujib replied that of course 'we'—the Awami League government—would carry West Pakistan with them: 'We will consult them. We will frame the Constitution. We will frame it on the Six Points. We will show a copy of the Constitution to you. There will be nothing wrong in it.' There was nothing for Yahya to be pleased about in the words used by Mujib, although the tone was apparently cordial enough—even honeyed, as when Mujib replied to Peerzada's remarks (although what a Staff Officer was doing making comments of substance on matters of national importance when attending on his President is another matter). When Yahya left Dhaka for Karachi on 14 January he was observed by Salik as seeming 'to have lost all hope for the future'.

After a meeting between Yahya and Bhutto at the latter's Larkana estate (in Sindh) on 17 January, Bhutto flew to Dhaka on the 27th to talk with Mujib. Positions were restated. Compromise was impossible. Mujib could not disagree with the oath taken by his Party's 417 politicians; had he even hinted at doing so he would almost certainly

have been overthrown as leader of the Awami League. Bhutto wrote
that,

> ...we put forward certain constitutional proposals but the Awami League
> leaders refused any discussion till the Six Points were accepted in toto. We
> pointed out to Mujibur Rahman that public opinion in the West Wing was
> against the Six Points...[Mujib] fully understood our difficulties but was
> not prepared to accept them...[6]

No other authority mentions the 'certain constitutional proposals', and
the Awami League version of the talks, which seems balanced, states
that the PPP had '...not prepared their draft [for discussions], and were
merely probing the Six Points as Yahya had done before them'.[7]

It seemed nothing could go right. Yahya, the trusted go-between in
negotiations involving China and America, did not appear to have the
delicacy required for subtle negotiations on his own or his country's
account. Bhutto did, but was not prepared to employ his talents to woo
Mujib; Bhutto wanted power, and Mujib stood in his way (and so did
Yahya). There were a hundred pinpricks that increased the alienation
of the Bengalis: Yahya went to stay with Bhutto, the minority leader,
at Larkana but, as a Bengali journalist pointed out: 'When Yahya comes
here [to Dhaka], one of his staff officers rings up Mujib, the majority-
party leader, to come and report to the President at the President's
house.'[8] A photograph of Bhutto and Yahya strolling in the grounds of
the Larkana mansion appeared in Dhaka newspapers. There could
hardly have been a more evocative picture: conspiracy was afoot,
thought the Bengalis. They were right, in a way: conspiracy was
certainly afoot, but it was not all on the part of the West Pakistanis.

On 30 January, an Indian civil aircraft was hijacked between Srinagar
and Jammu by two Kashmiris who ordered the pilot to fly to Lahore.
The men were accused by both India and Pakistan of being agents for
the other. They were. In the strange world of espionage, they had acted
as double agents, and it is not certain on whose side they were when
they hijacked the aircraft. It seems likely they were not, at that time,
employed by the intelligence services of either country[9] but were acting
simply as Kashmiris attempting to bring the plight of that region to the
attention of the world. What they succeeded in doing was to increase
tension between the countries and, of some importance, cause India to
forbid overflight of India by Pakistani aircraft. The ban resulted in
diversion via Sri Lanka, adding six hours to a flight from Karachi to

Dhaka. (The Pakistanis retaliated by forbidding overflight of their territory, which was mildly inconvenient for India.)

On 13 February, Yahya announced that the National Assembly would meet in Dhaka on 3 March. Bhutto then stated that the PPP would not attend the Assembly. He had reached his own version of compromise: the PPP should control the West and the Awami League the East. This was acceptable to neither Mujib nor Yahya, nor, of course, to those Pakistanis—the majority of the electorate—who had voted for government by the Awami League, albeit they were solely in the East.

* * *

It became apparent that West Pakistani troops would be required in greater numbers to carry out Operation *Blitz*, the counter-insurgency plan for the East, as Bengali troops could not be trusted to do so. The situation became even more tense at the end of February, when 22nd Battalion of the Baluch Regiment and 13th Bn. Frontier Force Regt. were flown to Dhaka to join 57 Infantry Brigade—whose brigade major (the senior staff appointment in a brigade HQ), a Bengali, was not informed of the reinforcement until after it had begun. PIA staff at Dhaka airport refused to handle the aircraft (and two Bengalis tried to blow up one of them) with the result that the PAF took over most airport duties and continued to perform them until the end of the war. The fly-in of the two battalions (about 1700 men) took place by PIA 707 aircraft between 27 February and 1 March—a swift move by the standards of the day, which leads to the belief that it had been planned for some time.

Then Yahya decided to postpone the meeting of the Assembly that was due to take place on 3 March. (He had been urged to again visit Dhaka by the Governor, the admirable Admiral Ahsan, but did not go.) On 28 February, on the telephoned orders of General Peerzada from Karachi, Mujib was called to Government House in Dhaka, where Ahsan told him of the decision. Mujib appeared relaxed about the postponement but said the election would have to be held in March if he were to be able to control the situation. If the date was to be in April, it would be more difficult. An indefinite postponement would be impossible. He was '...between two fires,' he said to Maj.-Gen. Rao Farman Ali, the political affairs officer at Martial Law HQ in Dhaka. 'I will be killed either by the army or extremist elements in my party.

Why don't you arrest me? Just give me a ring and I will come over.'
One does not know how much joviality there was in the comment, but
it would seem Mujib could not have expected to be taken seriously
about the arrest. There is little doubt he was earnest enough about the
killing part, however, as he knew how dangerous the situation was, and
how much more critical it could become. His reaction, and a plea by
Ahsan for inclusion of a date for the sitting of the Assembly when a
formal announcement was made, was cabled to the West Wing as soon
as it could be encoded and received the reply: 'Your message fully
understood.' One doubts if it was, for next day at 1:05 p.m. the radio
broadcast announcing that the Assembly would not meet on 3 March
did not include a date for its eventual sitting. Not only that, but the
message was delivered by an announcer rather than the President,
which created a poor impression. Mobs were out on the streets within
half an hour of the broadcast ending.

* * *

There was confusion in the following three weeks. The honourable
sailor Ahsan was replaced as governor by the honourable soldier
Sahibzada Yaqub Khan, who resigned on 5 March after failing to
persuade Yahya to visit Dhaka. There were killings, many by Bengalis
of any non-Bengalis on whom they could lay their hands, but most by
the security forces. West Pakistanis—or as many of those who could
afford it—began to flee by air. Awami League volunteers set up check-
points on roads to the airport to 'stop the outflow of Bangla Desh
wealth', and the security forces were unable to interfere.[10] Mujib
declared a general strike that was completely successful. For all
practical purposes he was the ruler of East Pakistan, as nothing could
take place in the province without his approval. On 6 March Yahya
announced that the Assembly would meet on the 25th, but it was too
late for this to be acceptable to the League or the population as a whole.
Mujib stated that he would make a speech in Dhaka the following day
at which he would demand acceptance of six points before he or his
party would attend the Assembly. But it was impossible for the central
government to agree to withdraw troops and permit law and order to
'be left exclusively to the police and the…East Pakistan Rifles, assisted,
where necessary, by Awami League volunteers,' as demanded.

Events were marching swiftly. Also on 6 March, Yahya sent a
teleprinter message in clear to Mujib urging him not to take a hasty

decision and assuring him that, 'I have a scheme in mind that will more than satisfy your Six Points.' His attempts at conciliation were too late and, in any event, the General Officer Commanding troops (GOC) in East Pakistan, Maj.-Gen. Khadim Hussain Raja, stated to two of Mujib's representatives (at 2 a.m. on the 7th) that, although he would be at the racecourse (where Mujib was to address the mass meeting later that day), 'to save him from the wrath of the extremists,' if he spoke 'against the integrity of Pakistan, I will muster all I can—tanks, artillery and machine guns—to kill the traitors and, if necessary, raze Dacca to the ground' (Salik [1978]). Maj.-Gen. Khadim Hussain Raja was undoubtedly under stress, but this was a dreadful thing to say. The meeting passed off quietly. An estimated million people gathered in and around the racecourse but Pakistan Radio was forbidden to broadcast the speech. (It was allowed to, next day.) The crowds dispersed peacefully, which should have been evidence enough to convince the central government that Mujib, and only Mujib, could control East Pakistan, but Lt.-Gen. Tikka Khan, who arrived in Dhaka that afternoon to assume command, was not known for a spirit of compromise, especially where malcontents or dissenters were concerned, and was unlikely to grasp the fact that his authority could be less than total.

In his capacity as commander 4 Corps in Lahore, Tikka Khan had been Martial Law Administrator of Punjab, in which appointment he was judged a hard man.[11] He was a good officer, loyal to the Constitution. He tended to see matters in black and white, which may or may not be a good thing in a soldier but is certainly not the most desirable attribute for a senior figure thrust into the political maelstrom of an incipient civil insurrection. He assumed the appointments of Chief Martial Law Administrator and military Commander Eastern Command but there was a problem about taking over as governor: the Chief Justice refused to swear him in. Eventually a form of words was composed that permitted his appointment by presidential fiat, but it was not an auspicious start to his six months of rule over the Province. (He was withdrawn by Yahya on 4 September.)

Killings grew in number and ferocity. Bengali officers and soldiers continued to prepare clandestinely for their 'war of liberation' against the detested West Pakistanis. Their activities were described in one account:

In the evening of March 6, I held a secret meeting in my office…with a few
of the reliable Bengali JCOs and NCOs to brief them about their tasks in
the future against the Pakistanis…I told them to be ready to strike at the
Pakistanis, to make a list of all non-Bengali EPR [East Pakistan Rifles]
personnel…and then join the fight against other Pakistani forces whenever
they were told to fight.[12]

The UN made arrangements to fly out the families of its employees,
and some foreign governments chartered aircraft to evacuate their
citizens. On 10 March Mujib issued a statement that, 'the responsibility
of the United Nations does not end with the evacuation of their
employees from a troubled area. The threat that we are facing today is
of genocide….,' but his speech at the racecourse, although refraining
from declaring independence for East Pakistan, had not been devoid of
emotional incentive to violence. It ended:

My request to you, under the leadership of the Awami League, [is to]
organize combat committees in every village…Arm yourself with whatever
you can get. Remember, since we have once shed blood, we shall have to
shed a lot more, but we shall free the people of this country, Inshallah.

This was clear enough. There were few courses of action open to
the central government—to Yahya—and Mujib knew this. He was
forcing Yahya into a corner but did not reckon on the ferocity of his
reaction or the manner in which his loyal subordinates would carry out
orders to suppress disaffection.

* * *

Yahya, after much vacillation, decided to visit East Pakistan and arrived
in Dhaka on 15 March. Five days before, in India, Mrs Gandhi's
Congress Party had won a massive electoral victory. This should have
given Yahya pause for reflection but there is no evidence it did. A
thoughtful politician might have concluded that the leader of a
neighbouring country who wins 350 out of 525 parliamentary seats
would be in a position to exert considerable regional influence and
would perhaps have adjusted national policies accordingly, but it
appears that tunnel vision had set in for good. The President and his
circle considered his authority to be absolute and ignored the fact that
for two weeks of chaos his writ had not applied in the East. He did not
imagine that India might give active support to the 'rebels', but this is

what they were about to do. To be fair to Yahya, Dr Kissinger thought
the same way and wrote that Mrs Gandhi, although,

> busy with the election campaign and its immediate aftermath…adopted a
> hands-off policy. As late as the middle of March the…head of the Indian
> foreign office, T.N. Kaul, told our ambassador in New Delhi, Kenneth
> Keating, that India wanted Pakistan to remain united. On March 17 the
> Indian ambassador in Washington, the skilful L.K. Jha, spoke in the same
> sense to me. Neither gave the slightest indication that India would consider
> the troubles in neighbouring East Pakistan as affecting its own vital
> interests.[13]

This was probably correct at the time, but both assurances were
given before Mujib's declaration of independence, and arrest, on the
night of 25/26 March. What Kissinger does not mention is that on 27
March the Indian parliament passed a resolution stating that: 'This
House wishes to assure them [the Bengalis] that their struggle and
sacrifices will receive the whole-hearted sympathy and support of the
people of India.'

* * *

Bhutto visited Dhaka, too, but with as little positive result as his
President, who left secretly—or as secretly as he could—on the 25th
having endorsed Operation *Searchlight*, the plan to enforce total martial
rule in the East Wing (replacing *Blitz*). How Yahya, a professional
soldier to his bootstraps, could have thought that some twenty units
(perhaps 16,000 combat troops) could control a country of over
70 million is a mystery. General Yaqub, before being replaced, had
resisted proposals for reinforcements to be flown in as he considered
this would further alienate the Bengalis. But it became apparent that
the Bengalis were already about as alienated as they could be and that
many more troops would be needed if the country was to be subjugated.
It may be that Yahya had already planned to increase the West Pakistani
military presence in the East Wing. If he had, nobody informed the
Chief of the General Staff in Rawalpindi. Bhutto left on the 26th, after
the brutal crackdown had begun, saying 'Thank God, Pakistan has been
saved.'[14]

* * *

The plan for *Searchlight* had been composed by Maj.-Gen. Rao Farman Ali (office of the CMLA) and Maj.-Gen. Khadim Raja (GOC 14 Division) on 18 March and cleared by Tikka Khan and Yahya on the 20th. Technically it was a good plan, taking into account the fact that so few troops were available. But practically (and morally) it was a disaster as it ignored the depth of feeling on the part of the Bengalis. The attitude on the part of (West) Pakistan's leaders appears to have been that the gun would conquer all.

Maj.-Gen. Khadim Raja was telephoned by Tikka Khan in the morning of 25 March to be told that H-hour for *Searchlight* was 0100 the following day. In the event, timings were brought forward because the Bengalis knew something was afoot and had stepped up preparations for confrontation, led by one Colonel Osmani, a retired officer. General Gul Hassan (in this instance perhaps a not altogether neutral commentator) observed that Osmani, '...though senior to me in service, was my deputy when I was the DMO in the early sixties. He had been superseded for good and was naturally bitter against West Pakistan officers, who dominated the Service.'[15]

One of the most extraordinary aspects of the whole affair was that the Chief of the General Staff of the Pakistan Army in 1971, General Gul Hassan, was not only unaware of the plan for *Searchlight* but did not know where his President was on 26 March; furthermore, he had '...some days previously discovered by accident that General Hamid had gone to Dhaka. He kept his movements secret, certainly as far as I was concerned. But I was in for a staggering surprise. I found out that Generals Eftikhar and Mitha had also gone to Dhaka but no one could educate me as to the purpose.' This was verging on the incredible, but more surprises were to follow for the CGS. One of these was the appointment of Lt.-Gen. A.A.K. Niazi as Commander Eastern Command. Gul Hassan's account of being told of the appointment (and his own promotion) is worth retelling:

'When did you see General Hamid [the Chief of Staff] last?' the President asked.
'I am coming straight from his office.'
'Didn't he tell you that you have been promoted?'
'No, Sir. Where am I going?'
'Nowhere.'
'Then why should I be promoted?'

'Because we are promoting Niazi who is junior to you. So we have had to give you the next rank.'
'Where is Niazi going?'
'As Commander Eastern Command.'
I swore audibly.
'This is what he thinks of my senior officers,' the President said, turning to Sultan Khan.[16]

That was indeed what Gul, and many other officers, thought of Niazi, who was assessed by Gul as having a professional '...ceiling... no more than that of a company commander'.[17] But he was Yahya's man, and could be relied upon to carry out orders. In fact, notwithstanding Gul's stricture, he was efficient in brutally subduing East Pakistan, although the combination of Niazi and Tikka Khan was to prove disastrous for the country as a whole. It was a truly terrible duo of appointments for the Bengalis.

Under command HQ 14 Division (Dhaka) and HQ CMLA the allocation of units and outline operational tasks in East Pakistan were (from Salik [1978] and other sources):

LOCATION	HQ	UNIT	TASKS
Dhaka	57 Bde.	43 LAA Regt.	Security of airport.
		22 Baluch	Disarm 5,000 Bengali soldiers (from 2 and 10 EB and HQ E. Pakistan Rifles) and Reserve Police. Seize wireless exchange.
		32 Punjab	Disarm 1000 'highly-motivated' police.
		18 Punjab	Secure Nawabpur and Old City areas.
		31 Fd. Regt.	Secure Second Capital (near airport) and adjoining localities.
		1 Coy. from each inf. bn.	'Flush' the university campus.
		Platoon of SSG (commando)	Raid Mujib's house and take him alive.
		M-24 tanks (about 10)	Show of force, but could fire if required.
Jessore	107 Bde.	25 Baluch 27 Baluch 24 Fd. Regt. (-) 55 Fd. Regt.	Disarm 1 East Bengal, Reserve Police, etc.; Secure town and arrest Awami League leaders; Secure communications facilities

Location	HQ	Unit	Tasks
Khulna		22 FF	Disarm Bengali troops; Secure town; Arrest Awami League students and communist leaders.
Rangpur-Saidpur	23 Bde.	29 Cavalry 26 FF 23 Fd. Regt.	Disarm 3 East Bengal; If possible disarm Sector HQ and Reserve Coy. at Dinajpur, or neutralize by reinforcing border outposts; Arrest Awami League and student leaders at Rangpur; Secure area and communications facilities; Secure ammunition dump at Bogra.
Rajshahi		25 Punjab	Disarm Reserve Police and sector HQ; Secure university and in particular Medical College; Arrest Awami League and student leaders; Secure communications facilities.
Comilla		53 Fd. Regt. 3 Cdo. Bn. (-) 11/2 mortar byts. Station troops	Disarm 4 East Bengal, Wing HQ East Pakistan Rifles, and Reserve Police; Secure town and communications; Arrest Awami League and student leaders.
Sylhet		31 Punjab (-)	Disarm Sector HQ East Pakistan Rifles and Reserve Police; Secure airfield, Koeno bridge, and communications facilities.
Chittagong		20 Baluch Coy. 31 Punjab Mobile column from Comilla: Brig. Iqbal Shafi with *ad hoc* HQ 24 FF. Tp. hy. mors. Fd. Coy. engrs.	Disarm East Bengal Regimental Centre (EBRC), 8 East Bengal (if loyalty detected as shaky), Sector HQ East Pakistan Rifles, and Reserve Police; Seize Police armoury (20,000 weapons); Arrest Chief Instructor EBRC; Arrest Awami League and student leaders; Secure communication facilities.

The West Pakistani troops carried out their tasks effectively, but there was much bloodshed. Siddiq Salik, whose book is probably the most balanced of subcontinent publications (and certainly the most readable) about the period, records that:

At about 2 a.m. [on 26 March] the wireless set in the jeep again drew our attention. I was ordered to receive the call. The captain on the other end...said he was facing a lot of resistance from Iqbal Hall and Jagan Nath Hall [of the University]...a senior staff officer snatched the hand-set from me and shouted into the mouth-piece: 'How long will it take you to neutralise the target?...Four hours!...Nonsense...What weapons have you got?...Rocket launcher, recoilless rifles, mortars, and...OK, use all of them and ensure complete capture of the area in two hours.' The university building was conquered by 4 a.m. but the ideology of Bengali nationalism preached there over the years would take much longer to subdue. Perhaps ideas are unconquerable.

Salik visited the campus later that morning and '...found three pits—of five to fifteen metres diameter each. They were filled by fresh earth. But no officer was prepared to disclose the exact number of casualties.'

There is no doubt that 'casualties'—deaths—were enormous, but it is difficult to determine how many there were. Foreign reporters had been discouraged from moving around the country and were evacuated from Dhaka on 26 March. There was no independent eye to confirm or confound claims by either the Bengalis or West Pakistanis. Naturally the world's media tended to accept what they were told by the Bengalis rather than by the Pakistan government. Both were suspect, but there was more resonance to Bengali claims.

Salik, trusted by foreign reporters, could have done much at the time to assist in painting an objective picture but was not permitted to do so. His account of the murders of West Pakistanis serving in 2 East Bengal Regiment—and their wives and children—is chilling:

...Subedar Ayub, who had served with the battalion for over twenty years, managed to escape...He asked for help...[a] company of [the] Punjab Regiment was despatched ...As the reinforcements reached the battalion headquarters they saw the most gruesome sight of their lives...five children, all butchered and mutilated, the abdomens ripped open with bayonets. The mothers of these children lay slaughtered and disfigured on a separate heap. Subedar Ayub identified, among them, members of his family. He went mad with shock—literally mad.

It was all too reminiscent of the 1947 massacres, but this time it was soldier of soldier and Muslim of Muslim—except for the religious and ethnic minorities, who were slaughtered by Bengalis with as great a gusto as they killed West Pakistanis. And West Pakistani soldiers in their turn (and even before their turn) murdered Bengalis with relish. No one can understand how our fellow human beings could act in such a fashion.[18]

Between 26 March and 6 April, two divisions arrived to join 14 Div.: HQs 9 and 16 Divs. brought five brigade headquarters, twelve infantry battalions, and a commando unit. These were followed by three more battalions on 24 April and two mortar batteries on 2 May. No armour or artillery was transferred from West to East at that time because it was assessed that internal security duties did not require such equipment (which is not always so). It was apparent that GHQ did not expect a situation to arise in which heavy weapons would be required. At that time, apparently, there was no thought given to the possibility of involvement by India.

India began a military build-up in the east in the latter part of 1970, but it appears this was caused by a requirement to counter Naxalite terrorists in West Bengal and other internal security considerations. There is no evidence that events in East Pakistan contributed to the decision. The emergency in West Bengal was a direct result of the fall of the State government and declaration of President's Rule, and several units of the Border Security Force (BSF) were sent, with some regular troops, to restore order.

After 25 March 1971, however, Indian officials acknowledged that the situation in East Pakistan was a matter for concern. Further troops were sent to West Bengal, Assam, and Tripura but,

> ...it should be noted in this respect...that when the service chiefs of the Indian military were consulted in late March 1971 about India's capacity for military intervention in East Pakistan, they informed the government that it would take several months before such intervention would be feasible despite the desertion of most of the East Pakistan military, para-military, and police units.[19]

This was prudent advice, but it should be remembered that India had speedily moved six divisions hundreds of miles to its western front in 1965, and that in the north-east of the country there were well-established formation headquarters and many units. Eastern Command HQ was in Calcutta and had two subordinate corps: HQ IV Corps at Tezpur with three divisions and XXXIII Corps at Siliguri with two. There were a further three divisions at Kohima, Kalimpong, and along the border north-east of Calcutta. All were mountain formations and had little or no armour, but then, neither had the Pakistan Army in the east got much armour.

The (West) Pakistan Army managed to impose martial law on the towns and cities of the East Wing but could not, of course, control the countryside. They had an impossible task, and their brutality encouraged the departure of refugees.

Mixed with the millions who fled to India were not only League leaders but Bengali soldiers, police, and members of the Mukti Bahini (the 'Liberation Force') and other militant groups. A 'Bangladesh Government in Exile' was formed in Calcutta, and guerrilla training camps were established along the border, under the tutelage and administration of the Indian army.

Colonel Osmani, the passed-over officer, was appointed commander-in-chief of Bengali forces on 14 April by the 'Provisional Government of Bangladesh'. Osmani was a complex character and not devoid of self-importance although, unlike many heads of irregular military organizations, he did not at once promote himself to general. His time would come, however, and in the months before overt intervention by the Indian Army he was energetic in organizing the Mukti Bahini, and in directing their operations in association with the Indians. He later became C.-in-C. in independent Bangladesh, which must have been sweet, indeed.

* * *

The West Pakistani authorities lacked information concerning such of Mujib's intentions as he did not publicly announce. After his detention, the security forces obtained little or no detail concerning the movements or intentions of resistance groups. There was no physical penetration of consequence of the Awami League, the Mukti Bahini, or any other element by the government's intelligence agency or military intelligence. In the cities the educated classes refused to talk with West Pakistanis. In the countryside there was no communication, not only because of resentment and demonstrable hatred on the part of the peasants, but because there was no language in common with the security forces. (English was the medium between educated Bengalis and West Wing Urdu or Punjabi speakers.) The West Pakistanis were conducting counter-insurgency operations in the dark. And neither did they have any idea as to how India was *really* thinking. But the White House did.

Several commentators have stated—based, apparently, on senior Indian sources—that Mrs Gandhi and her government (which meant her immediate coterie) had no intention of taking direct military action against Pakistan. Doubtless these sources gave their honest opinion reflecting what they knew of circumstances at the time. And the Pakistanis could base their actions only on what Mrs Gandhi was saying, which was that she did not contemplate military intervention. But the US had different information because, in addition to other intelligence, it had a source close to power in New Delhi.

Mr Morarji Desai was not personally close to Mrs Gandhi (loathing was mutual), but he was a member of her cabinet as well as being a paid agent of the Central Intelligence Agency.[20] It is likely that he provided information regarding India's military preparations to the CIA but, in spite of the drama (and success) of having such a highly-placed source, it would not have taken any intelligence organization long to discover that something was afoot. General Sukhwant Singh has described the preparations that began in spring 1971, and these are so all-embracing that it is difficult to see (even given the Indian proclivity for secrecy—witness the 1998 nuclear tests) how they could have been undetected by defence attachés in New Delhi, however little access they were given to military establishments.

The Chief of the Army Staff of India at the time was the admirable General S.H.F.J. (Sam) Manekshaw, who was also (as the senior Service chief by time in appointment), Chairman of the Joint Chiefs of Staff Committee. Manekshaw was not only a 'character', he was a highly efficient commander and staff officer. He had presence, as one might expect, but in addition to that he had the gift of enthusing his officers and soldiers to perform to the utmost of their abilities—without seeming to 'break into a sweat', as the Indian DGMO told the author in 1982.

When Mrs Gandhi indicated that she was on the warpath, Manekshaw advised caution: the country's war reserves were depleted; the army was jogging along, confident that there was no Chinese threat and that if the 'Paks' tried something they would 'sort them out' very quickly.[21] Turnover of units around the country was normal; extended leave was still being granted because there was no threat; the Territorial Army (TA, which manned much of the air defence system, but not the Soviet-supplied SAM sites) was disorganized; and there were deficiencies in the pay code, not the least being inadequate arrangements for widows' pensions—a matter dear to the heart of soldiers, who may hazard their lives for the sake of the Regiment but wish to be assured that if they make the supreme sacrifice, their dependants will not suffer.

Manekshaw changed all this in short order. The government was prevailed upon to adopt the recommendations of the Third Pay Commission, submitted in June, which improved many conditions of service; war reserve stocks were built up; new equipment was obtained (mainly from the USSR); unit turnover was reduced; and the families of soldiers in units suddenly posted to the border with East Pakistan were allowed to remain in accommodation that normally they would be expected to evacuate. TA training was reorganized to fit in as many consecutive days as would be permitted by harvest-time and other commitments, and training was improved by seconding above-average officers and NCOs, and especially JCOs, to TA centres; orders were issued for instructors at the Staff College, National Defence College, and other training institutions to be prepared to join units and headquarters when hostilities began. Implementation of these measures was an extraordinary and impressive administrative process which would deserve and receive admiration were it conducted by any army in the world, even today.

* * *

In contrast, in Pakistan, in GHQ, in General Niazi's headquarters, and in government, there was confusion in mid-1971. One problem was that General Hamid, although the Chief of Staff, refused to assume the mantle of Army Chief as such. This was not altogether his fault. He had been appointed COS, but the C.-in-C. was General Yahya Khan. So Hamid deferred to him in many matters. This might have been reasonable had the President maintained his interest in the Army and attended to its development, but instead he seemed to treat the military as a hobby. He interfered in promotions and appointments and appeared from time to time to look at stage-managed exercises, but he failed to provide the leadership which was so badly needed. Planning for operations in the east was left to Niazi and his staff, which caused concern to the CGS, Gul Hassan, but, apparently, to no one else in a position of power. While it would have been impossible—and improper—for GHQ in Rawalpindi to have involved itself in *detailed* planning for containment or defeat of the rebels (or whatever the aim was; that is unclear), it should certainly have been involved in overall planning for the security of the country. Niazi appeared to believe that there would not be an Indian invasion and, at least until September, structured his plans accordingly, in spite of the fact that Yahya had said on 19 July that if India attempted to, '…seize any part of East Pakistan… I shall declare war, let the world note. Nor will Pakistan be alone.'[22] Pakistan would certainly be alone, of course, even if US and Chinese messages appeared to be encouraging. But India would not be alone, and Yahya should have taken heed of the Indo-Soviet *Treaty of Peace, Friendship, and Co-operation* of 9 August which 'was received in India with great acclaim by all sections of political opinion' and with satisfaction by the army as it 'took care of the threat of Chinese intervention…and ensured better procurement of much-needed weaponry'.[23] (General Niazi published his memoirs in 1998 [*see*, Bibliography] but it must be stated, regretfully, that some statements in his book have to be treated with caution. The claim, for example, that 'The Russians used poison gas against my troops in the Mymensingh sector' cannot be verified.)

India, bolstered by the USSR's public support, and confident that the US and China could do nothing of consequence to help Pakistan in the light of increasing world concern about the brutality in the east, moved more troops east in mid-year and began open support of Mukti Bahini operations within the East Wing, including firing artillery over the border. Niazi's plan, according to what he himself stated after the war, was based on the understanding (or misunderstanding) that if India became involved, it would seek to take only a relatively small area, which would be handed over to the Provisional Government of Bangladesh. This was a poor appreciation of the courses open to India.[24] What would happen then? Would Indian troops stand by with folded arms if the West Pakistanis attacked the enclave? Could it be imagined that the Indians, once committed to invasion, would have confined their operations to limited tactical objectives? One is drawn to agree with Gul Hassan and Sukhwant Singh that Niazi's vision was indeed limited.

Descriptions of the battles fought by Pakistani forces are in the main tales of chaos ameliorated only by instances of individual bravery and determination on the part of units. Not only was there confusion, caused largely by General Niazi and his headquarters, but it was only too obvious (although apparently not to Niazi) that defence of the East was a forlorn hope. No army can fight without air support. When hostilities between the Indian and Pakistani armies began in November, there were sixteen F-86E fighters in the East, and no addition was possible, the Sri Lankan government, understandably, having prohibited transit through Colombo. 14 Squadron PAF shot down nine Indian aircraft for the loss of five Sabres[25] from 0730 on 3 December to mid-morning on the 6th. Tejgaon (Dhaka) airfield had been put out of action by bombing on the 6th but in spite of the craters being filled in overnight another strike at 0500 on the 7th made it totally unusable. The remaining 11 aircraft were disabled and the squadron's fourteen pilots were flown to Burma on 8 and 9 December to return to West Pakistan. They were an important asset but did not reach the West in time to make any difference. 14 Squadron had been outnumbered by ten to one and did an outstanding job in the circumstances, but it was unfortunate that they had been left alone to take on the Indian Air Force.

The Build-up to the Ground War in the East

Some months before overt hostilities began it became apparent to the Americans that India was intent on war. Kissinger was convinced by May that '...Mrs Gandhi had ordered plans for a lightning 'Israeli-type' attack to take over East Pakistan,' but that also, '...Indian military leaders thought Mrs Gandhi's proposal of an attack...was too risky'.[26] At that time, apparently, the CIA and the State Department disagreed with Kissinger that war was imminent (and they probably had enough sources in the Indian military and elsewhere to produce compelling arguments for their conclusion), but it soon became obvious that planning for war was well under way. The Manekshaw initiatives could not be kept secret indefinitely, and there were other indications of India's intentions.

In early July 1971,

Lt.-Gen. Jagjit Singh Aurora, General Officer Commanding-in-Chief Eastern Command, was brought into the [planning] picture [by Manekshaw] and...was given the task of destroying the Pakistani forces in the eastern theatre and of occupying the major portion of east Bengal...Manekshaw personally briefed Aurora, covering the political background, our aims...the outline operational plan, with...emphasis on the vigour and determination required for its execution...the machinery started moving for preparations for the war to liberate Bangladesh.[27]

On 1 September the US learned that India's forces were at a high state of readiness, and a week later, that 1st Armoured Division and an armoured brigade had moved to the border with West Pakistan. This, combined with support of the Mukti Bahini, increased cross-border shelling and incursions by Indian forces in the East, and troop reinforcements and massive logistic movement throughout the country, gave warning to the world that India was on the march. But even then the Pakistani government failed to take measures to try to safeguard the integrity of the East Wing—or of the West.

Mrs Gandhi's visit to the US in November was a presage of war, not an attempt to resolve matters diplomatically. After the first meeting between Nixon and Gandhi, Kissinger was '...convinced that Gandhi's aim was to destroy Pakistan,'[28] which was a fair summation of her ambition—that any India-watcher could have determined without the resources of the CIA, the analyses by the State Department, the tales of the traitor Morarji Desai, or knowledge of the surge in activity reported by defence attachés. The Nixon-Gandhi meeting took place concurrent with a massive airlift of Russian military equipment to India. Later that month, the Soviet air force chief visited New Delhi. It was obvious that Mrs Gandhi was playing the Soviet card for all it was worth, and this only reinforced Nixon's distrust of her.

Mrs Gandhi was determined to go to war, and nothing that was presented to her in an attempt to deflect her from her purpose could possibly have had any effect. Her purpose was firm. She had a national Aim, which was rather more than Pakistan had at the time—or later—and her army was ready to strike in both East and West. As it happened, the Pakistanis were unwise enough to engage in open warfare by attacking in the West. Not only was this militarily inept, it was political suicide for Yahya. Further, it played into the hands of India in more ways than tactically or strategically, by diverting attention from the provocative violations of Pakistan's territorial sovereignty that began in the East in November. Pakistan had come under increasing criticism for the brutality of its forces, but it was apparent that India's incursions were attracting adverse attention from world media. This was instantly diverted by Pakistan's reactive attack in the West, and the Indian invasion of East Pakistan was granted a legality it did not deserve.

* * *

Quantum and Quality of Forces in Eastern India and the East Wing

As recounted, the disparity between the countries' air forces in the East verged on the incongruous. So far as ground forces were concerned, the situation was slightly better—on paper. But West Pakistani troops had been fighting a counter-insurgency campaign for many months, a type of warfare that is particularly debilitating. They could not trust the local levies or indeed any 'Bingo' (as they called Bengalis), and this added to the air of unreality, confusion, and melancholy that pervaded Pakistan's forces in the East. The police and Frontier Corps troops brought from the West were efficient but poorly treated by the HQ in Dhaka over conditions of service; they objected and almost revolted. Army units received strange orders followed by bewildering counter-orders and exhortations to perform their duty, when what they needed were clear orders and definition of their Aim. Units were regrouped to come under command of unfamiliar headquarters; there were movements and redeployments for no apparent reason. *Ad hoc* formations without adequate staffs were created, and there were communication failures on the technical as well as the intellectual level. Two examples—of many—might serve to illustrate the confusion:

> 83 Mortar Battery moved from Lahore to Dacca in April 1971. It was to relieve 88 Mortar Battery. As [the] advance party...came off the plane it was detailed to guard the [airport] VIP lounge. A month later the twenty-odd men were flown to Comilla where with some men from 88 Mortar Battery they were thrown together in a troop. Captain Mohammad Anwar was put in command and the troop [sent] to Sylhet. They were reclaimed by 83 Mortar Battery in June....[29]

> [in November HQ Eastern Command]...asked for two more divisions. It got a promise of eight infantry battalions. Five of them arrived by the last week of November; the remaining three battalions, on arrival, were divided into companies and despatched to the areas under extreme pressure. They thus lost their identity as cohesive fighting units.[30]

All this to the drumbeat of relentless optimism by GHQ and General Niazi's headquarters.

Indian Forces Deployed in the East

All ground forces came under command of the redoubtable Lt.-Gen. Jagjit Singh Aurora at Eastern Command HQ, from which there was close co-ordination with the air force and navy. Aurora had at his disposal '…close to half a million men and women of the Army, para-military forces, and the Bangla Desh forces including the Mukti Bahini under his command, more than any lieutenant-general had ever commanded before or since.'[31]

CORPS/DIRECT COMMAND ELEMENTS	SUBORDINATE DIVISIONS AND CORPS SPT UNITS	SUBORDINATE BRIGADES AND UNITS	INVASION TASKS
II Corps, Krishangar, Lt.-Gen. Raina	4 Mtn. Div., Maj.-Gen. M. S. Barar	7, 41, 62 Bdes.	Advance to Jhenida, Magura, Faridpur to R. Madhumati
	9 Mtn. Div., Maj.-Gen. Dalbir Singh	32, 42 Bdes.	
	2 tank regts. (T-55/PT76), mdm. arty. regt. (D-130)		
IV Corps, Agartala, Lt.-Gen. Sagat Singh	8 Mtn. Div. Maj.-Gen. Krishna Rao	59, 81 Bdes.	Capture Kulaura and Shamshernagar
	23 Mtn. Div.	83 Bde., 'Kilo Force' (6 battalion brigade)	Capture Comilla and Maynamati; advance to Chittagong
	57 Mtn. Div. Maj.-Gen. Gonsalves	61 Bde. (initially Corps Troops); 181, 301 Bdes.; 311 Mtn. Bde. Gp.	Initially, assist 23 Div. at Comilla; then advance to Chittagong
	3 indep. armd. sqn., 2 mech. bns. 8 'Bangladesh' bns.		

Corps/Direct Command Elements	Subordinate Divisions and Corps SPT Units	Subordinate Brigades and Units	Invasion Tasks
XXXIII Corps. Silguri, Lt.-Gen. Thapan (strained relations with Manekshaw)	20 Mtn. Div., Maj.-Gen. L.S. Lehl	9, 66, 165, 202 Bdes.	Take Bogra and Rangpur, advance to Dhaka.
	71 Mtn. Bde. Gp. 340 Mtn. Bde. Gp. Bde. from 6 Mtn. Div. 69 Armd. Regt. (PT 76) Armd. Sqn. (T-55)		
101 Comm. Z HQ (*ad hoc* Div. HQ)		95 Mtn. Bde. Gp. plus Bde. equivalent	Take Jamalpur and exploit south
167 Mtn. Bde.			From Northern Command to assist II Corps
2 Parachute Bn.			Take Tangail

Sources: Salik (1978); Sukhwant Singh (1981); Islam (1974); Jackson (1975); Sarbans Singh (1993); Niazi (1998); Hamoodur Rehman Commission Report.

The above does not take into account regrouping, redistribution of units, or later reinforcements, but the number of formations gives an indication of the strength of Aurora's command compared with that of Niazi.

Pakistan's forces were spread all over the East Wing in a counter-insurgency posture, which Sukhwant Singh refers to as being in 'penny-packets', which is exactly what they were. Not only this, but East Pakistanis in para-military elements could not be relied on, sometimes, doubtless, unjustifiably. Members of the East Pakistan Civil Armed Forces (EPCAF) and other irregulars were in an awkward position, morally, physically, and geographically. Most were Bengalis whose loyalty was perforce divided between the central government (which paid them) and their homeland; if they carried out the orders of West Pakistanis to the detriment of their fellow-countrymen, their lives were at risk. If the worst happened, and East Pakistan managed to secede, there was nowhere for them to seek safety from the wrath that would surely fall upon them. Little wonder that they soft-pedalled and that their West Wing superiors did not trust them. So far as the

Order of Battle (ORBAT) and quantum of forces are concerned, EPCAF troops and *Razakars*, the other irregulars, can be discounted as effective fighting groups, although they were included on the ORBAT.

Niazi's plan, such as it was, depended on the fortress concept. Ten towns were selected to be fortified and held. The course of action for the defence of East Pakistan against Indian invasion was that:

> The troops on the border [the 'penny-packets' referred to by Sukhwant Singh] would fight on until...ordered by the GOC [Niazi] to withdraw.
> While withdrawing to the fortresses they would fight delaying actions so as to 'trade space for time'.
> Finally they would occupy and defend the fortresses to the end.[32]

This was a plan born of despair. Niazi at one point stated that, 'My troops in the border outposts are like the extended fingers of an open hand. They will fight there as long as possible before they fold back to the fortresses to form a fist to bash the enemy's head.' Salik, who quotes this startling statement, comments that he was '...fascinated by the simile. But I recalled his latest decision prohibiting any withdrawals unless seventy-five per cent casualties had been sustained. When three out of four fingers are broken is it possible to form a fist?' Salik was a remarkable PR officer.

The disadvantages of the fortress concept of operations did not register with Niazi, nor with his superior, General Hamid, when he endorsed it, including GHQ's recommendations that:

> Offensive action against English Bazar [in the area where the Indian 20 Mountain Division was concentrated] should be reinforced in the plan.
> The plan should incorporate a commando action to destroy or damage Farakka Barrage.
> One infantry battalion should form the nucleus in Chittagong (to be reinforced later by sea).
> Dacca should be treated as the lynch-pin for the defence of East Pakistan.[33]

These were extraordinary additions by, presumably, experienced staff officers. What troops, for example, could have taken 'offensive action against English Bazar'? It could not be unknown to GHQ that the area was held by an entire division of XXXIII Corps. What strategic advantage could possibly have accrued from the destruction of Farraka

Barrage? Reinforcement by sea?—the Indian Navy was presumably expected to allow that to take place. The vital ground was not Dhaka; but Niazi did not seem to know what 'vital ground' meant.[34] Nor, apparently, did his superiors in GHQ Rawalpindi. It seemed that Niazi wished to wear down his opponent—but there could be no war of attrition in East Pakistan.

* * *

General Niazi allocated his forces in and around the 'fortresses' of Jessore, Jhenaida, Bogra, Rangpur, Jamalpur, Mymensingh, Sylhet, Bhairab Bazar, Comilla, and Chittagong. Local commanders were ordered to develop other towns and villages as 'strong-points'. He created *ad hoc* divisional headquarters and brigades by removing staffs and units from other formations in a manner that might be described as cavalier if that word did not have the connotation of being at least stylish. '...The enemy,' he is quoted by Salik as saying, 'will be flabbergasted to see these additional headquarters. He will mentally multiply our strength accordingly. It will certainly be a deterrent to him.' As if the Indians had not kept track of units arriving in the East. Niazi's Concept of Operations was badly flawed.

Troop dispositions were:

Division/Location and Task	Subordinate Elements and Locations	Ad Hoc Arrangements
9 Division HQ Jessore (to Magura 3 Dec) Maj.-Gen. M.H. Ansari	107 Bde. - Jessore 57 Bde. - Jhenida In Direct Support: 49 Fd. Regt.	On 29 Nov the Col. (GS) 9 Div. was ordered to form an *ad hoc* brigade at Kaligari of two bns. (38FF, 50 Punjab), two
Task: Defence of Jessore Sector	55 Fd. Regt. 211 Mor. Bty.	105mm guns, and four 120mm mortars, taken from other brigades.

Division/Location and Task	Subordinate Elements and Locations	Ad Hoc Arrangements
	In support: 3 Indep. Armd. Sqn. (8 tanks)	
16 Division HQ Nator Maj.-Gen. Nazar Hussain Shah	23 Bde. - Rangpur/Dinajpur 34 Bde. - Rajshahi/Pabna 205 Bde. - Bogra area	
Tasks: Defence of North	In Direct Support:	

Division/Location and Task	Subordinate Elements and Locations	Ad Hoc Arrangements
Bengal	117 Mor. Bty. 80 Fd. Regt. 48 Fd. Regt. 29 Cav. Regt. (3 sqns.)	
14 Division HQ Dhaka Maj.-Gen. Abdul Majid Qazi Task: defence of Eastern border	27 Bde. - Akhaura (2 bns. + 2 coys.) 202 Bde. - Sylhet (1 bn. + 2 coys.) 313 Bde. - Maulvi Bazaar (1 bn. + 2 coys.) In support: 31 Fd. Regt. Two mor. btys. Troop of 4 tanks	36 'Division' - Maj.-Gen. Jamshed, MC (DG EPCAF) with under command 93 Bde. (33 Punjab, 31 Baluch from 14 Div.) Task; defence of Dhaka north.
97 Independent Brigade Brigadier Ataullah Task: Defence of Chittagong	2 Cdo. Bn. - Kaptai 24 FF - Chittagong 2 coys. 21 AK Regt.	39 'Division' - Maj.-Gen. Rahim Khan (DMLA) with under command 117 Bde (Brig. Arif; from 14 Div.); 53 Bde. (Brig. Aslam Niazi; 15 and 39 Baluch); 91 'Bde.' (Brig. Tasheen; EPCAF troops + 2 coys. 21 AK) Task: Defence of Comilla area.

Doubtless there are inaccuracies in the above summation. Published sources, unit histories (where they exist; units were ordered to destroy their War Diaries), personal recollections, intelligence summaries, and even the Hamoodur Rehman Commission Report, are at variance to some degree. This is not of major importance. What *was* important was that the higher command of the Pakistan Army in the East Wing and GHQ in Rawalpindi had lost touch with reality and allocated tasks that could not be carried out by the forces available. The defence of East Pakistan was so poorly planned that defeat by the vastly superior Indian force was inevitable. Devoid of air support; split into widely-separated elements of units and sub-units under unfamiliar commanders and headquarters; with 64 tanks (1950-vintage Chaffees and 12 Soviet PT-76s captured in 1965) whose unserviceability was a reflection of their age rather than the care of their crews and EME mechanics; and commanded, overall, by an officer whose military acumen can be described as limited, the soldiers of the army in East Pakistan were doomed.

The North-West Sector (Map 12)

Lt.-Gen. Thapan's XXXIII Corps undertook preliminary operations well before 'official' hostilities began on 3 December. These involved occupation of Pakistani territory in the north to give a springboard for a swift advance to Rangpur and Bogra when the time came. Thapan was a cautious commander who had fought well in the 1965 war but had little dash. His relations with Manekshaw were brittle—the latter had wished to place Thapan's chief of staff in command of operations within East Pakistan but, in an unusual display of indecision, allowed the status quo to apply when Thapan objected. Direction of the campaign in the north-west suffered in consequence, as Thapan's tendency to caution was exacerbated by his natural desire to avoid criticism by Manekshaw. This attitude appears to have influenced some of his subordinates, with the result that five defended localities remained standing at the time of the cease-fire on 16 December, including one, Rangpur, that had been given as a main objective to three brigades.

Maj.-Gen. Lehl's 20 Mountain Division moved against the Hilli area, which was defended by 4th Battalion Frontier Force (4FF) of 205 Brigade. Lehl had maintained pressure from the salient of territory facing Hilli since September and increased effort markedly from 21 November, when 7 Guards Battalion, with armour support, attacked and took a platoon position of 4FF at Qasim, two kilometres to the north.

The terrain in the north was suitable for the use of armour—or at least less unsuitable than in the south—and most of Pakistan's only tank regiment, 29 Cavalry, had been allocated to 16 Division, commanded by Maj.-Gen. Nazir (or Nazar) Hussain Shah. It had four squadrons, one of which was divided into troops and distributed elsewhere (one of the troops of four tanks was designated the Corps Reserve and held at Hardinge Bridge). Shah placed each of the remaining three squadrons under command of a brigade: 23 at Rangpur, 205 at Bogra, and 34 at Nator/Pabna. The *ad hoc* brigade covering Rajshahi did not receive any armour and would have been incapable of using tanks properly, anyway. The allocation was curious. It violated

MAP 12   **NORTH WEST SECTOR**

SIKKIM

BHUTAN

RIVER TISTA

NEPAL

SILIGURI
HQ XXXIII CORPS

INDIA

COOCH BEHAR
6 MTN DIV

9 BDE

RIVER
BRAHMAPUTRA
(JAMUNA)

BODA

71 BDE

DOMAR

THAKURGAON

NILPHAMARI

LALMONIRHAT

MANDALPARA

71 BDE

SAIDPUR

KURIGRAM

INDIA

RANGPUR
HQ 23 BDE

DINAJPUR

66 & 202
BDES

PIRGANJ
(FALLS 7 DEC)

20
MTN DIV
21 NOV

340
BDE

HILLI
4 FF BN

66 BDE
202 BDE

BORDER

RIVER
GANGES
(PADMA)

ENGLISH
BAZAR

185 BDE

340 BDE

NAOGAON

BOGRA
HQ 205 BDE
(FALLS 16 DEC)

INDIA

BORDER
FOLLOWS
RIVER

AD HOC BDE

RAJSHAHI

NATOR

HQ 16 DIV
HQ 34 BDE

Garrisons in Dinajpur,
Saidpur, Rangpur,
Nator and Rajshahi
held out until the
cease-fire.

40 KILOMETRES
25 MILES

HARDINGE
BRIDGE

PABNA

BORDER

the principle of concentration of force and, although it was undoubtedly difficult for Shah to predict enemy intentions, it should have been apparent from patrol reports and Indian activity that 20 Div. was poised to the west of Bogra/Rangpur and that these would be early objectives. 29 Cav. Regt. as a complete unit, even with its old tanks, would have been a useful force against 20 Div., which itself had only five squadrons of tanks (69 Armd. Regt. plus a squadron) at the time of the advance. It would be easy to be critical of Shah for his failure to employ armour effectively, and it is perhaps over-severe of Sukhwant Singh to state that Shah '...failed his country and his command'.[35] He obeyed Niazi's orders to combine internal security operations with the almost impossible task of repelling the Indian attack.

North of Hilli the Indian advance was conducted by 71 Mountain Brigade Group commanded by Brigadier (later Lt.-Gen.) P. N. Kathpalia, who wrote about his experiences.[36] Kathpalia was a good commander, perhaps even of the first rate, but naturally he does tend to concentrate on his own skill, the potency of the enemy (and thus the effectiveness of his 'relentless pressure' about which Sukhwant Singh expresses doubts), and the speed of his advance. In spite of differing opinions concerning his prowess, it is apparent that 71 Bde., more or less on its own until 5 December, when it came under command 6 Mountain Division (although allocated almost all 6 Div.'s artillery, two helicopters for artillery spotting, and considerable ground-attack aircraft support), achieved a mighty advance across difficult country against an enemy who was a determined defender, even if patchily deployed and lacking air cover.

Kathpalia's advance began on 26 November, and by 1 December his brigade had reached Boda, whose single-company position, of 48 Punjab, was taken by 21 Rajputana Rifles supported by a squadron of 69 Armd. Regt.'s PT-76 tanks. The company withdrew in good order to Thakurgaon. Kathpalia mounted a brigade attack on the 'uncoordinated and hasty defences' (his words) at Thakurgaon on 3 December, the day that 'the President now declared that India was at war with Pakistan'. But the attack was poorly executed. His lead battalions hesitated, especially 21 Rajput, which was 'not quite enthusiastic' about pushing on. The two companies of 48 Punjab in and around the built-up area managed to break contact and get away—an impressive feat in the face of a brigade operation which was supported by artillery, armour, and air strikes. It is a fair bet that the COs of 21 Rajput and 7 Maratha (which failed to establish a blocking position to cut off 48 Punjab's companies) had their careers cut short at Thakurgaon.

While Kathpalia was trying to transfer some of his boldness and enthusiasm to what appear to have been some fairly second-rate troops, 66 Brigade was having little success at Hilli, where it was besieging 4FF and its troop of tanks and four guns. (Two guns of 180 Battery moved there on the night of 3 December, followed by the others next day.) Ammunition for tanks and guns was of course restricted to 'first line'—the amount carried in the tanks and gun-towing vehicles. A company each of 13FF and 8 Baluch were deployed east of Hilli to counter a possible by-pass manoeuvre, an ill-advised action by the commander 205 Brigade, the urbane and popular Brigadier Tajammul. Two companies, four tanks, and four guns were not going to hold up a division for long, and it might have been better, by this stage, for Nazir Shah to have withdrawn his forward outposts, which were being defeated in detail anyway, to a well-prepared defensive position from which counter-attacks could be mounted. But his orders from Niazi gave him no leeway and the Indian advance, although hesitant, was of such size as to make local tactical adjustments irrelevant.

Hilli, occupied by a single company of 4FF (D Coy., which, to the mind of the writer, should have its own Battle Honour), had been attacked first on 23 November by 8 Guards supported by a squadron of tanks. The attack 'ended up a dismal failure because the armour was immobilised by the marshes and failed to support the infantry'. After that debacle, and subsequent failures to overcome Hilli's defences, it is further recounted by Sukhwant Singh that India's 'Command Headquarters [i.e. HQ Eastern Command in Calcutta], following the bitter struggle for the capture of Hilli by a direct attack, decided to switch over to the contingency plan. It was now decided to avoid capturing strongly-held defensive positions.'

It would seem that the entire Indian concept of operations was altered because of the resistance of a tiny Pakistani force in a minor defensive position—but it is difficult to believe that General Aurora would have changed his plans unless he had been given to understand that his enemy's numbers were much greater than they actually were and that the defended localities had artillery, armour, and air support. The comments of Lt.-Gen. Kathpalia concerning 'intelligence shortcomings' are relevant, in that he states that information gained by forward troops was exaggerated and that analysis was not carried out at unit level; but it appears there was not much analysis at higher levels, either.

* * *

71 Bde., held at Nilphamari, swung south towards Dinajpur where 26FF, supported by the six field guns of 177 Battery (48 Field Regiment) was in defence. Quite why it had been decided to hold terrain in that area is not clear. To the south-east, Hilli was being besieged; Rangpur was under threat from the north-east by 9 Mountain Brigade; and it was—or should have been—obvious that the vital ground (if that had indeed been identified) was nowhere near Dinajpur. There do not appear to be records of decision-making at the time in this sector, and it has to be assumed that the reason 26FF did not withdraw was simply because it could not. Niazi's orders for the fingertips to fold back to form a fist was all very well, but in several instances the fingers could not curl up. For 26FF to fall back to Hilli would have been hazardous, as the complex was surrounded by three battalions, there was no other route through enemy lines, and it was apparent that 16 Division's line of communications to the northern garrisons had been cut by 7 December. Shah himself narrowly escaped capture when his jeep convoy was ambushed on the Rangpur–Pirganj road on that day, at about the same time as a combat group of a 2/5 GR and 69 Armd. Regt. entered Pirganj without opposition. Once more the Pakistanis had made a clean break, but this was impracticable for the defenders at Rangpur. It might have been possible for HQ 23 Bde. and its battalion to have conducted a fighting withdrawal to the south-east if they had been confident that the Brahmaputra river could be crossed. They were not, and it was evident by now that, even if some formations of 20 Mtn. Div. were not good at pressing home their advantage or at mounting road blocks to cut off escaping garrisons, there was no need for Lachhman Singh to do either. Maj.-Gen. Shah had lost his Division: there was no contact between its brigades or between many of their component units, and no possibility of re-establishing links. All that 20 Mtn. Div. had to do was wait until the garrisons ran out of ammunition and supplies, which assuredly would not be long.

Shah tried to mount a counter-attack to take Pirganj and sent two 'task forces' commanded by Brigadiers Naeem (commander 23 Bde. at Rangpur) and Tajammul (205 Bde.) to move respectively from north and south. It was a move of desperation to attempt such a manoeuvre without artillery support. Neither force made contact with the enemy, which was probably fortunate, and 340 Brigade consolidated its position, regrouped, and moved towards Bogra, which surrendered on the 16th (although announcement of the surrender was made by All India Radio the previous day). It was too much for the remnants of 205 Brigade—8 Baluch, fragmented companies of 4FF, 13FF, and 32 Punjab, and minor elements of 32 Baluch and other units—to be expected to hold out indefinitely against 340 Brigade, which was on the outskirts of Bogra, the second main objective of 20 Mountain Division, by 12 December. (Sukhwant Singh is generous in his praise of 8 Baluch in stating that, 'however heroic' were its actions and those of its CO, 'they were not equal to containing a brigade group with a regiment of armour', which seems fair comment.) The soldiers of 205 Bde. had conducted fighting withdrawals for over fifty miles in position after position, knowing full well, as only soldiers can, that this was not a case of *reculer pour mieux sauter* (which is in any case a dubious tactic) but a retreat involving evacuation of territory that would never be recovered. 340 Bde. was a battle-worthy formation with an excellent commander, Joginder ('Jogi') Singh, whose energy and expertise had welded it together as an efficient fighting entity. His final manoeuvres around Bogra were skilled indeed. In the north, however, the same could not be said for the commander of 202 Bde. and his troops, or even for 66 Bde.

Lehl's revised plan, as of 8 December, was for 202 Bde. to capture Hilli, link up with 66 Bde., and then for both to turn towards Bogra, after mopping-up in the north, to join 340 Bde. (whose mission to capture Bogra was achieved without the assistance of either). It had appeared essential that 202 move to the assistance of Jogi Singh because HQ Eastern Command had ordered that 340 Bde. be made available as soon as practicable for the advance to Dhaka.

In prosecution of this plan, 66 and 202 Bdes. were ordered to take Rangpur, which was held by HQ 23 Bde. (Brigadier Ansari), 8 Punjab, and parts of other units deployed north (85 Punjab), west (48 Punjab), and east (25 Punjab) of Rangpur. Its other battalion, 26 FF, was engaged at Dinajpur, under siege by 71 Bde. (86 Mujahid was deployed in platoons and sections with other units.) 9 Bde. of 6 Mtn. Div. was advancing on Rangpur from the north-east. The situation for the Rangpur garrison was hopeless, faced as they were by a complete division.

The battalions of 340 Bde. had been scattered around by Lehl in order to bolster 66 and 202, but once Jogi Singh received orders to reconstitute his force and advance on Bogra, he did so with alacrity. But this left 66 and 202 Bdes. in the awkward situation of having themselves to regroup while maintaining pressure on Rangpur. Understandably, pressure relaxed and the regrouping took almost two days to effect. Jogi Singh dispatched units south as they came under command and regrouped on the way (a pretty skilled piece of work), but the commanders of 202 (Bhatti) and 66 (Sharma) seemed to lack the confident élan displayed by their counterparts in 71 and 340, and displayed reluctance to advance more energetically. Sukhwant Singh comments that, '...Bhatti's brigade never became effective in the offensive tasks of the division,' and that it appeared the spirits of his troops 'had been sapped in the defensive operations at Hilli'. This is an interesting statement, especially as the operations by 20 Mtn. Div. at Hilli were surely *offensive* in intent, and perhaps Sukhwant Singh is being kind to the memory of Bhatti and his men. But, no matter the ineffectiveness of some elements of 20 Mtn. Div., the war was over for Shah and his Division. The surrender on 16 December was of course a matter for rejoicing on the part of 20 Mtn. Div. and 71 Mtn. Bde., but it is questionable if the victory was quite as overwhelming as some commentators have claimed. Sukhwant Singh, deeply versed in the Profession of Arms, had his doubts. The fact remains that, although Shah's plans were flawed (for which much blame lies with Niazi), and in spite of the apparent dilatoriness of some of Lehl's subordinates, there was never any doubt about the outcome in the north-west sector. Had Shah been a more skilled commander he might have been able to inflict graver damage on 20 Mtn. Div.—but to what end? Sukhwant Singh says that 'the campaign in the north-western sector did not make a significant contribution to Niazi's collapse'. This may be so, but did operations in the other sectors contribute to his defeat? If not, what did?

The Northern Sector

'Sir, the locals say they are Chinese.'

But the parachutists were not Chinese; they were members of the Indian Army's 2nd Parachute Battalion, and their drop at Tangail on

11 December, although tactically irrelevant, demonstrated India's overwhelming superiority.

Pakistan's forces in the north that were intended to delay the Indian advance to Dhaka (Map 13) consisted of 93 *ad hoc* brigade of 36 *ad hoc* Division raised in mid-November and commanded by Maj.-Gen. Muhammad Jamshed, MC, former commander of EPCAF. These formations were incomplete, had never trained together, had units as unknown to their commanders as the reverse was true, and had neither artillery nor armour. The commander of 93 Bde. was the elderly Brigadier Qadir, a martial law administrator without experience of commanding a fighting brigade and about to retire on age. He tried hard but, as with so many of Niazi's notions, the appointment simply did not work. He had two full battalions, however, which was more than some other brigadiers had in the East, and they served him as well as they could, given the eventual confusion. His frontage was about 180 kilometres, an enormous length for a two-battalion brigade, and he decided to try to delay the enemy on the main approaches to Dhaka for as long as possible. (Quite what the advantages of 'trading space for time' might have been is not clear.) His units performed as bravely as could be expected in the circumstances, but it was unwise of Niazi and Jamshed to hope that two battalions, no matter how dedicated, could affect the Indian advance.

The Indian general to Qadir's north was also an administrator, but not of martial law; of logistics. He was the commander 101 Communications Zone (Comm. Z) with his HQ in Shillong. Essentially a 'housekeeper', responsible for the support of troops in the ethnically and tribally disaffected areas of the north-east, Maj.-Gen. Gurbux Singh Gill was a 'character' whose job, although not intended to be an operational command, was just as demanding as any divisional commander's; perhaps even more so. And divisional commander was what he became, for the Comm. Z was declared a fighting formation and given the resources with which to undertake the 'offensive tasks of destroying the Pakistani forces deployed in Tangail and Mymensingh districts within 14 days of the outbreak of hostilities' (Sukhwant Singh). *Battle Honours of the Indian Army* is more precise and indicates that Jamalpur was to be captured by D+7 (10 December) and Tangail by next day. Dhaka was to be 'contacted' by the 16th.

Gill had two main subordinates. Brigadier Hardev Singh Kler, commanding 95 Brigade Group, was a Signals' officer who had been a forceful—some might say brutal—commander of counter-insurgency

MAP 13   **DEFEAT IN THE NORTH**

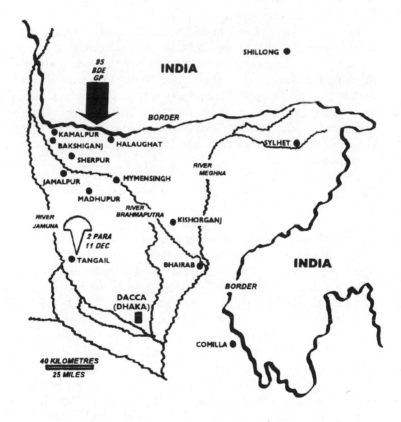

operations in Nagaland. His units were 13 Guards, 1 Maratha, 13 Rajput, and (from 9 December) 6 Sikh Light Infantry from 167 Brigade. Brigadier Sant Singh, commanding a group (a brigade in all but name, called FJ Force) of one regular infantry battalion (6 Bihar), 83 Battalion of the Border Security Force, and two units of Mukti Bahini, was a competent officer who, although not selected for a 'proper' brigade, proved himself a tough and intelligent commander. (167 Infantry Brigade was allocated from Northern Command on 9 December but only 6 Sikh LI saw action.) There was a group of Mukti Bahini based at Tangail under command of one 'Tiger' Siddiqi, lately of the Pakistan army.

The army's remarkable public relations officer, Siddiq Salik, as usual sums up pithily. In the north, he says, three memorable things happened: 'the tenacious defence of Kamalpur border outpost, the self-defeating withdrawal of 93 Brigade, and the Indian paratroop drop near Tangail'. To this he might have added the wounding of Maj.-Gen. Gill (by a landmine) and his replacement by the somewhat less competent Maj.-Gen. Gandharav Nagra on 5 December, and the ample support by IAF ground attack aircraft, which had opposition neither in the air nor from the ground.

The defence of Kamalpur, a hamlet on the border, by Captain Ahsan Malik and his 140 men would be an epic in any army's history. He had seventy soldiers of 31 Baluch and the same number of para-military troops; all fought well against great odds.

Attacks against Pakistani border outposts in the north had begun in July. These were mounted by Mukti Bahini, mainly former members of East Pakistan's regular forces, but failed to make any impression. Further attacks on Kamalpur, a kilometre from the border, came on 22 October and 14 November, the latter being made by 13 Guards Battalion (of Kler's brigade), which established blocking positions to the south. Malik was cut off and his CO, Lt.-Col. Sultan Mahmood, tried to relieve him and the other two outposts (Naqshi and Baromari, to the east) without success. On 29 November (all this before 'war' broke out) Major Ayub of 31 Baluch tried to resupply Malik's tiny garrison but failed. He tried again on 4 December and was killed.

Kler tried to take Kamalpur on the run, using Mukti Bahini troops, and failed. He then mounted a battalion attack by 1 Maratha Light Infantry on the forty men and four 120mm mortars of 83 Mortar Battery (whose soldiers we had last seen guarding the VIP lounge at Dhaka airport) and overran them, suffering one casualty. Kler then

'decided to lay siege to Kamalpur and break down its will to resist,'
according to Sukhwant Singh. 'Getting wary because of casualties,
successive failures and demoralisation among the attacking troops, he
decided to starve out the garrison by a prolonged siege.' A brigade is
demoralised by a company? Sukhwant Singh knew that there was no
Pakistani artillery in this sector, only two troops of mortars, but states
that Kler was,

> ...further handicapped inasmuch as one of his battalions had just been
> reorganised from [a unit] raised initially for counterinsurgency with no
> support elements. In tackling a weak platoon post, another battalion brought
> out some weaknesses of leadership under fire. The battalion reached its
> objective with relatively few casualties. As expected, the enemy turned
> artillery [he meant mortar] fire on the objective. A mortar bomb landed on
> the trench occupied by four men close to the commanding officer. He saw
> limbs fly and lost his nerve.

Captain Ahsan Malik did not lose his nerve when much worse was
happening in his area.

At about 0930 on 4 December, 'after withdrawing his troops from
close siege,' Kler 'hammered the post with seven sorties of MiG 21s
firing rockets and cannon and this was repeated twice later in the day'.
General Gurbux Singh himself entered affairs by sending Captain
Malik a note by a Mukti Bahini courier: '...whatever you decide to do
we have every intention of eliminating Kamalpur post. It is to save you
and our side casualties this message is being sent to you...' He sent
another note after a further air strike and this was met, as had been the
other messages, by increased firing by Malik's men. But it could not
go on. Malik received the order by radio to surrender, which he did at
1900 that day. 'He had,' as Sukhwant Singh goes on to say, 'put up a
courageous stand...and surrendered after holding a brigade of besiegers
for 21 days...Manekshaw sent a personal congratulatory message to
Malik commending his defiant stand.' (A gentlemanly gesture on the
part of a fine officer.) Maj.-Gen. Gurbux Singh decided to meet Malik
but, while being driven towards Kamalpur by Kler, their jeep went over
a mine. Singh was badly wounded in the feet and had to hand over to
Maj.-Gen. Gandharav Nagra of 2 Mountain Division (which was
outside the theatre of operations); Kler was also wounded but carried
on.

Sultan withdrew his troops to a line across Sherpur village and 33
Punjab conformed to the east. Brigadier Qadir was in a muddle and

ordered Sultan to recapture one of the positions from which he had withdrawn. This, of course, was impossible; not only that but 31 Baluch, widely spread out, were under pressure from 95 Bde. and were forced to withdraw lest they be cut off. Sultan fell back on Jamalpur on 6 December and Qadir ordered 33 Baluch to Mymensingh, these two towns being the final defensive positions planned for the north. Withdrawal went through road-blocks manned by Mukti Bahini, but there was no interference from them as, 'the Mukti Bahini felt that the strength of the withdrawing columns was greater than they could cope with' (Sukhwant Singh).

Kler closed up his brigade against Jamalpur on 7 December, maintained a frontal threat from the east with 13 Guards, moved his other two battalions round to the south, and brought in air strikes. On the other front, towards Mymensingh, FJ Force moved south more slowly. In Jamalpur, Sultan was prepared to fight it out in spite of being surrounded and without artillery or air support. 95 Bde. had displayed little urgency in following up 31 Baluch, and much has been made of the difficulty in overcoming water obstacles, of which there were certainly many, but 13 Rajput took 'more than 48 hours to traverse some 48 kilometres after fighting no more than one platoon action *en route*.' (Ibid.) 1 Maratha moved more quickly when presented with no opposition, and outflanked Mymensingh to create a roadblock, covering twenty-two kilometres in six hours. Sultan realized he was bottled up, but not by what strength, and sent out patrols to obtain information which was only too clear. But on 9 December, when Kler sent him a note demanding his surrender, Sultan replied, enclosing a bullet, that he hoped 'to find you with a sten in your hand next time instead of the pen you seem to have so much mastery over'. Cheeky; especially as Kler had been an instructor at the Staff College.

Kler appears to have been indecisive. He had three battalions supported by artillery, generous air support on call, and was in a position to assault the defended locality, but considered he had not enough force to do so. In this summation he was joined by his divisional commander, who asked HQ Eastern Command for more resources. On 10 December 'systematic air and artillery bombardment was kept up,' including napalm (which missed its target), and 167 Brigade was released to join Kler's forces. Its lead battalion, 6 Sikh LI, arrived at Jamalpur at first light on 11 December.

It was apparent that as long as Nagra's division was held up by the Jamalpur and Mymensingh battalion outposts there could be no advance towards Dhaka from the north, but it was obvious, even to Niazi, that he could not leave Qadir's brigade there to be overrun. So he ordered it to withdraw. Qadir tried to speak with Jamshed (in Dhaka) to seek further direction but was unable to contact him—not because there were technical difficulties, but because there were human ones. Jamshed did not make himself available to speak.

Qadir was in an awkward situation. If he ignored orders his command would remain besieged and there was no hope of resupply or reinforcement. If he obeyed, he might be able to withdraw the Mymensingh garrison, but then 31 Baluch would have to fight its way out against a force that, although seemingly reluctant to attack, was of much greater strength and would have little difficulty in disrupting the withdrawal. He obeyed.

On the evening of 10 December, 33 Punjab sent a company to the Madhupur road junction south of Jamalpur to establish a firm base for the two battalions to link and continue withdrawal. The Mymensingh troops, irregulars, and families managed to get to the RV and moved as quickly as they could towards Dhaka. Brigadier Qadir and his staff withdrew to Tangail with the company of 33 Punjab, commanded by Major Sarwar. 31 Baluch tried to fight its way out and was destroyed in detail. Sultan and about two hundred of his men, split into small groups, managed to get away.

Next afternoon Qadir and his dispirited staff were in the Circuit House in Tangail when the air drop began. Sarwar took his company to investigate and reported that the locals told him the parachutists were Chinese. The fact that Qadir could believe this for even 'an initial flurry of hope' is in hindsight almost incredible, but such was the proclivity for the Pakistanis to grasp at straws—especially Chinese straws—that in those days of despair there was real hope of Chinese and American intervention. Qadir and his men got out and walked south until their inevitable capture. Stragglers from his brigade reached Dhaka on 13 and 14 December in appalling physical condition. The northern approach to the capital was open.

Sukhwant Singh states that Nagra's performance was poor; he goes further and writes that, 'The Pakistani troops managed to impose a hold-up of more than 24 hours at every delaying position they occupied. At no time were they attacked or trapped, and managed to get away intact each time.' True, and a generous plaudit; but in the end valour counted for nothing against a numerically superior enemy who had command of the skies. There had never been a possibility that the *ad hoc* division and its *ad hoc* brigade could have held the north, and the fact they did for so long is attributable more to their individual courage and lower-level leadership than to the plans and command of Niazi.

The Jessore Sector

Pakistan's 9 Division was intended to defend a front of 600 kilometres with two brigades (an *ad hoc* brigade was also formed). This was not quite as bad as it sounds because the southern half of the area (Map 14) is marshland and jungle so criss-crossed by rivers and other water channels, large and small, that large-scale troop movement is almost impossible. That part was therefore ignored by both sides, but the front, even then, was more than a division could cope with. Jessore, the main town in the region, lies about forty miles from the border and its only route to Dhaka is by ferry across the Padma river.

Maj.-Gen. Ansari commanded 9 Infantry Division, which had been flown to East Pakistan in May without armour or artillery (and at the time under command of Maj.-Gen. Shaukat Riza). Its brigades, 57 and 107, both formerly of 14 Division, had been employed in the eastern border region on internal security duties and were moved to the Jessore sector when Niazi reorganized his forces. 57 Bde. under Brigadier Manzoor was responsible for the north (HQ at Jhenaida) and Brigadier Makhmad Hayat with 107 Bde. (HQ Jessore) for the south. The HQ of an *ad hoc* brigade of East Pakistani irregulars was at Khulna. Indian forces were II Corps, commanded by Lt.-Gen. T. N. Raina, who had under command 4 Mountain Division (Maj.-Gen. Mohinder Singh Barar) and 9 Infantry Division (Maj.-Gen. Dalbir Singh). Raina was a good officer who had performed well in the 1962 war when he was a brigade commander. Barar is described by Sukhwant Singh in terms only too familiar to many soldiers. He came to notice when he was Military Assistant to the Chief of the Army Staff, and his 'subsequent rapid rise had set a trend for the personal staff's divine right to find room in the higher command...' Dalbir Singh was a large man who exuded self-confidence to the point of aggression in social contact but seemed unable to transmit his energy downwards.

Indian operations against the small Pakistani force were fairly pedestrian, given the disparity in numbers. II Corps had begun operations before war was declared, and obtained lodgements within Pakistani territory in November at Garibpur and Darsana. Some of its

MAP 14   THE JESSORE SECTOR

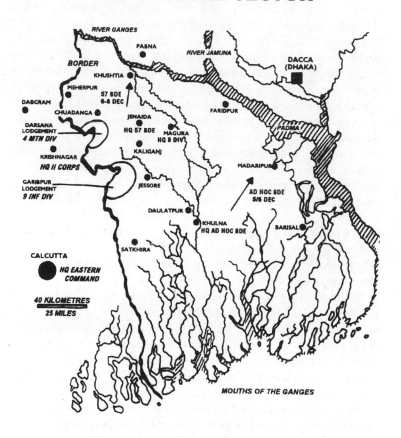

later movements were speedy, mainly because Pakistani garrisons
evacuated their positions before major force could be brought to bear
on them, but Dalbir Singh's Division took four days 'to cover a
distance of about thirty miles against an opposition of no more than
about one battalion strength' (Sukhwant Singh). The Garibpur
lodgement of 9 Division was faced by 6 Punjab (less two companies),
12 Punjab (complete), 21 Punjab (less two companies), and a company
of 22 FF, all of 107 Brigade, whose commander, Brigadier Hayat, was
a skilled tactician and a good leader. He had, in support, 55 Field
Regiment and two ancient M-24 Chaffee tanks. When it appeared likely
that Indian forces might be ready to break out of the salient, Hayat
wished to begin an orderly withdrawal from Jessore which was already
within range of Indian artillery. His divisional commander refused
permission, apparently because of Niazi's orders that no withdrawal
was to take place until 75 per cent casualties had been taken. (This,
when one thinks about it, must have been the most stupid order given
during the whole war. The signal included the edict that a general could
withdraw only a company and a brigade commander a screen. Hayat
calls it 'the notorious signal'.) So Hayat submitted to the inevitable,
but had to begin retreating after Indian pressure increased. In fact Hayat
intended, all along, to withdraw to Khulna, as he is said by Salik to
have told one of his COs on 5 December that, 'If we leave Jessore, we
go to Khulna,' but whatever his intentions, 9 Division moved inexorably
east and Jessore was vacated, in a clean break, on the morning of the
6th, although it was occupied by Indian forward troops only on the
afternoon of the 7th.*

While 107 Brigade was beginning its withdrawal, the *ad hoc* brigade
in Khulna had left for Dhaka, not having suffered 75 per cent casualties,
or indeed any losses whatever. At the same time the commander of the
naval base left in a patrol boat. HQ Eastern Command continued to
state that the battle for Jessore was continuing—until intrepid foreign
correspondents who had attached themselves to the Indian advance
arrived in Dhaka and 'ridiculed…[the] unrealistic claim'.[37] Dalbir
Singh's Division continued its slow advance towards Khulna and came
up against Pakistani defences at Daulatpur on 11 December. The whole
of 9 Division moved along the axis to perform a narrow frontal assault,
which was held by 6 Punjab, and although a move round to the flanks
was attempted on 15/16 December (and there was 'timely and close'

---

* Brigadier Hayat confirmed these details in a letter to the author in May 1998.

air support), Hayat and his brigade held out until the cease-fire. Hayat had conducted a masterly withdrawal and could probably have fought on longer in the Daulatpur-Khulna area but, as with all Pakistani forces, eventually his troops would have been overcome.[38]

Further north, Barar's 4 Mountain Division moved out of its lodgement in the Darsana salient against Brigadier Manzoor's 57 Brigade, whose HQ was initially in Jhenaida. Manzoor was a laid-back officer who seems to have lacked fire. (Salik refers to him as 'of mild disposition', but one officer who served in East Pakistan stated to the author that 'he wasn't up to it' as a commander.) His brigade had two battalions, 29 Baluch and 18 Punjab, along with two companies of 50 Punjab, a company of 12 Punjab, and a squadron of armour, twelve M-24s. It had a mortar troop from 211 Mortar Battery, and its artillery was 49 Field Regiment, equipped with 3.7 inch howitzers left over from the 1939–45 war. The regiment took over these guns from store on arrival in East Pakistan in August. They were not calibrated and lacked spares.[39] Manzoor failed to determine the Indian axis of advance and dithered. He knew they must be advancing *somewhere*, but, in the absence of hard information, concentrated his force around Chuadanga, where it waited for the enemy to come to it. The enemy, of course, did no such thing. HQ 9 Division was no more perceptive. It wasted resources by despatching a 'task force' (of 38 FF and two companies of 50 Punjab) under a senior staff officer, Colonel Afridi, to Kaliganj, where it did not good at all as the Indians were not obliging enough to advance that way, either.

On 4/5 December, the Indian 62 Mountain Brigade established a blocking position half-way between Chuadanga and Jhenaida with a battalion and a squadron of armour. Manzoor sent an officer, then a patrol, to investigate. On 6 December he sent a platoon to clear the area but withdrew it when it became obvious the Indians were there in strength. Manzoor realized he could not get to Jhenaida and withdrew his brigade north to Kushtia, which he reached on 8 December. The unfortunate Colonel Afridi withdrew to Magura, where, Salik says, the divisional commander was spending 'most of his time on his prayer mat,' and prepared a defensive position. On 15 December they were withdrawn to the area of Faridpur (to join divisional HQ), where they stayed until the cease-fire next day.

The only battle fought by 57 Brigade took place south of Kushtia on 9 December, when a company of 18 Punjab and two troops of tanks took on and held 22 Rajput, the advance guard of the advancing

62 Bde. The action was gallant (Major Zahid of 22 Punjab and Major Sher-ur-Rahman of 29 Cavalry were awarded the SJ for bravery), and gave the rest of the brigade time to prepare for retreat across Hardinge Bridge over the Ganges, which it began on 10 December. The IAF destroyed a span on 12 December but Pakistani Engineers established ferry points and took the remaining soldiers and many hundreds of anxious civilians east, until the last possible moment.

Pakistani defence in the Jessore sector was no more successful than elsewhere in the East, and there could have been no hope that it would be otherwise. Outnumbered as they were, with a few ancient tanks and even older guns, and without air support or air defence artillery, the units of 9 Division did as well as they could, given the lacklustre leadership of its GOC, Ansari, and the commander 57 Bde., Manzoor. It was all a waste of time. From the Indian point of view, Sukhwant Singh summed things up by writing that, 'the [II Corps] operations do not seem to have achieved results commensurate with the effort'. The same could be said for 9 Division.

East and North of Dhaka (Map 15)

Dhaka lies only seventy miles from the Chittagong–Tripura border, from which it was obvious that an attack would be launched. In fact, GHQ in Rawalpindi warned HQ Eastern Command in October to expect the *main* enemy thrust to be mounted from that direction. In the south, the Comilla area was identified as vital ground and the old British cantonment (barracks area) was developed as a 'fortress' and given supplies for a month by the commander 39 *ad hoc* Division, Maj.-Gen. Mohammad Rahim Khan, who established his HQ at Chandpur, sixty miles west. To the north, with its boundary beginning at Saldanadi, north of Comilla, was the area allotted to 14 Division, which was understrength, overstretched, and forced to withdraw to Sylhet, where it remained until the cease-fire.

39 Division was expected by Niazi to deny the eastern approaches to Dhaka with three brigades:

- 117 at Comilla, commanded by the former captain of Pakistan's winning Olympic hockey team, Brigadier Atif, was at almost full strength. 23 Punjab with 3 guns was deployed along the border from Chaudagram to Comilla, a distance of twenty miles, which

MAP 15 NORTH AND EAST OF DACCA

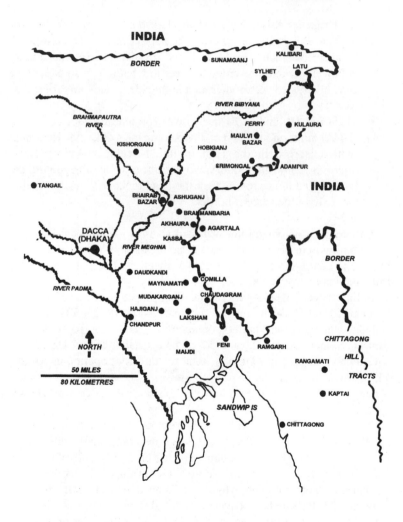

would have been a fair frontage for a division, given the terrain. 25 FF (5 guns) was south of Comilla; and 30 Punjab (3 guns) was to hold Mian Bazar-Kasba.

- 97 (Brigadier Ataullah) at Chittagong had 2 Commando Battalion at Kaptai to defend the Hill Tracts, and 24 FF at Chittagong, plus two companies of 21 AK Regiment and some *Razakars* and EPCAF.
- 53 (Brigadier Aslam Niazi; HQ at Laksham) was responsible for the Feni-Belonia area, covering the approaches to Chandpur, with 15 and 39 Baluch. The Indians had invaded the Belonia 'bulge' in November and presented a threat to Chittagong, so Niazi (the general) created yet another *ad hoc* brigade to deny this approach; so.
- 91 *ad hoc* (Brigadier Tasneem) was formed and allocated some EPCAF units and the HQ and two companies of 21 AK Regiment (which arrived in the East in late November)—more Niazi improvisation which, oddly, worked for a while in deceiving the Indians that larger forces than they had reckoned on were facing them along the eastern border.

The concept of operations was faulty: all brigades were forward, with nothing in reserve, and there was no depth other than that afforded by troops guarding the lines of communication. The outcome of the Indian advance was inevitable.

India's IV Corps at Agartala (Lt.-Gen. Sagat Singh), hard by the border, had three full-strength mountain divisions (8, 23, 57) and eight Bangladeshi battalions under command. Its task was for 8 Div. to 'invest' Sylhet and for 23 and 57 to take Chandpur and Daudkandi (twenty-five miles from Dhaka), then to 'develop' operations to take Chittagong. Of course this was nonsense, as admitted by Sukhwant Singh, who knew Sagat Singh well. The real objective was Dhaka. 'Leave it to me,' said Sagat Singh. 'I will get there.'

After preparatory operations in November to secure firm bases on the enemy side of the border, Sagat Singh began his main attacks on 3 December. That night, 62 Mountain Brigade hit 25 FF south of Comilla. Its CO and the two forward companies surrendered, exposing the northern flank of 23 Punjab, which was being attacked by 301 Mountain Brigade. 23 Punjab had to retreat to Laksham, which it did with difficulty as its rear area had been penetrated. There was no communication between 53 and 117 Bdes. and the former was ordered by HQ 39 Div. to withdraw to Laksham, which it did—but 301 Brigade got behind it. Brigadier Niazi then tried to extricate his brigade and managed to get much of it to Maynamati on 8 December. 301 Brigade advanced quickly to Hajiganj, where there was heavy fighting resulting in the withdrawal of two companies of 21AK and the commandos on 8 December. The whole 'front' had crumbled to Indian troops who were skilled, brave, and well-led.

The garrison in Laksham was surrounded by 181 and 301 Mountain Brigades but managed to make a clean break on 7 December. Two groups were organized: one composed of the remnants of 21 AK and 23 Punjab, and the other of two companies of 15 Baluch. They were intended to clear the enemy from Mudafarganj, where 39 Baluch were besieged. They failed. 15 Baluch were ordered back to Laksham and the other column to Hajiganj, only twelve miles from Chandpur. 21 AK and 23 Punjab had a nightmare march, split up, and were both captured on 10 December, early on which day General Rahim's HQ tried to leave Chandpur for Dhaka by local river-craft, escorted by a gunboat. The convoy was attacked by two IAF MiG-21s which killed several people.

On 9 December, 61 Mountain Brigade under the formidable Tom Pande took Daudkhandi after an impressively fast approach march during which it encountered only one delaying position. Pande began to besiege Maynamati (where there were some 4,000 troops) whose commander, Brigadier Atif, refused to surrender and held out until the cease-fire. Sukhwant Singh states that Comilla fell on 9 December, and up to a point he is correct: the town was occupied, but the cantonment held out until the 16th. Although some strongpoints remained intact, the battles for the eastern routes to Dhaka were decisive for India. Indeed, it might be concluded that if other Indian forces had done nothing else but contain Pakistani troops in the north and west, the fall of Dhaka would have been ensured by IV Corps. Sagat Singh had been confident he would succeed, and he was right.

* * *

Further north, Maj.-Gen. Krishna Rao's 8 Mountain Division had been ordered to clear the region around Sylhet and advance on Maulvi Bazar. The division carried out cross-border operations in November and began its advance on 2 December, taking until the 7th to move up to Maulvi Bazar, having encountered stiff resistance on the way.

81 Brigade was held up by two companies, one each from 22 Baluch and the Tochi Scouts, and then by a company of 30 FF, but their efforts, although gallant, were wasted. The Indians were able to move 4/5 Gorkha Rifles of 59 Bde. by helicopter to the south of Sylhet which, according to Sukhwant Singh, was being 'saturated daily with napalm'. Pakistani forces comprised HQ 14 Division of 27 Bde., 313 Bde., and 202 *ad hoc* brigade with a total of about six reduced battalions. 202 was defending Sylhet, to which 313 fell back. The 6,000-strong garrison was besieged by Krishna Rao and held out until 17 December, when it surrendered following the cease-fire the previous day. Sukhwant Singh summed up the campaign in the north by writing:

> The battle of Sylhet, like that of Khulna, was lost by Pakistan elsewhere. It was remarkable that, despite battle fatigue and the prospect of an unequal fight, a company each at Shamshernagar and Kalaura, with a few para-military troops and very little artillery and air support [in fact, no air support] held Krishna Rao's brigades for days. And in spite of the great odds against them they managed to slip away to Sylhet.

But Sylhet proved—if any proof were necessary—that the fortress concept did not work. Fortresses may have held up a lot of Indian troops, but there were even more troops available to carry out the aim of overcoming Pakistan's army in the East. Pakistan's 27 Bde. (about a battalion strong, of 39 Baluch and some para-military troops, commanded by Brigadier Saadullah) fought delaying actions in the Ashuganj-Bhairab Bazar area, and reached the former on 7 December after an epic fight by 39 Baluch which captured seven PT-76 tanks of 63 Cavalry when fighting through Indian positions. This local success was not enough to deter the massive Indian forces, of course, and the brigade withdrew westwards, leaving 57 Mountain Division commanding the line of the Meghna River by 9 December. The way to Dhaka was open on any axis the Indians chose to take.

The retreating Pakistanis had blown the bridge between Ashuganj and Bhairab Bazar, but Sagat Singh assigned his fourteen Mi-4 helicopters, along with all water transport he could lay his hands on, to ferry 311 Mountain Brigade over the Meghna River. The use of the Mi-4s was impressive—they flew some 110 sorties—but Maj.-Gen. Ben Gonsalves (another first-rate general), commanding 57 Mountain Division, was unable to move enough troops in a balanced manner to immediately begin the advance to Dhaka. No movement plan, given the extraordinary mix of transport means, could have coped with transporting, for example, a battery of guns over the river at the same time as their prime movers and ammunition trucks. It simply was not possible to marry up forces and equipment in an organized fashion. But it didn't matter, anyway, as the cease-fire was declared before 57 Div. was required to advance on Dhaka.

* * *

'The sahibs are crying inside.'

On the evening of 7 December it became apparent to General Niazi that all was lost. The Governor, Dr A. M. Malik, an avuncular figure of seventy-four who had taken over from Tikka Khan on 3 September, tried to comfort him, but, as noticed by the servants, Niazi broke down while briefing him, the content of the discussion being such that Malik said, 'I think I should cable the President to arrange a cease-fire.' He did; but Yahya took no notice. For the next three days Niazi appeared to be in a state of collapse. Dhaka was under constant attack by the IAF and, although the news of the Indian advance from east, north, and west was appalling, Yahya seemed to be placing his hopes on intervention by China and the US. Gavin Young, the brilliant reporter and author, who was in Dhaka at the time, wrote

> ...later I attended the 'surrender lunch' with the victorious Indian and defeated Pakistan generals. What the Pakistan generals told me then was at that time not generally known...What they said was that the war could have ended a week earlier (and many lives been saved) had...Yahya...not cabled his hopelessly outnumbered and surrounded generals in Dacca with the misinformation that they only had to hang on and America and China would come to their aid.[40]

There was no possibility that either China or the US would come to the aid of Pakistan against India. Yet Yahya appeared to think — hope against hope — that his allies would support him. Niazi's cable to him on 9 December was as redolent of despair as of fantasy:

> One: regrouping adjustment is not possible due to enemy mastery of skies...population...providing all out help to enemy. [No aircraft] mission last three days and not possible in future. Two: extensive damage to heavy weapons and equipment due enemy air action. Troops fighting extremely well but stress and strain now telling hard. NOT slept for last 20 days...

Three: situation extremely critical. We will go on fighting and do our best.
Four: request following immediate strike all enemy air bases this theatre.
If possible reinforcements airborne troops for protection Dacca.

The request for an air strike on Indian air bases was almost as
ludicrous as that for airborne troops. Yahya replied to Malik, copy to
Niazi, that any decision taken on 'your good sense and judgement'
would be approved. The Army Chief, Hamid, sent a message to Niazi
containing such gems as, '...it is only a question of time before the
enemy...will dominate East Pakistan completely,' and advising him to
'attempt to destroy maximum military equipment so that it does not
fall into enemy hands'.

Meanwhile, during 11 and 12 December, HQ Eastern Command
tried to obtain troops to defend Dhaka. Brigadier Atif was asked to
move from Comilla; Maj.-Gen. Qazi from Bhairab Bazar; Maj.-Gen.
Nazar Hussain to send 57 Brigade. There was no possibility that any
of these moves of troops towards Dhaka would have succeeded. The
fact that the requests were made is evidence of both panic and
misappreciation of what was going on in the field.

It was decided to send another message to the West advocating
surrender. Niazi wanted it to be sent from Government House rather
than HQ Eastern Command. Maj.-Gen. Rao Farman Ali, in charge of
Civil Affairs at Government House, was not prepared to accept this.
He had been authorizing officer for previous signals composed by
others, and was not happy about sponsoring another request to
surrender.[41] The matter was resolved by the Chief Secretary, Muzaffar
Hussein, who agreed that the message should be sent. The reply (to
Niazi) of 1530 (Eastern time) on 14 December was unclassified and
unambiguous:

Governor's flash message to me refers. You have fought a heroic battle
against overwhelming odds. The nation is proud of you and the world full
of admiration. I have done all that is humanly possible to find an acceptable
solution to the problem. You have now reached a stage where further
resistance is no longer humanly possible nor will it serve any useful
purpose. It will only lead to further loss of lives and destruction. You should
now take all necessary measures to stop the fighting and preserve the lives
of all armed forces personnel, all those from West Pakistan and all loyal
elements. Meanwhile I have moved U.N. to urge India to stop hostilities in
East Pakistan forthwith and to guarantee the safety of armed forces and all
other people who may be the likely target of miscreants.

Later that day Niazi asked the US Consul-General, Mr Spivack, to send a message to Manekshaw asking for a cease-fire. Spivack, of course, sent the message to Washington, but it was not long before Manekshaw replied that the cease-fire was acceptable. Sam Manekshaw was a warrior and a great man. He did not wish to prolong the conflict, gave a guarantee of safety to Niazi and all his troops and associated elements, and provided a radio frequency on which HQ Eastern Command could be contacted to arrange details. The final, formal, surrender of East Pakistan took place at the racecourse in Dhaka on the afternoon of 16 December, some hours after Maj.-Gen. Rahim Khan[42] and some others were flown by helicopter to Burma. (Unfortunately, eight nurses were left behind, but the decision to save the helicopters was the right one.) The war in the East was over. Some 90,000 civilian and military prisoners would remain in captivity in India for over two years (contrary to the Geneva Convention), and Pakistan suffered a severe blow to national pride from the loss of its Eastern Wing.

It is fitting, in ending a description of the war in the East, to recount the words of the indefatigable, intelligent, and admirable Siddiq Salik, whose common sense was obviously admired as much by the Indians as it was ignored by Niazi and others. On 20 December, Salik accompanied Niazi and his four most senior officers when they were flown to Calcutta. Soon after arrival in Calcutta, Salik, 'took the opportunity of discussing the war, in retrospect, with General Niazi before he had the time, or the need, to reconstruct his war account for the enquiry commission in Pakistan'. Salik's verbatim account of the discussion is illuminating. Niazi 'talked frankly and bitterly. He showed no regrets or qualms of conscience. He refused to accept responsibility for the dismemberment of Pakistan and squarely blamed General Yahya for it....'

Certainly, Yahya bore overall responsibility for what befell his country; but General Niazi was the commander who lost the war in the East.[43] The war in the West was another matter.

NOTES

1. Since this chapter was written I have had many communications from kind critics (and some not so kind, but thanks to them as well), which have been most helpful in correction of errors of fact. 'The Report of the Hamoodur Rehman Commission of Inquiry into the 1971 War' was released by the Government of Pakistan and published by Vanguard Books in 2001. It is temperate and impartial, and an invaluable source. Its Conclusions are damning.
2. Hersch (1983).
3. Wolpert op. cit.
4. *Dawn*, Karachi, 15 January 1971.
5. Salik (1978). Siddiq Salik was a Public Relations Officer in East Pakistan throughout the period. His book is detailed, humorous, and well worth reading. It is unfortunate that, being a junior officer and a near-civilian (both dreadful things to be), his wise counsel was unheeded. Alas, he died in the aircraft crash with Zia in 1988.
6. Bhutto (1971).
7. 'Negotiating for Bangla Desh: A Participant's View', *The South Asian Review*, London, July 1971.
8. Salik op. cit.
9. According to a former senior intelligence officer. A Pakistani inquiry found they were acting on the part of India.
10. When Yahya eventually decided to visit Dhaka Mujib agreed to remove a check-post on his route from the airport 'to avoid embarrassment to his guest'.
11. Judgements on Tikka Khan's character were gathered throughout Pakistan in the years 1980 to date. In 1990, when he was once again Governor of Punjab, the author spoke with him about his tour of duty in East Pakistan.
12. Islam op. cit.
13. Kissinger op. cit.
14. According to Bhutto himself, quoted in Wolpert op. cit., he said, 'by the Grace of God Pakistan has at last been saved.' In *The Great Tragedy*, Bhutto wrote that, 'In my heart I hoped and prayed that I was right.' One wonders. Bhutto was a clever man and it is unlikely he could have ignored the fact that his police escort in Dhaka flew Bangla Desh flags and wore black armbands. See also, R. Khan (1998) for a first-hand description.
15. See also, Z.A. Khan (1988). Osmani, when Deputy DMO, tried to have a tank regiment located in East Pakistan.
16. G.H. Khan op. cit. In fact, according to another senior officer, speaking with the author, what Gul said was, 'Shit!'
17. Sukhwant Singh (1981) considered Niazi to be '...essentially a battalion commander in general's uniform' and incapable of thinking '...beyond the deployment of companies and platoons, an unfortunate trait of senior infantry officers in both India and Pakistan'. 'Sukhy' Singh was an admirable and honourable officer.
18. One appalling comment was recorded by Maurice Quintance of Reuters (see 'Demons of December' by Hamid Hussain in Pakistan *Defence Journal* December 2002). A Pakistani senior officer in Khulna told him 'It took me five days to get control of this area. We killed everyone who came our way. We never bothered to count bodies.' The parallels with the conflict in Iraq in 2003-2005 are macabre.
19. Sisson and Rose op. cit.

20. Hersch op. cit.

21. Indian Army officer to author.

22. Interview with the *Financial Times*, London. See *Asian Recorder*, Vol. XVII, No. 36.

23. Sukhwant Singh op. cit.

24. The indictment of Niazi in the Hamoodur Rehman Commission Report, in the section on 'Professional Responsibility of certain Senior Army Commanders', is, inter alia, that he 'displayed utter lack of professional competence, initiative and foresight expected of an army commander of his rank, seniority and experience, in not realising that the parts of his mission concerning anti-insurgency operations and ensuring the 'no chunk of territory' was to be allowed to be taken over by the rebels for establishing Bangladesh, had become irrelevant in the context of all-out attack by India on or about November 21, 1971, and that the most important part of his mission from that juncture onward was 'defend East Pakistan against external aggression', with the result that he failed to concentrate his forces in time, which failure later lead to fatal results.'

25. See 'The Story of the Pakistan Air Force'. I am indebted to Mr Usman Shabbir for pointing out an error in the original text in which I stated that two Sabres had been destroyed on the ground. See also internet site www.pafcombat.com.

26. Kissinger op. cit. Hersch op. cit. Walter Isaacson, Kissinger, Simon & Schuster, 1992.

27. Sukhwant Singh op. cit.

28. On 4 November. At the meeting the following day the subject of Pakistan was not raised.

29. Riza (1980).

30. Salik op. cit.

31. Sarbans Singh (1993).

32. Salik op. cit.

33. Ibid.

34. Vital ground is 'Ground of such importance that it must be retained or controlled for the success of the mission.' But there has to be a clear enunciation of what the mission is.

35. The Hamoodur Rehman Commission's conclusion about Major General Shah and two of his fellow commanders, Major Generals M.H. Ansari (9 Div.) and Qazi Abdul Majid (14 Div.) was that 'adverse comment reflecting on their suitability for retention in military service [after the surrender] would not be justified.' This should not be taken lightly. The Commission's findings concerning other major generals, notably Mohammad Jamshed of 36 Div. and Rahim Khan of 39 (see note 38), were scathing and employed such descriptions as 'lack of courage' and 'cowardice'.

36. Kathpalia (1986).

37. Ibid.

38. See Brigadier Hayat's excellent description of the Khulna battles in *Defence Journal*, Karachi, March 1998. He gets a pasting in the Hamoodur Rehman Commission Report because it is alleged that he, amongst other things, 'shamefully abandoned the fortress of Jessore...' I simply don't agree. And Jessore wasn't a 'fortress', except in the eyes of Niazi.

39. In 1971 the process of calibrating a gun-ensuring its rounds would fall accurately-took many days of tests which, in the circumstances, could not be conducted.

40. Gavin Young, 'The Bangladesh War, 1971,' *Worlds Apart*; Hutchinson 1987. Young
     was given the 1971 Journalist of the Year Award for his reporting.
41. Major General Rao Farman Ali was the subject of 'a lengthy cross-examination' by
     the Hamoodur Rehman Commission which found he had 'functioned as an
     intelligent., well-intentioned and sincere staff officer in the various appointments
     held by him and at no stage could he be regarded as being a member of the inner
     military junta surrounding and supporting General Yahya Khan.'
42. In its *Supplementary Report* of 1974 the Rehman Commission recommended that
     Rahim Khan, by that time serving as Chief of the General Staff, be tried by court
     martial (along with several others, including Niazi), for what were quite obviously
     most serious breaches of discipline. Little wonder the Commission's Report was
     kept secret for so long. Unpalatable as its findings are, it is hoped that the Report
     will be studied by young officers in order to learn from the past.
43. But see his own explanation of affairs in Niazi (1998) and in public
     pronouncements.

9 War in the West—and the Fall of Yahya

The question now arises as to India's further intentions. For example, does India intend to use the present situation to destroy the Pakistan army in the west? Does India intend to use as a pretext the Pakistan counterattacks in the West to annex territory in West Pakistan? Is its aim to take parts of Pakistan-controlled Kashmir contrary to the Security Council resolution of 1948, 1949, and 1950? If this is not India's intention, then a prompt disavowal is required. The world has a right to know. What are India's intentions? Pakistan's aims have become clear: it has accepted the General Assembly's resolution passed by a vote of 104 to 11. My government has asked this question of the Indian government several times in the last week. I regret to inform the [Security] Council that India's replies have been unsatisfactory and not reassuring.

US Ambassador to the United Nations, George Walker Herbert Bush, 12 December 1971.[1]

The Indian invasion of East Pakistan had been planned for many months and was preceded by considerable cross-border activity in November. It was legitimized by Pakistan's—Yahya's—barely credible decision to attack India from the west on 3 December.

Pakistani plans had been prepared for a 'counter-offensive' in the West, to take effect if India invaded the East Wing. These, in the words of Lt.-Gen. Gul Hassan Khan, then Chief of the General Staff at GHQ, in his *Memoirs*, 'contained two ingredients: first, formations other than those in reserve were to launch limited offensives; secondly, a major counter-offensive was to be launched concurrently into India'.

Gul Hassan was a hawk. He wanted to deal a decisive blow against the Indians but he did not take into account, to the extent merited, the fact that a quarter of the army was in the east. And he discovered, too late, that many formations in the west were badly short of equipment. On realizing this, his enthusiasm for an attack on India rapidly waned, as well it might, for Yahya had taken it upon himself to alter the plan by ordering that the counter-offensive, the thrust into India, should take place *after* local operations had secured ground. He thus denied his forces the advantage of confusing the Indians about the direction of his main attacks. The offensive was doomed, not least because the Indians were well-prepared for war and had large forces along their western border ready for anything that Pakistan could move against them. There was little hope that Pakistan would gain international support for their attack, even with evidence of Indian provocation in the East Wing.

The campaign was a disaster for Pakistan. Poor planning, indecision about deployment, hasty and countermanded regrouping, inadequate or even non-existent co-ordination between formations, inability to seize the moment for exploitation, lack of co-operation between GHQ and Air HQ, bungling of movement control procedures—the list of failures is long. Had nothing been done in the years 1965–71 to hone the skills of the Pakistan Army? It certainly seemed so.

* * *

Indian western forces also had problems, especially in leadership and logistics, but not to the same degree as their opponent. India's Western Command was responsible for the border from Anupgarh in Rajasthan to the Cease-fire Line in the far north of Indian-administered Kashmir and Ladakh (Map 16). It had three corps: XV in Kashmir, I in northern Punjab, and XI covering southern Punjab and Rajasthan as far south as Anupgarh. Southern Command had 11 and 12 Infantry Divisions and a large number of Border Security Force troops (about a division equivalent, but with only light weapons) to cover the area from Anupgarh to the coast. Advance parties of II Corps began arriving in Punjab from East Pakistan on 13 December.

The Pakistanis had three corps, and three infantry divisions commanded directly by GHQ. On paper they appear well-balanced, but there had been many last-minute alterations to groupings, and insufficient attention had been paid to detail in attempts to rationalize manning and equipment.

23 Division did indeed take Chhamb, which remained in Pakistani hands until the cease-fire, but, as in 1965, there was no exploitation of the gain. The Indians took territory (Maps 17 and 18) at Kargil, Tithwal, and Poonch in Kashmir, and Shakargarh, Sehjra, Islamgarh, and Chachro further south: a total of about 7,000 square miles, much of it desert—but all of it important to the national morale of Pakistan.

MAP 16

INDIAN AND PAKISTANI FORCES IN THE WEST

Corps	Subordinate Formations	Tasks
I – Sialkot Lt.-Gen. Tikka Khan	6 Armd. Div. 8 Inf. Div. 15 Inf. Div. 17 Inf. Div.	Counter-offensive
IV - Lahore Lt.-Gen. Bahadur Sher	10 Inf. Div. 11 Inf. Div. 8 Armd. Bde. 105 Indep. Bde. 212 Bde. 25 Bde. Gp.	Defence of Lahore; advance over border.
II - Multan Lt.-Gen. Irshad Ahmad Khan	1 Armd. Div. 7 Inf. Div. 33 Inf. Div. (strategic reserve) 12 Inf. Div. 18 Inf. Div.	Strike force in the south. Take Poonch Forward defence of Karachi; changed to: take Jaisalmer.
	23 Inf. Div.	Take Chhamb

War began at 1747 hours Pakistan time on 3 December, when the PAF mounted a simultaneous attack on airfields at Amritsar, Avantipur, Faridkot, Pathankot, and Srinagar. (It can be argued that this offensive was undertaken with too few aircraft, and on the wrong targets; it did not interfere markedly with IAF capabilities.) The Indian Navy promptly sank the submarine PNS *Ghazi* off Vishakapatnam in the Bay of Bengal. (A Pakistani submarine sank the Indian frigate INS *Khukri*, but the overall contest was one-sided.) But instead of attacking immediately with concurrent massive strikes into Indian territory to catch the opposition off-balance, the Pakistanis began a piecemeal series of land battles. 1 Armoured Division was not used. Amazingly, it saw no action during the course of the war.

* * *

News of the attack was received quickly in the US, where the Assistant to the President for national security affairs called a meeting of the Washington Special Action Group at 11 a.m. local time. The minutes of the meeting[2] are illuminating: Dr Kissinger informed the gathering that he was 'getting hell every half-hour from the President that we are not being tough enough on India...He wants to tilt in favour of Pakistan'. It was not clear who had taken action first. Kissinger wanted to know if it were possible that 'the Indians attacked first and the Paks simply did what they could before dark in response?' The Chairman of the Joint Chiefs of Staff, Admiral Moorer, helpfully observed that this was 'certainly possible', but the tone of the meeting had been set by Nixon—get the Pakistanis off the hook. They didn't, of course, and ended up frustrating Nixon, disappointing Pakistan, infuriating India, confirming the USSR's long-held conviction that US imperialism was unprincipled, and demonstrating to the world that the US could not, when the chips came down, act unilaterally in support of a friendly state.

* * *

In the far north, India's Ladakh Scouts advanced up the Shyok valley, and 3 Infantry Division took 36 Gilgit Scouts' posts in the mountains north of the old Cease-fire Line. The Indians feared reinforcement of the area from Gilgit, but there was no real threat of that, simply because there were not many troops in the north—and even if there had been it would have taken them weeks to redeploy to the Cease-fire Line. XV Corps had five divisions: 3 in Ladakh; 19 in the Valley; 25 in Rajouri; 10 in Chhamb; and 26 in the Jammu sector (Map 17). The last two were to advance towards Sialkot concurrent with an attack on Shakargarh by 36, 39, and 54 Divisions of I Corps.

12 Division failed to capture Poonch, which was well-defended. The extent of the defences was known by GHQ, where the DMO argued that, as the operation required additional troops to be brought from other sectors, and would take a long time, it would endanger the areas from which these troops had moved. A good point—but the Chief of Staff disagreed. The result was that when Indian probes took place further south, concurrent with the advance being held up, the reinforcements had to be sent back to their parent formations. 26 Brigade tried to link up with a company of the Special Services Group which had infiltrated over the border, but was prevented from doing so by Indian counter-attacks supported by IAF sorties. The SSG suffered heavy losses. There was penetration by 12 Div. on a frontage of perhaps twenty miles across the Cease-fire Line, with some elements

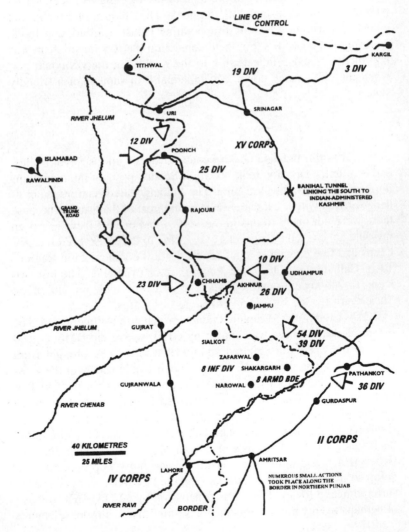

MAP 17   **KASHMIR AND NORTHERN PUNJAB**

MAP 18   THE SOUTHERN SECTOR

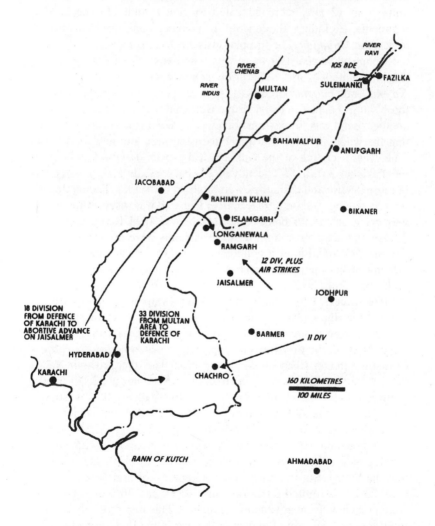

getting as far as Rajouri,[3] but the impetus was lost. 12 Div. was driven back, and the Indians gained territory.

There was more, but limited, success in the Chhamb sector. 23 Div. (Maj.-Gen. Iftikhar Janjua) was told on 30 November that D-Day was 3 December, H-Hour 2100. The VCGS, Maj.-Gen. Anwar Qureshi, flew in on 2 December to confirm the orders. In addition to integral artillery, units from 17 Div. were allocated to give a total of nine artillery regiments, excluding sixteen old 17-pounder guns manned by local levies, the *Mujahids*. The fire plan was due to start half-an-hour before the troops advanced. But there was a nonsense about timing, a thing that all Gunners, world-wide, pride themselves on—usually justifiably. An exuberant *mujahid* fired his 17-pounder ten minutes early. All right; these things happen in every army. But what was unfortunate was that another round was fired, from somewhere. What was unforgivable was that the whole divisional artillery then followed suit and fired before time. The discipline of the Gunners had broken down—a sad day for the Pakistan Artillery. The advance went well at first, but fighting became intense and casualties were high on both sides. The battle went on, see-sawing, and on 8/9 December Chhamb was taken. A lodgement was made on the far bank of the Munnawar Tawi River, east of the village, but after more fighting the Pakistanis were driven back. Next day the GOC died after a helicopter crash. The front stabilized on 12 December, but there was no possibility of further advance by 23 Div. with the forces available. Both sides strove to obtain advantage, without success. Direction from GHQ in Rawalpindi was negligible. It seemed that the Chhamb operation might be a side-show; perhaps a diversion from a greater and more decisive offensive by the strike force. Not so. The division was expected to penetrate far enough east to disrupt Indian lines of communication with the Kashmir Valley. (This would not have had much effect on the fortunes of 12 Div. further north, as India had ample supplies in the Valley.) It was strange, however, that the PAF was not tasked to deny the approaches to the tunnel leading into Indian Kashmir at Banihal. The PAF flew 85 interdiction and 19 ground attack sorties in support of 23 Div., to considerable effect, but there was no attempt to block the only road into the Valley. But there was a development—or non-development—from 23 Div.'s limited territorial success: 10 and 26 Indian Divisions were prevented from advancing on Sialkot. This was probably the most important tactical turn of events of the war in the West—even if it had not been planned that way.

GHQ was not only irresolute about reinforcing the relative success in Chhamb, it was incapable of seizing the moment to commit the armour positioned further south. It had, however, ordered 18 Div. to advance to Jaisalmer, which would seem to have no strategic or any other significance (Map 18). GHQ had been warned by the Assistant Chief of the Air Staff (Operations) in August that if 18 Div. were committed to offensive operations (rather than its original task of defending Karachi), Air HQ should be given notice so that Jacobabad airstrip (a bare base) could be activated. Came the day, and no such warning order had been given. Worse, a senior staff officer of the division went to GHQ on 30 November and showed the CGS a list of equipment that had not been delivered, in spite of the Army Chief's assurance, some weeks before, that it would be. When Hamid was tasked with this by Gul Hassan, the COS was insouciant. Four days later the division was committed to battle.

On 4 December, India's 12 Div. advanced north along the Jaisalmer-Rahimyar Khan axis and captured Islamgarh by 0400 next day. At about the same time, a patrol of 23 Punjab, which had a company at Longanewala, reported the advance of an armoured column which proved to be 18 Div. The Indians called for air support, which arrived at dawn and was effective.

Gul Hassan states in his *Memoirs* that, 'Having learnt yet another lesson in my dealings with the COS, I was naturally anxious to keep a wary eye on the operations of 18 Division, which began crossing our border into India early on 4 December'—but he also says he did not know about the PAF's reservations concerning 18 Div.'s mission. *The Story of the Pakistan Air Force* recounts that:

Ill fate had nothing to do with the failure of 18 Division's attack against Ramgarh [forty-five miles north-west of Jaisalmer]. The air chief was in GHQ on the morning of 4 December when he heard that 18 Division was to launch an attack towards Jaisalmer. He asked the CGS...why the army was springing this sudden surprise on the PAF. Gul Hassan replied that the divisional commander had a good plan and that 'he will jump into Ramgarh one day and the next day will be in Jaisalmer'. Greatly disturbed, the air chief told the CGS that the area was out of reach of the PAF both from Sargodha and from Karachi, whereas the IAF had at least 3 airbases around Jaisalmer from where it could give a severe pounding to 18 Division. But his warning went unheeded and GHQ allowed the operation to proceed. [Also] the 2 Brigades were neither equipped nor prepared to undertake a penetration in the desert...water, fuel and ammunition soon ran out...

pandemonium prevailed...There was no PAF aircraft based within 250 miles
to provide air support to the division whose commander clearly had the
responsibility to have established this fact...it took just 4 of the 6 enemy
Hunters based at Jaisalmer to destroy or disable most of the Pakistani tanks
on 5 and 6 December...The division withdrew...and a new commander
(Major-General Hameed) took over on 7 December. Thereafter the front
became inactive.

It might be inferred that the front 'became inactive' because of
Maj.-Gen. Hameed's inactivity—but there was not much he could do,
given that his division had lost at least seventeen tanks destroyed (and
others damaged) along with over twenty other vehicles.

General Gul Hassan is a trifle more discursive concerning the fate
of 18 Division. 'The rate of advance,' he wrote, ' indicated that, despite
little enemy opposition on the ground, it was the terrain that was
obstructing the move.' This, with the greatest respect to Gul Hassan,
is incorrect, especially as he had been 'handed a message saying that
the division had lost some twenty tanks...through enemy air action'.
The disaster was nothing to do with terrain: it was entirely to do with
lack of air cover by the PAF, which had warned against the very
situation that occurred.

Gul Hassan, without reference to the Chief, gave orders through the
DMO for the division to withdraw to the border. The COS agreed, but
sacked the GOC, Mustafa, and replaced him with Maj.-Gen. Abdul
Hameed Khan. If Mustafa had gone out on a limb and stated,
beforehand, that his division could not advance without air cover and
with inadequate equipment he would, of course, have been sacked at
once; but he didn't, and was sacked eventually. That was the way the
army was being run, and the CGS, the honourable Gul Hassan, wrote
that, 'For the débâcle in the desert I hold myself as blameworthy as the
COS.' Well, maybe. He could, perhaps, have defended Mustafa...As it
happened, 12 Division failed to follow up the advantage conferred on
it by the IAF, and did not resume its advance. Further south, 11
Division had 'unforeseen administrative problems' that prevented it
advancing towards Hyderabad, after its initial successes along the
border—which was fortunate for Pakistan because the strategic reserve,
33 Division, took several days to be redeployed from the Multan area
to defend the Karachi sector.

Another example of erratic management of the army by the President
(still C.-in-C.) and General Hamid, the army Chief of Staff (who did
not know exactly how much latitude he had in decision-making, and

apparently never sought to have his position clarified) is described in *The History of Pakistan Artillery*:

> On 20 November General Yahya and General Hamid visited 8 Division [near Sialkot, which] was commanded by Maj.-Gen. Ehsan-ul-Haq Malik. Gen. Yahya pointed out to Ehsan that one approach was rather thinly held. 8 Division had three brigades and had to defend a front of approximately 120,000 yards. Ehsan replied, 'Sorry, sir, nothing can be done about it. I have three brigades which I have disposed of as best I can. If this approach is to be held in greater strength I need one more brigade.' Ehsan was promptly replaced by Maj.-Gen. Abdul Ali Malik and 8 Division was given two additional brigades.

This sort of action was, regrettably, not unusual in the years between the wars and especially, it appears, in the months immediately before Yahya's strike across the eastern border.

* * *

8 Div. (Maj.-Gen. Malik) captured a small enclave on the River Ravi during 4/5 December as part of the 'offensive-defensive' operations in northern Punjab dictated by GHQ, but the division then took much of the brunt of the attack mounted by India's I Corps into the Shakargarh salient the next night. There were two main Indian thrusts: the northern advance of 54 Div. aiming to cut the road between Shakargarh and Sialkot east of Zafarwal, and that of 36 Div. due east, directly at Shakargarh, with, presumably, the intention of exploiting to the Grand Trunk Road. The area was mined and defence was dogged. The PAF flew 206 sorties in support, of which 51 were ground attack. The Indians were stronger, but, in the words of Major Sarbans Singh, 'I Corps could not make much headway; it advanced 13 kilometres in 12 days and failed to capture even the initial objectives.' This is correct, but the fact remains it gained 750 sq. km. of territory—and the defence involved heavy losses in men and *matériel* by Pakistan, at least some of which could have been avoided. 36 Div.'s attacks 'all ended in fiasco due to incompetence at brigade and divisional levels,' wrote India's chronicler of *Battle Honours*, but there was nothing 8 Div. could do to take advantage of the Indian failures. There were no forces available for exploitation or counter-attack, nor was there any move by GHQ to provide them.

On the morning of 15 December, 8 Armoured Brigade (Brigadier Mohammad Ahmad) moved to counter-attack the Indian thrust. The operation was disastrous.

First, according to the artillery history (Riza [1980]), Ahmad was ordered to 'restore the situation with minimum force'. It is difficult to understand this order. No soldier, other than on UN duty or 'In Support of the Civil Power', can expect to be told to employ minimum force. But let us say it was a misunderstanding for 'use what you have, there is no more...' — even then, it was known by 14 December that the last minefield had been gapped and that the enemy was preparing to move through. It was hardly likely the Indian 54 Division would attempt to advance with a small force. Ahmad was told he faced 'a troop of tanks and approximately one infantry company,' which anyone who had been in the area for over a day should have known was incorrect.

No request was made for close air support, and only one artillery unit (61 [SP] Regiment) was allocated. Its CO did not attend the brigade commander's Orders Group. (How he was meant to co-ordinate fire support without details of start lines, bounds, limits of exploitation, and so on, is nowhere recorded.) The commander did not conduct a personal reconnaissance. No counter-attack force or reserve was nominated.

On 15/16 December, 13 Lancers and elements of 31 Cavalry performed their very own Charge of the Light Brigade, straight into the killing ground of the Poona Horse, 4 Horse, and a brigade's worth of infantry. 62 Field Regiment was within range of the battle but no orders were given for it to be involved. When a 'Uniform Target' (all artillery in the Corps) was ordered at a particularly dicey moment, in support of 13 Lancers, the only guns that could respond were 61 (SP) and a battery of 12 Medium Regiment. By last light the two gallant armoured Regiments were left with six tanks each. The day had been a shambles. Dozens, perhaps scores, of individual acts of bravery took place, but to no purpose. The cream of Pakistan's armoured corps was destroyed.

Ninety miles south, in the Kasur sector, 106 Brigade (Brigadier Mumtaz) of Maj.-Gen. Majid's 11 Div. moved across the border on the night of 3 December, took the bridge over the River Sutlej, and captured Hussainiwala, two miles over the border and five miles north-west of Ferozepore. The Indian counter to this was to move into the Sehjra salient, between Ferozepore and Khem Karan, on 5/6 December.

It was impossible for 11 Div. to advance, with the Indians lodged on their left flank. There was stalemate.

A further sixty miles south, at Sulemanki, 105 Brigade (Brigadier Amir Hamza, who was awarded the HJ for bravery) gained a lodgement on the far bank of the River Sutlej, during which Major Shabbir Sharif (FF Regt.) displayed formidable leadership, for which he was awarded a posthumous NH, the highest gallantry award. But in spite of individual acts of courage, and over fifty F-86 sorties in support, the brigade could not advance further; Amir Hamza had no exploitation or counter-attack forces—but the Indians had, and used them to drive the brigade back from Fazilka.

There were other piecemeal operations in Sindh (in addition to the 18 Division debacle), where Indian activity was also fragmented and unstructured, but 11 and 12 Divisions managed to take 4,765 square miles of Pakistan territory, albeit all desert. The hasty move of 33 Division for the defence of Hyderabad was necessary because 18 Division's move north had left the Karachi area without forces to counter an Indian thrust. This left the strike corps without a major infantry component. There had been a grave misappreciation by GHQ.

The whole sorry tale of operations may best be summed up in the words of Maj.-Gen. Shaukat Riza:

In 1971, while neck deep in the quagmire of civil war, the Army was hurled against an enemy better equipped, better organised, better trained and larger in numbers.

And to crown everything we seemed to have no national objective except a cease-fire.

* * *

The cease-fire in the East took effect in the afternoon of 16 December. That evening, only hours after the destruction of two of his finest regiments, President Yahya Khan broadcast to the nation that, 'In such a great war a setback on any one front does not mean that the war has come to an end...have confidence, the war continues.'[4] At about the same time Mrs Gandhi announced a unilateral cease-fire, to begin next day at 8 p.m. (7.30 p.m. Pakistan time). After consultation with his intimates, Yahya decided to accept the inevitable. His forces could not fight on. This time, however, he did not deliver the message in person;

at 3.30 p.m. on 17 December Pakistan Radio broadcast a statement to the effect that Pakistani forces should reciprocate the cease-fire at the time given by Mrs Gandhi. The war was over.

* * *

Yahya was disenchanted with the US and China, and it is difficult to find fault with him for that—although their efforts at the UN, and bilaterally with other nations and with India itself, had been of considerable assistance in persuading Mrs Gandhi to curtail India's objectives. But they had not come to his aid in the manner that he, a simple soldier (and that is a fair description),[5] expected. He had given the impression to Niazi in the East that 'friends' were coming to the aid of Pakistan,[6] and naturally enough, rumours to this effect spread in the West Wing. He could not have imagined that China would commit troops to battle (they would have found it difficult to cross the passes in winter, anyway); but he might have expected a little pressure, a tweaking of Indian uneasiness, in the territories disputed between the two countries. The move of a Chinese brigade (or even a few combat aircraft) in Aksai Chin or towards the border in Sikkim or Arunachal Pradesh would have created panic in New Delhi and, of more importance for Pakistan, would have had the effect of diverting troops and aircraft to the supposedly threatened regions. It was only nine years since the PLA had given the Indian Army a trouncing; nine years since the citizens of Delhi and Calcutta were taking air raid precautions against a Chinese attack. *Any* action on the part of China would have concentrated the Indian mind on the northern borders, and greatly assisted Pakistan. But China sat on the fence, in spite of making some belligerent statements.

The US President, to be sure, made a gesture in sending an aircraft carrier group—Task Force 74—into the Bay of Bengal. This move was puzzling. Kissinger claims that 'our objective was to scare off an attack on West Pakistan,' which is barely credible as the countries were at war by the time the Task Force was identified by the Indians. Sir Morrice James, Britain's High Commissioner to Pakistan in the mid-Sixties, wrote that, 'Anyone who is more than superficially acquainted with... South Asian history must consider Henry Kissinger's thinking on this matter shallow and ill-informed and the Seventh Fleet's despatch to the Bay of Bengal as misguided.' True; even the clever Kissinger was not an expert on South Asia. His endorsement of Nixon's decision to send the *Enterprise* to menace Mrs Gandhi was justified by him in hindsight as 'sober calculation',[7] but another phrase he used in his memoirs, albeit as rhetoric, might be more apposite: 'Had we,' he posed as a hypothetical media question, 'lost our minds?'

The end of Yahya was the beginning for Zulfikar Ali Bhutto. The loss of the East Wing was Bhutto's political gain. He did, indeed, become 'leader of the people of West Pakistan' that he had claimed to be when he appeared at the UN General Assembly, because Yahya, despondent and defeated, stood down on 20 December. Bhutto went to call on him at the Presidency in Rawalpindi as deputy prime minister and foreign minister. He left the house as President of Pakistan.

There was no longer a general ruling the country. But there was no democracy, either.

NOTES

1. Quoted in Kissinger, *From Turmoil to Hope*, Weidenfeld & Nicholson 1979.
2. *New York Herald Tribune*, Paris edition, 6 January 1972, quoted in Jackson (1975).
3. The author spent several weeks in Rajouri in 1980. At that time there was a curious and moving ceremony every evening at an ancient and deserted fort about 500 feet above the river. On the ramparts an Indian flag was flown. At sunset, to a bugle call, it was lowered in memory of those who had died in the battle for the area. It is hoped the tradition continues to be observed, as it is one that all soldiers would respect.
4. Quoted in Jackson (1975). Full text in *Pakistan Horizon* XV, No. 1.
5. Although I stand by this overall description, it must be pointed out that the Hamoodur Rahman Commission stated, with incontrovertible evidence, that Yahya had the morals of an alley cat. The Commission Report notes that his 'scandalous way of life had a direct impact on General Yahya Khan's ability and determination to lead the nation in war.'
6. Most sources. But Niazi is especially forthright about this, as well he might be.
7. 'It was also Chou En-Lai's judgement, as he later told Bhutto, that we [the US] had saved Pakistan. The crisis was over [on 15 December 1971]. We had avoided the worst—which is sometimes the maximum statesmen can achieve' wrote Kissinger in *From Turmoil to Hope*. Pompous and self-serving, but he probably believed it.

10 Zulfikar Ali Bhutto

I have been summoned by the nation as the authentic voice of the people
of Pakistan by virtue of the verdict that you gave in the national
elections...I would not like to see Martial Law remain one day longer than
necessary...We have to rebuild democratic institutions...we have to
rebuild a situation in which the common man, the poor man in the street,
can tell me to go to hell....

Address to the nation by Zulfikar Ali Bhutto,
20 December 1971[1]

O f course Yahya had to go. There was no alternative to that,
other, perhaps, than an army *coup*, and that way would lie
disaster. The army was unpopular and there would have been
trouble if soldiers had been deployed on the streets. And there was no
alternative to Bhutto as Yahya's successor. Bhutto was brilliant. Bhutto
was the man for the time. But Bhutto was deeply, irrevocably,
disastrously flawed. There was no person in Pakistan who could tell
Zulfikar Ali Bhutto to 'go to hell' and remain free from vindictive
retribution.

The days immediately after the cease-fire—the surrender—were
confusing for all Pakistanis, not only those in uniform. Half the country
had vanished. It wasn't that Bengalis as such had meant much to
Punjabis or Pashtuns or almost anyone else in what had been the West
Wing; but it was hard to come to terms with the fact that after twenty-
four years the country had ceased to exist in the shape and size in
which it was founded. Pakistanis had always considered themselves
superior to Indians, and most considered the outcome of the 1965 war
to have been bad luck. A defeat that was so open and dramatic and final
was difficult to swallow.

The army felt betrayed by its commander-in-chief, to the extent that
in at least one garrison, Gujranwala, there was near mutiny. Just why
General Hamid chose to address the officers of GHQ in Rawalpindi on
19 December is inexplicable. Perhaps he thought it was 'the thing to
do'. The officers were silent at first; then restless; then vociferous and

interruptive; finally, abusive. Hamid was shocked beyond speech. Gul Hassan Khan, still CGS, escorted him to the platform in the National Defence College auditorium but had little recollection of what went on other than, 'The one incessant demand of the audience that I vaguely recall was that all officers' messes should be declared dry.' (As he also states in his *Memoirs*, it is difficult to see how this would solve anything either immediately or in the future, but some officers had seen Yahya the worse for drink and word had got round of his alcohol problem.[2] This, and a dash of over-zealous religion, and the writing was on the wall for the old-style messes—although prohibition was imposed five years later by none other than the Scotch-drinking Bhutto.) There was worse: the Quartermaster-General (QMG), General Mitha, was a close crony of Yahya's and decided to meddle in affairs by ordering a company of the Special Services Group to be moved to Rawalpindi 'for the protection of the President, COS, and GHQ'. The man he approached to carry out his wishes was the commander of the SSG, Brigadier Ghulam Mohammad Malik, 'GM',[3] who declined the order and at once reported to Gul Hassan. There was no good reason for a company of SSG to be used for close protection, and anyway the QMG had no business issuing orders of this type. Gul Hassan assured GM that he had acted properly. The exact nature of the conspiracy is not known (and conspiracy there undoubtedly was) but it is likely, according to several retired officers, that the COS and his QMG had ideas of ensuring that the President (who may or may not have known of the SSG affair) should remain in power. There was no hope whatever of this and the attempt showed that the two officers were as inept at reading the mood of the nation—and plotting—as they were at running an army. At the time, Bhutto was on his way home from the US, having first taken the wise precaution of telephoning Mustafa Khar, his close friend (then) and an astute politician, to ascertain whether it was safe for him to return in the PIA aircraft sent by the Chief of the Air Staff (and Gul Hassan) to fetch him from Rome. He was assured he would come to no harm.

When meeting with Nixon in Florida on 17 December, Bhutto apparently was given assurance that Pakistan would receive 'military and monetary support'—a promise Nixon would find hard to honour, as his policy during the war had little Congressional or popular backing. The gesture was welcomed by Bhutto in spite of his preoccupation with his own immediate political future. What seemed to be important was that he, Bhutto, was on cordial terms with the

President of the United States—who, he perhaps did not know, was just as devious, untrustworthy, and amoral as Bhutto himself.[4]

* * *

One of the first things Bhutto did as President was to dismiss Hamid as COS and appoint Gul Hassan to take over on 20 December. Swift work; but Bhutto made up his mind quickly. The circumstances of the appointment took a strange form, of which the best description is in Gul Hassan's *Memoirs*.

Bhutto wanted to broadcast the appointment that night and sent for Gul Hassan to tell him of his proposed elevation. Hassan was hesitant, but after about forty minutes contemplation he told his President he would take the job—on four conditions:

- The COS should be in the rank of lieutenant-general, not general, as there had been too much 'rank creep', a request to which Bhutto 'consented with alacrity'. (Gul would find out almost as quickly just why he was so enthusiastic.)
- There must be disengagement of troops along the border, an important consideration when they were so physically close and emotionally tense; and the prisoners of war should be returned as soon as possible. Bhutto said he was working on this.
- It was time to lift Martial Law. Bhutto said that once a Constitution was composed [by a committee of his own nomination...] and passed 'by all the political parties' [presumably meaning the National Assembly] 'he would bury Martial Law forever'.
- Last, said Gul Hassan, showing his firmness and complete lack of understanding of his President's character, he wanted 'no interference from anyone, himself or any of his ministers included'. Bhutto 'smiled and assured me that was the reason why he had selected me for the job'. Accepting this at face value showed that Gul did not know Bhutto. There was no possibility that any subordinate of Bhutto's would be allowed to run his own show without interference. And not only interference: strict, down-the-line obedience to decision and personal whim was demanded, however illegal or base these might be. Those who would not conform would be dismissed—or worse.

But there it was: the conditions were composed after less than an hour's thought by an honourable man who, before meeting Bhutto that evening, did not even know he was the new President (although some, including Niazi, allege that it was Gul Hassan who forced Yahya's resignation and ensured Bhutto's rise to power.)

* * *

That night Bhutto made his broadcast to the people of Pakistan, about two hours later than had been notified, but nobody minded. The saviour of the nation was to appear and would reassure them about the future. The new President would 'pick up the pieces' and would make 'A Pakistan envisaged by the Quaid-e-Azam' (the much-lamented Mohammad Ali Jinnah), with the co-operation of the people. This was precisely what the citizens of the new Pakistan wanted to hear. There had been mismanagement, exploitation, suffocation, but he, Zulfikar Ali Bhutto, although 'no magician', would lead his country from the squalor of recent years to recreate its pristine origins, from where it would develop, under the calm and majestic guidance of its new leader, to be once again the Land of the Pure. And in his first communication to the nation—and everyone was listening, some watching, too—he told a lie.

Gul Hassan had good reasons for asking to be left as a lieutenant-general rather being promoted to four-star rank. Bhutto said,

> I have asked General Gul Hassan to be acting Commander-in-Chief. He is a professional soldier. I do not think he has dabbled in politics and I think he has the respect and support of the Armed Forces...But he will retain the rank of lieutenant general. We are not going to make unnecessary promotions. We are a poor country, We are not going to unnecessarily fatten people....

'This,' wrote Gul Hassan in his *Memoirs*, 'was out-and-out cheek'. Perhaps it was; but it was certainly an out-and-out lie by Bhutto for the sake of creating an impression *that he didn't need to make*. Bhutto didn't need to enthuse anyone about the new army chief. If he had announced that Gul would be promoted field marshal or demoted to corporal because he, Bhutto, considered that the most appropriate rank for the post, the people of Pakistan would have shouted approval until they were hoarse. Bhutto was a populist—but he didn't really

understand, *au fond*, the feelings of the people he so desperately
wanted to have follow him. He desired dramaturgy for its own sake.
They did, of course, follow him—until his arrogance became too much
for them; and so did Gul Hassan, with the difference that the arrogance
showed itself to him rather sooner than it did to those whom Bhutto
wanted to 'tell him to go to hell'. 'Why,' asked Gul Hassan of Bhutto,
'had [he] deliberately told a lie about my rank?' To Bhutto this was a
strange question. He had made a statement; its content was therefore
unassailable. His answer was that his new army chief did not understand
politics, which was certainly true. But Gul Hassan then ensured his
later eclipse and banishment by telling Bhutto that, '...he should keep
politics out of his dealings with me or he was at liberty to get someone
[to be army chief] who was familiar with such language'. Bhutto did
not reply (and probably could not even begin to conceptualize how
politics could be kept out of any of his dealings with anyone), but,
according to a public figure still active in Pakistan, he began to think
again about his new army chief and to consider with whom he might
replace him. Tikka Khan, the general who carried out orders without
question, might be an alternative, thought some of Bhutto's
associates.

   Bhutto had appointed a man of honour as head of the army, but,
being Bhutto, he did not—could not—understand that anyone could
serve him and not be plotting against him. The army's chief would be
especially suspect. He was to be lucky, for a while. Gul Hassan was
loyal, as was his successor. The problem for Bhutto came when he
appointed a Chief of the Army Staff whom he considered pliable or
even quiescent but who, deep down, was a smarter player than the
brilliant Bhutto.

                                    * * *

Bhutto wanted to get rid of the old title of 'commander-in-chief', a
hangover from British days. This was an ideal time to do so, with the
armed forces at their nadir of popularity and Bhutto at his zenith, but
he waited until he could also get rid of Gul Hassan who, Bhutto
belatedly realized, was not the pushover he wanted. The army, thought
Bhutto, should be put in its place, which was firmly under control of
the civilians. This is a proper thing in a democracy, but Bhutto was no
democrat. He proposed that the army be sent in to Karachi to enforce
discipline amongst the restive work force; Gul disagreed and said the

police should be used. Bhutto wanted to release National Cadet Corps members (students—PPP supporters) who had deserted and been imprisoned after court martial; Gul refused. Bhutto wanted to go with Gul on his first visit around the army; Gul was firm: 'As of tomorrow,' he said, 'I begin my visits to units, and alone.' Gul's days were numbered. And Bhutto, quietly and unheralded, visited units and headquarters on his own account. There were many pinpricks, many other instances of attempted interference by Bhutto, but two in particular showed his mindset: according to Gul, he proposed that all army officers should be 'screened by the police or intelligence, and those with political leanings or connections would be kept under surveillance'. This, too, was rejected by Gul, who was satisfied with the normal vetting process and, in any event, did not countenance 'meddling in politics'—but Bhutto would not be deflected from his desire to impose a personal mark on the army. He wanted to attend a promotion and selection board due to sit on 5 February 1972.

After the war it was obvious some officers would have to be retired. In the army twenty-nine senior officers were relieved of duty: two generals, eleven lieutenant-generals, ten major-generals and six brigadiers. (The navy and air force each lost their chiefs and six others.) Once the Military Secretary had done all the paperwork involving marshalling confidential reports, career outlines, vacancies, and the promotion plot, a meeting of the senior generals was called to consider promotions between the ranks of lieutenant-colonel and major-general. They, in turn, would place recommendations before government in the normal way. Gul would chair the meeting. Bhutto told him he wanted to attend it, and, when Gul demurred, reminded him that he had been asked to attend cabinet meetings—as if there were any similarity between the two. Annoyingly for Bhutto, Gul had refused his invitations to go to cabinet meetings, so was able to parry that one, but in any case Gul was adamant: the President could not, would not, attend meetings of promotion boards. And it was so.

A strike of police in Peshawar took place at the end of February and Bhutto, not unnaturally, wished to have it resolved. His approach was much the same as he intended concerning the Karachi workers: force. Force against the 'common man', the people who could tell Bhutto 'to go to hell'. Gul had refused to co-operate concerning Karachi, but he was not consulted about the intention to employ military force in Peshawar. The National Security Adviser ordered deployment of two field guns to Peshawar from the School of Artillery at Nowshera, about twenty-five miles away on the Grand Trunk Road. He also ordered the move of a number of recruits from the Punjab Regiment Centre at Mardan, north of Nowshera, to Peshawar. Gul's staff told him of the orders, which he promptly countermanded. He was then surprised to receive a visit from a figure (of cabinet rank) who was none other than former Maj.-Gen. Akbar Khan, he of the 1951 'Rawalpindi Conspiracy' (Chapter 2), for which he had served a token period in prison. Akbar tried to browbeat the Commander-in-Chief but was sent off with a flea in his ear to (presumably) report to the President, whose confidence he had. Just what a bunch of recruits and two 25-pounder guns would have achieved in Peshawar is not clear (chaos, most likely), but the orders show that Akbar was probably as expert in putting down disturbances as he had been at planning them.

Had Gul been more of a political animal, had he been devious and out to save his professional skin, he could have thwarted Bhutto—even to the extent of toppling him. Reports came to him that the police strikes, spreading throughout Punjab, had been engineered by Bhutto's People's Party in order to get the army involved and 'furnish Bhutto with a pretext to defame it beyond redemption'. Perhaps; perhaps not. But whatever was going on, it was nasty.

Some young officers indicated that he had only to say the word and they would 'sort out' Bhutto, an offer which appalled Gul, who calmed them down and sent them on their way. Matters were coming to a head. Given Bhutto's network of informers, it is reasonable to believe that he got to know, if not about this particular incident, then about the feeling in some sections of the army concerning himself. Little did he know—he was incapable of realizing—that he had a loyal chief who would brook no interference with government by the army. Gul simply wasn't interested in what to Bhutto was lifeblood: the manipulation of people and events. Bhutto seemed to attribute to everyone he met the more sinister characteristics he himself possessed; it appeared he was unable to believe that anyone could be disinterested enough to serve their country without an eye to the main chance.

The end for Gul came after he refused to provide a briefing on contingency planning for all ministers, especially as it was to be conducted, on Bhutto's orders, at a police facility (nice touch) and not at GHQ, where such briefings normally took place. This, combined with his refusal to become involved in putting down the police strike, and his remonstrance when Bhutto proposed creating the Federal

Security Force, a para-military organization intended for such creative activity as strike-breaking, sealed his downfall.

On 3 March, a national holiday declared by Bhutto to mark the introduction of land reforms two days before, Gul Hassan and the Air Chief, Rahim Khan, were sacked. The drama—the 'needless drama', Gul called it—is described in detail in his *Memoirs*, but Bhutto's radio address to the nation that evening, in English, deserves to be recounted. He said, in part:

> My dear friends, citizens, the interests of this country are supreme, and it is in the interests of the country and the interest of the armed forces of Pakistan that today we have taken the decision to replace the commander-in-chief of the Pakistan Army and the commander-in-chief of the Pakistan Air Force. Both of them have been replaced by officers who are familiar with the armed forces [*sic*] and who have kept working with them with devotion and with splendid records. Replacements have been made on merits and in the highest consideration of the country and the armed forces.
>
> By now you must have heard that Lieutenant-General Gul Hassan, who resigned this afternoon, has been replaced by Lieutenant-General Tikka Khan and Air Marshal Rahim Khan...by Air Marshal Zaffar Chaudhury. From today we will no longer have the anachronistic and obsolete posts of commander-in-chief...so we have changed the colonial structure of the armed forces of Pakistan and injected a truly independent pattern into these vital services... And you must remember, my friends and compatriots, that the people of Pakistan and the armed forces themselves are equally determined to wipe out Bonapartic influences from the armed forces. It is essential so that these tendencies never again pollute the political life of this country. Bonapartism is an expression which means that professional soldiers turn into professional politicians. So I do not use the word Bonapartism. I use the word Bonapartic because what had happened in Pakistan since 1954 and more openly since 1958 is that some professional generals turned to politics not as a profession but as a plunder and as such, the influences that crept into Pakistan's socio-political life destroyed its fabric as the influences of Bonapartism had affected Europe in the eighteenth and nineteenth centuries....[5]

This was a fascinating insight into the man Bhutto. Not only did he use historical references to a defunct European emperor to make his points—a ludicrous choice, as only the highly-educated would know what on earth he was talking about—he was deliberately and without conscience slandering Gul Hassan whom he had forced to 'resign'. But it was all over, at last. Tikka Khan, the hard and loyal man to whom a superior's order was the final word and never to be questioned, took over as Chief of Staff and would remain so for exactly four years, at that time the tenure for the heads of the three Services.

* * *

Over the next six years, until Bhutto's fall, several measures were taken to modify, and in some instances improve, the structure of the armed services. It appears, however, that at least some of these moves were made for the sake of consolidating Bhutto's control, rather than by reason of improving efficiency.

The move of naval headquarters to Islamabad from Karachi in 1974 made sense in that the chief and his staff would be more readily available to government and the other Services and could contribute better to overall defence planning and preparedness. There are those who argue that the place for NHQ is Karachi where the fleet is based, especially as the navy's part in conflict as fought in the subcontinent would not involve a great deal of 'jointery'—intimate co-operation with the other Services—and would never be required to be extensive. In the particular strategic circumstances of Pakistan this is a compelling point of view, but on the principle that all Service HQs should be collocated, the decision was proper.

There were many arguments about how far 'jointery' should be carried. The debate is usually fierce and sometimes emotional in all staff colleges and at any gathering of professionals—but in Pakistan in 1972 it was flaccid and undirected.[6] Proponents of joint doctrine went largely unheard. The half-hearted outcome was the appointment of a uniformed Chairman of the Joint Chiefs of Staff Committee on 1 March 1976[7] (until which time the chairman was the defence minister, who was Bhutto), but General Mohammad Sharif and his successors were not given the opportunity to mould their headquarters into a true command HQ.

The army seemed to have focused inwards, which is understandable in the circumstances (and might have been no bad thing had it lasted only for a year or so), but it needed a leader who had broad, bold vision so that it could break free from introspection and parochialism. Tikka Khan was a solid soldier, a firm believer in Constitutional propriety, a stickler for procedures and the chain of command. An original military thinker he was not.

* * *

The composition of the 1973 Constitution was to reflect Bhutto's preoccupation with the loyalty of the military, but before endorsement of that document by the National Assembly there was another conspiracy to be dealt with. In early 1973, 14 Air Force and 21 Army officers were arrested on charges of plotting to overthrow the government and went before separate Service courts martial. One army officer was acquitted and the others received punishment ranging from life imprisonment (2) to stoppage of promotion (3). The air chief acted harshly. The case against one officer had been dropped and nine of the others were found not guilty, but Air Chief Marshal Zafar Chaudhury ordered retirement of all fourteen. His order was overruled by government in the case of seven officers. He resigned. 'In fairness to him,' says *The Story of the Pakistan Air Force*, 'it must also be stated that his abrupt departure may have been precipitated by the anti-Qadiani sentiment [Chapter 2] sweeping the country at the time...' Things are not always what they seem. The trial of the army officers was presided over by a Maj.-Gen. Ziaul Haq, who reported to Bhutto, frequently in person.

The conspiracy case showed that the Services were not inclined to support calls for revolt against the government. They had, after all, detected the plot themselves and brought the offenders to justice. It seemed they could be trusted to remain outside politics and act against any within their ranks who would seek to do otherwise. Bhutto may or may not have agreed that this was so, but in any event he made sure that the 1973 Constitution authorized the Parliament to pass laws for the punishment of those found guilty of treason, and included an oath to refrain from indulging in political activity. The old tradition that officers did not involve themselves in politics was not enough: the Constitution formalized it:

> I...do solemnly swear that I will bear true faith and allegiance to Pakistan and uphold the Constitution of the Islamic Republic of Pakistan which embodies the will of the people, that I will not engage myself in any political activities whatsoever and that I will honestly and faithfully serve the Pakistan Army/Navy/Air Force as required by and under the law.

The trouble with an oath of this nature is that it can make it attractive for an autocratic regime to destroy those whom it fears. 'Any political activities whatsoever' is a catchall phrase. With checks and balances, a strong and independent judiciary, a parliament monitored by a free

Press, and a sense of honour and responsibility on the part of political leaders, a phrase like this may have meaning (it will also, probably, be redundant). It does not appear to be recorded if the oath was taken by General Ziaul Haq.

Bhutto realized that he could not remain as unelected (indeed, self-appointed) President indefinitely. The Constitution would be of dubious legality were it not to be endorsed by an elected Assembly, and in any event the people wanted an end to autocracy. Memories of 1958 had faded. The 'social vermin' to whom Ayub had referred at that time had been replaced by Bhutto's military 'traitors' who had 'beaten the workers...lashed the peasants'[8] and, in his eyes, deserved their relegation to the blacker pages of Pakistan's short history. But martial law suited Bhutto. He was able to enact legislation as Chief Martial Law Administrator that would have been impossible, or at best extremely difficult, to push through a democratically-elected assembly, even were the Pakistan People's Party to have a majority. He begged protesting students and striking workers to 'Give me some time' to introduce democracy, largely because the powers of martial law were required 'for the sole purpose of bringing...basic reforms...Once this first phase of reforms is over...the ground would be laid for the full flowering of democracy.' Fair enough, one might think, after such a long period of rule by diktat: use the methods of the autocrats to nurture the long-dormant seeds of fairness, equity, civil law, and freedom for the masses. But it didn't work out quite like that.

Pakistan's economy was placed under severe strain by the nationalization of hundreds of private enterprises. Its international standing (and credit rating), already low in spite of Bhutto's charisma, took a hard knock. The army, of course, was not involved in the nationalization process—but in later years it was to reap benefits by undertaking, through its charitable agency, the Fauji Foundation, many commercial enterprises which were exempt from imposts paid by businesses that had been re-privatized.[9] Nationalization was unpopular with industrialists and businessmen, many of whom sent much capital abroad. In some cases the entrepreneurs themselves went, too; a grave loss for Pakistan and, perhaps strangely, a loss for the army. The army's officers were being recruited in increasing numbers from the middle class rather than the landed gentry and the aristocracy, and the introduction of middle-class young officers was a good thing. Ayub and Yahya had encouraged the grandees to send their sons to serve for at least a few years—like the old British system. And Ayub and Yahya were, in fact, just a wee bit snobbish about it all. Neither were of the real aristocracy—but Bhutto was; and he cared about the middle class just as little as his predecessors had. In a society such as Pakistan's, it was a real step forward to broaden the social base of the officers corps, but the flight of so many of the middle classes meant a reduction in the number of educated young men from whom officer selection could be made.

Martial law was unpopular with the army, which does not seem to have disturbed Bhutto greatly, but it was also unpopular with his political supporters, especially the young. That was serious. In April 1972 its retention was about to come under attack in the Supreme Court: not critical, but definitely annoying for Bhutto. So on 14 April he announced that Martial Law would be repealed a week later, which it was. But he did not give publicity to the fact that the Interim Constitution, proclaimed concurrently, omitted to guarantee Fundamental Rights. These were suspended under a Proclamation of Emergency. Bhutto was not yet prepared to be *entirely* democratic.

The army was occupied with internal reform. Tikka Khan could be relied upon to reorganize it without drama and without creating any political waves. It appears that Bhutto did not again insist on attending a P&S committee meeting, but there would have been no need for that, anyway—Tikka would ensure that only those whom he considered politically reliable would be promoted or appointed to sensitive posts. But there was one thing that even the loyal Tikka could not equivocate about: the prisoners of war. Of the 90,000 POWs held by India contrary to international law, some 70,000 were military, the others being civil servants, military dependants, and private individuals. Article 118 of the Third Geneva Convention (1949) states that, 'Prisoners of War shall be released and repatriated without delay after the cessation of active hostilities,' but Mrs Gandhi ignored the Article, just as she ignored Security Council Resolution 307/71 of 21 December, which called for her forces to be withdrawn and for compliance with the Convention. Tikka Khan was not much of a one for humanitarian Conventions, any more than was Bhutto, but he knew it would be difficult to concentrate the minds of the army on re-equipping and reorganizing while his officers and men fretted about their comrades in Indian prison camps. He wanted action and, for different reasons, Bhutto also wanted their return. His electoral support would depend on such things; therefore, the sooner the POW problem was resolved, the better. In the short term it was as easy as it was justified to blame India, but Bhutto knew that odium could soon begin to shift.

Bhutto released Mujib from confinement (he could hardly have done otherwise) and the erstwhile captive became the President of Bangladesh, with whom Bhutto wanted to have talks as well as with Mrs Gandhi. But Mujib wanted some POWs to be tried as alleged war criminals, which made it difficult for Bhutto to propose including him. Mujib, too, was under pressure at home: the Bengalis considered Bhutto just as much an oppressor as Tikka Khan and Yahya, so it would be politically unwise for Mujib to have talks with Pakistan. Mrs Gandhi, alone, it had to be.

They met at Simla on 28 June and signed an agreement on 2 July.[10] The woman whom Bhutto had described as being 'mediocre...with mediocre intelligence...she'll never succeed in impressing me...' negotiated with the national leader she had described as '...not a very balanced man...' who, 'when he talks, you never understand what he means'.[11] A lovely couple.

The accord was cobbled together without benefit of reasoned input by Bhutto, whose efforts were limited—naturally—by the fact that he was more a supplicant than an equal party to negotiations. He had to get *some* sort of agreement. Bangladesh was not discussed, and there was therefore no mention of the POW question because Mrs Gandhi refused to permit this unless Bangladesh was recognized by Pakistan— a diplomatic venture that Bhutto could not possibly make only seven months after East Pakistan had been lost. For want of something better, Bhutto accepted the Simla (now Shimla) Accord, which the Indians seized upon as justification to treat the Kashmir question as bilateral— nothing to do with Kashmiris and certainly no business of the UN, whose 'good offices' were forever eschewed. The Security Council Resolutions concerning the holding of a plebiscite (agreed by Nehru) were, to the Indian mind, 'overtaken' by this bilateral accord—as curious an interpretation of the Simla Agreement as it was of UN procedure. India's contention that the Accord invalidates UN involvement in the Kashmir issue is, apparently, based on paragraph (ii) (under the heading 'Harmonious Relationship'), in that:

> ...the two countries are resolved to settle their differences by peaceful means through bilateral negotiations or by any other peaceful means mutually agreed upon between them....

This does not expunge, cancel, amend, or deny the Security Council Resolution about a plebiscite, any more than it excludes the UN from involvement in the Kashmir dispute. India holds that 'mutually agreed' is in some fashion equivalent to 'bilateral'. The 'peaceful means' must be bilateral or...well...bilateral. 'Mutual agreement' will, of course, never obtain about 'any other peaceful means'—so far as India is concerned. But this does not make it irrelevant; nor does it render UN resolutions or involvement inapplicable. The fact that the UN Mission in Kashmir remains in existence is evidence that the UN Security Council, although unable or unwilling to enforce some of its own most important Resolutions, confers legitimacy upon its involvement in Kashmir, even if by omission rather than commission. India can hardly renege—formally at least—from the first Simla agreement: 'That the principles and purposes of the Charter of the United Nations shall govern the relations between the two countries,' but it is probable there will continue to be arguments between India and Pakistan about the main paragraph of the Simla Accord, the other terms of which are anodyne. But what is decidedly not anodyne is the *'Delineation of the Line of Control in Jammu and Kashmir Resulting from the Cease Fire of 17 December 1971 in Accordance with the Simla Agreement of 2 July 1972'*.

This document, composed by twelve army officers (six from each country), is, so far as it goes, unambiguous. Its territorial precision is remarkable. It contains such descriptions as:

> The Line of Control runs from NR 313861 to NR 316865, thence to NR 319867, thence EAST to NR 322868, thence NE to NR 331872, thence to a monument on ridge line at NR 336874 approximately five hundred yards SE of Point 10008 (NR 3387), thence to a point NR 338881 on the Nullah such that point NR 336874 and point NR 338881 are connected by a counter clockwise arc with a radius of five hundred yards, thence NE to junction....

What was not precise, unfortunately, was where the termination of the Line should be in the east. To be sure, the description ended with a grid reference: NJ 980420—but what then? There was a cairn erected in 1972 at 980420; it was still there in 1982; it may still be there now; but there was, and is, about a hundred miles of mountainous snow and ice between 980420 and the border with China—at the junction with Aksai Chin, a large area in dispute between India and China (Map 2).[12]

What was to be done about allocation of this area? It was of no commercial advantage, and of interest only to the most dedicated mountaineer. Dull rock, jagged ice, deep snow, foul weather. There could be no attraction in the region. And as such it was described to the author by one of the signatories to the *Description of the Line of Control* (short title).

Lt.-Col. B.M. Tewari was one of the Indian representatives who held meetings (nine altogether) with their Pakistani counterparts from 10 August to 11 December 1972. Ten years later, a brigadier, he was garrison commander in Srinagar (in Indian-administered Kashmir) and, like most Indian officers, genial, comradely, and good company when sure that the intelligence services were not looking over his shoulder. And Tewari said that delineation of the Line of Control was effected in the most gentlemanly manner and the reason the description of the Line stopped at grid reference NJ 980420 was that nobody in their right mind (or words to that effect) could possibly want any of the land between there and the Great Wall of China, and that they (the Indian officers and their Pakistani colleagues) agreed that anyone who wanted to lay claim to ice, snow, and rocks was welcome to them.

Nobody, at that time, imagined that there might be military confrontation in the area. It would be futile to attempt to wage war at such heights, at the end of long lines of communication, with no strategic or even tactical aim, in an area in which mere existence (and no-one lived there) would involve great hazard in moving tiny distances. Who would send troops to occupy a terrifying wasteland where there was no threat of invasion or even territorial infringement?

Mrs Gandhi.

* * *

Sensible but incomplete delineation of the Line of Control sowed the seeds of the Siachen Glacier confrontation of 1984, but in the 1970s there were other external and internal factors that affected reorganization of the army and the attitude of its leaders.

Bhutto took Pakistan out of the Commonwealth on 30 January 1972 (because Commonwealth nations had recognized independent Bangladesh), which had the effect of denying the army and the other services co-operation at the very time when this would have been most welcome. His decision to withdraw from SEATO (7 November) was less sensitive and was based on his wish to begin to play a part in the non-aligned movement, which would be difficult for the leader of a country aligned with the west and not sympathetic to the Soviet Union; but in any event SEATO was dying and was wound up three years later. Withdrawal resulted in the cutting of links with other SEATO nations (who were disinclined to continue them on a purely bilateral basis with Pakistan), but so far as practical planning for war was concerned, SEATO had never mattered greatly to Pakistan. Bhutto also wanted to withdraw from CENTO and sent word of his intention far and wide, but never got round to it. (That grouping was also moribund and finally collapsed on 15 March 1979.) 'Clearly,' say Burke and Ziring, 'Pakistan's continuing presence in CENTO was an expression of friendship towards Iran and Turkey rather than a commitment to the American anti-Soviet policy,' which Bhutto considered irrelevant to Pakistan. The army's leaders had not been enthusiastic about either organization since it had become apparent that they would be of no consequence in a conflict with India.

It was necessary to rebuild the army to be capable of planning and fighting a conventional war. Mrs Gandhi said she had no further territorial designs on Pakistan, but the Kashmir problem had not gone away—if anything it had been exacerbated by the terms of the Simla Accord—and Pakistan was right to be wary of what might happen next. In fact, there was little need to be concerned about India's rearmament programme in the early Seventies. The view of the authority Chris Smith is that, 'it seems that through the 1970s India's defence procurement policy was low key, especially with regard to the army,' and that, although the only reliable and comparatively inexpensive supplier of weaponry was the Soviet Union, availability of equipment was limited.[13] This, combined with the fact that India's army had not appeared overwhelmingly efficient during the war (although some units and formations conducted operations with distinction), might have been enough to convince Bhutto that there was no threat from across the border. He had other ideas, and in June 1972, just before going to Simla, produced an intriguing document on military strategy based on having 'read quite a bit on military matters and warfare....' He wrote that India had about 975,000 troops, 1,050 combat aircraft and 1,650 tanks (all of which figures were exaggerated),[14] and, dangerously, that India would depend 'largely on material superiority and not the human factor, upon technique and not the force of an ideal. In this can lie their weakness and our strength'.[15] This rubbish was followed by the contention that there should be plans for an offensive against Delhi, a thrust in the south to cut off Bombay, and a 'massive wave of raiders', similar, presumably, to those who conducted unsuccessful forays into Kashmir in 1965 during Operation *Gibraltar*. In this one might detect the advice of failed coup-leader Akbar (now defence adviser to the President), as he had been involved in (badly) training the unfortunate 1965 raiders who went bravely but fruitlessly to death or capture. This was to be 'people's war' — but with what aim was not made clear. Was Pakistan to defeat India militarily? Occupy it? What was to be gained by waging all-out war? GHQ was making plans anyway — that was its job — but the idea of Bhutto becoming involved in the higher direction of war was alarming. Bhutto had been a hawk in 1965 and 1971; it seemed that he had not learned from his country's defeat. But (perhaps fortunately) he and Tikka Khan were to be more concerned about alarms within the country.

In Balochistan in December 1972 the Marri tribe attacked settlers in the area of a disputed canal. At about the same time, the Bugti tribe tried to force the resignation of Ahmad Nawaz Bugti, a minister in the Provincial government. There was general unrest. Troops were deployed but not committed; but in February next year an insurrection began, caused mainly by Bhutto's dismissal of the Provincial government. (He also 'swept aside' that of the North–West Frontier Province, both having a majority of the National Awami Party, opposed to the PPP).[16] The army was used vigorously by Tikka Khan (who became known as 'the Butcher of Balochistan') until the revolt was put down and operations ceased, officially, at least, on 15 May 1974. It was a (relatively) short and a bloody campaign, and thoroughly alienated much of the Baloch population which, fortunately for Pakistan, was tiny, numbering only 2.4 million.[17] According to a retired senior officer, about twenty battalions were deployed in the Province (although it is not clear whether they were all there concurrently) at a time when the army should have been concentrating on training for conventional operations. One benefit, as in all counter-insurgency campaigns, was improvement in junior leadership; but it would have been better had there been improvement in senior leadership.

Bhutto became prime minister on 14 August 1973 (and a new President, Fazal Ilahi Chaudhury, was elected by the National Assembly and the Senate), but there appeared to be no change in his methods of governance. He retained the defence portfolio and appointed a Minister of State for Foreign Affairs and Defence, Aziz Ahmad, to undertake business not appropriate for a prime minister, and it was Bhutto who went to Delhi to negotiate the POW repatriation which finally took place in April 1974. An exchange of POWs taken on the western front had been effected on 1 December 1972, and Bangladesh (which Bhutto recognized in February 1974, immediately before chairing an Islamic summit conference in Lahore) agreed to drop charges against the 195 alleged war criminals. 72,795 POWs and 17,186 civilians came home. (Some had come home earlier: six officers and soldiers escaped and walked back over the Himalayas—a considerable feat.)

Absorbing the returnees was not easy. Some, of course, did not wish to continue to serve and were pensioned off. Others were unsuitable, mentally or physically, to undertake military duty, and still others bore resentment against the government which, they thought, had not done enough to secure their release. Problems abounded, but Tikka Khan and his staff rose to the occasion and, by a combination of sympathetic treatment, allocation of money for resettlement, and the embrace of the regimental system, managed the transition well. Army strength was maintained at about 300,000, including 25,000 Azad ['Free'] Kashmir troops recruited in their eponymous area and to all intents and purposes regular soldiers. (AK battalions and brigades have fewer heavy weapons than other units.) The loss of the East Wing had little effect on recruiting, as there had been few Bengalis in the army, but it did have considerable effect on the Gross National Product of the new Pakistan (and on the new Bangladesh, too).

Defence expenditure rose in the 1970s, as might have been expected, but authorities differ as to the increase in percentage of GNP, with one claiming that it went up to 9.2 in 1972 from 3.7 the previous year. Figures below are those of Omar Noman and are considered accurate.

The defence budget was modest. There was no alternative. The country had grave economic problems, but it seemed that Bhutto thought he could achieve growth by nationalization alone, which would result, he was convinced, in greatly expanded production and export of manufactured goods. Subventions by such luminaries as Colonel Gaddafi of Libya were forthcoming, but it must have been apparent that the economic management of the country could not depend on irregular subsidies. The fiscal base was tiny and skewed, and financial management was badly affected by Bhutto's virtual disbanding of the Civil Service of Pakistan and his appointment to responsible positions of PPP loyalists with few or no qualifications in administration.

Another destabilizing factor was the Federal Security Force. It appeared that its role was to enable Bhutto to deal with politically motivated violence, or the threat of it, without having to resort to the army. It was 'responsible only to the Prime Minister and its actions were not subject to scrutiny or debate by Parliament, nor, as matters worked out in practice, was it inhibited by too nice a regard for the law.'[18] Had he been army chief, it is likely Gul Hassan would not have permitted the FSF to exist, but Tikka Khan had no such qualms. What Bhutto ordered, Bhutto got. The FSF was raised without parliamentary endorsement in October 1972, and came into being officially by an Act of Parliament in June the following year. Equipped with automatic weapons and rocket-launchers as well as rifles,[19] its strength in 1974 was almost 14,000: 8,000 in Punjab, 4,000 in NWFP, 1,100 in Sindh, 300 in Azad Kashmir, 200 in the Tribal Areas, and a mere 23 in Balochistan. (Bhutto did not need to cow Balochistan any more than it had been by the army's brutal suppression.) 'The ranks of the FSF,' says Lawrence Ziring, 'were filled by generally repulsive former members of the police and military communities...,'[20] but its significance lies not only in its creation as an unsavoury parallel institution to the armed forces and its entirely unconstitutional use as a private army (ironically, such elements had been explicitly banned by Bhutto), but because its Director-General, Masood Mahmud, a former policeman, eventually testified that Mr Bhutto had ordered the Force to murder one of his political opponents. The perceptive Hasan Askari Rizvi wrote in 1974 (and courageously republished in 1976, at the height of Bhutto's revengeful viciousness) the observation that, 'Once the political leadership [of Pakistan] is sure of the military's support, they assert their authority in society and deal with [political] opposition effectively,' which was precisely what Bhutto did.

So Bhutto intended and largely succeeded in having the army divorced from enforcing civil law, or the version of it applying at the time, and military re-equipment and training programmes went ahead, although not without some interruption. Floods and earthquakes in 1973–5 required support to the stricken populations of Punjab, Sindh, and NWFP, the earthquake in Swat and Hazara of December 1974 being the worst calamity, with over 5,000 dead. The army provided aid and also undertook road, well, and dam building. Gradually the army regained the trust of the people.

Military hardware is not difficult to obtain on the world market, providing the purchaser has hard currency with which to buy it. There are some problems with western suppliers, such as reluctance of governments to permit exports to regimes of which they do not approve (or if they consider that selling arms to these countries would cost them votes), and a proclivity to deny spares or replacements at the time they are most needed. But Pakistan could not afford to pick its suppliers. China had given assistance, but it was European and US systems the services wanted—although some had been obtained via Iran, some directly from France. President Nixon wanted to help, but was involved with Vietnam and Watergate and had to chose his moment carefully. On 14 March 1973 he partially lifted the embargo in effect since 1971, and military sales were resumed on a case-by-case basis to an initial value of $14 million, which would, in 1973, purchase a lot of equipment, especially if prices were kept low by benevolent suppliers. Holdings of some main equipments in 1972 and 1976 were:

Equipment	1972/3	1976/7
M-47/M48 tanks	200	250
T55/T59 tanks	250	750
M-113 APCs	250	400
Naval patrol boats	1	17
Mirage aircraft	approx 30	approx 60
MiG-19 aircraft	approx 50	approx 80

Source: *Military Balance*, International Institute for Strategic Studies.

The table does not show changes in artillery inventories. Chinese and US 105, 122, and 155 mm guns were acquired in lieu of older pieces such as 25-pounders, which were phased out of front-line service. The difference in quantity was small—900 in 1972 and 1000 in 1976—but quality was much superior. Army strength increased from 278,000 to about 400,000 in the same period, and military expenditure surged immediately after the war but levelled out later:

Year	Amount (US $ millions)	As % of GNP	As % of Budget
1969	350	5.0	55.52
1970	372	4.8	53.91
1971	436	5.6	56.17
1972	522	6.7	59.10
1973	522	6.6	58.10
1974	572	5.7	53.22
1975	569	6.3	53.41

Reproduced from *Pakistan—a Political and Economic History*.

The armed forces were gradually regaining self-confidence and seemed less perturbed about India's nuclear test on 18 May 1974 than was the prime minister. India protested to the US about the resumption of defence co-operation with Pakistan, especially as it involved training as well as supply of equipment, but its complaints seemed less convincing when the 'peaceful' twelve kiloton device exploded in the Rajasthan desert. It was, said the chairman of India's Atomic Energy Commission, 'a part of the research in peaceful uses of nuclear explosives'. A later, independent comment was that, 'Besides claiming that their bomb was a strictly peaceful one, which was as stunningly hypocritical as it was brazen, New Delhi also boasted that, "Not a single thing in it was foreign".'[21] But Pakistan could not ignore the bang: the existence of a nuclear weapon over the border meant a rethink of defence policy. The cost of defence against nuclear attack would be impossible to meet, and it seemed that the only counter to a hostile nuclear state was possession of a similar weapon. India was instrumental in causing the nuclear arms race in the subcontinent on which both countries have spent billions of dollars at the expense of human development. Bhutto was vehement about India's perceived intentions. Two weeks before the test he had indulged in barbed comment at a banquet in Beijing (after the Indian ambassador left in diplomatic dudgeon because a reference to Kashmir had been made by Deng Xiaoping) by asking, 'Does India want conflict and confrontation instead of co-operation and friendly relations? If India wants that, then I can tell you Pakistan is prepared for it.' Which it wasn't, of course, any more than it was prepared for a new Ice Age—but after the explosion Bhutto became even more defiant and '...conscious of the dire necessity of our having a coherent nuclear programme'.[22] Pakistan was already engaged in nuclear research, with a focus on electricity generation centred on the Canadian-supplied 'Candu' reactor in Karachi which began operating in 1972 and was subject to IAEA inspections. The weapons programme began in earnest in 1974–5, and gathered pace in the following decades.[23]

Some officers were concerned about the way India was being run. Mrs Gandhi had made belligerent statements about Pakistan and Kashmir and it was feared that, in order to restore her waning popularity, she might manufacture an incident from which conflict could erupt. Neither the army nor the other services were in good enough shape to fight another war. The army's senior officers were being selected increasingly for their docility and perceived allegiance to the 'Quaid-e-Awam' (or 'Leader of the People', as Bhutto had taken to calling himself) rather than for ability to command troops in battle. But it was apparent that the army was beginning to resent the selection process. Even the iron man Tikka Khan had been given a rough time when addressing groups of officers in 1975.

On 12 June 1975 Mrs Gandhi was found guilty of electoral corruption. On the 26th she declared a State of Emergency, arrested 676 of a later total of several thousand political opponents, imposed censorship, and damaged (but only temporarily) her credibility as a democrat. GHQ warned units along the LoC and the border to be vigilant, and the PAF increased combat air patrols and surveillance (using its newly-delivered French Mirage IIIRPs) to monitor Indian movements. But Mrs Gandhi had more than enough problems to deal with in New Delhi and elsewhere to give her attention to Pakistan.

Bhutto had a good year, diplomatically, in 1975. He obtained assurance from President Ford that Pakistan was important to the US, which resulted in the complete lifting of the arms embargo of 1971 that had been partially lifted in 1973 (but see Note 22); pushed along an agreement with France for supply of Crotale missiles, more Mirage aircraft, and more helicopters; discussed regional security with the Shah of Iran, including Bhutto's proposal for a conference of Indian Ocean littoral states on the subject; and tabled a resolution in the UN General Assembly about safeguarding the integrity of non-nuclear states which was adopted unanimously. Pakistan was making its mark in the world, and when the meeting of Islamic countries' foreign ministers agreed at Jeddah in July to support Pakistan's candidature for a vacant seat on the Security Council, Bhutto's cup was made full. But at home, Bhutto was not doing so well. Bombings, assassinations, plots, political mayhem were rife. The former Bhutto loyalist Mustafa Khar (whom Bhutto had telephoned from Rome to find out if it was safe for him to return to depose Yahya Khan) tried to play Bhutto at his own game of unscrupulously manipulating political affairs, as he had tried to do in 1973, and again lost. The political scene resembled that at the court of a particularly paranoid and malevolent Kabuli chieftain.[24]

General Tikka Khan retired on 28 February 1976 from the position of army chief (to become Special Assistant to the Prime Minister on Defence and National Security), and was succeeded by General Ziaul Haq. (Bhutto had wanted the COAS to remain for another year but it had become apparent that an extension of Tikka Khan's tenure would not be well-received in the army, which was conscious that it was being politicized.) Zia was not Tikka's choice by any means, but Bhutto wanted him.[25]

It seems Zia was thought to be a reasonable fellow who, while deeply religious, was apparently not a zealot, and Bhutto considered he would not question his authority. At the time, he was commander II Corps, the armour-heavy 'strike force' based in and around Multan. An officer who had been on his staff at that time told the author in the early 1980s that Zia was a good corps commander who let his staff get on with what they should be doing while 'doing the right thing' by getting around visiting units and assessing their capabilities. Zia's exercises were perforce small-scale, but seem to have been realistic enough, and his corps was as effective as it could be in the circumstances. He seemed the ideal man to be Chief of the Army Staff, as the seven officers senior to him either had political question marks against them or were disliked by Bhutto (same thing, in the end), who had dossiers on them all.[26] He was fifty-two, a good age for an army chief, not yet being in the bracket that could be called old and out-of-touch, yet not so young as to attract the 'wet-behind-the-ears' calumny. (Yet he had one remarkable deficiency for an army officer: he was hopeless at adhering to a timetable or keeping appointments, and sometimes exasperated his staff by forgetting engagements arranged days in advance. This trait became even more marked—and exasperating—in later years.)

Zia made no waves on arrival in GHQ at Rawalpindi. He seemed 'a bit withdrawn at first,' according to one of his staff officers, but soon settled in to run a fairly humdrum headquarters whose officers had not been encouraged to indulge in original thinking or question conventional wisdom as to what the army was all about and where it was going. And he did 'run' it: he wanted to know who was doing what and why— although he seemed to have an unfortunate proclivity for 'sitting on' files. Initially he did not wish to delegate to subordinates too much of what he saw as important. In later years he changed completely, and, in spite of being an autocrat, delegated a great deal to his Chief of Staff, General K. M. Arif, who has written a detailed and valuable account of his association with his master (see, Bibliography).

In GHQ there was no 'Mission Statement' (not that the phrase existed then), and training directives produced by the Military Training Directorate were decidedly low-key, even banal. Operations Branch had a lot to occupy it, what with Balochistan, Sindh, the Afghan border, but planning was poor. Nobody quite knew what would happen if the Indians were to commit their armour in Punjab, or try a 'vertical envelopment' (the OK phrase of the day, meaning a parachute drop) to cut the road to Karachi, or simply engage in a war of nerves along the border. (There was already a war of nerves along the Line of Control in Kashmir, but the orders to troops there consisted, basically, of 'if you are fired at, fire back, but make sure the UN Observers are informed as soon as possible'. Which was one reason why the UN Mission in Kashmir was so unpopular in India. An examination of its independent reports on cease-fire violations makes interesting reading.) The War Book, as such, had given way to contingency plans, but these were pedestrian, imprecise, and seemed in many ways impractical to some who had to examine them. Unfortunately, Zia was not the man to inject imagination into the minds of the planners. They carried on churning out what they considered to be staff college solutions to problems they had not examined in a spirit of challenge. But Zia did no harm to the army in his first fifteen months as COAS. He did not take over a happy team, but that was not his fault, and he tried to place it back on the rails in the best way he knew: with calmness, professional integrity, a genuine religiosity that struck a favourable chord with many of the younger officers and most of the soldiers, and a middle-class pragmatism that was beyond the comprehension of his mentor, Zulfikar Ali Bhutto.

One of Bhutto's concerns was the approach of general elections, and it is puzzling why he appeared to be so worried about what was bound to be a victory for the PPP. At the end of 1976, the *Far Eastern Economic Review* commented that, '...even his staunchest rivals conceded privately that he did not face any serious challenge. Considering the plight of the Opposition, brought about partly by Bhutto and partly by its own...political ineptitude, its despondent mood seemed fully justified.' But it seemed that Bhutto wanted overwhelming endorsement by the people. This he was determined to achieve.[27] It is difficult to disagree with Ziring that, 'He not only wanted to defeat his adversaries, he was determined to destroy them forever.'

* * *

During 1976, an agreement with the US was signed for the supply of arms worth $38.6 million, and Congress was asked by the Administration to approve a further $79.5 million. The equipment took some time to work its way through the pipeline, but it played a part in convincing the Services that they were not being neglected. Of considerable importance to the armed forces, Bhutto decided to provide plots of land at give-away prices to Junior Commissioned Officers because they were 'not financially well-off and their continued service to the country should not go unrecognized' — and nor should the thoughtfulness (in the months before elections) of Zulfikar Ali Bhutto, who hoped that Zia would 'let [the grants] be known to all ranks of the Pakistan Army'.[28]

Bhutto's despairing comment in mid-1977 that, 'there has been complete polarization—both horizontal and vertical—and it has left hardly any walk of life unaffected,' was quite true, but he would not admit to responsibility for this polarization any more than he could admit that the resurgence in political opposition owed much to his own confrontational stance. He had treated the opposition parties with contempt and was surprised when they established an alliance, the United Democratic Front, to fight the elections of 7 March. In spite of this development, the PPP would probably have won the elections even had they been conducted fairly.[29] It seems that in much of Sindh and the North-West Frontier Province the ballots were as fair as possible in the circumstances, but nobody believed that the results in Punjab were anything but well and truly rigged. General Gul Hassan, ambassador in Athens, and his close associate Air Marshal Rahim Khan in Madrid, resigned as publicly as possible, but there were no major outbreaks of discontent in the country until the middle of April. Then the real trouble began.

The country was riven and shaken by demonstrations. By mid-June, more than 11,000 people were in prison. Leaders of the opposition Pakistan National Alliance (PNA), the coalition of nine opposition parties (the 'gang of nine' as Bhutto referred to them) were as unprincipled as the prime minister in encouraging violence throughout the country. Once it became apparent that violent agitation was working in their favour, they refused to negotiate with Bhutto, who at first prevaricated about discussing the rigged election, then arrested many of the PNA's leaders. Bhutto banned demonstrations and, in a desperate throw for popularity with the Islamic parties, declared the prohibition of alcohol and gambling.[30] Mosques became centres of agitation. Congregations were whipped to fury at Friday prayers and then held demonstrations which were suppressed by the police and, later, by the army. In an attempt to influence the population, the Chairman of the

Joint Chiefs of Staff Committee and the Service Chiefs issued a statement towards the end of April declaring that Bhutto's government had the loyalty of the armed forces. It was ignored. Immediately after this, Bhutto declared martial law in Hyderabad, Karachi, and Lahore (and later Multan), and the army imposed a curfew on these cities. Three brigadiers, all in 10 Division in Lahore, refused to involve themselves or their troops in putting down riots, as this would almost certainly have involved killing civilians.

The country was becoming ungovernable, but it seemed that Bhutto did not realize that time was running out. The PNA wanted his resignation, the formation of an interim government, and fresh elections. After much behind-the-scenes negotiation (including mediation by some Arab countries), the PNA dropped the resignation demand, agreeing that the Constitution required a PM to be in office until election of a successor (as pointed out by the wily Bhutto), and even compromised on their insistence on an interim government. They could not have gone much further, and Bhutto was forced to consent to hold elections on 8 October. But the two sides could not continue to agree on anything for any length of time and kept altering their positions. The country was seething with dissatisfaction. A crisis was approaching. The President, Fazal Ilahi Chaudhry, was unable to resolve matters because the Constitution forbade any action on his part except on the advice of the prime minister. As the prime minister was a major part of the problem, the President was powerless.

On the evening of 4 July 1977, the Chief of the Army Staff called a meeting of senior GHQ officers, having already discussed the nation's predicament with his corps commanders. Both sides in the political struggle, said Zia, had weapons. There was danger of a full-scale civil war. Operation *Fair Play* had begun. The army was going to take over.

NOTES

1. Radio and TV address, quoted in Wolpert op cit.
2. The Hamoodur Rehman Commission Report goes into this in some detail, as it does about Yahya's womanising. Chapter 26 of the Report, 'The Moral Aspect' makes sad reading, as it deals with widespread moral decay in the army as well as making observations about Yahya himself. The statement that he 'was extremely friendly with a number of ladies of indifferent repute' is substantiated by the visitors' log of the President's House, Karachi. It was all sordid stuff.

3. 'GM' was Director Military Operations (a brigadier's appointment) in the early 1980s when the author first made his acquaintance. Amongst later appointments he was Commandant of the Military Academy and commander X Corps in a very sensitive period. He had been awarded the Queen's Medal at Sandhurst and never looked back. A man of deep religious conviction and complete integrity.

4. See also, R. Khan op. cit. for descriptions of Bhutto.

5. Rizvi op. cit.

6. Discussions with senior officers of Joint Staff HQ, 1990–94.

7. As recommended by the Hamoodur Rahman Commission.

8. Speech in Karachi, 3 January 1972, quoted in Wolpert op. cit.

9. In 1997 the Fauji Foundation owned ten industrial and commercial projects. Sales in 1994–5 were almost a billion dollars. A description of its organization was given by M. Ziauddin in *Dawn* of 28 April 1997. The Fauji network of business, educational and other enterprises is now enormous, and, for example, the Fauji Fertiliser Corporation had a share capital value of 3 billion rupees ($50 million) as at March 2005.

    The US magazine *Business Week* of 12 November 2001 carried a major piece on the Foundation. It began 'It's early morning in Islamabad, and a middle-class child sits down for breakfast. He pours sugar refined from Fauji Sugar Mills into a bowl of Fauji oatmeal, which his mother cooked using gas bottled by Fauji LPG. In the next room his father logs onto his computer running on electricity produced by the Fauji Kabirwala power plant and clicks onto a program that uses Fauji software. The house they all live in was, of course, built with Fauji cement. The Fauji group is as pervasive a commercial presence in Pakistan as General Electric is in the US. And the Fauji companies, all part of the Fauji Foundation, are closely linked to an even more ubiquitous institution--the Pakistani military, itself a formidable force in the economy.' See http://www.businessweek.com/magazine/content/01_46/b3757138.htm.

10. One of Mrs Ghandi's advisers, Parmeshwar Narain Haksar, told her that the object was not to humiliate Pakistan but to create confidence and trust. 'You must not forget the Versailles Treaty [that humiliated Germany in 1919 and led to the second World War],' he said. 'You don't trample a man who is down and out.' See *Indira*, by Katherine Frank (HarperCollins 2001), an elegant and most readable account of Mrs Gandhi's life.

11. Oriana Fallaci (trans. John Shepley), *Interview with History*, New York, Houghton Mifflin, 1976.

12. Which, if it ever went to international arbitration, would probably be awarded to India. But India has spoiled its chances of international arbitration over Aksai Chin (and other areas in dispute with the PRC) by refusing such on Kashmir. Hoist by its own petard, India can attempt only bilateral negotiations—and China will not mention Aksai Chin.

13. Smith (1994).

14. The IISS *Military Balance* for 1972–3 gives the figures as 960,000 troops, 650 combat aircraft, and 1,490 tanks.

15. Wolpert op. cit., who records that the content of Tikka Khan's reply to the memo is not known.

16. Ziring op. cit.

17. The army was assisted in its operations by Iranian helicopter gunships (supplied by the US) provided at the orders of the Shah who did not wish tribal troubles to spread to the Iranian provinces of Balochistan and Sistan. In 2004-2005, as serious tribal and religious violence began again in Balochistan, its self-appointed leaders of dissident groups lost no opportunity to recall the events of the 1970s.
18. James (1993).
19. Arif (1999).
20. Ziring op. cit. Also M. A. Khan (1983) for descriptions of how the FSF operated.
21. William E. Burrows and Robert Windrem, *Critical Mass*, London, Simon and Schuster, 1994.
22. Wolpert op. cit.
23. In 1976 Dr Henry Kissinger, on behalf of the Ford administration, offered Pakistan 'a substantial conventional arms package' if Bhutto agreed to forgo the reprocessing plant. (Dennis Kux, *The United States and Pakistan 1947-2000.*)
24. Kux (for example) states that Bhutto 'was acting more like a feudal autocrat than a democratic political leader.'
25. There is an account, perhaps not altogether unbiased, in Chishti (1996) of the selection process.
26. Arif, op. cit., recounts that Bhutto made 'unsavoury' comments about all seven.
27. He had also learned about propaganda, and the PPP produced thousands of little red booklets on the lines of Mao's *Thoughts*, entitled *Bhutto Says: a Pocket-Book of Thoughtful Quotations and Writings of Chairman Zulfiqar Ali Bhutto.* In 1980 the author asked a PPP loyalist (who had prudently decided to move out of Rawalpindi to his house on a Kashmiri hillside) if the title was really intentional, or had someone been ironical and the joke got out of hand? No, no, said the former politician, the whole thing was genuine enough—but, anyway, those who could read were already convinced that Bhutto would win.
28. Wolpert op. cit.
29. In *Years of Upheaval*, Kissinger observed that 'Bhutto destroyed himself by seeking a popular mandate too rapidly and then manipulating the electoral result.'
30. A close associate of Bhutto, Colonel Ismail Khan, described the institution of Prohibition to the author on several occasions over many years. He and Bhutto 'cracked a bottle of Scotch' to celebrate.

11 The Years of Zia

The experience of Pakistan, however, suggests that it might be easy for a disciplined army to take over the reins of government in a developing country...but the military cannot solve all the problems facing a new nation. It may check instability, introduce certain social and economic reforms and accelerate the rate of economic growth but it cannot tackle the real problem which leads to a *coup d'etat*—creation of a viable framework of political action which can function smoothly without the backing of the military commanders...

Hasan Askari Rizvi, 1976

Rizvi forecast correctly on all counts: the army's take-over in 1977 was easy (and without violence); instability was checked; social and economic reforms were introduced; and the rate of economic growth was accelerated. But there was no development of an alternative system, the 'viable framework' of civil government that would serve the country without the threat of bayonets in the background.

Zia was not prepared in any way to run a country. He had no concept of the intricacies of government; no agenda for social reform (at first); and no training in economics (which he found boring). But for many years under his rule the country was prosperous and comparatively stable. Certainly he told a lie when he first promised to hold elections. Was it a lie at the time he told it? Or did it become a lie when, after a few weeks, he realized that elections would free the vicious and unforgiving Bhutto to stomp the country with his private army, making rabble-rousing speeches which would be equalled in ferocity by his political opponents? It is tempting to be drawn into description and comment on Zia's governance, but this is the story of the army's development, and, while there will be observations on martial law and other social and foreign policy matters relevant to the army, it would be inappropriate to attempt examination of the country's history. It is contended, however, that improvements to the lot of the average Pakistani were greater in Zia's time than in any previous period. Certainly there were undemocratic fiats that restricted personal freedoms, and there were judicially-awarded punishments that appalled the liberal west. Emergence of religiosity of a weird and wonderful brand was undoubtedly at Zia's behest, and the seeds of future discord and violence were well and truly sown by his encouragement of Islamic bigots. But in the villages and towns and cities the people could relax for the moment, at least—provided they did not indulge in political machinations—and begin to enjoy life free from surveillance by Bhutto's FSF and the PPP petty functionaries who had delighted in their power over the man in the street—those whom, only six years ago, Bhutto said he wanted 'to be able to tell him to go to hell'.

The Zia regime lasted from 5 July 1977 to 17 August 1988. In these eleven years the army grew from 400,000 to 450,000 and its inventory of equipment increased in quantity and quality. The outlook of the army altered. Its members were encouraged by the example of the COAS to pay more attention to religion, which some did as lip-service, some as genuine devotees. Some, of course, ignored the call, and were quietly shunted sideways or out. Some ignored the call and were too valuable to dismiss. There was a gradual growth of national pride within the officer corps. They came to consider that although America had influence over their country, they could take as much US advice as they wished and discard the rest. China was an ally, although at times it appeared reluctant to offer more than token approval for Pakistan's policies—perhaps because America was so much to the fore—but the Chinese did not have much effect on military doctrine or training. The days of hankering after a 'people's army' were over. But the army was weakened, especially at the beginning of Zia's regime and in the early 1980s, by the requirement for officers to be involved in martial law. A constant complaint was that many good officers who should have been gaining command experience were forced to have their postings cut short or disrupted by 'double-hatting'—carrying out administration of martial law in addition to normal military duties. It is impossible to quantify this, but it is obvious it existed.

The President, Fazal Ilahi Chaudhry, remained in office, to the satisfaction of Zia, who gave him the respect he almost invariably afforded older and wiser men. The position, however, was a hollow one, just as Bhutto intended it to be, and Ilahi was a tired man. He had borne with equanimity the insults of Bhutto and his henchmen ('...no ministry...should in future deal directly with the President's Secretariat...'[1]), and wanted to leave at the end of his tenure in September 1978 in spite of Zia's sincere request that he remain. Under the Constitution, his successor should have been elected by both Houses of Parliament, but martial law overrode this, and on 16 September Zia was sworn in as Pakistan's fourth military President.

He charted the way ahead in his first speech to the nation on 5 July (written by the talented Salik, who we last saw accompanying General Niazi into captivity in the East)[2], of which one theme was the lack of political ambition on his own part: 'My sole aim is to organise free and fair elections which [will] be held in October this year. Soon after the polls power will be transferred to the elected representatives of the people. I give a solemn assurance that I will not deviate from this schedule.' They weren't; it wasn't; and he did.

Zia formed a military council of the Chairman of the Joint Chiefs of Staff Committee (who was senior to Zia) and the three Service Chiefs of Staff, of whom he was but one—but it was obvious who was calling the shots, because he announced that the Chief Martial Law Administrator was to be Chief Executive of the Nation and that Martial Law Orders and Regulations were not to be challenged in any court of law. By proclamation he suspended the Constitution, dissolved the federal and provincial assemblies, sacked the prime minister and all ministers (federal and provincial), dismissed the provincial governors, and brought the entire country under martial law. All within forty-eight hours of taking power. Interesting stuff, especially as replacements were needed at once for a large number of experienced officials. Which makes one imagine that Operation *Fair Play* might have been thought out in detail over a considerable period. Some sources state that Zia was in the hands of junior officers—majors and colonels—who forced him to go ahead with the *coup*. Perhaps; but, interestingly, Zia had been keeping track of young officers' career profiles for many years. When he was the senior administrative staff officer on the HQ of 6 Armoured Division, it was noted by a fellow officer who had known him for many years that he 'paid a lot of attention to the confidential reports' of officers in the formation, which was not what administrators normally do.[3] His dislike of files did not seem to extend to detailed examination of personal records. And, later, he was very careful in selection of officers when it was within his gift to do so. One wonders whether Zia might have been planning ahead in some way...

The stage was set for a restoration of stability and then progression to what one might call the Third Republic. But Zia discovered two things: that Zulfikar Ali Bhutto had been even less principled than had been supposed—to the point that he was strongly suspected of ordering a murder; and that he, Zia, thought he was rather good at governing the country.

The rights and wrongs of Bhutto's trial and execution are neither here nor there so far as this narrative is concerned, save to state that the army itself acted with propriety and dignity. There were many wild allegations made concerning the circumstances in which Mr Bhutto died, and for these Ms Benazir Bhutto can be excused, speaking as she did when overcome by grief.

The system of martial law throughout the country was consistent with the military chain of command. Initially the corps commanders were appointed province governors in each province (except Balochistan, which at that time did not have a Corps HQ in the capital, Quetta). This resulted in protocol problems and was also unwieldy. Dignity was at stake, of course, when a governor who was a lieutenant-general considered that he should be treated as senior to a full general when the latter was a visitor in the former's province...The somewhat bombastic (but, to the author, at least, most likeable) Lt.-Gen. Fazle Haq of the North-West Frontier Province objected when the Deputy Chief of the Army Staff, General Muhammad Iqbal, was to be given precedence over him at a passing-out parade at the Pakistan Military Academy. Fazle Haq refused to attend the parade, but Zia took no notice and continued to place confidence in him. It became necessary to appoint full-time governors from the army, which was done in NWFP (Fazle stayed), Punjab, and Sindh. Balochistan continued to be governed by Lt.-Gen. Rahimuddin Khan, Zia's son-in-law. The insurrection in Balochistan was ended, simply, by ceasing military operations, granting amnesties, and turning 'confrontation into reconciliation'.[4]

The federal cabinet, at first styled the Council of Advisers, did not originally include many military officers, and in its final composition had none at all. Many members were able enough but had ideas above their station and became embarrassing, and some outstanding ones left because they considered they were wasting their time. The retired Lt.-Gen. Habibullah Khan, an industrialist of energy, honesty, and wealth, became weary of having his advice ignored and went home to Peshawar. The minister for finance and planning, the sagacious Mr Ghulam Ishaq Khan, became President of Pakistan in later years, and some others continued to exercise their talents in the interests of their country, but it cannot be said that the cabinet was a happy organization (perhaps few cabinets are). The army, too, began to lose direction. It became unsure of itself, and the chain of command became imprecise and unclear. Perhaps it became unsure of itself *because* the chain of command was unclear. It had a chief who was also President, which resembled a re-run of the Yahya period, when it seemed the President was never quite sure about which hat he was wearing at any given time. Zia had to concentrate on running the country, which was his own choice and nobody else's, but surely, thought the army,[5] he should pay attention to reorganization, re-equipment, and getting rid of 'Bhutto-boys'.

In fact, Zia had got rid of several 'Bhutto-boys'. Some were included in the first bunch of thirty or so that he ordered sidelined or sacked when he sent for the Military Secretary to talk about the career plot the day after he took over, and some others went later. 'Bhuttoism' did remain in the army (and more so in the Air Force), but was of little consequence. (The navy ignored all this vulgar stuff.) In spite of this, Zia was never quite sure about some senior officers who remained in command positions and made it clear they were on probation. Those who seemed to be in the pattern of the old Ayub and Yahya style were suspect—although Fazle Haq and some others were undoubtedly in this mould.

Of the many Zia loyalists, few were more dependable than Lt.-Gen. Muhammad Sawar Khan, who was appointed governor of Punjab in 1978. He performed the difficult task of managing the province for two years and was then made Vice Chief of Army Staff—a new appointment redesignated from Deputy Chief—which carried the rank of full general. The duty statement of the Vice Chief was: 'To exercise and perform all the powers and functions vested in the Chief of Army Staff under the law, rules, regulations, orders and instructions for the time being in force.' Further, the Vice Chief was allowed all facilities 'as authorised to the Chief of Army Staff for so long as the COAS holds the office of the President.'[6] He was head of the army—but not altogether, because he could not take independent action in matters that Zia considered his sole province, such as senior promotions and appointments. Zia had three hats: COAS, CMLA, and President. The anomaly that, although senior to the Chairman of the Joint Chiefs of Staff Committee by virtue of being President, he was his junior in military appointment and length of service, was overcome by tinkering with the Constitution. He based his right to do so on the dubious Supreme Court decision that imposition of martial law was validated 'as it was found to be dictated by considerations of state necessity and public welfare'—although the nine judges rejected the argument that legitimacy of the *coup* (or any *coup*) was conferred by success.[7] The judgment resulted in modifications to the Constitution that were designed to legitimize and prolong Zia's Presidency. They included amendment of Articles governing senior military appointments, which suited Zia's purposes but were untranslatable when the country reverted to parliamentary rule, and almost caused a constitutional upset when Benazir Bhutto, as prime minister, attempted to exercise what she considered her powers to appoint a Chairman of the Joint Chiefs of Staff Committee in 1989. In any event, the amendment to the Constitution that was relevant to Zia's Presidency and the armed forces was that: 'Without prejudice to the generality of the foregoing provision [that the Federal Government shall have control and command of the Armed Forces], the Supreme Command of the Armed Forces shall vest in the President.'[8] So Zia was senior to the Chairman, after all.

It has been claimed that Zia was a hypocrite as regards religion, but it is difficult to find a convincing argument for this contention. Allegations are usually based on the fact that the regime was harsh and that many PPP adherents suffered because of their connections to Bhutto. The regime *was* harsh on those who sought to undermine it; and PPP loyalists *were* treated badly in squalid jails. (And it should be remembered that many of them had behaved outrageously, illegally, and brutally during the time in power of their protector.) But this was hardly un-Islamic *per se*. Zia was a genuinely religious man, and tried his best to encourage the people of Pakistan to observe the Faith. In the army this had mixed results.

The problem is that there can be conflict between encouragement, suggestion, discipline, and obedience. In a strictly structured military society there is little room for exhibition of originality. In modern times, eccentricity is distrusted and conformity approved. And there is a fine line between the highest level of conformity and the lowest of compliant obsequiousness. Once that line is crossed, the subject can move quickly to ever-greater levels of ingratiation, thereby compromising integrity in the desire to appear efficient. It can appear to junior officers that sycophancy is not only acceptable, but that without it the road to advancement is blocked. In an officer corps this can be a speedy way to disaster. It is not detectable at first; but once it becomes apparent it is usually too late to alter course without a wholesale cleansing, which usually means excision of some of the innocent along with the guilty, and also of some who could be saved by restoration of good practices.

This does not mean that the holding of religious beliefs and their practice are in any way undesirable in a defence force. It *does* mean that the flaunting of religious belief in the hope that this will meet with the approval of superior officers is unhealthy. But there are problems here, too. Common worship in Islam is desirable because it 'strengthen[s] the awareness of one Muslim for another in times of gain or of adversity. In many respects [acts of common worship] serve to cement communal bonds by stimulating the individual's sense of belonging.'[9] So where is the line between public worship because it is an essential part of religion, and public worship because it is a good thing to be seen by a senior officer performing one's devotions? The answer lies in the application of common sense by all concerned — but as this is unlikely to obtain at all times, it must be accepted that a military hierarchical system with theocratic overtones will be difficult to manage.

Many of Zia's new senior officers were by upbringing and education more inclined to religion than their worldly predecessors whose secular approach he had long distrusted. (Even as a divisional commander he had banned alcohol in officers' messes.) Omar Noman wrote that,

> One of the first changes made by Zia, after his appointment as COAS, was to upgrade the status of the maulvis attached to each army unit. Hitherto they had been regarded as comic figures which the military elite tolerated as a gesture to religious obligation. Zia integrated [them] into the everyday ethos of the military and made it compulsory for them to go into battle with the troops. This initial gesture was a harbinger of things to come. Thus, when the military-bureaucratic apparatus regained power in 1977, it was the religiously inclined generals who were dominant.

— Well, not altogether. There were several influential senior officers who, while perfectly good Muslims, had a more lenitive interpretation of what their leader required. It seemed, however, that the writing was on the wall for those who wanted wider and more secular horizons. But events moved in favour of wider horizons, at least. First, most religious parties objected to martial law (for reasons that would take too long to examine) and were unwilling to support Zia; and outside developments took place that perforce encouraged a less conditional approach to the Profession of Arms.

It was Zia who furthered polarization between Shia and Sunni Muslims. Little as this was his intent, he exacerbated the problem (never far below the surface) by introducing *zakat*, an Islamic wealth-sharing arrangement which was objected to by Shias. He then reversed his decision (not for nothing was CMLA known as Cancel My Last Announcement), thereby alienating extremist Sunnis. The short-term result was the usual rioting, but the effects lasted and the Sunni-Shia divide is a matter for serious concern in modern Pakistan.

Zia was helped in development of the country by instability across the western border. When the Soviet Union agreed to provide Afghanistan with 'urgent political, moral and economic aid, including military aid' in 1979, it was obvious that a Soviet military take-over was in progress. On 1 January 1980 the Kabul government admitted it had 'invited' Russian troops into the country 'in view of the present aggressive actions of the enemies of Afghanistan', without specifying who these might be and ignoring the fact that the need for Soviet intervention stemmed largely from the Afghans' own proclivity for internal strife. Events then moved quickly. Thousands of refugees (soon to be over three million) began to cross the border into Pakistan (and some hundreds of thousands to Iran). President Carter said the US would provide defence equipment;[10] Saudi Arabia and the Gulf States sent donations, the former giving $100 million in its first tranche; the EEC promised $20 million in refugee assistance; China said it backed Pakistan 'against foreign aggression and interference' and, in one of the more improbable developments of the era, later received indirect CIA funding for provision of weapons to the freedom fighters, the *mujahideen*; Japan signed a $50 million aid package and gave $1.5 million for the refugee programme; the world was beating paths to Zia's door. The economy of Pakistan, in reasonable shape but already skewed by such fiscal subsidies as the earnings of Pakistani workers in the Gulf, was put even further out of kilter by these donations, and by an outflow of capital caused by fear of the Russian presence. It is now known 'that the leaders of the Soviet Union never wanted to invade or occupy Afghanistan,'[11] but the fact remains that they did occupy it. And so far as most of the rest of the world was concerned the situation was grave, for what other sovereign country might be invaded by a stronger power in the future?

The Services benefited greatly from the quantities of money and weapons that began arriving in the early Eighties. Pakistani officers were once again welcome in the US for briefings, training, and visits concerned with provision and use of weapons and intelligence. The threat of terrorism (as much from the Al Zulfiqar organization[12] as from across the border) brought a British team of 'mountaineers' to instruct the Special Services Group in some of the arcane skills employed by Britain's counter-terrorist experts.[13] Zia even went to the US to have talks with Mr Carter in October 1980, and a year later Mrs Thatcher visited Pakistan and recorded that, 'Pakistan's was an unsung story of heroism, taking in hundreds of thousands of refugees and bordering the world's greatest military power...if Pakistan was to stand as a bulwark against communism it would need still more help from the West.'[14] (Mrs Thatcher did not like Zia,[15] but her support for him was to bear fruit during the Falklands Campaign, when he refused to sell Exocet missiles to Argentina in spite of approaches by a European country which was supposedly an ally of the UK.) When President Reagan entered the White House in January 1981 there was a surge in support and especially in provision of military equipment, including F-16 aircraft, much to the vexation of India.[16] The CIA, according to Brigadier Mohammad Yousaf of the Afghan Cell in ISI, '...supported the Mujahideen by spending the American taxpayers' money, billions of dollars of it over the years, on buying arms, ammunition and equipment...A high proportion of CIA aid was in the form of cash. For every dollar supplied by the US, another was added by the Saudi Arabian government...'[17] Pakistan was full of dollars, international goodwill, spooks of all nations, and amazement that the world suddenly seemed to care about what was going on in their country and to its west.

* * *

The Pakistan Army had produced plans, years before, to take account of a threat from the west (other than the perennial one from the tribes). These involved positioning of artillery and armour units in the NWFP and Balochistan, and reinforcement from the Multan-based 'strike force'—even were there a concurrent threat from India—and creation of a corps HQ in Quetta, which was undertaken. If the Soviets crossed the border, the tactical plan was to hold the Khyber and Bolan passes and then strike into Afghanistan with special forces and ground attack aircraft. (There had been a request for provision of Crusader aircraft on Pakistan's wish-list for a long time but the US would not provide them. They had been part of the offer by President Ford as a quid pro quo for agreeing to cease nuclear weapons' development, but Carter withdrew the carrot).[18] The rest of the army would have time to deploy westwards and would be able to hold the advance. Enemy air attack in the passes would be suicidal at low level and ineffective from high altitude. Attempts at outflanking would be dealt with by ambush—just as they had been by the tribes in the days of the British. There was to be no reliance placed on foreign troops or aircraft. Pakistan would be on its own, and could handle matters nicely, provided it had the equipment. This time, of course, it could be assured that the supply of spare parts would not be cut off.

The Americans had a plan, too. US forces were to be involved, but it is not known from where and how quickly they would come, the closest troops other than Marines being in Germany. The Soviets were to be permitted to advance through the passes and to 'fan out' on the plains, where they would then be defeated by overwhelming US military might. It is not known whether the Pakistanis were officially informed of this.[19] It is doubtful if the DMO in the early 1980s would have paid much attention to such a scenario, other than, with characteristic politeness, to thank the Americans for such original thought. Zia thanked the Americans for their largesse and laughed up his sleeve about their change of policy. The defence forces of Pakistan increased in size, capability, and credibility. The mid-1980s saw a remarkable change in all three, but, all the same, one had reservations about the effectiveness of collective training and the quality of leadership. Statistics covering the decade show the difference in holdings:

YEAR	1979	1989
STRENGTH/EQUIPMENT/ ORDER OF BATTLE		
Army	400,000	450,000
Air Force	17,000	17,600
Navy	12,000	16,000
Army Corps HQ	3 plus 2 forming	7
Infantry Divisions	16	17 plus 1 eqvt. (North)
Armoured Divisions	2	2
Armoured Brigades	3	4
Infantry Brigades	3	8
Tanks	900	1,600
Artillery Pieces	1,000 (many obsolete)	1,200
Armoured Personnel Carriers	500	900
Advanced Combat Aircraft	–	39
Other Combat Aircraft	250	300
Surface-to-Air Missiles	1 battery	7 batteries

Sources: based on IISS, *The Military Balance*, amended by later information.

The Pakistan Military Academy increased its intake but had to lower its standards in quality of instructors and the educational standard of entrants. Expansion of the army meant much more than a mere increase in quantities of advanced weapons: it required more officers and soldiers, of course—but it demanded a commensurate improvement in technical skills, which depended on an education base Pakistan did not possess. The Education Corps was hard pressed to keep up with instruction in English, the language needed for understanding foreign manuals and for communication at higher levels. One of Zia's priorities was the use of Urdu as the national language. English was to be downgraded. Regional languages were to be acknowledged, but Urdu was to be paramount. Remonstration was useless so far as Zia was concerned. He was as happy in Urdu as he was in English and failed to grasp, or perhaps didn't want to grasp, the implication of the comment by Dr Abdul Qadeer Khan, the now-disgraced nuclear expert, who is said to have observed that there were few textbooks about nuclear technology written in Urdu. (One of Zia's doctors told the author that he mentioned that there weren't many medical books in Urdu, but Zia just grunted.) Higher education in Pakistan was set back considerably by the introduction of 'Urdu-medium' schools that emphasized religious instruction. It became noticeable in the 1990s that many cadets entering the Service academies required coaching in English (just as they do, unfortunately, in many western colleges and universities, such has been the deterioration in education standards.)

The army could not be directed properly with only a few Corps headquarters. There was a limit to how many divisions could be commanded by a single HQ or be under effective direct command from GHQ. Both wars had shown that arrangements were inadequate. Expansion would exacerbate difficulties if more headquarters were not raised. In the late 1970s this was begun, and the army gradually took the shape shown in Map 19. It was necessary to take account of the threat from the Soviets to the west, but planners realized that the defence of Karachi and the routes linking the industrial centres of Pakistan with its only port must be given greater priority than had hitherto obtained. The Indians had doubtless learned their lesson and, if there were another war, it could not be expected that the failure in 1971 of India's 11 and 12 Divisions to press their advantage would be repeated. In any event, India's Southern Command had been overhauled and was better organized to conduct offensive operations. It was not enough for Pakistan to have only an incomplete division to hold the southern sector. There had to be more troops and a higher HQ to command them and to act independently of GHQ if necessary. Tanks from the US and the workhorse Type 59s from China permitted the formation of more armoured regiments, and Pakistan complemented foreign weapons by giving emphasis to indigenous production of small arms under licence (such as the German G3 rifle) and manufacture of ammunition.

The influx of weapons had many effects on Pakistan, which had never been a country where the carrying of arms was unusual, especially in the Tribal Areas and North-West Frontier Province in general. Large stocks of small arms and other weapons were built up, with suitable quantities of ammunition, by many tribes and groups. The Afghan factions increased their armouries, with some weapons being used against the Soviets and the Kabul regime—but many being stockpiled for use against each other when the day came that the Soviets left Afghanistan and the real fight for control of the country would begin. The Al Zulfiqar organization obtained weapons, too, including an SA-7 shoulder-fired anti-aircraft missile which was used on 7 February 1982 against a Falcon aircraft just after take-off from Islamabad/Rawalpindi.[20] It was carrying Zia, who was unperturbed about the attempt on his life but disconcerted that a missile could be

MAP 19   **PAKISTAN
CORPS HEADQUARTERS**

launched so close to the airport. Some wild rumours flew round at the time, as Zia was loath to have the incident publicized yet ordered improvements in security which were implemented without explanation. More SA-7s were discovered later, including two in a private house in Lahore. Pakistan was becoming an ever more dangerous place, courtesy of western, Chinese, and Saudi support for the war against the Soviets in Afghanistan.

On 16 January 1983, the first three F-16s arrived in Pakistan, a symbol of US commitment to Pakistan, irrespective of the government in place. This support was a matter of concern not only to India but to the opposition political parties which had formed an alliance named the Movement for the Restoration of Democracy (MRD). They had hoped that the Zia regime would not receive so much backing, but reckoned without *realpolitik*. Zia was intent on retaining power for some years to come, but was also trying to come to terms with transforming martial law into a regime more akin to civilian rule. This was impossible, as Bhutto had discovered. It had to be one thing or the other. For Pakistan there was no middle way; no possibility of melding the civil infrastructure and the military ethos on the lines of Indonesia— to which Zia was drawn but realized was impracticable in Pakistan. So he tinkered with alternatives and announced a three-phase programme of elections: municipal in 1983; provincial the next year; and federal in March 1985. The problem was that the MRD was excluded from taking part as it was an illegal organization. Disturbances began in August, and anti-government rallies were held throughout the country resulting in several hundred deaths (official figure 61) and the imprisonment of thousands of demonstrators and political activists, mainly of the PPP, whose leader, Benazir Bhutto, called on the army to overthrow the President. This caused Zia, in a display of severity (and showing a lack of understanding of the country at large), to ban political activity by the PPP for a further ten years. But in spite of the violence encouraged by the PPP, there was considerable satisfaction with the Zia regime. Very many Pakistanis were enjoying prosperity such as they had never known before, much of it engendered by the spin-off from the Afghan war and the benefits accrued from Saudi approval of Zia's theocratic approach to government. Not only were there substantial subsidies with no strings attached, but Pakistani workers were employed in large numbers throughout the Kingdom, adding to an already increasing flow of cash from the extensive

Pakistani diaspora. There was also a Pakistan military presence in Saudi Arabia which grew to over two divisions, some 40,000 men.

So far as the US was concerned, Zia was in a similar position to Nixon's Yahya Khan. Deference and dignity were the keywords. He was being treated as a world figure, an important personage in international relations. George Shultz, a civilized man, recounts in his book *Turmoil and Triumph* that he met Zia in Delhi at the time of Indira Gandhi's funeral, then at Chernenko's in March 1985: '...the vice president and I visited President Zia...Chancellor Kohl...Prime Minister Thatcher...' At the funeral itself, 'I stood beside Zia and Yaqub Khan of Pakistan to show our unity in opposition to Soviet occupation of Afghanistan...' This would turn the head of most Third World rulers. It did not turn Zia's. He knew exactly the motivation of the US—and it certainly was not to support Pakistan because of sympathy for a developing nation. He had seen how American policy towards his country had changed over the years. He was grateful for the aid—and actually liked the style of many Americans—but knew it would end the moment the US ceased to be concerned about Russia's activities in the region.

The navy and air force faced more problems with the introduction of new systems than did the army. There were advanced detection devices fitted in the navy's surveillance aircraft and in the F-16s, whose radar was the most advanced in the world (and to whose provision the USAF objected but was overruled). The French Mirage Vs were equipped with Exocet missiles, and Harpoons were provided by the US. There had to be expansion of technician training and many were trained overseas, but even with this assistance there was strain placed on facilities and training systems.

India was worried about all this new technology. The fact that Soviet aircraft were violating Pakistan's territory was neither here nor there so far as India was concerned: New Delhi considered that additions to or improvement in Pakistan's military hardware presented an increased threat to India. And that point of view was reasonable. Although there was belligerence on the part of India (especially during Rajiv Gandhi's election campaign in late 1984), and while it was becoming an ever more close associate of the USSR, which was still perceived as the aggressor rather than an unwilling participant in the Afghan mêlée, it was apparent that Pakistan's *army* improvements were greater than could be justified by Soviet adventurism—although in 1986 the Soviets had some 250 combat aircraft and 140 attack helicopters in

Afghanistan.[21] There was an increase in army strength in Balochistan and some upgrading of capabilities in North-West Frontier Province, but most improvements were taking place in Punjab and Sindh, on the border with India. Little wonder India was worried—but it compounded its own fears by increasing its own military capabilities, which caused Pakistan and its Western backers to be even more suspicious about its intentions and those of its Soviet ally, for such the USSR was perceived to be.

In spite of Ms Bhutto's encouragement to rise up and depose Zia, the army remained loyal to the President (who was also commander-in-chief), although there were some problems. There had been arrests of several officers in January 1984 following a shooting incident in Lahore Cantonment, and the army was worried that her call to overthrow the regime might be heeded, especially by younger officers. In some cases it appeared that this was so. Several officers had heard they were to be arrested on 3 January and managed to leave the country, perhaps with the help of the Al Zulfiqar organization (which had contacts in Islamabad and Karachi airports, including some PIA staff), but others were detected and a few attempted to fight it out. All appear to have been junior officers, but they had received encouragement from some senior figures whose involvement could not be completely proved. Several officers were tried by court martial and served their sentences in Attock military prison. Others were encouraged to quit the service. Zia remained in power—threatened by PPP/MRD extremists; suspicious of some of his officers (especially in the air force); dubious as to how he should continue to govern the country; confused by the religious political parties' failing to give him the support he had expected would be forthcoming; wary of permitting political activity lest it get out of hand; and worried about the enormous number of Afghan refugees within the country. He had not lost his sense of humour, however. On one occasion he had to fly to Saudi Arabia at short notice to argue that the Pakistan Army contingent's Shia Muslims should be permitted to serve in the Kingdom.[22] The diplomatic corps were present to bid him farewell, as were the most senior officers, one of whom, to his surprise and not to his delight, had been appointed to act as Chief Martial Law Administrator in Zia's absence. Brigadier M. A. Durrani, Zia's senior aide, watched the aircraft take off and, as the wheels left the ground, turned to the acting CMLA and asked for orders. 'Ah,' said the officer, 'I've only got one: Prohibition is repealed at once.' Zia heard the story, of course, but, in spite of his anti-alcohol stance, laughed about it and never let it interfere with his dealings with the officer concerned (a close friend of the author).

Zia had a lot on his plate in the mid-1980s, including the Indian occupation of Siachen, in what had been regarded as Pakistan-controlled territory. Most cartographers had drawn the Line of Control as extending to the Karakoram Pass leading to China, and mountaineers wishing to attempt peaks further north went through Islamabad rather than Delhi to obtain clearance. This appeared to vex Mrs Gandhi.

As foreshadowed, an Indian force advanced from Ladakh to the northern end of the Siachen Glacier in the spring of 1984, there having been a lodgement the previous year. New Delhi could have made a reasonable case in international law for a claim on the region, but chose to use force rather than negotiation. Its agreement at Simla, 'That the two countries are resolved to settle their differences by peaceful means...,' was apparently annulled by contemporary considerations whose urgency and essentiality has never been satisfactorily explained.

India's claim was based on the fact that the Line of Control ended, as agreed by representatives of India and Pakistan, at Grid Reference NJ980420, there being no further delineation in any direction. India came to consider, eleven years after agreeing with Pakistan about the Line of Control, that because there was no formal accord governing the barren lands between the end of the Line and the Karakoram Pass, the area should belong to India. No attempt was made to enter the contiguous Aksai Chin area occupied by China.

Of some consequence in the Indian position—had it been decided to follow diplomacy rather than take military action—would have been the fact that Pakistan and China concluded an agreement on 2 March 1963 concerning demarcation of territory between Xinjiang Province and Pakistan-controlled Kashmir, a sensible arrangement to which India took exception at the time.[23] It could be argued with some reason that Pakistan and China had no right to apportion territory to each other (1,350 sq. m. to Pakistan; 2,050 to China) while some of it was, possibly, in dispute with a third party. A case could have been made for adjudication by the International Court of Justice, or even by an independent body of assessors, but India, since the decision of the tribunal concerning the Rann of Kutch in 1968, has resisted mediation or 'good offices' intended to defuse tension in the subcontinent. One Indian argument was that,

The strategic Tibet-Sinkiang road passes through territory captured by
China east of Siachen. Northwards we have the new road from Pakistan
going through the Khunjerab Pass. These form a noose round India's
jugular. If they took Siachen they would be holding a dagger to our backs
in the Nubra Valley.[24]

There is no point in examining this contention (by a general, alas), as
anyone knowing anything about the region would ridicule it.

The Siachen dispute continued, with many casualties on both
sides—most caused by respiratory ailments, frostbite, avalanches,
crevasses, and losing sense of direction in white-outs. 'We take Siachen
as a test case,' said one supporter of India's thrust. 'We want to assert
that the Indian strategic doctrine of the '80s goes way beyond the
docility of the '50s and '60s, that it is no longer possible to gnaw at
our far flung territories and then get away with no more than filibustry
at the United Nations...'[25] The cost to both countries has been
enormous in lives and money. Indian defence attachés around the world
were tasked to buy sleeping bags, high-altitude tents, boots, clothing,
and snow vehicles. Pakistan was more fortunate: it had much cold-
weather gear in store, and received more from friendly nations.
Instructors in mountain warfare came to Pakistan, and Pakistani officers
and soldiers went to the UK, the US, Germany, France, and Italy for
such training. Many countries regarded India's foray into the wastes as
ridiculous and, although there were few protests, made it clear that
Pakistan would receive assistance if requested.

The Pakistan army has a major advantage: its lines of communication
to Siachen are much shorter than India's. It does not require the
Sno-cats and other expensive equipment needed by India to supply its
troops along the glacier. India's expenses in maintaining its presence
in the north are immense. One intelligence estimate in the early 1990s
placed them at $100 million a year, as against one-tenth of that for
Pakistan. Pakistan has one brigade of three battalions, an artillery
regiment, and a company of SSG in the area, while Indian strength is
about twice that. The conditions in which the soldiers live (as witnessed
by the author on the Pakistani side, and there is no reason to believe
they differ on the Indian side) are the harshest in the world. There are
no soldiers, anywhere else, who undergo the privations of the men at
Siachen. At heights of over 20,000 feet the soldiers of both sides
display great tenacity and courage—over a dispute which the politicians
could settle in ten minutes.[26]

Zia was concerned about his soldiers in the north. The author was his guest in September 1985 and, during discussions, Zia expressed regret about the futility of operations in Siachen, but, he said, what else could be done other than to counter the Indian advance? What might come next? The move of the Indian army towards Skardu? What, he was asked, if an offer were made to India to have the Line of Control declared the international border? Would not that solve the whole Kashmir problem? No, Zia said. He had a political problem anyway with the Kashmiris and didn't want an uprising, as would surely happen if they thought he was dealing with India behind their backs.

This is one of the main difficulties. India's insistence on bilateralism excludes Kashmiris from discussion about their own future. In December 1985 Zia went to Delhi to talk with the new Indian prime minister, Rajiv Gandhi. They agreed that there should be a peaceful solution to the Siachen Glacier confrontation, but later meetings of defence secretaries ended in the usual inconclusive manner.

In 1985 Zia ended Martial Law. He had received a 98 per cent approval vote in a referendum (of very low turnout) on 19 December 1984 asking if the electorate approved Islamization of the state. This he interpreted as endorsement of his rule. The poll was undoubtedly rigged, but he went ahead in March the following year with elections, permitting no political parties as such to participate. All candidates were 'independents', but political parties were allowed to resume their functions in 1986. The Prime Minister, Mr Mohammad Khan Junejo, assumed leadership of the Pakistan Muslim League (PML), and in the same period the PPP of Benazir Bhutto began to conduct itself again as a normal political party (although it excluded itself voluntarily from the National Assembly). There was a move towards polity by Zia, but the military scene was giving cause for some concern.

Relations between India and Pakistan were poor in the mid-1980s. There were allegations by New Delhi that Pakistan was involved in an assassination attempt on Rajiv Gandhi by Karamjeet Singh, a Sikh; there were more clashes in Siachen, and neither Gandhi nor Zia appeared willing to compromise over the dispute; India, having exploded a nuclear device in 1974, criticized Pakistan for having a nuclear programme; Zia brought up the subject of Kashmir at a non-aligned conference in Harare, immediately after which Gandhi criticized Pakistan's counter-terrorist assault on a hijacked aircraft at Karachi airport. Neither country was behaving well.

Outside influences contributed, too, to distrust: the US arranged a further aid package for Pakistan in March 1986, for $4.02 billion. Mr Gorbachev visited India in November and had the pleasure of hearing Rajiv Gandhi criticize the US for assisting Pakistan. This did not appear to cause Pakistan much concern but annoyed the US which, in turn, criticized the Soviet Union for not making genuine efforts to quit Afghanistan, which it was trying to do without losing face.[27] Altogether the subcontinent was in a mess and did not need another drama, especially one that might seem to be over-played by some domestic and foreign observers.

In the second half of 1986 the Indian Army began a major exercise, *Brass Tacks*, which has been the subject of intriguing comment concerning Indian intentions and Pakistani reaction. Curiously, *The Economist* did not cover the matter in spite of having both a 'Survey' of Pakistan and a cover-piece on India in January 1987. The *Far Eastern Economic Review* first mentioned the exercise on 12 February in the context of a meeting between foreign secretaries in Delhi earlier that month that was aimed—and successful—at easing tension. It appears that the whole affair was given rather more attention than was warranted, but it was and remains difficult to sort truth from unsubstantiated allegations.

Both sides over-reacted; their media, including government-controlled radio, was often irresponsible;[28] and both sides told lies. Pakistan was not given official notification before the exercise began, although the *Pakistan Times* carried a report on 14 November that, 'The major manoeuvres of the Indian armed forces will last four months, an unusually long time.' The Indian defence ministry would neither confirm nor deny, on 11 November, that an exercise was scheduled, as reported by AFP and other agencies. Next day New Delhi 'categorically denied reports that India has massed troops on its western borders for major manoeuvres,'[29] which, as events showed, was patently untrue. According to *India Today*, a critic of Delhi's handling of *Brass Tacks*, Rajiv Gandhi forbade telephone contact between the two Directors-General of Military Operations which, if correct, was a lamentable way for him to behave.[30] When it became apparent that Indian troops were indeed massed for large-scale manoeuvres, the Pakistan government—Zia and his prime minister—at first reacted cautiously, but, in response to the unscheduled move of more troops in India's western sectors, later sent forces to the border area. The affair is perhaps best summed up by the International Institute for Strategic Studies' *Strategic Survey*

1987–88, which noted briefly and pithily that the two countries 'demonstrated that their mutual antipathy could be contained when they backed away from a major build-up of forces on their border which was the result of poor communications and some posturing on both sides'. A storm in a teacup? Not quite. Although the antipathy was 'contained', there remained grave distrust. Zia was as placatory as he could be in February when he said that the agreement to end tension along the border was 'proof of the wisdom of the Prime Ministers of the two countries,' which he may or may not have believed but was a generous public statement.[31]

Zia scored a propaganda success by visiting Jaipur in February for a Pakistan-India cricket match at which Gandhi had to meet him. Zia was no cricket fan, but used the opportunity to score runs which annoyed Gandhi but placed him in a position in which he might appear churlish if he objected to the approach. Zia was demonstrating that he was not concerned about India's military manoeuvres, but might not have been so sanguine had he known of India's plans. A week later, Gandhi's budget increased military spending by 43 per cent to about $10 bn a year. This, given friendship prices and other arrangements for Soviet equipment (the first Kilo Class submarine had just arrived), did not reflect true military expenditure. Pakistan's defence budget was artificial, too, because of aid and other subventions. It is impossible to calculate the real expenditure of either country during the cold war years; only since the early 1990s can reasonably accurate, unclassified estimates be made, and these, of course, do not take into account nuclear programmes.

The Indian government enjoyed irritating Pakistan (and the US) about the situation in Afghanistan. The external affairs minister, N.D. Tiwari, visited Kabul in early May 1987 for the seventh session of the Indo-Afghan Joint Commission and held a press conference. Pakistan, he said, was obtaining weapons 'clearly designed for use against India' and not against the Soviet Union or 'any hypothetical threat from Afghanistan'. There have been many outrageous statements made by representatives of both governments over the years, but this minister deliberately tried to undermine what consensus had been obtained during discussions about troop withdrawal from Afghanistan by stating that, 'Pakistan has not shown the degree of flexibility that was expected of it at the proximity talks,' on which record the signatures were barely dry. This was bumbling stuff, and it is hardly surprising that the US Administration was exasperated with such meddling and continued assistance to Pakistan in spite of knowing full well about its nuclear programme. US concerns rose in June, when India sent fighter aircraft to escort its An-32 transports that violated Sri Lankan airspace to drop supplies to rebel Tamils in Jaffna—and threatened to shoot down opposing aircraft. The *Guardian*'s Derek Brown, who travelled in one of the transports, wrote that he flew 'through Sri Lankan airspace where we have no right at all to be,' and that, '...the mission is a spectacular success. Not as a relief operation, for 22½ tonnes of supplies won't feed...many people, but rather as a message to Colombo that it can no longer defy the regional superpower.'

Pakistan, too, got the message, as did other regional countries and several further afield: India's fast-growing military capabilities seemed to be intended for power projection.

India was 'invited' by the government in Colombo to send troops to Sri Lanka to intervene in the campaign against Tamil terrorists. The Indian Peace-Keeping Force (IPKF) was disorganized, poorly-trained, and unprepared to fight the guerrilla war in which it became involved. In spite of much bravery by individuals, the IPKF—the cream of the Indian Army, eventually over fifty thousand of them—suffered terrible casualties, including some 1,500 killed. They withdrew in 1990.

GHQ Rawalpindi was aware of Indian problems of poor leadership, bad planning, almost no training in counter-revolutionary warfare, and a 'very peculiar, off-beat command and control structure,' as they were of Indian tactics being 'predetermined, strait-jacketed, predictable and reactive'.[32] But that was in Sri Lanka. Would the Indians display similar incompetence on the plains of Punjab and Sindh where their tanks, outnumbering Pakistan's in 1988 by about 2:1, with massive close air support, might swamp Pakistan's defences? It was time to construct better plans for the defence of Pakistan. But who would put forward such plans? The new Vice-Chief in 1987, a small, rather unsmiling (enigmatic, some thought), and energetic man called Aslam Beg might be the fellow to do this, thought the bright young officers.[33]

* * *

Prime Minister Junejo was trying to interfere in the army's internal affairs, which its chief, the President, could not permit. Amongst other things, Junejo insisted on the removal of General Akhtar Abdul Rehman as Director-General of Inter Services Intelligence and questioned the promotion of two officers to be corps commanders

(Pir Dad Khan and Shamim Alam Khan, both admirable officers). Zia considered that Mr Junejo, nice fellow as he was, was becoming too big for his boots and dismissed him, with his Cabinet, on 29 May 1988, on the grounds that:

> Whereas the objects and the purposes for which the National Assembly was elected have not been fulfilled
> And whereas the law and order in the country have broken down to an alarming extent resulting in tragic loss of innumerable [sic] valuable lives as well as loss of property
> And whereas the life property honour and security of the citizens of Pakistan have been rendered totally unsafe and the integrity and ideology of Pakistan have been seriously endangered
> And whereas public morality has deteriorated to a serious level
> And whereas in my opinion a situation has arisen in which the Government of the federation cannot be carried on in accordance with the provision [sic] of the Constitution and an appeal to the electorate is necessary
> Now therefore I, General Mohammad Zia-ul-Haq, President of Pakistan in exercise of the powers conferred on me by Clause (2)(b) of Article 58 of the Constitution of the Islamic Republic of Pakistan hereby dissolve the National Assembly with immediate effect and in consequence thereof the Cabinet also stands dissolved forthwith.[34]

Zia's speech to the nation in Urdu on 30 May was poor.[35] 'Life,' he said, 'continues normally. There is no ban on political parties or political activities. The press is free, as usual... The only difference is that the National Assembly and all four Provincial Assemblies and Federal and Provincial cabinets have been dissolved...' He reminded listeners that in 1977 his 'sole purpose was to hold free and fair elections'—without mentioning the ninety-day caveat—and went on to emphasize that an Islamic form of governance was paramount and that the Junejo government's 'greatest crime was that the enforcement of Islam was put aside'. He was floundering. His speech was full of inconsistencies.

Benazir Bhutto tried to bring her supporters into the streets to show popular condemnation of the government. Only a few thousand people demonstrated against Zia, but there was a groundswell of opinion against the President, even if it was not necessarily in support of the PPP. He was becoming unpopular, and the army was restive. His death on 17 August 1988 caused little mourning.[36]

NOTES

1. Letter from the Cabinet Secretary, Waqar Ahmad, of 19 December 1974, quoted in Wolpert (1993).
2. General Arif had been told to write the speech but found it difficult to find 'populist phrases', and was in any case writing in English, so Salik was brought in to write it in Urdu, which he did very well. *See*, Arif op. cit.
3. Discussion with colleague of Zia, April 1988.
4. R. Khan op. cit.
5. Discussions with many officers serving at the time.
6. Arif op. cit.
7. *Introduction* by Makhdoom Ali Khan (also editor) to *The Constitution of the Islamic Republic of Pakistan 1973*, Karachi, Pakistan Law House, 1986 (1990 edition).
8. Amended 1973 Constitution, Part XII, Chapter 2, Article 243 (1) and (1A).
9. *Islam*, Caesar E. Farah, New York, Barron, 1970.
10. On 4 January. The amount—$400 million—was deemed 'peanuts' by Zia and was increased to over 3 billion in 1981.
11. *See*, Martin Walker, *The Cold War*, London, Fourth Estate, 1993.
12. 'Al Zulfiqar' was an amateur terrorist organization formed by Bhutto's sons. *See*, Anwar (1998) for a description of this extraordinary organization.
13. The final exercise in 1982, the storming of a PIA aircraft parked on the PAF side of Islamabad airport, went well. The SAS officer and the British Defence Adviser then went to Army House to be congratulated by Zia.
14. Margaret Thatcher, *The Downing Street Years*, London, HarperCollins, 1993.
15. Letter from senior Foreign Office official, February 1988.
16. It is often claimed that India's acquisition of Mirage 2000 aircraft from France was caused by the provision of F-16s to Pakistan. In a way this is correct: the F-16 agreement was signed in December 1981, but the Mirage negotiations had been under way for over a year before this—although the final signature was not applied until January 1982.
17. Brigadier Mohammad Yousaf and Mark Adkin, *The Bear Trap*, Lahore, Jang Publishers, 1992.
18. Dennis Kux, *The United States and Pakistan 1947-2000*.
19. The author learned of this in the US in 1993.
20. There had been an attempt in the previous month. Both tries failed because the firers were poorly trained. See Anwar (1998).
21. *Strategic Studies*, Islamabad, Winter 1986. The Institute had excellent sources.
22. He lost, and withdrew almost the entire force—a principled action.
23. *See*, *Sino-Pakistan 'Agreement' March 2, 1963, Some Facts*, Ministry of External Affairs, Government of India, 16 March 1963.
24. *India Today*, New Delhi, 31 July 1985.
25. Ibid.
26. I am grateful to Usman Shabbir for drawing my attention to *Fangs of Ice* by Lt.-Col. Ishfaq Ali, which gives details of engagements in Siachen.
27. See Diego Cordovez and Selig Harrison, *Out of Afghanistan*, OUP, 1995. Myra Macdonald of Reuters is writing (march 2005) a definitive book on Siachen which will cover all aspects of this tragic and senseless adventure.

28. *The Washington Post* was not blameless in the period. It carried a story on 3 November, quoting an alleged intelligence report, that Pakistan had 'tested the bomb' between 18 and 21 September.

29. BBC *Summary of World Broadcasts*, 12 November 1986 (henceforth *SWB*).

30. *India Today,* 15 and 29 February 1987. The edition of 15 February is remarkable for its estimate that, 'The Cost of a Day's Fighting,' excluding deaths and injuries, would be 'around Rs 4,700 crore [about $3.4 bn at the then rate of exchange], a horrendous expense that neither side can realistically afford'. It also noted that there 'are now no outstanding international issues over which the two countries could be propelled into a war'. *India Today* was a sensible magazine and robust about Indian policies as well as being forthright concerning Pakistan. Unfortunately it has now become more of a Bollywood Gazette.

31. Karachi Home Service, 7 February 1987; *SWB*.

32. Lt.-Gen. S.C. Sardeshpande, *Assignment Jaffna*, Lancer, New Delhi, 1992. A summation of Indian army capabilities by an honourable and most capable officer.

33. Base on conversations with many of them in following years.

34. *The Pakistan Times*, 20 May 1988.

35. SWB, 2 June 1988.

36. In the original editions of this book this chapter ended with the words 'but he left his country in better shape than he had found it eleven years before.' The distinguished academic, Dr Ian Talbot, told me I was talking rubbish. He was quite right, so I have omitted it from this edition and, after more research, altered some observations on Zia in the text.

12 Democracy Again

In 1988 the US was trying to sell M-1 Abrams tanks to Pakistan. Production tanks were provided for trials and evaluation (which did not go well). Zia wanted to attend a demonstration of the Abrams at the Bahawalpur field firing range and flew there on the morning of 17 August in a PAF C-130 transport, callsign Pak One. The US ambassador, Arnold Raphel, and his senior military sales officer, Brig.-Gen. Herbert Wassom, were present, as were some twenty Pakistan Army officers who were to fly back to Rawalpindi in Pak One with Zia. The aircraft left Bahawalpur runway at 1546, carrying, in a late arrangement, Raphel and Wassom. The aircraft crashed, killing all on board. The US/Pakistan Inquiry determined that there had been sabotage. There is no point in attempting to theorize about what occurred.[1] The Vice-Chief, General Aslam Beg, in another aircraft which had taken off at about the same time, flew on to Rawalpindi and, after consultation and deliberation, announced that the days of military dominance were over. This was a historic decision, and a wise one on his part. The Chairman of the Senate, Ghulam Ishaq Khan, was appointed President, as provided for by the Constitution. A caretaker National Emergency Council was formed, and elections were scheduled for November.

The Pakistan People's Party, although well-organized to conduct electioneering, did not win an outright majority in spite of the split in the Pakistan Muslim League (which must have had a death wish to indulge in internal quarrels at such a time). Benazir Bhutto became prime minister following the elections. There was hope throughout the land that, this time, there would be a new dawn for Pakistan. Not only had the armed forces left the scene of governance (and were happy to do so), but the politicians had surely learned their lesson and would not behave irresponsibly and fall again to the temptations of deceit and corruption. It was thought that ministerial selection would be on merit, and that there would be no attempt to politicize the Civil Service. The atmosphere in Islamabad, amongst the educated classes at least, was euphoric. When a PTV female announcer appeared on the screen to read the news without her head-scarf there were telephone calls all round the capital. It seemed there might be relaxation of Islamic laws and practices, especially as the religious parties had not done well in the elections.[2]

Unfortunately, the PPP did not meet the expectations of most people. President Ghulam Ishaq Khan dismissed it on 6 August 1990. There is little doubt that the leaders of the armed forces were involved concerning the President's action, which was lawful under the Constitution even if it was not in the spirit of the times. The government had had many problems, not the least of which was the Senate, which had been appointed during Zia's time and was opposed to the PPP. Ms Bhutto concentrated her energy on preserving her narrow majority in the National Assembly, and the long-awaited reforms were not introduced. There was no legislation of any importance passed, and the country's economic and social problems worsened to an alarming extent.

One of the problems was the situation in Sindh Province. The *Guardian* (UK) reported on 16 July 1990 that some 3,000 people had been killed in communal violence in Sindh since 1985, mainly involving *mohajirs*—settlers from India at Partition-time—and Sindhis. The PPP ran the Province and was in direct confrontation with the Mohajir Qaumi Movement (MQM). On 10 February 1990, an incident occurred which perhaps encapsulates the bizarre situation. Armed activists of the PPP and MQM had each kidnapped about a dozen of the other's supporters. In the office of commander V Corps in Karachi, the leaders of the parties arranged an exchange of twenty-seven hostages.[3] The significance is twofold. First, that leaders of political parties were involved in patently illegal affairs; second, that the army was being drawn into civil matters once again.

The army had enough to worry about concerning increasingly bellicose statements from New Delhi, which had become concerned about the insurrection in Indian-administered Kashmir that began in 1989. The Kashmiris, indignant about years of Congress (I) Party ballot-fixing, lack of political representation, and the arrogance with which they were governed, had finally had enough. India immediately accused Pakistan of involvement. The 'foreign hand' was once again blamed for India's ills; but it was nonetheless serious, for all the Indian posturing, and tension was high along the Line of Control. Cease-fire violations increased, and there were incidents of firing on 'Azad' Kashmiri demonstrators by Indian soldiers. Both countries sent reinforcements to the Line and the international border. Pakistan was certainly not involved in the insurrection to begin with, but there is no doubt there was later and very deep dabbling when the indigenous rebellion was hijacked by jihadi militants whose motive was not so much freedom for Kashmiris as establishment of fundamental Islamic rule throughout all Kashmir.

The army was also concerned about two figures close to the Prime Minister: her special assistant, former Maj.-Gen. Nasirullah Babar,[4] a close confidant of Z.A. Bhutto, and the adviser on defence, former Maj.-Gen. Imtiaz Ali, who had been Z.A. Bhutto's military secretary, with neither of whom was there an easy relationship. (Babar considered Beg 'a coward'.) Accusations were made that the army chain of command was being bypassed and that decisions were being taken on defence procurement matters without consultation with GHQ.[5] The chain of command is sacrosanct in any armed force. If it is ignored, there is a danger that orders will not be carried out. If it is bypassed by what is perceived to be a legal authority, it places subordinates in a difficult position: whom are they to obey if they receive conflicting orders?— their superior officers or the political associates of a government? Meddling with the military chain of command is a dangerous thing for politicians to do. It creates confusion and resentment. An intriguing development was that on 24 May, Ms Bhutto dismissed the Director-General Inter Services Intelligence, Lt.-Gen. Hamid Gul, and replaced him with Lt.-Gen. (retd.) Shamsur Rehman Kallue. Gul was appointed commander II Corps at Multan. He was a hawk concerning Afghanistan, and his support for the more fundamentalist political groups did not meet with the approval of some members of the PPP (or with many other people, for that matter); but the manner of his going—although completely lawful, as ISI was a discrete government body—did not give the army confidence that the government wished to refrain from interference in military affairs as much as the army wished to stay out of politics.

In mid-1990 the PPP government appeared to be rudderless. This was regrettable, although hardly cause for its dismissal, but the President gave detailed reasons including allegations of 'persistent and scandalous 'horse-trading' for political gain', breakdown of law and order in Sindh, corruption and nepotism, and use of statutory corporations, authorities, and banks for political ends and personal gain. A state of emergency was declared and a caretaker administration under Mr Ghulam Mustafa Jatoi was appointed. It governed until elections were held in October, when the Islami Jamhoori Ittehad (IJI)[6] an alliance of parties led by Nawaz Sharif obtained 105 seats, Benazir Bhutto's People's Democratic Alliance 45, and the MQM 15 (all in Sindh). The election was conducted fairly.[7] It seemed that the new government, with a large majority, might be able to concentrate on domestic reforms and urgent foreign policy affairs that demanded its immediate attention.

* * *

Ms Bhutto blamed the army for her dismissal from power. At a press conference on 8 August 1990, she stated that, 'military intelligence forced the President to make this decision,' and that the army had, 'from the first day [of her government],' planned a conspiracy against her. She asked why, if there was no military involvement, the army had seized records of the Intelligence Bureau (the civilian counter-intelligence organization) and why troops had been posted at radio and television stations.[8] 'Within two to three weeks they'll roll back and it will be proper martial law.'[9] These were grave allegations and deeply resented by many in the armed services who considered that strain had been placed on their loyalty by the activities of some people in or associated with government in the recent past. There had been disagreements between the prime minister and the President (in his capacity as commander-in-chief) and, in spite of efforts to stay outside politics, the army considered it should take a stand. Whether this was justified or not, is another matter.

In August 1989, Ms Bhutto had sought to appoint a new Chairman of the Joint Chiefs of Staff Committee in place of Admiral Iftikhar Sirohey, who had succeeded to the position in November 1988. It seemed clear from the usual interpretation of tenure that he would serve until November 1991, when he would retire after his three-year tour. In any case it was the prerogative of the President to appoint a new Chairman.[10] On 8 August, Begum Nusrat Bhutto, mother of Benazir, told a reporter that the Admiral had 'completed his three years' and stated that her daughter was attending a meeting concerning 'the security of our country and democracy,' a remark, according to one newspaper, 'which only added to the impression of a crisis being played out behind the scenes'.[11] The prime minister had chosen to interpret the three-year tour as being from the date of Sirohey's promotion on 14 August 1986, when he took over as Chief of Naval Staff. If implemented, such a procedure could be awkward, as an officer appointed to one of the senior positions might already have held four-star rank (general, admiral, or air chief marshal) for some time before assuming his new position, and it was reasonable to expect him to carry out a full tour in the new job. But it seemed there might be another factor.

General Aslam Beg had been a four-star general since 1987 but COAS only since 1988. If the government was successful in restricting Sirohey's term, would it then insist that Beg retired in March 1990 instead of August 1991, citing curtailment of the Chairman's tour as a precedent? There were rumours that Ms Bhutto wished to side-line Beg to be Chairman (a non-executive post) and replace him by Lt.-Gen. Ahmed Kamal Khan, the Deputy Chief, because of his perceived loyalty to the PPP. This was sensitive stuff.

In the end the prime minister had to back down. The President handled the affair gracefully (although, as the perceptive journalist Mushahid Hussain pointed out, he had been in favour of Junejo's position concerning military appointments in 1987—which contretemps with Zia contributed to Junejo's dismissal) and the matter came to a close. It petered out rather than ending on a conclusive note of agreement by the President and the prime minister, but it was evident that the government had failed in its attempt to control military appointments, and the armed forces and the PPP were wary of each other from that time on. The President resented the attempt to encroach on his authority and prerogatives (as he saw them) and bided his time.

* * *

The armies of Pakistan and India still faced each other in Siachen. Casualties in the icy wastes mounted as the years went by. There was no possibility of a military solution. Neither side could advance beyond the areas they held. There was stalemate—until mid-1989, when a breakthrough took place. Or seemed to take place. An excited journalist (well, as excited as that phlegmatic race can be) contacted the author on 17 June and said he had just sent a piece to the effect that the Indian and Pakistani foreign secretaries (respectively Mr S. K. Singh and Mr Humayun Khan) had agreed that troops would be withdrawn to the positions occupied at the time of the Simla Accord. The journalist said it was a final agreement that was, obviously, authorized by the two governments and only needed the armies to implement it forthwith. A major occurrence in the subcontinent, he said; at last an indication that the countries seemed to be serious about *rapprochement* and working for peace; there might even be a new era of trust and co-operation. (He was quite enthusiastic, for a journalist.)

The BBC reported that the foreign secretaries

> had been meeting for two days and their discussions set the seal on the earlier meetings...between the defence secretaries. At a joint news conference Mr Khan announced that both sides have now decided to withdraw to the positions that they held at the time of the Simla Accord.

A corresponding report was broadcast in Urdu on government-controlled All India Radio.[12] It seemed, even to the most sceptical observers in Islamabad and New Delhi, that, at long last, senior representatives of the countries were not only sitting down and talking about matters of substance, they were actually authorized to take decisions that would smooth the way for further confidence-building measures. Wrong.

A 'clarification' was issued by the Indian Ministry of External Affairs. The 'chronology of events', said a spokesman, had been 'muddled and confused'. He went on to state that, 'The Indian foreign secretary had endorsed the Pakistani foreign secretary's observations on their talks, whereas the report has made out as if he had endorsed the Pakistan foreign secretary's remarks on the defence secretaries' talks.'[13] Which statement was, of course, not muddled or confusing. The Indian government denied 'that Pakistan and India had reached an agreement on this [Siachen] issue'. The foreign correspondents in

Islamabad shrugged their collective shoulders. 'What,' asked one of them, rhetorically, 'can you expect of a bunch of people like that?'*

If there has been one occasion, a single identifiable point, a precise moment in the history of the subcontinent at which India and Pakistan might have been placed on the road to establishment of reasonable relations, it was that day in June 1989. An agreement such as the one that was reached and then denied would have saved hundreds of soldiers' lives and cost nothing in national pride. The strategic positions of the countries would not have altered one jot. The accord would have proved to the world that bilateralism actually worked (a real winner for Indian objectives concerning Kashmir), and terminated an unjustifiable drain on national budgets (India's much more than Pakistan's). But New Delhi blew it.

* * *

The Doctrine of 'The Riposte'

> If a war is thrust on us then the broad strategy we are going to follow is that, while defending all territories of Pakistan, including Kashmir, the Pakistan Army plans to launch a sizeable offensive, thus carrying the war into Indian territory.
>
> General Aslam Beg, 13 September 1989[14]

The author attended exercise *Zarb-i-Momin* (the Believer's Blow) from 17 to 20 December 1989. There were several foreign observers, some of whom saw more of the exercise than others, and the consensus was that the Pakistan Army could fight a conventional war against India for several weeks, and stood a reasonable chance of carrying war into Indian territory but for one thing: insufficient attention to the enemy air threat. There was not enough PAF participation at all levels.

Battle procedures were effective much of the time but on occasions were poor. This gave the observers some confidence in what they were witnessing, in that, of course, real exercises generally have almost as many snafus as real battles. An exercise that goes exactly to plan is not without its uses—but mistakes show what commanders and staffs at all levels are made of, when they have to sort things out quickly. There is nothing like pressure for revealing proneness to panic. In *Zarb-i-*

---

* He did not say 'people'.

Momin there were some nonsenses, one caused by elements of the 'enemy' armour becoming over-enthusiastic and advancing to overcome positions that should have remained inviolate until the following day. The exercise was, after all, they thought, the first trial of *Riposte*—the quick and devastating thrust into enemy territory—why not press on? This was the greatest fun for the visiting generals, many of whom had been in similar circumstances, and resulted in later exchanges of confidences about how poorly written exercises were these days, and how they (the Pakistani commanders and observing generals), would have dealt with things had they (the planners) been better organized. A telling comment was made by one visitor after we had bumped around in four-wheel drive vehicles for three hours without seeing an 'incident' of note (other than a fire caused by an unfortunate cavalry subaltern who was, apparently, trying to dry out his bedding). 'This,' he said, 'demonstrates the emptiness of the battlefield.'[15] To see this emptiness was of considerable value to commanders and staffs—and to participants at more humble levels. It is not often an exercise can give the 'feel' of the battlefield and show that engagements are rarely fought concurrently all over the area of operations.

Planning for the exercise began soon after Beg took over as COAS, and care was taken to notify India several months before it started. Maps were provided that included directions of advance and withdrawal—north-south—lest there be any misconstruction placed on Pakistan's putting over 200,000 troops in the field. *Zarb-i-Momin* was a very large exercise. It was perhaps too big, too extensive in its objectives, to be valuable in all aspects of tactics, and many soldiers were bored for long periods. This was realistic, but the troops were out of barracks for too long. But it had value in many other ways. It showed that the Pakistan Army was now out of the business of martial law, once and for all, and could concentrate on training. It gave the message to India that enormous numbers of troops could be moved quickly and with 'notional' ammunition (represented by sand-filled ammunition boxes), rather than causing alarm by moving real ammunition (which would deteriorate, anyway, due to handling and exposure to climate, as the Indians experienced during *Brass Tacks*). It was a good exercise whose main results, following analysis by GHQ and input from elsewhere, included improvement in armour tactics, better passage of intelligence, enhanced co-operation with the PAF, creation of Air Defence Command, and introduction of higher-level co-ordination of artillery.

Thus far in his term as Chief of Army Staff, General Aslam Beg had proved to his army and to outsiders that there was some original thought in GHQ, an organization that had been singularly lacking in vision for some years. But the COAS had some other ideas that did not sit quite so comfortably with the government or with some other countries. These included the concept of 'Strategic Defiance'.

* * *

General Beg spoke to the Press frequently and did not appear to realize that he was not always reported accurately and that on occasions he went further than he should. Sometimes his statements irritated the government. Had some of them been made by his counterparts in the US or the UK (for example), they would have swiftly become his former counterparts.

On 2 December 1990, exactly four months after Iraq invaded Kuwait, Beg gave a talk at the Pakistan Ordnance Factories' annual seminar at Wah Cantonment near Islamabad. Those present prepared themselves for the usual comments about how efficient Pakistan defence industries had become, and other mandatory platitudes. They sat up when he began speaking about the Gulf, and even more interest was displayed when he mentioned Iraq in terms of approbation in relation to defiance of 'the mightiest of the mighty'. He also said words to the effect that the audience should not mention what he had said once they got outside the auditorium—fat chance of that, especially as there were reporters and defence attachés present. Later, the office of Inter Services Public Relations was swamped by telephone calls from reporters, diplomats, defence attachés (and even, it was said, staff officers from GHQ), asking for copies of the speech. There wasn't one, said the harassed voice at the other end of the telephone. Why? Well, because there isn't. And it seems there wasn't. The Chief of the Army Staff appeared to have been speaking off the cuff. A version of his speech was produced[16] but nobody had a definitive copy. Outside the hall, when asked by reporters why the US was discriminating against Pakistan concerning aid (which the Bush administration had cut off in October), he said, 'I think I have spoken enough,'[17] which indeed he had.

A leader in *The Muslim* on 4 December was encouraging about the General's speech:

...his extempore remarks at a seminar in Wah Cantonment on Sunday with
reference to the current Gulf crisis represent a forceful and highly significant
reminder of the premium the Chief of the Pakistan army continues to place
on strengthening collective defences of regional Muslim countries....

Well, yes; he had gone on record almost two years before with the
notion that regional Islamic nations should present a united front of
some sort, and had named Iran and Turkey (and, optimistically, a
peaceful Afghanistan) as possible partners in a security arrangement.
Pakistan is narrow, east to west, and Beg had some idea of using Iran
as 'strategic depth', which was a woolly concept and unlikely to attract
much support in Teheran. And he wooed Iran assiduously. 'Iran,' he
said on 13 September 1989, 'has gone through a revolution and after
great sacrifices has emerged stronger in spite of the fact that many
countries of the world joined hands to destroy the revolution.' Iran was
ambivalent about strategic consensus, in spite of being willing to accept
whatever assistance Pakistan could offer in provision of defence
equipment and training (and wishing to exercise influence concerning
the rights and treatment of Pakistan's Shia minority). Beg may have
believed that some senior Iranians approved of his enthusiastic
proposals. The Chairman of the Joint Chiefs, Brig.-Gen. Shahbazi, said
that Iran 'would appreciate such co-operation amongst the Muslim
countries,' and the Revolutionary Guards' minister, Ali Shamkhani, said
that Iran and Pakistan 'will form an important part of the Islamic
defence line in the region,' neither of which statements meant anything
definitive to anyone versed in international relations, which Beg was
not. Neither was Turkey enthusiastic. As a secular nation drawing
closer (it hoped) to Europe than to poor eastern countries that had little
to offer it, it distanced itself from Beg's proposal. This was no CENTO,
with US approval and all the backing that went with that dubious
accolade. Beg's ideas had little support within Pakistan, either, although
some half-baked ideologists seized on his apparent fervour for Islamic
solidarity to push their own theocratic barrow. No; 'Strategic Defiance'
was not born out of 'strategic consensus', as it was known in some
circles. It was a new concept and, given the manner in which it was
presented, apparently not well thought-through.

The Muslim sounded a note of caution—although that was not what
the writer of its editorial intended in the penultimate sentence: 'It is
striking that, though apparently in agreement with this [Beg's]
approach, the political government of the day has not so far come out

with such a clear statement of national policy....' Wow. The *political* government. Was there another one? Three days later *Dawn* commented, 'That the Chief of Army Staff chose to announce the policy, which in a civilian democratic set-up should normally have been the prerogative of the prime minister, is...understandable. After all, Mian Nawaz Sharif does not mind keeping a low profile.' This was becoming dangerous. There was no one in authority in Pakistan who appeared to disapprove of this alteration in the nation's defence policy—or, if there was, they were not able or willing to speak out against it. Further, and of greater importance, it is not 'understandable' that policy should be notified by a general, no matter how eminent. It is the responsibility of government and *no one else* to do so. Beg was quite wrong to make the announcement. Even had the policy been agreed with government and the President (still the supreme commander of the armed forces), it was not for the COAS or anyone in uniform to announce it to the world at a technical seminar, however prestigious.

But what did the concept, possibly the new defence policy of Pakistan, actually mean? It had a challenging ring about it, certainly. Strategic Defiance—'Come the three corners of the world in arms, And we shall shock them....'[18] Stirring; nationalistic; even xenophobic... Was it self-reliance? If so, this was dreamtime. There was no possibility that Pakistan could become self-reliant in all or even most aspects of defence production. Well, then, was it based on refusal to accept assistance from larger powers—specifically the US, which had in any case curtailed its aid on the grounds that it believed Pakistan to be a nuclear weapons' state, like Israel and India? Not much point in that: it was only from more sophisticated industrial economies that advanced weapons systems could be obtained, and the armed forces badly needed such equipment. It was difficult to pin down, this doctrine, unless it was—but surely not?—a catch-phrase looking for a policy?

Beg said, 'We do not say no to friendly offers of assistance but that does not mean we can be dictated terms which I believe are not in the best interests of the country.' Referring to the 1965 and 1971 wars, he pointed out that US military aid had been suspended and 'we were left high and dry but we managed to live and the aid cut-off did not affect us'. This is simply not correct. The cut-off had a severe effect on the country's war-fighting capabilities and would have been critical had cease-fire arrangements not come into force. What was Beg trying to illustrate by this assertion?

The Nation was in a reflective mood by 4 December.

While one should stand by everything that is being said about not allowing the nation's sovereignty to be compromised, the question is whether the acceptance of aid, or loans to be exact, really compromises our sovereignty? It has not, so far. Again, since a US aid negotiations team is expected to be here soon, wouldn't it be better to wait and see if any demand against our national interests is made?

The editorial went on to question the right of the COAS to pronounce on foreign policy, and indicated that his 'view on the Gulf conflict could be at variance with our declared position on Iraq. It would have been better if all organs of the state were to be seen to speak with one voice, if all of them have to speak on national issues.' The responsible Press of Pakistan had engaged gear. But it made no difference. 'Strategic defiance' was the jargon of the moment—whatever it meant—and the country's policy was not to become engaged in the Gulf War, for which the build-up in the Arabian Peninsula had almost ended.

It should have been worrying for Pakistan that in December the US Assistant Secretary of Defence for International Security, Henry Rowan, and a large delegation visited New Delhi to discuss ways of improving defence co-operation, but it seemed that neither Beg nor the government was perturbed about this development, or about others of considerable international significance.

The Cold War had ended. On the day that Beg delivered his speech at Wah, Presidents Bush and Gorbachev, meeting in the port of Marsaxlokk, declared its demise. Pakistan's value to the US as a counter to what had been perceived as Soviet expansion in Afghanistan had disappeared, and the end of the Cold War meant that Pakistan had no further strategic value for the US. India could no longer count on receiving weapons from the Russian Federation at the bargain rates of former years—but if the US were to distance itself from Pakistan and move closer to India, as seemed to be happening, then Pakistan could find itself in a difficult situation economically, and could have an even worse problem so far as defence was concerned. This may not have escaped the professionals in Pakistan's Foreign Office but, unfortunately, neither the government nor the army seemed to be paying attention to what was happening, at amazing speed, in the outside world.

Pakistan and the Gulf War

Pakistan did not join the coalition that provided troops to fight against Iraq in 1991. In a particularly maladroit manner, it compromised by sending, initially, 12 Independent Armoured Brigade Group to Saudi Arabia to 'guard the Holy Places'. The US was unpopular in Pakistan, for obvious reasons, and Iraq, under the unbeliever Saddam Hussain, was considered by many semi-educated people (and some educated ones, too) to be the aggrieved party.[19] They thought Saddam should be congratulated on his defiance of the mighty US-led coalition which, in any case, was only going to help the arrogant Kuwaitis who treated the rest of the Arab and Muslim world with contempt. It would have been difficult (but not impossible) for the government to justify committing troops under command of a power that had dumped Pakistan as an ally.

A hiatus in foreign policy decision-making was probably inevitable in this period that saw so many important international events and developments. The PPP government had been dismissed just at the time of the Iraqi invasion; the interim government was not in a position to take decisions that, in any case, would not have been binding on their successor; and the new government of Nawaz Sharif was finding its feet and lacked expertise in foreign relations. Into the vacuum where Pakistan's foreign policy should have been there came Aslam Beg, and it would have been better for the country had he refrained from trying to fill it.

Not only was the dispatch of the brigade to Saudi Arabia politically inept, it was an operational and administrative disaster. Had Pakistan acted under the aegis of the Gulf Coalition, it would have been welcomed with equipment and generous support. It would have been doubly welcome: its very presence would have demonstrated Pakistan's solidarity with important nations; and its expertise and professionalism would have contributed to the coalition's war-fighting capability. An armoured brigade is a potent force, and commanders, no matter how many troops they have, can always find tasks for more. The brigade would have fitted well alongside any of the coalition's forces and would doubtless have distinguished itself. But it was treated coolly by Saudi Arabia (although Saudi aircraft transported Pakistani soldiers) and, barely credibly, was almost ignored by GHQ. Immediately before the attack began, Beg went to Coalition HQ for a briefing which, according to US military officers, 'shook him'. (He was not given details of timings for the advance.) He had no idea what to expect and was amazed at the size of the build-up in spite of having been briefed on its progress by US officers in preceding weeks. He avoided discussion of Pakistan's reluctance to become involved in the coalition and appeared 'sort of apologetic, but he didn't say that'.[20] Beg had visited his troops, which by now included 330 Independent Infantry Brigade Group as part of the GCC element, but was seemingly not disturbed that morale was low and that his soldiers were poorly-equipped and lacked proper clothing.[21] Their mission was unclear (Saddam would have been insane to have attacked the holy places, even if his army could have crossed the Saudi border) and their rules of engagement non-existent. They were moved hither and thither throughout the country and were unpopular with almost everyone. There was not much evidence of 'Strategic Defiance' in this. Pakistan had distanced itself from the coalition that it was prevented from joining by a combination of reluctance on the part of Beg, and Iraqi propaganda. A government in Islamabad that was settled in power and had foreign affairs experience might have overcome the problems associated with propaganda, which was extremely effective. It could have employed all the publicity means at its disposal to counter pro-Iraqi agitators (many of whom were simply trouble-makers, but no less effective for that), who chose to ignore the fact that Saddam was no more a Muslim than he was a soldier—although he was portrayed as a defender of the Faith and a mighty warrior in all the material circulating in Pakistan.

The Gulf War was a sad chapter for Pakistan. India, too, had problems with *Desert Shield/Desert Storm*, but somehow they were overcome. The minority government of Prime Minister Chandra Shekhar had allowed US aircraft to refuel in India *en route* to the Gulf but rescinded permission when there was (quite cynical) objection from, amongst others, Rajiv Gandhi. This did not affect the burgeoning of US–Indian relations because Washington wished to believe the best of 'the world's largest democracy' and was happy to ignore the decades of support by and for the Soviet Union. (Not much happened, in the end, on the defence scene. India's paranoia about secrecy exasperated American delegations, who reported to the State Department and the Pentagon that co-operation on the scale proposed by the Administration would present more difficulties than it would reap benefits. Some members of the US defence staffs in New Delhi had warned that this would be the outcome.)

Rumours of War

In 1990 tension rose between New Delhi and Islamabad. The main cause was the uprising in Indian-administered Kashmir. There were Indian allegations of Pakistani support for Kashmiri armed separatists. Representatives of the two countries indulged in unhelpful public comments, as in the cases of Indian Prime Minister V.P. Singh and Pakistani Chief of Army Staff General Aslam Beg. Mr V.P. Singh was asked in April if he could 'at this stage rule out an armed conflict with Pakistan.' 'You see,' said V.P. Singh,

> it is all one-sided. All action you see is the asymmetry of the action. It [Pakistan] is sending weapons of the highest calibre across the border: machine guns, anti-tank mines, rockets [sic] launchers, and even surface-to-surface missiles according to our intelligence sources. It is also sending armed and trained infiltrators in a well planned move to instigate insurgency [in Kashmir] while we are doing nothing like this on their side.[22]

It is charitable to imagine that Mr V.P. Singh may have been tired at the time of this comment, but only a few days before he made it, he said in the Lok Sabha that, 'We have the capability to inflict a very heavy cost on Pakistan for its territorial goals against India,' when he was in possession of a prepared statement. On the same day, 11 April, General Beg said that deployment of the Indian Strike Corps between Suratgarh and Bikaner was 'most threatening' and the Pakistan army had to take measures to counter it. The army did no such thing, as was made clear a week later by Lt.-Gen. Alam Jan Mahsud, commander IV Corps in Lahore, when he said that the army remained in peacetime locations. One might ignore the hyperbolic statements of the Indian prime minister—for he, after all, had a domestic constituency to address, placate, and enthuse. But what constituency was Aslam Beg speaking to? Further, what message was being given to India by conflicting statements about Pakistan's preparedness to meet the move of an Indian division and a brigade[23] close to the border? Who spoke for Pakistan? Was it the government in Islamabad (still, in early 1990, that of Benazir Bhutto), or was it the generals in Rawalpindi? Who was calling the shots in Pakistan?

* * *

Tension continued to increase. It appeared there was a harder line being taken in India because the uprising in Kashmir was gaining momentum. Pakistan was being increasingly blamed for the insurrection, as the foreign minister Inder Kumar Gujral alleged on 8 May. Pakistan, he said, 'is aware it cannot take Kashmir by force. Its real design is to foment communal tension and to create a situation of 1947.'[24] (Mr Gujral's opinion of Pakistan did not undergo much modification during the 1990s. He became prime minister in 1997—albeit for only seven months—and on 31 July, the day after India announced it was reactivating its intermediate-range ballistic missile programme, he said that Pakistan was spreading hostile propaganda, taking provocative actions, and stockpiling arms: 'The government is aware that Pakistan maintains a military arsenal far in excess of its legitimate defence requirements.')[25]

Eventually, Pakistan moved some units close to the border. There was not much secrecy about the deployments. In fact, it appeared that Pakistan wished it to be known—or did not care if it were known—that reinforcements were on the move. The author witnessed the entrainment of an artillery regiment in Karachi which took place with all the clandestinity of a National Day Parade. Diplomats and defence attachés in Islamabad were aware of what was taking place and received information from many sources in addition to raw and processed intelligence. They concluded that tension was high but that the situation was not dangerous. It appears that some other people considered it to be dangerous to the point that a nuclear weapons exchange could take place.

On 16 February 1994, a meeting of eighteen experts on the subcontinent took place at Washington's Henry L. Stimson Center, whose President is the highly-respected Michael Krepon. The aim was to 'set the record straight' as to whether there was a 'near-nuclear war between India and Pakistan in 1990'. Participants included former ambassadors Oakley and Clark, who had been US heads of mission in Islamabad and New Delhi at the time, their then defence advisers, Colonels Jones and Sandrock, and General Sundarji, former Indian army chief. The key findings included that:

- By all accounts the Gates Mission was extremely helpful in defusing the crisis (*see below*), and
- The participants knew of no credible evidence that Pakistan had deployed nuclear weapons during the crisis.[26]

Pronouncements by both sides appear to have relied on national intelligence assessments which, given the means at their disposal, could not present a full picture of each other's intentions. Commercial satellite photography was available but was neither high quality nor timely. There was confusion as to whether troop movements were exercises or operational deployments. Human intelligence sources were unreliable, and, even if credible, far from timely in the passage of information. Communications intercept was fragmented. Intelligence analysts were confused because movement was carried out using identical security measures whether it was operational or for exercise purposes. It may be that if the countries had had better intelligence systems, then mutual confidence would have been more readily established.

Apparently it was fear of a nuclear exchange that prompted the visit to Pakistan and India of a delegation led by Mr Robert Gates, deputy national security adviser to President Bush, from 19–21 May, an activity that intrigued several journalists.[27] India greeted the visit cautiously, stating that, 'We have friendly relations with both the US and the Soviet Union, but there is no question of mediation by the US,' and Pakistan, which had been expecting yet another visit by the egregious Stephen Solarz, was grateful to be spared the latter[28] but did not know what to make of the former.

From 15–24 May, Ms Bhutto visited Iran, Turkey, Syria, Jordan, Yemen, Egypt, Libya, and Tunisia seeking support for Pakistan's stance on Kashmir. It was strange that the prime minister was out of the country when the emissary of President Bush came calling to stop a nuclear war, but Mr Gates met the President and COAS and, from what we are told,[29] convinced them that Pakistan should not proceed with plans for employment of nuclear weapons. It is said he achieved his objective in India as well. And, to be sure, there was no recourse to the atom; no nuclear Armageddon. But there are doubts as to whether there *were* any plans to employ nuclear weapons, or even intention to do anything, very much, in the conventional field.

Pakistan moved troops in Punjab and Sindh but was careful to avoid closing right up to the border itself. India was cautious, too. The Punjab canals are a double-edged obstacle: good for defence when your forces are on the home side; good for attack if your forces cross to the far bank within your territory to give them an advantage once the balloon goes up. Indian troops did not cross to their own far bank. Such an operation would have been practicable without interference; Indian troops could do what they liked in their own country. It would have signalled to the Pakistanis that war might be imminent, and who knows what might have happened then?—but nothing happened. The armies moved closer to their borders, but refrained from provocation. There were no incidents of cross-border firing (there were many of firing over the Line of Control, but this was normal), and it was apparent to observers that, although the mood was one of disquietude, there was none of the expectant exhilaration that might be the prelude to operations. Satellite imagery and communications intercept provided an important part of the picture but could not tell the attitude of human beings. Washington knew the locations of tank squadrons and all sorts of other units—and it should have known the opinion of experienced observers on the ground concerning the behaviour of the army's leaders; but if it did, it paid more attention to the former than the latter. A photograph can indicate the position of a tank, and much else besides, but it cannot (yet) see if there is the light of battle in the eyes of its commander.

During the period of heightened tension there had been little evidence of leadership on the part of the government. A ten-day, eight-country tour by the prime minister to encourage support for Pakistan's stance on Kashmir was hardly a substitute for firm direction on the home front. General Beg had made pronouncements of national sensitivity that seemed to be at variance with the facts as reported elsewhere. His opposite number in India also made comments—but they reflected his government's position. In Pakistan, it seemed, important pronouncements were left to the military. Oddly—well, perhaps not so oddly—many people felt comfortable with that.

US intercession probably provided a fig leaf for both sides to calm down and withdraw troops without suffering loss of pride. The confrontation with India fizzled out—just in time for a row between the government and the army about the future of a corps commander and over the legal powers of the army in connection with the terrible violence in Sindh Province.

Army Appointments

On 10 July, the author paid a call on the commander IV Corps in Lahore, the genial and extremely competent Lt.-Gen. Alam Jan Mahsud, whose tour was about to end. His successor had been named and Alam Jan was preparing to retire. But there were rumours that he might be retained. What, he was asked, was the future? It all depended, he said, 'on the lady'. It appeared he had been told by someone—not in GHQ—that the prime minister wished him to become deputy chief of the army staff (as distinct from vice-chief), a post that had not been filled since the retirement of the previous incumbent, Lt.-Gen. Ahmad Kamal Khan, some seven months before. It was Ahmad Kamal, so rumour had it during the Sirohey debacle, who was Ms Bhutto's choice for Chief of Army Staff had Beg moved to become Chairman of the Joint Chiefs of Staff Committee, had Sirohey been retired as Ms Bhutto wished. All very complicated and smelling nastily of political meddling. Alam Jan would have made a good deputy chief (although one doubts if his heart would have been in it, as administration was not his scene; he was a soldier's soldier) and would not on any account have dabbled in politics—but what was going on was quite improper. He knew it, and was embarrassed; and the COAS knew it and was determined that no officer should be extended beyond retirement age and especially that no officer should be appointed to *any* post because a politician wanted it. It was no fault of Alam Jan's that he had been placed in this position, and he retired the next week, after General Beg prevailed, but it left a nasty taste in the mouths of many people. What was going on between the government and the army? Especially, what was going on between them concerning the situation in Sindh?

A Province in Chaos

The armed struggle between the sides in Sindh, and especially in Karachi, had almost developed into civil war. Dreadful things were happening, and it seemed the central government was powerless to control events. At the end of May 1990, when, allegedly, Pakistan was sharpening its nuclear talons, the respected Senator Mohsin Siddiqi was shot dead by a sniper in Karachi when returning from a visit to the scene of disturbances in which over forty people had been killed. On 4 June (about the time when he was supposed by some people to be considering nuclear war), General Beg toured the worst areas with the Corps Commander Karachi, Lt.-Gen. Asif Nawaz. It was obvious that firm action was needed if there was not to be anarchy. The trouble was that the PPP government felt itself unable to act decisively because of political complications. Earlier in May there had been some plain speaking at a meeting of the Defence Committee at the Prime Minister's Secretariat. The army was involved in Sindh—it had to be, simply because it was the only element that could combat organized terrorism (the police were politicized and ineffectual and the para-military Rangers lacked authority)—but the army wanted power to arrest and detain malefactors. The government wanted malefactors to be arrested and dealt with—provided they were MQM malefactors.[30]

During a call on Commander V Corps on 17 July the author was told the nature of some of the problems in Karachi and Islamabad, and specifically about relations with the government.

At a further meeting of the Defence Committee, ten days before, General Asif Nawaz had been handed a list of persons against whom there were *prima facie* cases to answer concerning plans to disrupt affairs in Sindh. Certainly it seemed that all on the list belonged to the ungodly. Their detention would assuredly assist in restoring order in Karachi. There was only one problem, said the general to one of the ministers, in front of his prime minister and his chief (neither of whom took part in the subsequent exchange of views): all the names on the list appeared to be MQM adherents. Were there not any persons of evil intent who had other political allegiance? Like, for example, those on this list he happened to have with him, that contained not only many of those on the list of the minister, but the names of some who were of other political persuasion? There was strong disagreement. And Lt.-Gen. Asif Nawaz said it would not be proper for the civilian authorities to arrest only some of the alleged criminals and, in any case, the army could not arrest *anyone* under present legislation. Where did they stand? If the government wanted the army to act, as it seemed it did, why did not the government permit the army to have the legal authority to take action? (The answer, of course, was that the army, if Asif Nawaz had anything to do with matters, would act against PPP thugs as well as MQM thugs.) The meeting ended in complete understanding and mutual antagonism. Two days later, a PPP spokesman in Karachi issued a statement urging the COAS 'not to indulge in politics'. Now, the COAS had undoubtedly been indulging in politics for many months. He had said what he should not have said on some occasions; he had explored the fascinating world of foreign affairs and enjoyed the heady brew of headlines; he had spoken without reference to government on matters that were the province and prerogative of government alone; he had taken unto himself the might and majesty of a national leader rather than a servant of the civil power who by virtue of his appointment should enjoy a proper dignity and respect—and no more. But the PPP had gone too far, in the eyes of the President and his Chief of the Army Staff.

The Government was bad. The deliberations of the cabinet, solemnly issued to the Press, included matters so petty and inconsequential as to be embarrassing. There had not in eighteen months been a major piece of legislation that might have improved the lot of the common man or, especially, woman. Citizens in Sindh went in fear of their lives. Corruption was rampant, as the old Z.A. Bhutto loyalists claimed their rewards and the new adherents to 'BB' climbed on the gravy-train. The country was becoming—had become—tacky, squalid, sordid, venal, and dangerous to live in. BUT—the PPP government had been elected by the people and had a mandate that had not expired. What had expired was the patience of the President and of the Chief of the Army Staff, neither of whom was prepared to have their powers reduced or even questioned. The army, in spite of wishing to stay out of matters affecting the governance of the nation, was being drawn back into power-politics by its chief—and it did not like it.

Change of Government

After Ms Bhutto and the PPP government were dismissed in August 1990, Mr Nawaz Sharif and his coalition were elected in October with rather more than a two-thirds majority in the National Assembly. Mr Sharif had been a protégé of General Zia (and was still young, at forty), but had little political baggage to encumber him. He was a populist, naturally, but had, perhaps, something more to offer the country. He had, after all, actually *run* something. He was an industrialist, albeit scion of a business family, but he had also run the province of Punjab, a major undertaking, and had done it well. In fact, considering the confrontationist stance of the central government and the machinations of his enemies, he had performed very well indeed, as he had always to keep an eye over his shoulder to watch for the next political dagger thrust.

On 10 November, the day that Mr Sharif and his cabinet were sworn in by the President, a compromise prime minister was selected in India. Unlike Mr Sharif, Mr Chandra Shekhar had no popular mandate, nor a guaranteed majority in parliament, but within two weeks they met at a SAARC gathering in the Maldives and arranged for a meeting of foreign secretaries in December to 'discuss confidence-building measures'. There was no headway on Kashmir as, in spite of the Indian prime minister finding his counterpart 'very co-operative,' they both stuck to their briefs, which meant, in Pakistan's case, the raising of Kashmir as a problem to be discussed in the context of UN Security Council resolutions, and, on the Indian side, restatement of the stand that there must be 'no interference in India's internal matters'. Still, it was better to talk peace than shout about war. But at this juncture General Beg began to speak of 'strategic defiance', which left the Indians guessing just as much as everyone else. The foreign secretaries' talks included arrangements for weekly telephone links between the Directors-General Military Operations in Delhi and Rawalpindi, which was a step forward, and there was agreement to exchange the *Instruments of Ratification of the Agreement on Prohibition of Attack against Nuclear Installations* of 31 December 1988, which was largely symbolic, but nonetheless welcome evidence that agreement could be reached about *something*. It was unfortunate for the foreign policy of Pakistan that there had been a government upset in a crucial period, just as it was unfortunate for India that there had been eleven ministers and ministers of state for external affairs in the period January 1986 to January 1991. Construction and continuity of measured, farsighted, prudent policy was difficult for both countries in these circumstances. There appeared to be little *gravitas* in their exchanges. There were self-righteousness and mutual castigation in abundance; there were misunderstandings, wilful and otherwise and to spare; there may even have been a subliminal desire to seek resolution of their differences. But without governments on both sides that, concurrently, had massive popular support and an unassailable majority in both houses of their parliaments, there could be little progress.

After Aslam Beg (1991–3)

In mid-1991 the Islamabad rumour mill was working hard. General Beg, it was said, did not wish to retire in August. He wanted to stay as army chief, to take over as executive Chairman of the Joint Chiefs, to reintroduce martial law, to take over the country. Wild interpretations were placed on the fact that the US ambassador said he was remaining in Pakistan until August rather than returning to Washington on the date his tenure ended. In Delhi, government-controlled All India Radio claimed that Beg wanted to invade and capture Kashmir before he retired. Nothing, it seemed, was too far-fetched to be retailed and, by some, at least, believed. Then it all stopped. It was announced on 12 June that Lt.-Gen. Asif Nawaz was to be appointed COAS on 17 August. General Beg would retire on time—but not before he made some startling pronouncements.

In July he stated that the situation in Kashmir could make it 'quite likely that in sheer desperation India could lead to (*sic*) venture against Pakistan,' which statement was 'clarified' by a foreign office spokesman who explained that the army chief was not speaking about the immediate situation but was 'referring to problems being faced by India which could lead to a certain course of action in the long term....' Undeterred by clarification, the general returned to his theme of regional bonding. On 3 August he said, 'the tripartite accord reached by Pakistan, Iran, and the Afghan *mujahideen* to reach a peaceful solution of the Afghan issue (although abrogated almost immediately by the Afghans) was a prelude to achieving strategic consensus and regional security linkage between the three countries'— which was a strange statement to follow that by the Iranian ambassador on 20 June when, at a news conference, he said, 'any sort of defence agreement was out of the question' because the country's Constitution excluded any such arrangement. Game to the last, a few days later the general said that 'the enemy' had 'launched a calculated campaign of disinformation to sabotage the political stability of Pakistan,' which prompted *The News* of 10 August to note in an editorial that, 'all too often we have chosen to externalise problems of our own making...the danger lies in beginning to believe our own propaganda,' which was sagacious, perceptive, unbiased, and probably completely ignored by all but a few, and they the wrong people.

It was small wonder that there was a sigh of relief from the bureaucracy and not a few politicians when Beg handed over. The new chief, Asif Nawaz, was different. Where Beg was taciturn, even enigmatic, when meeting with those whom he did not know well (and especially those whom he distrusted), Asif was straightforward and prepared to exchange views. Beg enjoyed publicity and the sense that he was at the centre of events. Asif eschewed the media and cared little for influence for its own sake. He was interested in foreign policy and relations, of course, but had no intention of making the first or interfering with the second. He liked senior members of the ministry of foreign affairs, respected their expertise, and recognized that there should be closer consultation. Beg had given approval for a strategy review to have input by the ministry and Asif was happy to endorse this. There was a changed atmosphere in the capital and in GHQ. No theatre; no thrilling statements—and no 'strategic consensus' or 'strategic defiance'. These inventions were quietly laid to rest.

This is not to denigrate the achievements of Aslam Beg, which were many. He placed the country back on the road to democracy when he could have continued in the shoes of Zia. It was not his fault that democracy was limping along, stricken by the perennial diseases of corruption, petty infighting, and shallow thinking. He had interfered in politics, of course: his agreement with the President concerning the dismissal of the PPP government was improper—but what else could he have done? The President had been adamant that the government must go. The Eighth Amendment to the Constitution placed the loyalty of the COAS firmly at the office of the President, the supreme commander, who could 'act in his discretion in respect of any matter in respect of which he is empowered by the Constitution to do so'. The empowerment included dissolution of the National Assembly. But, although Beg interfered with the governance of the country, he was apolitical in the strictest sense. Never did he give the impression that he favoured one political party over another. He disliked and distrusted some members of both governments during his tenure, but did not let this affect the manner in which he carried out his duties. In fact, some said he should have been more resolute when the MQM's activities in Sindh began to resemble insurrection, but he was reluctant to commit the army wholesale to taking over from the civil power. Amongst other things, he introduced improvements in administration and operational planning. Promotion and selection procedures were speeded up, the role of administrative areas was examined and aligned with operational requirements, surface-to-surface artillery was included in tactical planning, armour tactics were re-examined, command and control of artillery was enhanced by introduction of the artillery division HQ, and air defence was given a much-needed boost in priority and inter-service liaison by the establishment of Air Defence Command. Not bad for three years in which he had a multitude of other matters to attend to. If only he hadn't talked so much and got himself more deeply involved in politics than was necessary.

* * *

General Asif was a tough man. The political parties were aware of his stance: he was uncompromising about aid to the civil power in that, if it was deemed necessary by the supreme commander, then it should be introduced by the parliament and implemented vigorously by the army. There could be no half measures. Asif preferred to keep out of things in Sindh, but, if there were no other means of controlling the vicious killers in the Province, then the army it would have to be—but without its hands tied. And he would make sure there were no favourites. There would be no question, either, of criminals coming to arrangements of mutual benefit with politicians, the police, or anyone else.

Unfortunately the prime minister dithered, probably because the MQM was an asset in the Assembly, and the lawlessness continued. The Chief Minister of Sindh, Jam Sadiq Ali, was a political ally (and a former PPP man), but when the province was faced with even more violence after he died (of natural causes) in March 1992, Nawaz Sharif continued to dither. Along with growth in politically-motivated violence, there was a surge in 'ordinary' criminal activity. Dacoits— bandits—took advantage of the situation to indulge in rape, robbery, kidnap, extortion, drug-smuggling across the border with India, and general disorder. It was unsafe to travel by road and even by train, for gangs boarded coaches and stole what they could from the passengers— usually, of course, the poor. The rich travelled by air, or by road with well-armed bodyguards. The main sufferers were the villagers, and their plight did not matter. There were not, after all, elections in the offing.

By the end of May the President had had enough. On the 28th he ordered Operation *Clean-Up* to begin, following a 'request' from the Sindh government. Article 147 of the Constitution[31] was invoked, and GHQ issued orders to Commander V Corps (Lt.-Gen. Nasir Akhtar; just the man for the job) accordingly. The army began with operations against dacoits in an area along the Hyderabad–Lahore road, and along the railway. Asif Nawaz insisted that all operations be conducted 'in consultation with the civil administration,' and whenever possible this was done; but sometimes it was difficult to distinguish between some members of the civil administration and those who were flouting its authority. Para-military Rangers were employed in conjunction with regular troops; curfews were imposed; the army was in control—but still without legal cover, which Asif continued to insist was necessary. The President finally agreed, and issued a retrospective ordinance on 19 July to the effect that when troops were involved in police work such as search and arrest, they would be immune from legal procedures.[32] The President and the army had got what they wanted, but the prime minister was faced with problems of changing political alliances in the light of the crackdown. He had to perform a balancing act which took much time that should have been devoted to legislation, administration, and national leadership.

Disagreement between some members of the government and the army arose in September, when the country was hit by floods. *The News* of 25 September reported that the prime minister, although pleased with the way the emergency was dealt with by the army, was under pressure from some political colleagues to remove troops from relief work. Several million people lost their homes; livestock deaths and flooded farmland caused grave destitution; and the army worked wonders in cleaning up, restoring bridges, repaving roads, and administering distribution of relief moneys and supplies. But in one incident, local politicians informed the garrison commander in Multan that troops were no longer needed and that they should be withdrawn.[33] The order was rescinded, but there was unease locally and in the rest of the country about the motives behind such action. The sensitive aspects of this crisis, alas, were nothing to do with alleviating the distress of poor people rendered destitute, or with methods of restoring drowned land to productivity. Neither did they concern the best means of reconnecting canals, wells, sewage, tracks, roads, power supplies, and telephone lines. They were to do with how relief aid could best be distributed in order to make it appear that a beneficent government was the sole agency involved in succouring the common man.

The army tried to ignore this sort of nonsense. It had a job to do and was getting on with it efficiently. If a politician wanted to strut into one of his villages and claim that what was being achieved was entirely his doing, then by all means let him. It was nothing to do with the army, provided he did not interfere. But if relief money and material was being diverted by local functionaries to their own benefit, the army was going to have none of it. The petty official concerned would get short shrift and might even be clapped inside for a while to show that, although he might be a big man to the peasants, he was not going to be allowed to get away with dishonesty. The army did not understand politics. It was vital to a local politician that he be seen to be helping the voters. It was traditional, and for him essential, that largesse be seen as coming directly from him or from the people appointed through his influence. The army might be a bit feudal in its approach to discipline and its place in society, but it did not subscribe to feudalism if the poor were going to be even further disadvantaged by the actions of pompous little men who were lining their own pockets.[34] Ms Bhutto, leader of the Opposition, wanted to visit the afflicted areas but was denied a helicopter by the government. This did not make much difference to her popularity—may even have enhanced it or at least not reduced it—because the prime minister had been hissed and booed when he arrived from the skies in one stricken village, and the chief minister of Punjab had been stoned in another. Political mileage should not be gained by Ms Bhutto if the government had anything to do with it—but if their own people were to be put in the shade by the army, things were getting dangerous.

In November 1992 the author attended a divisional exercise in Balochistan. The Commander XII Corps, Lt.-Gen. Abdul Waheed, was his usual jovial self but had a sense of humour failure when watching a television broadcast on the 18th which showed preparations for a 'Long March' by the PPP on the capital. The government made much of the threat to law and order and prevailed upon the COAS to have troops stand by in case of emergency. General Waheed, in what he expected to be the final posting of his career, was critical of both government and opposition. They were putting the country in an impossible position, he said. Let them have disagreements, of course, but don't let one side force the other to take action that set Pakistani against Pakistani. This was an interesting comment that showed the way Waheed—and the COAS and probably most of the army—felt about politics. It was an unsettling period for the government, which seemed to be unaware that the Army took law and order very seriously indeed.

On 31 October 1992, Major Arshad Jamil was sentenced to death by a Court Martial in Sindh. Thirteen of his soldiers received life imprisonment. In June they had killed nine people in the village of Tando Bahawal, about ten miles from Hyderabad, on the pretext of their being dacoits, while the real reason was a land dispute to which the major was privy. It was appalling that the slaughter had taken place, but the fact that it was reported, investigated, and dealt with gave a message to the nation that the army was resolute about administration of the law. If the army could mete out punishment to an officer and his men, then, so notice was given, it could deal similarly with any who might fall within its jurisdiction. Curiously, this manifestation of respect for the law did not strike a resonant chord with either government or opposition.

1992 was a poor year for internal stability and it was cyclic externally. The army remained alert in Kashmir but refused to be drawn into internal security affairs when the Jammu and Kashmir Liberation Front stage-managed a march intended to cross the Line of Control. One interesting aspect of the Kashmir dispute that year was the apparent but unintended *volte-face* by India regarding bilateralism. New Delhi slipped up in its conduct of relations with Pakistan by holding individual discussions with the permanent members of the Security Council in an attempt to persuade them of the justice of India's cause concerning Kashmir. Demonstrators crossing the Line of Control would be fired on, said its representatives. Pakistan's foreign ministry chuckled and went for the jugular. How principled, how proper, that New Delhi should enlist the support of the Security Council concerning Kashmir, they said. There was a still-extant Security Council Resolution about a plebiscite, was there not? If India was so concerned about the disputed territory of Kashmir as to lobby the Great Five, then perhaps it might give similar attention to other matters, such as that?[35] The government did not seize this public relations advantage and Pakistan lost the opportunity to make a telling point—although it would have only been a PR victory, and nobody would have paid attention to it, so perhaps it didn't matter, anyway.

There had been many casualties in Siachen, but discussions in November were a waste of time. Neither government appeared anxious to reach a solution. Both had problems at home, and it seemed that political survival had priority over any initiatives that would save lives but endanger majorities.

Relations between the government and the army were looking shaky. While General Asif was on an overseas visit, the government replaced the Director-General Inter Services Intelligence, Lt.-Gen. M.A. Durrani,[36] by Lt.-Gen. Javed Nasir, a bearded *Tablighi*[37] engineer officer with no intelligence background. It was the government's prerogative to appoint the DGISI, but it was not tactful to do so while the Army Chief was out of the country. It looked ... contrived.

Then there was the rumour that a senior figure allegedly close to government had approached two (perhaps three) lieutenant-generals to ask them whom they would recommend to be Chief of the Army Staff if General Asif Nawaz was in some unspecified way to vacate the appointment in the near future. Would it, they were asked by the emissary, be regarded as a serious upset were General Asif to be replaced? When the army chief was informed of the approach he chose to ignore it, although his language was ripe and his suspicions were confirmed. He was, in any event, becoming disenchanted about some government activities, especially the attempt to prosecute *The News* newspaper for sedition. The government backed down, eventually, after pressure, but Asif was worried that the prime minister might have been hijacked by some of his more aggressive colleagues and convinced that there was a Press and army plot against him.

In the land of the conspiracy, nothing is impossible, of course, to the paranoid mind—but an army chief's plot was inconceivable. The idea that the chief editor and the editor of *The News* could be plotting against the government was also ludicrous—but a charge had been laid and the process of prosecution was taken a long way before it was dropped. The public was becoming restive about allegations of corruption and mismanagement. *The Muslim* commented on 9 October that over a million dollars had been spent on sending politicians and bureaucrats overseas for medical treatment. 'Try as one might,' ran the editorial, 'it is impossible to unearth a single [medical] facility in this country which is not being misused... What is happening in the corridors of power is downright dishonest...' *The News* reported two weeks later that the seats in the executive jet purchased for the prime minister had been replaced at a cost of two million dollars. A week later came the revelation that a ski resort had been sold to an entrepreneur of most dubious antecedents for a fraction of its value. The man-in-the-street was becoming irritated about the extent of corrupt activities and one heard it suggested, more and more, that it might not be a bad thing if the army took over again.

General Asif Nawaz died of a heart attack on 8 January 1993 and was succeeded by General Abdul Waheed, commander XII Corps in Quetta. Much was made of the fact that six officers were senior to him, and there was in fact a considerable difference of opinion between President and prime minister concerning who should be the next Chief. The President had selected the CGS, General Farrukh Khan, but when he informed Nawaz Sharif of his choice, the prime minister was violently opposed. Farrukh, alleged Sharif, 'had been responsible for all his problems with the late General Asif Nawaz'.[38] This was true, to the extent that Farrukh had been totally loyal to Asif. The President compromised and, after discussion with Roedad Khan, a close friend of many years, decided on General Waheed.

Whatever anyone expected of General Waheed, they should have known he would be his own man. Unfortunately for the ambitions of both President and prime minister—and most fortunately for the country—General Waheed brought hard common sense to the post of COAS. He was neither ideologue nor demagogue nor theocrat; no wild and dramatic ideas came from GHQ during his tenure. He was completely apolitical and determined that he and the army should remain so. He wanted the best for his country, and if he was forced to intervene he would become involved only in strict accordance with the Constitution. Some observers commented that his outlook was narrow. Well, it may have been; whatever it was, it was a blessing for his country.

The President dismissed the government of Nawaz Sharif on 18 April 1993 on the grounds that it was corrupt and had mismanaged the country. An interim government headed by a feudal landlord, Balakh Sher Mazari, took over at an undignified ceremony and set about creating a cabinet of fifty-eight members—a record number— whose usefulness was entirely dubious. On 26 May, the Supreme Court ordered the reinstatement of Nawaz Sharif and his group. The situation was developing into chaos and Pakistan was becoming a laughing stock. General Waheed, by a combination of tact, forcefulness, honour, and tenacity, convinced the President and the prime minister they should stand down, which they did on 18 July. A caretaker administration led by Mr Moeen Qureshi, another luminary of the World Bank, took over and was, it has been argued, the best government Pakistan had experienced since the country was created. He was, sums up Lawrence Ziring, 'an effective, efficient, no-nonsense and dedicated administrator'. In three months (the time laid down in the Constitution for elections to be arranged) Qureshi introduced many proposals aimed at restoring probity to the conduct of the country's affairs. Unfortunately these were discarded by the next government—and the decision to cap the expensive nuclear programme was also rescinded.

* * *

After three successful years as Chief of the Army Staff, General Waheed handed over to General Jehangir Karamat, an equally forceful and forthright character, in January 1996. His tenure had been successful but not without grave problems. There had been, for example, the matter of the failed coup.

Maj.-Gen. Zaheerul Islam Abbasi always appeared to the author to be a competent officer of some charm. As Director of Infantry he was, in the early and mid-1990s, in a position that any infantry officer would welcome. The incumbent could have great influence on his Corps, and could introduce—or at least endorse and fine-tune—many improvements. In tactics, leadership, equipment acquisition and structure he could contribute much to development. Unfortunately, Abbasi thought he could and should do more than was permitted an officer in influencing military affairs. He wanted to influence political affairs, too—and dramatically.

General Waheed had made it clear he would not countenance officers interfering in politics or becoming involved with contentious matters outside their profession. Let them argue about river crossings by all means, and give their opinions on deficiencies in training—but don't let them put their noses into affairs that might be considered even remotely connected with politicians. He dismissed from service the popular, intellectual, and most competent Lt.-Gen. Asad Durrani (see Note 36) for daring to involve himself in politics. Well-intentioned as Durrani was, he had to go (and told the author two days after his dismissal that it was 'a fair cop'). But Abbasi was not trying to be an honest broker. He was involved in Islamic extremism and thought he might be able to overthrow what he saw as an unIslamic government. He and another thirty-five officers were arrested on 26 September 1995, having failed to carry through a plan to kill all those attending a Corps Commanders' Conference (chaired by the COAS) and then eradicate the cabinet. The government tried to play down the significance of the attempted coup, which was made public three weeks later, but there is no doubt it was serious. Equally, it had no chance of success. The government of Benazir Bhutto was not anti-Islamic, any more than it was pro-anything other than staying in power, but the army was not prepared to have dissidents in its midst. Punishment was swift. The three dozen were dealt with, and others suspected of having connections with extremism were moved sideways or out. The coup attempt had effects throughout the army but was far from being an all-embracing defect.

Islam was not a 'problem' in the army. It could hardly be that, because the army is, after all, one of the armed services of The Islamic Republic of Pakistan. But those who advocate *extreme* Islam are a problem, as are bigoted militants who espouse extreme Christianity or extreme Hinduism or extremes in other religious and political beliefs, because those who advocate immoderation and intolerance, and condemn others for failing to adhere to their own particular beliefs, have lost touch with human purpose and dignity. The army does not seem to have gone overboard about religion, but there are lingering doubts, even in 2005, about the cumulative effects of the Zia years and the persistent efforts of the ultra-religious political parties to influence those whose primary duty it is to defend Pakistan.

In the early 1990s, during an exercise, I crawled 100 metres to a dug-in artillery observation post where a young officer showed me a laser range-finder with which I busied myself. After congratulating him on his device I was treated to an exposition on how, in fact, there is no need for advanced technology providing one believes in Allah. On another occasion I was informed gravely by a junior officer that the beard of one of his soldiers (the luxuriance and shade of which had attracted my admiration) had turned red of its own accord because of the piety displayed during his Haj. His commanding officer buried his head in his hands, but made no comment. In more recent years I have met middle-ranking officers and been told in some detail of more senior ones (only a few) whose approach to their military duties has been based entirely on their interpretation of Islam, to the point of subordinating the relevance and practicability of military doctrine. I do not say that these officers are typical; but I do say that their attitude is disconcerting.

* * *

In spite of these problems, General Karamat took the reins easily and continued his predecessor's policy of improving the army's capabilities and keeping it out of the running of the country, although he himself was forced to play a part in the next constitutional crisis—and the one after that.

* * *

The PPP under Ms Benazir Bhutto won eighty-six seats in the October 1993 elections, which were conducted fairly, under the eyes of the army and independent observers, of whom the author was one. The Pakistan Muslim League of Nawaz Sharif obtained seventy-two seats. Ms Bhutto managed to construct a coalition with 121 seats and achieved government on 19 October. On the election of her candidate for

President, Farooq Leghari, a PPP loyalist, Ms Bhutto stated that it was a triumph for democracy. Mr Leghari, she said, would contribute to the country's stability.

Mr Leghari dismissed the government of Ms Bhutto on the night of 4/5 November 1996. There was little condemnation. The country had become nigh on ungovernable. One senior politician told the author later in November in Lahore that 'all is not lost' but that it had been a near-run thing. Anarchy had loomed, he said, and, with that, intervention by the army, as 'there would have been no alternative'. Mr Nawaz Sharif's Muslim League was voted in to power on 17 February 1997 with 181 seats in the 217-seat lower house. He faced enormous problems, as the country was on the verge of bankruptcy, but, with his huge majority, it seemed that Pakistan might be on the way to stability as he could take action and institute reforms that would be impossible for a weak government to consider. Pakistan, thanks to the army, had avoided civil war (although Karachi resembled a battlefield later in the year, and clashes between Sunni and Shia fanatics in Punjab were mindlessly savage), and appeared to be able to start— once again—the long haul to stable governance thanks to an electorate that had become sick of corruption and mismanagement, and had voted for change.

In August 1997 the former caretaker prime minister, the wise Moeen Qureshi, sounded a note of caution. 'This is,' he said, 'the last chance for the parliamentary form of government of the kind we have now in Pakistan. I have often said before, if this experiment does not succeed, then I think we must consider a presidential form of government.' He was saying that the future of Pakistan lay in the hands of Mr Nawaz Sharif's government. He was right: but the hands eventually donned the iron gloves of autocracy. And the army would once again take over.

NOTES

1. An excellent account of the crash is contained in *On the Grand Trunk Road*, by Steve Coll, Times Books, 1994. *See also*, Arif op. cit.
2. In the original editions, this was followed by 'They never do', which, alas, was proved incorrect in the 2002 elections when the MMA grouping of six religious parties achieved enough votes to govern in NWFP, which has set development and social welfare in the province back by about fifty years.
3. *Gulf News*, 7 March 1990.

4. The *Globe* (Pakistan) of May 2001 carried a remarkable interview with General Babar, which is well worth reading for an intriguing interpretation of events in this period. http://www.paksearch.com/globe/2001/may/babar.html.

5. 'In 1995, a leading French military contractor, Dassault Aviation, agreed to pay Zardari and a Pakistani partner a $200 million commission for a $4 billion jet fighter deal that fell apart only when the Bhutto government was dismissed'—John F. Burns, *New York Times*, 9 January 1989. I have a copy of that edition of the NYT, given me by Burns, the Pulitzer Prize-winning reporter. Its front-page headline is 'Bhutto Clan Leaves Trail Of Corruption.' Inside there are two pages under the banner 'The Bhutto Millions: A Name That Stood For Democracy and Greed.' Two entire pages of *The New York Times* were given to such pieces as 'Powerful Clan in Pakistan Is Stained by a Vast Record of Corruption', and 'A Pakistani Fortune Amassed From Graft Left Its Tracks Round the World'. The paper's libel lawyers went through his copy most thoroughly before publication.

6. The Islamic Democratic Alliance was not, in spite of its name, a religiously-based grouping, although it included the fundamentalist Jamaat-i-Islami, which left the coalition in May 1992.

7. Or fairly. It was admitted by Beg in 1994 that the disreputable banker, Yunus Habib (jailed in 1995), had provided 1.4 million rupees to Beg in 1990 and that ISI spent part of that during the elections. See editorial in *Dawn* of 25 April 1994 and a more detailed description in *Islamic Pakistan: Illusions and Reality* by Abdus Sattar Ghazali, http://ghazali.net/book1/Chapter11a/page_4.html and published by the National Book Club (Pakistan).

8. The author went to the radio and television studios that day. At the entrance to each establishment there was a solitary soldier, looking bored. On being asked his duties at the TV station, the soldier appeared unsure of what he was about other than to 'help the police'. There were eleven soldiers outside the Prime Minister's house, who left in the early evening.

9. All newspapers, 9 August 1990. Steve Coll (*International Herald Tribune*, 8 August) was of the opinion that, 'This was the Benazir Bhutto who ruled shakily over Pakistan for 20 months, who had difficulty sharing power, and who seemed increasingly to view the world as composed of two groups: those who were with her and those who were against her.'

10. 'The President shall, subject to law, have power...to appoint in his discretion the Chairman Joint Chiefs of Staff Committee, the Chief of the Army Staff...', *Constitution of the Islamic Republic of Pakistan*, Article 243 (2)(c).

11. *Dawn*, 11 August 1989; *The Nation*, 23 August; and Mushahid Hussain in *Gulf News*, 16 and 20 August.

12. Also carried by *Deutsche Welle*, Radio Australia, and the Voice of America.

13. A recording was made of the press conference (in the VIP lounge at Islamabad airport) by, amongst others, the VOA correspondent. Mr S.K. Singh said: 'I would like to thank Foreign Secretary Dr Humayun Khan, and endorse everything he said.' Mr Singh was an experienced diplomat who well knew how to choose his words. There is an excellent description of the affair in the *Indian Express* of 5 August 2004, by Jyoti Malhotra—http://www.indianexpress.com/print.php?content_id=52397.

14. Press briefing. Full statement in *Globe*, Karachi, November 1989.

15. Maj.-Gen. Murray Blake, MC, Land Commander Australia.

16. *Defence Journal* [of Pakistan], Vol. XVII, Nos. 6–7 of August 1991.
17. *Gulf News*, 3 December 1990. All Pakistani newspapers.
18. Shakespeare. *King John*, V.vii.112, if you really want to know.
19. The bazaars in Peshawar and other cities had many stalls with posters and badges portraying Saddam Hussein. Uniline Badges of Faisalabad produced a particularly provocative 'Love For Saddam' badge which was worn by many schoolchildren.
20. US officer to author, January 1991.
21. The author read a report on the brigade's tour in Saudi Arabia.
22. The Indian reporter Anand Sagar recorded an exclusive interview with V. P. Singh, *Gulf News*, 30 April 1990.
23. Foreign country intelligence report.
24. *Gulf News*, 19 May 1990.
25. Reuters, 30 and 31 July 1997.
26. *Conflict Prevention and Confidence-Building Measures in South Asia: the 1990 Crisis*, The Henry L. Stimson Center Occasional Paper No. 17, April 1994, edited by Michael Krepon and Mishi Faruqee. The author is grateful to Khurshid Khoja of Stimson for providing a copy.
27. *See*, USIS transcript of a press conference given by White House spokesman Marlin Fitzwater on 15 May 1990.
28. Only temporarily. He came on the 27th. Mr Solarz was disliked in Pakistan. As Chairman of the Asian subcommittee of the House Foreign Affairs Committee he appeared to have some influence on US policy, but his self-importance was hard to bear. There was much rejoicing when he failed to be re-elected. A proposal for his appointment as ambassador to India fell through.
29. In *For the President's Eyes Only*, Christopher Andrew HarperCollins 1995. I wrote to the author about the apparent discrepancy, mentioning I was writing this book, but did not have the courtesy of a reply.
30. *Trial and Error* (Oxford 2000) by Iqbal Akhund, Benazir Bhutto's National Security and Foreign Affairs' Adviser places a rather different emphasis on the Sindh problem, and blames the army for failing to adhere to the law when troops were deployed after police had fired on a crowd in Hyderabad.
31. '...the Government of a Province may, with the consent of the Federal Government, entrust, either conditionally or unconditionally, to the Federal Government, or to its officers, functions in relation to any matter to which the executive authority of the province extends'.
32. The Criminal Procedure Code was extended to the military. Sections 46–9 dealt with powers of arrest; 53, 54, 55(a) and (c), 58, and 63–7 with seizure of illicit arms; and 100, 102, and 103 with powers of search.
33. *The News*, Lahore, 25 September 1993.
34. The author drove down the Indus plain on 13–14 September and *en route* was given the views of some army officers concerning flood relief.
35. 'PTI said India asked the five permanent Council members to persuade Pakistan to 'cease and desist' from escalating tension over Kashmir.' The request 'did not amount to an appeal for intervention by the Security Council members'. *Gulf News*, 7 February 1992.
36. There are two General Durranis relevant to this narrative, both outstanding officers: Lt.-Gen. Durrani, the ISI head (later ambassador to Germany and then to Saudi Arabia), is no relation to the Durrani who was Zia's PSO and later Chairman of

Pakistan Ordnance Factories. The latter is author of, amongst other things, *India and Pakistan, the Cost of Conflict, the Benefits of Peace* (Johns Hopkins 2000).

37. The Tablighi Jamaat is a Deobandi proselytising religious movement. See *The Origins and Development of the Tablighi Jama*, Yoginder Sikand. New Delhi, Orient Longman, 2002. An NBC news item of 18 January 2005 indicates the level of suspicion with which the Tablighi is regarded in the US. (http://msnbc.msn.com/id/6839625/).

38. R. Khan op. cit.

13 Karamat to Kargil

Change of Army Chiefs

General Jehangir Karamat took over from General Waheed in January 1996 and continued his predecessor's policies almost unchanged, but with the vigour and fresh personal approach that an energetic new appointee always brings to a demanding task. He saw his mission as being 'to put the army through a consolidation phase' because of the hiatus imposed by the coup attempt of Maj.-Gen. Abbasi, and severe financial constraints, and told the author his priorities were:

- Improving the institutional strength of the military system; and
- Enhancing operational readiness and establishing a sound command and staff environment.

The consolidation phase 'enabled us to make up shortfalls, improve manpower induction through a new short-term recruitment policy, and vastly improve our functional procedures.'[1]

There was much to do in the army, but it had to be done in a period of reduced activity. Major exercises, involving a division (which means more troops and staff officers are required from elsewhere to enable testing of the formation being exercised), were few and far between because there was not enough money to conduct them. One result of the nuclear tests in 1998 was to further reduce national defence capabilities, in addition to cancellation of defence cooperation by several countries. President Clinton told Nawaz Sharif by telephone that if Pakistan did not emulate India and explode nuclear devices, then the Administration would make every effort to have the F-16 ban lifted and would engage in a massive programme of military and other aid. The chiefs of the armed forces were in a difficult position, but 'internal dynamics made it inevitable that the nuclear programme would advance to conducting tests. Thus there was no room for dissent'.[2] (In fact the overwhelming majority of Pakistanis approved of the tests. Even some highly intelligent people were enthusiastic, and beside main roads entering many cities there were constructed celebratory artificial slag heaps purporting to be replicas of the test site at Chagai. The national mood was decidedly in favour of advancing to nuclear holocaust, and the author observed in a BBC interview that this was because most people had no idea of what nuclear fallout effects might be, and imagined nuclear bombs simply made a bigger bang.)

A major concern for the chiefs was that a new strategy was required if the country's defence was perforce to involve a nuclear posture. It had been much simpler before the tests (just as it continues to be for Israel), because the rest of the world was kept guessing about intentions and could even turn a (fairly) blind eye to what was going on.[3] Now that everything was public there had to be hard thinking concerning nuclear theory that would lead to doctrine, but first there had to be decisions about who would forge this doctrine. It could not be left solely to politicians and scientists. There would have to be a body established to define it, but its membership would have to reflect the responsibility of the military in development and employment of weapons as well as overall civilian control. In this context it is well to remember that military doctrine is:

> The combination of principles, policies and concepts into an integrated system for the purpose of governing a military force in combat, and assuring consistent, coordinated employment of these components. The origin of doctrine can be experience, or theory, or both. Doctrine represents the available thought on the employment of forces that has been adopted by an armed force. Doctrine is methodology, and if it is to work, all military elements must know, understand, and respect it. Doctrine is implemented by tactics.[4] [Doctrine can also take outside advice into account; but there was no possibility of that being offered by anyone.]

General Karamat's view was that the Defence Committee of the Cabinet, chaired by the prime minister, should be the 'apex body' (his words), with the Defence Council of the Ministry of Defence as the next tier. The Chairman of the Joint Chiefs of Staff and his headquarters would be the inter-service coordinator, but there would be input by the military at the level of a National Security Council.

The former Army Chief stated that 'My views were well known and I had discussed them with the PM often',[5] but the problem that resulted in his resignation was more complex than reasoned debate concerning one of the most important issues facing the country. It concerned his frustration with the country's governance as such, which was a fundamental matter—and one that the prime minister could not regard, in any circumstances, as being open to question.

Pakistan had enormous problems in 1998. In the words of one reporter it was suffering 'the worst financial crisis the country has faced, sanctions imposed for nuclear tests in May, and allegations and counter-allegations by the government and opposition of massive, systematic corruption.'[6] To this one might add *The Economist's* comments on 17 October that:

> Almost anywhere but Pakistan the plug would surely be yanked out. With days to go before an IMF mission was due to put the finishing touches to a rescue package, the prime minister, Nawaz Sharif, announced a 30% increase in electricity charges. This is lunacy of a high order: Pakistan's utilities are already losing enough money to sink the foundering economy... But Pakistan is no ordinary deadbeat debtor. It is a nuclear power engaged in a low-level war with another nuclear power, India, over the disputed province of Kashmir... Every newspaper carries a litany of murder prompted by greed or group hatred. An economic implosion would make things worse... the Sharif brothers seem to think that Pakistan can have Sharia and constitutional democracy, holy wars and a peaceful society, economic populism and an IMF bailout. The bet on the bailout is a long shot. The other gambles are doomed.

This was blunt condemnation of the country's government, but seemed to be shrugged off by Mr Sharif (and his brother, in theory confined to Punjab's administration, but whose national role was growing). It was in this period that General Karamat gave an address to the Naval College. Amongst other sensible observations he said that Pakistan 'cannot afford the destabilizing effects of polarization, vendettas and insecurity-driven expedient policies', and while there must be 'a neutral, competent and secure bureaucracy' there was need for 'a national security council at the apex', backed by advisers, to 'institutionalize decision-making'.[7] A senior figure of the establishment had spoken out. Having done so, he could not remain a member of the establishment—or, at least, not of Nawaz Sharif's establishment. He resigned.

There were many rumours following the resignation. Islamabad was rife with talk of an army take-over, pending constitution of a non-partisan government, and there were many who would have welcomed this. The Nawaz Sharif regime was all-powerful, politically, yet it was incapable of solving even the most basic economic problems, and corruption scandals were of such magnitude the IMF wanted to walk away and wash its hands of the country, and in October said it was doing so, although it changed its mind. (US influence was brought to bear, on the grounds that total collapse would not solve anything and that it was better to bail-out than to try to pick up the pieces afterwards.)[8] The independent press was under threat from Sharif's hoodlums (and later suffered grave assaults on its freedoms), and the bureaucracy was becoming increasingly politicized. Many distinguished civil servants were sidelined because preferment was being given to cronies of the brothers and their circle. But General Karamat is adamant that he was not forced out of his appointment:

> Dear Brian, [There was] no mystery or intrigue...My comments were blown out of all proportion by the media and exploited by people in a politically unstable environment to target the government and create an army-government rift—the start point for all our problems. [The speech] was wrongly interpreted as a 'bid for power' by the military and a criticism of the government, which it was not—it was a review of the state of affairs and the [social and political] environment for which many governments and political factions were responsible—even past military rule.
>
> I left at my own request, to save my institution from controversial and uninformed public debate...There was no conspiracy, no ambition and never did the PM ask me to leave. I acted in what I thought were the best interest of the army and the country at that time. Personal opinions should not plunge institutions into controversies in a politically divided atmosphere, because institutions suffer—individuals have to step aside.

This is an admirable explanation of what went on, by the man at the centre. Honour may be rare in politicians, but still exists in the military.

And yet…one wonders what Mr Sharif might have been thinking at the time. He has an unforgiving and vindictive nature, as was shown by his treatment of many loyal servants of government, not least being one unfortunate diplomat who was high commissioner in London during Mr Sharif's first tenure as prime minister. The Karamat episode was distasteful and served to accentuate the opinion within and outside Pakistan that the prime minister had become too powerful for the good of the country. One highly placed individual wrote to the author to say that the 'great fear' was that checks and balances to prevent further lurches to erratic autocracy had been eroded to the extent that not only was the National Assembly becoming irrelevant, but also the office of the president was seen as merely an extension of the ruling party's policy machine.

Consequential appointments came quickly. As General Karamat went into honourable retirement,[9] Lt.-Gen. Pervez Musharraf was appointed COAS, superseding Lt.-Generals Khalid Nawaz (QMG) and Ali Kuli Khan Khattak who, as CGS, was considered the obvious choice to follow Karamat. Both Khalid Nawaz and Ali Kuli took the honourable course and resigned. They were regarded by foreign observers as well above average, although the betting was on the latter to succeed as COAS in the normal course of events. He, however, being of the opinion that he had the distinction of being detested by both Benazir Bhutto and Nawaz Sharif,[10] had no illusions as to his future under either, especially as the president was without influence in military appointments (or, indeed, anything of importance).

Musharraf had as many outstanding credentials as those whom he superseded. His career[11] had been 'conventional-supersonic' according to a fellow officer, and this is an accurate comment, given that he went up the command chain with excellent reports (two tours as CO of artillery regiments; command of divisional artillery and an infantry brigade; command of an infantry division and II Corps), as well as serving with the SSG and in all the 'right' Operational staff jobs in which he did well. His report from the Royal College of Defence Studies in London was glowing and it was obvious that he was a front-runner for the highest rank. His considerable charm might also have been a factor, although he is nobody's Yes-man. He settled in quickly and brought in or moved some of his own team, promoting Muhammad Aziz Khan to Lt.-Gen. as CGS (posted from ISI, where he headed the Afghan desk—a surprise) and appointing Lt.-Gen. Muhammad Akram as QMG. The chain was not controversial, although there were some disappointed faces around. As in all good armies, the shake-up did no harm, although the DG ISI, Lt.-Gen. Ziauddin, was a government appointee and there were some raised eyebrows—not because of any lack of competence on his part but because he had not been thought of as a 'Nawaz man'. Now that the president was out of the loop, senior posts, except DG ISI, were the result of the recommendation of the COAS and the decision of the prime minister. (The ISI chief has always been a direct appointment as he answers only to the PM and not, in theory at any rate, to a military superior, which is of interest when considering developments in October 1999.)

Less than two weeks after the upset it was announced by the then Minister for Power, Gohar Ayub Khan, that military personnel would be seconded to electricity distribution regions because, according to the prime minister, 'WAPDA [the Water and Power Development Authority] itself could not contain line losses, pilferage and inefficiency'. The minister said 'We have to admit the fact that there is corruption in every cadre'[12] which was a remarkable admission, given the much-publicized announcement of a campaign against corruption. The power sector was a shambles, but the army was not the long-term answer to appalling problems of institutionalized improbity. The solution lay in the hands of government, and it was the responsibility of the country's leaders to revitalize public utilities. The band-aid approach could work for a while, but unless there were culling and retraining at all levels in WAPDA (and in many other enterprises) the country would continue to be ripped-off and would stagger along in the business-as-usual mode of extreme inefficiency which had come to be accepted by all but a few bold figures—and those were voices in the wilderness of venality that characterized Sharif's Pakistan. The views of General Musharraf are not known concerning the intervention to which he acceded, but other officers commented discreetly that it is not the business of the army to become involved in such tasks. They are right, for it is not in the best interests of the nation that the armed forces be associated with wider functions than national defence. Military involvement in detecting 'ghost teachers' (who were drawing pay for non-attendance, particularly in rural areas where they were most needed) was also regrettable.

However efficient the army might be in eradicating poor practices in civilian sectors, there is always a deferred price to pay, usually in reduced efficiency in the military element so employed. Units and formations have a 'training cycle' which, within a finite budget, is intended to improve standards. Not every type of skill can be practised within the training year, so there is emphasis, from cycle to cycle (and dependent on location and primary operational tasks), on different demands. To put it simply, it might be the Attack one year, then Defence the next. As every commander knows, the desirable number of months in a training year is thirteen plus, and any interruption of the cycle causes disruption. When units and individuals are required to serve with the UN, or natural disaster relief, or on internal security duties in aid of the civil power, they require much shaking-down when they get back, because they have concentrated on acquiring and practising skills which are not their bread and butter. Some units, such as engineers, transport and signals, may have been demonstrating their particular expertise in bridge laying, logistics, communications—but they have been doing this in a totally different environment and not within a structured fighting force. There is a world of difference for a signaller between reading and resetting an electricity meter that has been retarded by a Member of the National Assembly and manning the communications network for an armoured attack.

The armed forces are efficient, and are capable of managing almost any other institution, but that is not their job. If the government cannot run the country in the best interests of the people, and if the rule of law and provision of education, water reticulation, electricity and other services are so bad as to require the intervention of the armed forces, then it could be argued that one might as well have full martial law and have done with it—but this is not what democracy is all about.

One result of the government's deliberations about law and order was the Pakistan Armed Forces Ordinance, 1998, signed into law by President Mohammad Rafiq Tarar on 20 November. The Ordinance[13] was intended to legalize harsh counter-measures against terrorism and general mayhem in Sindh and especially Karachi (there is an excellent examination of armed forces' involvement by the ever-watchful Brigadier A.R. Siddiqi in *The Nation* of 13 January 1999), but the main features were disturbing. The old Article 245 of the Constitution,[14] one would have thought, would have met most requirements, in that:

(1) The Armed Forces shall, under the directions of the Federal Government, defend Pakistan against external aggression or threat of war, and, subject to law, act in aid of [the] civil power when called upon to do so.

(2) The validity of any direction issued by the Federal Government under clause (1) shall not be called into question by any court.

This was deemed inadequate by the government and it tried to bring in a new set of laws, seemingly without seeking legal advice from those best qualified to give it. Tinkering with the Constitution was a hobby of General Ziaul Haq, who sought to maintain his autocratic power by equating legality with personal ambition, and to that end demanded that lawyers discover language whereby the convergence might be furthered. It seems that this inclination had not deserted Pakistan's leaders in 1998 (and it might be remembered that it was Zia who appointed Nawaz Sharif Chief Minister of Punjab in 1985), for the Ordinance gave authority for the convening of military courts 'to try offences trialable [sic] under this ordinance', and declared many activities as not only illegal but deserving of severe punishment. The terms of Section (3)(1), were Draconian enough to have been constructed by the Raj in some of its worst moments of retribution against malcontent natives:

> 6. Creating Civil Commotion: 'Civil Commotion' means creation of internal disturbances in violation of law or intended to violate law, commencement or continuation of illegal strikes, go-slows, lock-outs, vehicles snatching/ lifting [sic], damage to or destruction of State or private property, random firing to create panic, charging bhatha, acts of criminal trespass (illegal qabza), distributing, publishing or pasting of a handbill or making graffiti or wall-chalking intended to create unrest or fear or create a threat to the security of law and order or to incite the commission of an offence punishable under Chapter VI of the Pakistan Penal Code (Act XLV of 1860 [sic].)

> 7. Punishment for creating civil commotion: Whoever commits an act of civil commotion shall be punished with rigorous imprisonment for a term which may extend to seven years, or with fine, or with both.

The ukase was as vicious as it was all embracing. Legally-appointed enforcers of the Ordinance could interpret a chalk mark on a wall as 'incitement' just as those zealous in enforcement of *Sharia* could declare an innocent person a defiler of the Quran were he or she to offend against a landowner's local decrees, however contrary to the true precepts of the holy book and its interpretations their own actions might be. The Constitution was being violated, and the army was being drawn into endorsement of its violation—and the army did not relish its role as courts-martial provider to the nation.

In February 1999, the Supreme Court ruled against the use of military tribunals, and there was nothing—for once—that Mr Sharif could do about a body that went against his express desires. It was unfortunate that in the meantime tribunals had ordered the death penalty for two offenders and that the hangings had been carried out, but the prime minister's opinion was that the military courts had 'shown good results' and that 'terrorists must take this idea out of their minds that they will be able to regain their foothold. Civility, truth and justice will be victorious in every circumstance. My mission is only peace and justice...'[15] was interesting, given that two months before, Mr Sharif had said 'Murderers and rapists roam around freely for years. Such people should be hanged publicly and their cases decided in twenty-four hours, three days or seven days'.[16] It seemed that justice in the eyes of Pakistan's government was to be weighed in favour of *Sharia* law, objection to which Bill, according to Sharif, would indicate that the opponent was not a true Muslim. (It is presumed that Sharif did not mean that rapists should be hanged publicly *before* their cases were heard, but merely that hearings should be conducted rapidly.) It has to be said that the number of killings in Karachi and elsewhere in Sindh did decline markedly in the period of quasi-martial law, and did not again reach the appalling levels of 1998 (when there was a total of over 800 murders), but the human rights' connotations of the Ordinance and the illegal actions taken as a result of its promulgation cannot be ignored. The army had been assured that its role was beneficial to the country, which it undoubtedly was, in the sense that malefactors were punished and removed from the society on which they preyed, but procedures were not satisfactory in law. As observed by the perceptive Brigadier Siddiqi, 'The question...is whether the army is to be used for law and order enforcement and administration of summary justice, or to settle old political scores' and it was this latter aspect with which the army was less than satisfied, according to one senior officer who wrote to the author at the time. Much of the slaughter was politically motivated, and was it right to place the army in the position of being associated with political matters, even if the overall benefits were tangible?

The army was to have other challenges in the coming months, not the least of which was the curious affair of incursions into Indian-administered Kashmir which gravely heightened tension in the subcontinent and led to even greater mistrust of Pakistan by India.

Kargil

The illegal incursion into Indian-administered Kashmir (Map 3) in early 1999, undetected by Indian forces until 6 May, was an aberration on the part of Pakistan. The aim of the operation has not been enunciated, and it is doubtful if it will ever be revealed—perhaps because the whole affair just seemed a good idea at the time, and got out of hand.

Analysis of the logistics of the incursion has drawn western observers to the conclusion that planning and preliminary operations began during winter 1998/99, with movement of mujahideen from camps in Afghanistan for training by the Northern Light Infantry (NLI) around Skardu,[17] and considerable movement by the NLI and other Pakistan Army troops in the areas of Astore, Skardu, the Deosai Plains, and forward to the Line of Control (LoC). In the event, mujahideen were not involved in organised combat.

I have walked and climbed in the precise areas in which movement across the LoC took place, in the course of a two-week visit to 3 NLI, based at Gultari in the Shingo Valley. I visited the Battalion's picquets at heights up to 14,000 feet overlooking the LoC (some are 2000 feet higher). The terrain is as beautiful and impressive as it is daunting and dangerous. Although the Line is not marked on the ground it is described fully in a document dated 11 December 1972[18] and soldiers would find little difficulty in establishing where it runs *vis-à-vis* map and ground. It is incorrect to claim that the Line is indistinct. There can be no plausible claim made that the intrusion was in some manner justified because there is dubiety or confusion as to the Line's location.

Pakistan stated that no regular troops were involved in the incursions. Strictly speaking this might be so, at least initially, because the NLI is in theory subordinate to the Ministry of the Interior, but the Force Commander Northern Areas (HQ Gilgit) commands the NLI through the brigades in Astore and Skardu, and he, in turn, is subordinate to Commander X Corps in Rawalpindi. Almost the entire NLI was involved in one way or another with the incursion, together with other infantry units. Fire support was provided by regular army artillery units whose guns were moved along the Shingo Valley.[19] Stockpiles of ammunition were brought forward from Gilgit and from the south via the Skardu road along the Indus.

It appears that only a few militants were involved in the incursions, and that several hundred NLI and other regular soldiers occupied about 130 picquets on the Indian side of the Line from late March to early May. Indian troops had begun thinning out from the higher positions the previous September, as is usual, and completed their withdrawal at the end of October. The commander of 121 Brigade (HQ Kargil), Brigadier Surinder Singh,[20] is said to have written to his superiors concerning his threat perception in the area. This would be a normal action, as any commander in a sensitive sector would keep his higher HQ informed as to his appreciation of the situation (in the military term), but what is contentious is the substance of his communication. The war of words over the brigadier's dismissal in early June and his claim to have informed his superiors of an unusual threat in his tactical area of operations will probably continue, but if he claimed (as has been leaked by official sources) that he was not permitted to send out reconnaissance or fighting patrols to check the area, then both he and his superiors are on dangerous ground. No commander requires permission to send out patrols unless this caveat has been included in formation Standing Orders or a specific directive to him. He would inform higher HQ and flanking formations of his patrol plan, but the converse is that if no patrolling had been done then the commander and staff at the higher HQ (3 Division, Maj.-Gen. V.S. Budhwar) should have been uneasy that there was no information coming in about an important sector. It would be standard operating procedure to report on snowmelt, for example, if for no other reason than to give adequate notice to units about when they would be expected to re-occupy their summer positions. Commanders are (or ought to be) unhappy if there is no regular flow of information about terrain and movement conditions, for they never know when they might be required to commit troops to battle. The Line of Control has never been a holiday resort, and patrols from both sides have tended to stretch the envelope and even trail their coats by what General Pervez Musharraf called 'aggressive patrolling'—in other words, moving across the Line.

No matter the outcome of Indian official inquiries[21] into the matter, the fact is that there was failure of intelligence. Quite why some elements in India have tried to place the blame for this upon the intelligence services themselves is unclear, because it is the duty of soldiers on the ground to report on what is occurring—or not occurring—in their area. Intelligence agencies can employ many means of surveillance, but nobody expects a RAW (Research and Analysis

Wing) or IB (Intelligence Bureau) man to be leaping from peak to peak at 16,000 feet while soldiers are snug in base camps below. If the US, with its enormously sophisticated technical intelligence methods, did not detect the build-up and incursions, it is hardly fair to blame IB and RAW.

No outside observer appears to have been aware of the movement to the Line of Control. While this is a sad commentary on the effectiveness of the Central Intelligence Agency (which at one time would have had at least a man in Skardu, where there was much activity before the incursions began, but mistakenly de-emphasized 'humint' sources during the disastrous tenure of Admiral Stansfield Turner, during the Carter presidency), it is also an interesting facet of the operations of the United Nations Military Observer Group in India and Pakistan (UNMOGIP) which maintains observers in Astore and Skardu during the summer months. (It had a field station in Kargil, but Indian pressure and UN weakness led to its closure in the mid-'80s.) It is the task of UNMOGIP to 'observe and report on the quantum of forces' on each side of the Line, but India forbids it to perform its duties in Indian-administered Kashmir (where it 'maintains a presence'), although Pakistan facilitates the 'field tasks' (patrols) carried out by observers on its side of the Line. The problem is that the Mission is only forty-four strong, because of Indian pressure, and does not have enough observers to man its posts all the time, never mind increasing their number to a desirable level. Pakistan, of course, would not have been happy about United Nations officers sitting in Astore, Skardu, Minimarg, Gultari or Dalunang in early 1999, because they would have detected movement and notified United Nations HQ in New York, whence this information would have quickly reached New Delhi. It is ironic that the very element so vehemently opposed by India, had it been adequately constituted and properly deployed, could have alerted India to the fact that something untoward was taking place in the Kargil–Dras sectors. (The statement by Pakistan's then foreign minister that 'no one knows where they [the infiltrators] come from and who they are'[22] is, with respect to Mr Sartaj Aziz, quite unbelievable.) There is also the aspect of 'open-source' information. General Pervez Musharraf visited the Northern Areas/Pakistan-administered Kashmir twice during the winter. Defence attachés (DAs), whether Indian or of other nationalities, generally maintain a log of movements of senior officers in their host country and try to find out what they are doing. (This can pay remarkable dividends.) Disruption to a pattern sends signals, and even if the DA himself cannot determine why a senior officer should make a certain visit, his alerting of other of his country's agencies as to unusual movements can result in closer examination, perhaps leading to interesting revelations.

First reports in the Indian media were optimistic about how the militants were being dealt with during Operation *Vijay*, as the Indian military action was named. There was talk of 'mopping-up', but the mood soon changed as casualties rose and Indian aircraft were shot down. Missiles destroyed a Mi-17 helicopter and a MiG-21 fighter, and another fighter crashed through technical failure. The MiG-21 is a singularly inappropriate aircraft to commit to tactical air support in high mountains, and it is not surprising that operations had to be scaled back, in order to keep up morale-boosting appearances. Contrary to Indian press reports, Mirage 2000 sorties using 'laser-guided bombs' were ineffective. It is questionable that such ordnance was used, as there do not appear to have been electronic intercepts of the readily identifiable procedures that would have been employed. India's command system was inadequate in many ways, not the least being the inability to use combat air support until the return of the army chief from an overseas visit. The infiltrators were dug-in and capable of maintaining most positions indefinitely, as they had a plenitude of rations and other stores, but, contrary to the opinion of some commentators at the time (including myself on BBC radio and other international media), not all of this came over the LoC, because much had been left behind by Indian troops the previous year. There was no point in removing it, as it would have had to be carried back again when the positions were re-occupied, so there were considerable quantities of food and heating oil available. This, and the fact that most of the bunkers were strongly constructed of concrete with metal reinforcement, caused speculation that the operation must have involved much more effort than it did. Certainly it was an impressive and major undertaking, involving much carriage of rations and stores, but most bunkers appear to have been existing Indian positions that had been developed over decades.

The matter of alleged torture of Indian soldiers was important because of its effect within India. I wrote at the time that:

> The temperature in the mountains is zero and below but has risen markedly in New Delhi and Islamabad, in part because Pakistan reported that India has used chemical weapons, and largely because of Indian allegations of

torture of prisoners of war. The former claim is nonsense, for many
technical reasons, but the accusation of torture is more serious, if only
because it has inflamed public opinion in India. There is not an Indian who
disbelieves that the half-dozen soldiers whose bodies were delivered to the
Indian army (across the Line from the Pakistani side, to the significance of
which little publicity has been given) were tortured and put to death after
capture. There is no point in attempting to question the Indian version—
although any soldier who has seen the result on a human body of
concentrated firing from an ambush will know that the victims resemble
pulped and messy colanders of meat, with eyes and teeth shattered and bits
of flesh torn away by the lacerating impact of point-blank bullets. It was
the fact that eyes had been destroyed—'gouged out'—that particularly upset
Indian public opinion.[23]

It has been acknowledged in some quarters in India that the claims
were exaggerated, but the damage has been done and it would be a
brave Indian commentator who would deny that torture took place. The
Kargil episode confounded what little trust India had in Pakistan (as
established by the Lahore meeting between Prime Ministers Nawaz
Sharif and A.B. Vajpayee in February 1999), and it was easy to believe
what was being retailed in the media as a result of statements by
government spokesmen. There may have been hesitancy, later, about
the truth of the stories, especially as the matter was not taken up by
the international media (which would have been more than happy to
expand on such a juicy story had they considered it credible), but tales
of atrocities are easier to spread than to deny, even if the originator
sincerely wishes to do that.

There was terrible irony in the gleeful description in *India Today* of
the body of what might have been a soldier of the NLI:

> He is a prized possession. The sight of him motivates the men and gears
> them for the next round of battle. Seeing him at the make-shift army
> headquarters in Dras sends their adrenaline pumping. The dead Pakistani
> Army regular—hung on a tree before his body was buried and a grid
> reference made on the map in accordance with the Geneva Convention—
> was a morale booster. More than 439 Pakistani casualties so far.[24]

This is crass. No soldier worthy of the name would have his morale
boosted by the sight of a rotting corpse, and it is ghoulish and macabre
to claim that they would. They might—such is the way of soldiers in
all armies—have a joke about it to try to reassure themselves that death
will never beckon them, but anyone who receives a pump of adrenaline

from seeing a dead body would be a seriously disturbed person. And the Geneva Convention does not approve of bodies being hanged on trees. That reporter was sick.

At the end of May it was recognized by Nawaz Sharif that the incursion was regarded in the US and elsewhere as a desperate gambit on the part of Pakistan to do something about Kashmir. It did not appear to be understood exactly what Pakistan was trying to achieve, but then, it seemed not be to known within Pakistan itself what the government wished to do. It is difficult to accept that the operation was conducted without the knowledge of Mr Sharif and his small circle of advisers, if only because the prime minister did not deny it (and, after all, the head of ISI, an important man in this affair, was his personal appointee). He had achieved the departure of a president and a chief justice and declined to refuse the resignation of a popular army chief; he was the most powerful prime minister in the history of Pakistan, and if he considered the Kargil venture to be an erratic initiative on the part of the army he was quite capable of dismissing its chief if he so wished. He stated on 2 June that the Lahore process was 'in grievous danger of being derailed',[25] which was ludicrously at odds with reality because the understanding reached at Lahore was already stone dead, but continued that 'The urgent necessity is to defuse the current situation' which nobody would have denied. The problem for Sharif was how to do it, because New Delhi was in no mood to compromise on anything.

India was angry, and had every right to be. The Union Home Minister, Mr L.K. Advani was outspoken concerning Pakistan's perfidy and reflected what was in the minds of many by saying 'It is a case of an armed intrusion by Pakistan, amounting to armed aggression'.[26] India was determined to evict the invaders, but was finding this difficult. 'The armed forces did not quite anticipate this battle and were unprepared for it,' wrote the respected defence analyst Manoj Joshi in August,[27] and listed some of the major deficiencies that caused the campaign to drag on and cost so many lives. These included lack of cold-weather clothing, protective vests, surveillance equipment, high-altitude helicopters, and radios. There was no excuse for the shortages, because the Indian army has nine mountain divisions and should have had stocks of equipment suitable for operations in their eponymous terrain. The fact that there were no night-vision devices is a reflection of grave incompetence within the procurement system, and Joshi is absolutely right to castigate politicians and senior officers for 'pushing big-ticket items instead of investing in equipping the soldier better'. There is much glamour in the thunder of a Su-30 combat aircraft, but little in a decent rifle, which is badly needed by the Indian army. There was no lack of courage on the part of Indian troops of all ranks, and, as always happens in good armies, there was a high ratio of young officers killed compared to the number of deaths of the brave soldiers they led so well.

The Northern Light Infantry and other Pakistani troops were brave, too, and casualties were considerable.[28] But Indian soldiers were at a disadvantage in fighting over unknown terrain, for most troops were brought in from elsewhere—which was why they were amazed, initially, at the militants' dug-in positions, not realizing that many of these were well-established Indian defended localities. The bunkers were small, difficult to locate, bristled with weapons, and had steep and difficult approaches, some of which were mined. Attacking such positions would be a nightmare for any soldier. It was doubly difficult for units that were brought in to the area hastily and whose men were not fully acclimatized, and it is regrettable that some were required to operate at these heights without acclimatization, which is a comparatively long process. They would be fit, of course, and would adjust more readily than most to the demands imposed on them, but committing them to battle before they were ready, and without adequate equipment and clothing (as evidenced by reporters and official photographs), was an act of desperation. It is not known what part was played by prompting from New Delhi in the early stages (and there is little of relevance in the Kargil Commission Report),[29] but it can be surmised that military leaders were under pressure to evict the intruders, in addition to their own natural inclination to get on with the job. It is easy to be critical, afterwards, but there are disturbing facets of this campaign that are reminiscent of the 1962 period, and it is hoped for the sake of the Indian army that its internal investigations result in forthright recommendations that will be adopted by the politicians and pushed through the moribund civil service system, which is more to blame for equipment deficiencies than either politicians or generals.

One thing for which the bureaucrats in New Delhi cannot be blamed was the shortage of spares for Bofors 155mm guns, which was caused by an embargo that followed bribery in contract negotiations. Depots and barracks in India were scoured, and over a hundred guns were cannibalized to ensure that those hastily moved to and around Indian-administered Kashmir could continue firing. Ammunition was a problem, too, and expensive to acquire at over $1000 per round. Conversely, Pakistan had few problems with artillery, not only because it had adequate spares, but also most of its ammunition is manufactured by Pakistan Ordnance Factories,[30] as are spare parts for many equipments, of which there was a considerable stockpile. It is of course bizarre that these members of the Commonwealth should have been shelling each other and causing so much destruction and loss of life—but the whole affair was verging on the surreal.

Pakistan kept on talking about talks, and one could not but feel an occasional twinge of sympathy for spokesmen who were trying to defend the indefensible against a growing barrage of adverse observations around the world. Some foreign comment was muted or disguised, with the intention of defusing an ugly situation, but India sometimes claimed support where none was evident, and on occasions damaged international goodwill by putting into headline news a 'spin' on statements that was undesirable from the point of view of those making them. Comments by the G-8 nations were one instance of this, and a source close to their deliberations informed the author that there was no need for India to 'reinterpret' what the G-8 communiqué had said, 'weak as it was', because the Group's critical stance had been made 'crystal clear' to Pakistan. Matters were becoming serious for Pakistan on the political front, although the intruders were difficult to dislodge and Indian casualties continued to rise. A distinguished Indian defence analyst and commentator, V.R. Raghavan, observed that 'The Kargil aggression has inevitably ended the good faith and trust which was painstakingly built up over the last few years' and that talks were 'an essential medium for understanding each other's needs and demonstrating the willingness to go the extra mile'[31] but, understandably, there were political considerations on the Indian side.

Mr Vajpayee was facing elections in September and it would have been impossible for him to appear to be backing down in the face of aggression, especially as public opinion was hardening as time went on, and voices advocating war were raised throughout the land. Bodies were being delivered to families in villages, towns and cities, and resentment against Pakistan was high and growing more intense as the weeks went by. The political problem was to keep channelling this resentment towards the 'enemy' and not to let it be deflected towards the government. Up-beat briefings, playing down equipment deficiencies, infusion of the idea that objective comment was not acceptable because this would be criticizing the gallantry of 'our boys' (a cynical political ploy not confined to India)—all these were important to the BJP's election campaign. At all costs the momentum had to be kept up against the invaders, but the problem was that they were so difficult to dislodge that casualties would undoubtedly increase—which they did, alas, dramatically—and it was difficult to gauge just how much the Indian public would stand.

As it happened, the Indian public would stand a great deal, and the government was able to maintain pressure on Pakistan to withdraw without making any concessions itself. The US endorsed a proposed visit by Pakistan's foreign minister to New Delhi, and then agreed to further the proposal that Mr Sharif himself should go there for talks, but although this was initially acceptable to New Delhi, the government read the mood of the country otherwise—and correctly. On no account could there be a visit by the prime minister of Pakistan. The manner in which the initiative was killed was as Byzantine as might be expected in the circumstances, but Islamabad continued to be optimistic about talks and was living in a dream world, as evidenced by the cabinet's 'serious concern' about 'the unwarranted Indian military operations in the area across the Line of Control involving heavy artillery, helicopter gunships and jet aircraft'.[32] This was ridiculous, as was known by India and the rest of the world. (In fact, there were no gunships: the Indian Air Force's Mi-25 attack helicopters cannot fly above 12,000 feet, and although it was claimed by India that troop-carrier Mi-17s were used as gunships, and there was a photograph of one apparently firing rockets, the official record shows that there were only 31 sorties by Mi-17s throughout the whole period.) The US became exasperated; as well it might, but eventually got Pakistan off the hook—and India, too, because in spite of the hype about success, Operation *Vijay* was a horrible, brutal slog in classic infantry fashion. The operations of 18 Grenadiers in the battle of 'Tiger Hill' (to take but one example) were superb, but were immensely costly against well dug-in and strongly supported NLI troops.

There were unofficial attempts to end the fighting, amongst which was despatch of the distinguished Indian journalist R.K. Mishra and a notable diplomat, Vivek Katju to Islamabad, reciprocated by a visit to New Delhi by Pakistan's former foreign secretary, Niaz Naik, an admirable emissary of dignity, acumen and experience. Openings to dialogue were effected, but the moves resulted in internal criticism in both countries and, although valuable in establishing a modest approach to future personal contact, had no chance of success.

In the end, Mr Sharif, failing to obtain support of any sort, even from China (whom one would have thought might not be averse to making things difficult for India, given its own little-reported incursion at Daulat Beg Oldi on the Indian side of the Line of Actual Control in Aksai Chin), had to crave audience with the American president to obtain a fig-leaf that would enable him to order retreat with a semblance of dignity.

There had been fears that clashes could spread to the point that forces along the border would become involved, and that this might lead to a nuclear exchange. Much pressure was brought to bear on India and Pakistan (in spite of what is claimed to the contrary) to refrain from widening the conflict,[33] and although both sides claim that the 'nuclear deterrent' ensured that their governments behaved 'responsibly' the fact is that existence of basic nuclear devices served to push much of the rest of the world to exert influence on the countries to refrain from taking more aggressive steps.[34] It was assessed that a nuclear war in the subcontinent, especially given the lack of systems for weapons' control, would be a world disaster and not just a local one. It was not deterrence in the classic sense, although Islamabad and New Delhi tried to present their avoidance of conflict-expansion in the context of Cold War nuclear theology.

A worrying aspect of the conflict was an increase in attacks by militants within Indian-administered Kashmir, especially against what are considered 'hard targets'—security forces' fighting patrols and well-guarded camps. There were instances of merciless murder of civilians, especially in Hindu villages and hamlets, but the aim appeared to be to demonstrate the militants' ability to extend their fight to debilitate and demoralize paramilitary forces, especially the Rashtriya Rifles who were bearing the brunt of internal security duties in the absence of regular troops redeployed along the Line of Control. Escalation of these operations was disconcerting because India, with good reason, stated that Pakistan was supporting the militants, and there was even further distrust of Islamabad by New Delhi.

In the Kargil affair Pakistan behaved outrageously and contrary to international norms—and, of some importance, inconsistently with the Simla Accord of 1971.[35] India, in spite of politically motivated bluster and understandable but excessive nationalism, had its confidence shaken by the Kargil debacle. Over 600 soldiers were killed[36] and some 1800 wounded in a few weeks, as against 1150 dead and 3000 incapacitated in almost three years in the disastrous 'peacekeeping'

operation in Sri Lanka (July 1987–April 1990). This is a dreadful toll
to be exacted, and it would have been very much higher if the intruders
had not withdrawn as a result of mediation.

Senior Indian figures stated flatly there was no outside mediation
concerning the Kargil affair, but President Clinton spoke with Mr Sharif
and Mr Vajpayee at length. While Mr Vajpayee did state to Mr Clinton
that 'there is no question of mediation' he cannot deny that he was
informed that Mr Sharif would be going to Washington, that he (Mr
Vajpayee) was told he was welcome should he wish to pay such a visit,
and that Mr Clinton was going to use his good offices to persuade
Nawaz Sharif that the bloodstained disaster had gone on long enough
and that withdrawal of the Pakistanis had better take place *ek dum* (or
words to that effect). And so it happened, after the 4th of July
meeting.

The Indian army's assaults on the heights in the Dras and Kargil
sectors cost its gallant regiments dearly. The NLI and other Pakistani
soldiers fought well and tenaciously before evacuating the fourteen
posts from which they were driven. Withdrawal from the remaining
120 or so defended localities was on orders from the Pakistan side of
the Line of Control. Casualties were high, perhaps as many as 400,[37]
and many of these know no grave, no honour, and receive no
acknowledgement of their dedication. May they all, of both sides, rest
in peace, and may their families take consolation in the fact that they
were doing their duty according to their code and oaths, whatever these
may have been, of whatever faiths they espoused. It was not their fault
that Kashmir is a disputed territory whose status could have been
resolved long ago were it not for the intransigence of successive
governments in both countries.

The Indian government issued a statement on 5 July concerning the
withdrawal from Indian-administered territory in Kashmir. It was
ungracious, as might be expected from an offended party, and had a
sting in the tail for those countries who wish India and Pakistan well,
and who would be more than happy to offer their assistance in
furthering good relations between them.

We have seen the US–Pakistan joint statement issued in Washington
yesterday. Our US interlocutors have informed us that 'concrete steps'
referred to in the statement mean withdrawal by Pakistan of their forces
from our side of the Line of Control in the Kargil sector.

We have also noted the sequencing of steps agreed to in the statement, that only after withdrawal is completed will other contemplated steps be initiated. We hope Pakistan will heed this call immediately. We will be watching developments on the ground.

We reaffirm that Pakistan's armed intrusion and aggression has to be vacated.

Our military aggression [*sic*] in the Kargil sector, which has been initiated for this purpose, is making steady progress.

It will continue with full force until the aggressors are cleared out, and the *status quo ante* on the Line of Control fully restored.

One word about the Lahore process. It is direct and bilateral. In this process there is no place whatsoever for any third party involvement. The same is true for any other aspect of India–Pakistan relations.[38]

There was no need for this sort of pietistic stuff, and (although there may have been chuckles about 'our military aggression') Washington considered its tone inappropriate. (A US diplomat in Washington informed me at the time that India's attitude of jubilation was 'unfortunate'.) The invaders regarded it unfavourably, and a spokesman for the United Jihad Council wasted his breath by stating that 'A withdrawal from Kargil would be detrimental to the freedom struggle for Kashmir and…the mujahideen will fight to their last breath to free their motherland from Indian forces of aggression'.[39]

India was entitled to be satisfied that the intruders had been withdrawn, but political point scoring was difficult to resist. The BJP and its allies were determined to be seen as the winning team and the perceptive Dinesh Kumar wrote that 'They are bound to hold celebrations like they did after the May 1998 Pokhran explosions, and would, in keeping with the nature of politics in the country, even seek to capitalize on the 'victory' keeping the forthcoming elections in mind'.[40] The interim government did indeed claim that the Kargil 'war' had been 'won' by the all-seeing BJP coalition, and on at least one occasion placed enormous photographs of the service chiefs and an *Agni* missile on an election platform. The mood of belligerence was fostered in many quarters, and although in Pakistan there was a fair amount of war-talk, there were fears, too, that India might go the extra mile—not towards talks, but towards conflict. The army chief made speeches emphasizing that the country was prepared to defend itself, but the mood in the army seemed to vary from outright bellicosity to fairly strong criticism of the Sharif government for getting the nation into a difficult position.

The government in Islamabad tried to put as brave a face on the debacle as it could, but the mood within Pakistan was largely of confusion. The army was shaken, and young officers, especially, felt betrayed. There was some plain speaking when the Chief of the Army Staff toured military bases, and morale was badly affected in some units. The entire episode seemed so unnecessary and harmful to Pakistan's already shaky image abroad that explanation appeared at best superfluous and at worst mere political ground shifting. Mr Sharif's national broadcast on 12 July[41] was worth giving, however, even if it was shaky on the aim of the invasion. He acknowledged that there was 'no secret that the threat of a big war with India was looming, by the way things had deteriorated between India and Pakistan', which he could hardly deny, but then he said that 'I think the basic purpose of the mujahideen occupation of Kargil was to attract world attention to the Kashmir issue... They have fully succeeded in that objective and they have also practically proved our stand that the Kashmir issue is a nuclear flashpoint'. Of course no Pakistani troops occupied Kargil but the question must be put as to when did Mr Sharif know of 'the basic purpose'? He approved of it, but did he approve the means of achieving it? There was not much point in 'proving' that Kashmir is a nuclear flashpoint, as many concerned people have been saying this since the time of the nuclear tests[42] — and there is a danger that proof might one day be obtained with unexpected finality.

There is little wonder that Mr Vajpayee's vexation with Pakistan was not diminished by the address, because Mr Sharif stated that 'During talks in Lahore I told Indian Prime Minister Vajpayee that we have achieved nothing through war, and after every war we moved to another war'. This is mind-reeling stuff, on the same level as India's contention that it exploded nuclear bombs in order to further the cause of nuclear disarmament. Deep talking to deep, obviously. General Talat Masood, sagacious as ever, wrote that:

> The Kargil crisis has once again exposed the bankruptcy of Pakistan's national policy. Events in and around Kargil brought India and Pakistan dangerously close to an all-out war, dealt a shattering blow to the peace process, have done immense damage to the already faltering economy, isolated Pakistan internationally, and proved highly divisive internally....[43]

Dr Maleeha Lodhi analysing the affair in a wide-ranging document, included the observations that:

> The failure to objectively assess national strengths and vulnerabilities during the Kargil crisis was in large part a consequence of...unstructured, personalised decision-making, and led to the avoidable diplomatic debacle... In using with an international audience the same propaganda techniques and tools, even idiom, that the government believes serves it so well in the domestic sphere proved utterly and predictably counterproductive....
>
> In the post-Kargil situation, Pakistan faces critical choices on both domestic and external fronts...Policy clarity is urgently needed about which direction the leadership wants to take the country. Playing holy warriors this week and men of peace the next betrays an infirmity and insincerity of purpose that leaves the country leaderless and directionless. But if flip-flops and government by muddling through, cum policy reversal continues, the dangers to Pakistan's stability will only mount.[44]

These sobering observations (much resented by the Sharif brothers and their henchmen) are applicable to government direction of the armed forces, and she notes that it was only on the eve of Mr Sharif's visit to Washington that there was a meeting of the Defence Committee of the Cabinet (DCC) which, almost unbelievably, was the first of the year.[45] It is essential that the higher direction of war should be understood by those in government whose duty it is to direct the armed forces (when democracy returns), and that the entire command and control system of the services be restructured.

Command and Control

Now that India and Pakistan have a nuclear capability and appear hell-bent on continuing development of nuclear-tipped surface-to-surface missiles, aerial delivery systems, and in India's case, breathtakingly expensive and complex maritime equivalents, it is important that their command and control systems be scrutinized. This is not to endorse the nuclear weapons race, which is a disaster for the subcontinent and will keep hundreds of millions in excruciating poverty; but if the countries are to establish a practicable nuclear doctrine—a labyrinth of intellectual contradictions through which even well-established nuclear powers continue to seek their way (and stumble from time to time)—there must be rationalization of their higher defence structure. The first step, in both countries, should be establishment of a Joint Commander.

For the purposes of modern war it is imperative that the armed services of Pakistan be placed under a single officer, with a staff designed to assist him in his command and other functions. The present Joint Staff Headquarters would be a start, but is physically far too small and lacks the number of officers required to function properly as a command HQ. The duty statement of the Chief of Defence Force (CDF) should be simply

To command the armed forces of Pakistan.

There should be no equivocation about this, and the words 'chairman' 'committee' and 'staff' should be eschewed in the title as well as in practice. Senior officers would give advice (especially concerning employment and deployment of their own services), which is what they are there for; they may even argue their positions to whatever extent the CDF might consider reasonable; but decisions are for the CDF and him alone. His is a non-executive board, save when he delegates action to be taken.

So far as the higher direction of war is concerned, the CDF should be the adviser to government on strategy, which is where a National Security Council (NSC) is important. As Talat Masood wrote:

> The argument that the Defence Committee of Cabinet can serve the same purpose as a National Security Council is inherently flawed... The DCC generally addresses issues at a time when a particular crisis has already become intractable or the policy has failed to deliver. The NSC, on the other hand, meets at regular intervals and can [also] be convened at any time in event of an emergency. There has to be continuous flow of information...on the basis of which sound policy options can be evolved and implemented. This can only happen if there is institutional back up of the NSC.

A National Security Council was established by Act of Parliament in April 2004, but it appears it is not in quite the form recommended by General Masood. It first met on 24 June and the *Pakistan Observer* of 2 July recorded that:

> [The] meeting addressed Pakistan's deteriorating law and order situation, the weeks of killings in Karachi, and anti-Al Qaeda operations on the Afghan border, Karachi turmoil, Sui explosions, WAPDA towers blown,

Christina Rocca's Congressional hearings, ongoing confidence-building talks with India, agreement between India and Pakistan to open consulates in Karachi and Bombay, and the lingering Kashmir entanglement.

Pakistan's top civil-military body including the then Prime Minister Mir Zafarullah Khan Jamali, National Assembly Speaker Chaudhry Amir Hussain, chief ministers of Punjab, Sindh and Balochistan, Joint Chiefs of Staff Committee Chairman and the Services Chiefs attended the meeting as its members while ministers for Interior and Foreign Affairs, the NWFP governor and Vice Chief of Army Staff attended the meeting on special invitation. They vowed to rid the country of terrorism and religious militancy that has claimed more than 60 lives since May. 'If there is a threat to Pakistan it is from (the) internal security environment,' said President Pervez Musharraf, chairing the first meeting of the National Security Council (NSC).[46]

It is for the senior figure in government to decide how much influence the NSC should have, and at present in Pakistan that is the President—but it is essential he puts in place a system that will be applicable to a future civilian government, whatever form that may take, including that of an executive presidency. The discussion points for the first meeting, noted above, are daunting and arguably far too all-embracing to produce Talat Masood's 'sound policy options', and refined procedures should reflect this. In the context of the direction of defence matters, the deliberations of the NSC should result in overall strategic objectives being conveyed to the Chief of Defence Force. It is then up to him to translate these into tactical (or operational) concepts. He must be undisturbed by government and bureaucracy once the national strategy has been spelled out. (There is nothing politicians love so much as being pictured as decisive commanders. When they are involved in military matters, they take on a particular look of macho determination for the cameras and do their best to combine a furrowed brow, jutting chin, and steely eyes.) Deployment and command of forces are the CDF's responsibility, although he will discuss matters with the NSC. All of this takes many years to hone to efficiency, but the government of Pakistan should no longer resist creation of a CDF and a Joint HQ. It will be costly, but there is no point in having expensive weapons and large forces if they cannot be directed properly. The manpower would come from the existing Service headquarters—from which source much resistance can be expected.

In the Joint HQ/CDF concept the service chiefs would have responsibility to 'raise, train and provide.' They would not be in the operational chain of command, but would be single-service advisers in what might be called the CDF's Advisory Council. Their own headquarters would shrink accordingly, for there would be no requirement for many of the staff branches that now exist. Single service operations branches, these sacred bodies to which the best and the brightest aspire, would be disbanded and reconstituted within the tri-service HQ, and this is why there would be so much opposition within the services. Using the well-tried strategy of divide and rule, the bureaucrats (whose own power would be reduced) would enlist doubters amongst the politicians and try to influence government against any moves towards creation of a CDF, saying that because the three services were having the mother of all turf wars about jointery, there would be no point in going further with the proposal. (Which is exactly what has been taking place in India. That saga is depressing.) This way lies disaster for the armed forces. I have been present at a creation, and saw officers disagreeing so violently about allocation of particular appointments to this or that Service that friendships of years were sundered.[47] It can be a messy business, but it is the only way to go.

After Kargil

In 1999 the country was far from stable: corruption continued on a massive scale, the economy was in tatters and the rule of law was all but defunct. The 'Anti-Terrorism Act 1997 (amendment) Ordinance' was repressive and reminiscent of the worst periods of martial law. Press freedom was under continuous threat, and it was only international outrage that resulted in the release of the courageous publisher and editor, Najam Sethi, and cessation of harassment of various newspapers, especially the Jang Group. The threats made against the editor of *The News*, Rawalpindi, and Dr Maleeha Lodhi, by a member of the government were bizarre, and resembled those of the Nazis against the German press in the mid-1930s. There was a nation-wide strike caused by proposals to institute a sales tax. The government's aim appeared to be to enunciate grandiose projects of which nothing more was heard after headlines had been obtained. There was no credible political Opposition, and religious militancy was on the rise.[48]

Little wonder that a diplomat on leave in his home country in 1999, when asked exactly where Islamabad was located, replied that it is 'twenty kilometres from Pakistan'.

NOTES

1. General Karamat to author, 23 August 1999.
2. General Karamat to author, 22 August 1999.
3. The US and several other countries were aware of detail concerning the nuclear programme. It was surprising—and fascinating—just how much was known. The US, in consequence of this knowledge and Congressional requirements, had to curtail all aid. Other countries did not have such legislation and could continue as if there were no nuclear programme, although they conducted a robust diplomatic campaign behind the scenes. The G-8, and especially Japan, were most active.
4. A US definition, as covered in most advanced military colleges.
5. Correspondence with the author, 18 August 1999.
6. 'Pakistan Army Chief quits amidst controversy', Andrew Hill, Reuters, 13:25, 10-07-98.
7. Press Release by the Directorate General of Inter Service Public Relations (ISPR), 6 October 1998.
8. See the excellent chronology in *Pakistan 2000*, Craig Baxter and Charles Kennedy (eds.) (OUP 2001); also Kux (2001). The IMF cancelled a mission to Pakistan in October 1998 but in November the US leant on the IMF/WB and a $5.5 billion bailout package was arranged.
9. From which he was appointed Pakistan's ambassador to the US in 2004, an admirable choice.
10. Conversation with the author.
11. See http://www.presidentofpakistan.gov.pk/Biography.aspx.
12. 'Power companies to be handed over to army', *The News*, 23 October 1998.
13. 'Text of Pakistan Armed Forces Ordinance, 1998', *Dawn*, 21 November 1998.
14. *The Constitution of the Islamic Republic of Pakistan*, Edited and introduced by Makhdoom Ali Khan, Pakistan Law House, Karachi, 1990. The 14th Amendment curtailed the powers of the President, the 15th sought to establish the 'Supremacy of the Quran and Sunnah' (*see*, 'Implications of the 15th Amendment, Asma Jahangir, *The News*, 13 September 1998), and further restriction was placed on the President on 24 December 1998 (*See*, 'President's powers further curtailed', *The Nation*, 25 December 1998.)
15. 'Pakistan PM bows to ruling against military courts', Raja Asghar, Reuters 11:12, 01-19-99.
16. 'Pakistan PM calls for Taliban-style laws', Andrew Hill, Reuters 08:50, 11-17-98.
17. Report of a conversation between a British visitor to Pakistan and two mujahideen in Gilgit in July, supplied to the author on 16 August 1999. They had been in militants' camps in Afghanistan during the US cruise missile attacks and stated that there were 'British Muslims' amongst the mujahideen at Kargil, a claim supported by a senior officer of RAW in New Delhi in a telephone conversation with the author, 24 August 1999.

18. *Delineation of the Line of Control in Jammu and Kashmir Resulting from the Cease Fire Line of 17 December 1971, in Accordance with the Simla Agreement of 2 July 1972.* (UN Document dated 11 December 1972. The author has copy No. 14.)

19. *Kargil, The Impregnable Conquered* by Lt-Gen YM Bammi (Gorkha Publishers, Delhi, 2002) is 558 pages of relentless praise for Indian forces, but in the case of Pakistan artillery is perhaps a trifle inaccurate when stating that in August 1998 there were 'Chinese manning Pakistani guns'.

20. Ibid., pp. 492 and 493. General Bammi points out that Brigadier Surinder Singh was criticised by the Kargil Review Committee in its Report. It appears the brigadier was the only officer in the entire Indian Army who performed inadequately. Bammi points out that the Committee 'did not comment upon the threat assessments of his higher commanders and how [they were] monitoring [the situation].' See also *New Chief for Army* by Praveen Swami in *Frontline* of January 18-31 2003 at http://www.flonnet.com/fl2002/stories/20030131005403400.htm.

21. See, for example, http://www.southasianmedia.net/index_opinion4.cfm?id=38377 for comment by Kanwar Sandhu of the *Hindustan Times*, 4 August 2004.

22. 'Indian jets fire on Kashmir', Arthur Max, Associated Press AP-NY-05-26-99 1256 EDT.

23. 'Kashmir with a capital N', Brian Cloughley, *Canberra Times*, Australia, 5 July 1999.

24. 'Kargil War: Battlefront', Harinder Baweja, *India Today*, 12 July 1999.

25. 'Kashmiri Militants Dismiss Offer', Kathy Gannon, Associated Press, AP-NY-06-03-99 2252EDT.

26. 'Sharif responsible for aggression', *The Hindu*, 3 June 1999.

27. 'The Kargil Syndrome', *India Today*, 5 August 1999.

28. General Bammi states that '... the award [of a decoration] to only one lieutenant colonel of infantry indicates that after initially deploying their units, the Commanding Officers [COs] of Pakistan Army did not come forward to fight or direct operations.' This is not only an unseemly and vulgar insult but is rubbish, militarily. For a CO to come forward and 'fight or direct operations' unless he is mounting a battalion attack is to interfere with his company and platoon commanders. If a CO has to use his personal weapon in a battle, there is something very badly wrong. This sort of nonsense began in Vietnam, when unit and even brigade commanders used helicopters to hover near platoon engagements and thoroughly confuse things by giving orders to hard-pressed subalterns. Pakistani COs were doing what COs ought to do: visiting the troops whenever possible and directing war at battalion level. The standard and credibility of Bammi's book can be summed up in his statement that 'The operations of 9 Mahar and 13 Kumaon... showed that with adequate planning Pakistani troops can be defeated in any terrain. Unfortunately, operations of 3 Rajput did not go well.' But he doesn't say what happened to 3 Rajput.

29. There are balanced accounts of the Kargil affair in *Dateline Kargil*, by Gaurav Sawant (Macmillan India, 2000), and *A Soldier's Diary* by Harinder Baweja (Books Today, New Delhi, 2000). A Pakistani book by Dr Shireen Mazari, *The Kargil Conflict 1999* (Institute of Strategic Studies, Islamabad, 2003) is on a par with *Kargil: The Tables Turned*, edited by Maj.-Gen. (retd.) Ashok Krishna and Dr P.R. Chari (Manohar, New Delhi, 2000) which, with *Kargil: Blood on the Snow*, by Maj.-Gen. Ashok Verma (Manohar, New Delhi, 2000) are well reviewed in *Frontline*

of November 22-December 05, 2003 by A.G. Noorani http://www.frontlineonnet. com/fl2024/stories/20031205000507300.htm. Other essential reading is *The Kargil War* (New Delhi: South Asia Publishers, 1999); Ashley Tellis, Christine Fair and Jamison Jo Medby, and *Limited Conflict under the Nuclear Umbrella: Indian and Pakistani Lessons from the Kargil Crisis* (Rand, 2001). *Kargil: Pakistan's Fourth War*, Jasjit Singh [ed] (New Delhi: South Asia Books, 1999) adds some other perspectives.

30. POF is a Pakistan success story. Probably its most outstanding Chairman (of some very high-grade officers who occupied the position), Lt.-Gen. Talat Masood, who later became Secretary Defence Production, brought the organization to a peak of efficiency which has been maintained. It does not manufacture 'big-ticket' items but concentrates on ammunition, for which it has a significant export market, and spares for all types of equipments. Heavy Industries Taxila (HIT) manufactures and upgrades armoured fighting vehicles.

31. 'The larger purpose in Kargil', *The Hindu*, 5 June 1999. General Raghavan is Director of the Delhi Policy Group and a former DGMO. His columns in *The Hindu* are always worth reading, being wise and succinct.

32. 'Pakistan urges urgent world steps to end escalation', *Dawn*, 6 June 1999.

33. Diplomatic and defence attaché sources of several countries to the author, June–August 1999.

34. General Bammi claims that in July 1998 there was 'Deployment of M-11 missiles at Deosai Plains' by Pakistan. The M-11 is the export version of the Chinese CSS-7, essentially a Scud-B, which has a trailer-erector-launcher 13.36 metres long and 3.03 metres wide. The TEL weights 37,400 kg with missile. The approaches to the track across the Deosai plains are difficult for a jeep to negotiate.

35. One of the interesting items in a telephone conversation during the conflict between General Musharraf (in China) and the CGS, Lt.-Gen. Aziz, recorded by the Indians (transcript in Bammi, Annex 15), is that the former is heard to say '[it] is in Simla Agreement that we cannot go for UN intervention', which is not so. There is nothing in the Simla Accord that states any such thing.

36. See http://www.subcontinent.com/sapra/military/kargil11.html quoting the Times of India on 6 and 9 July 1999.

37. Sources in Pakistan.

38. Reuters 08:38, 07-05-99.

39. 'Kashmir combatants make conflicting claims', Reuters 13:19, 07-10-99.

40. 'Kargil was a lapse. Halt the celebrations', Dinesh Kumar, *The Times of India*, 15 July 1999.

41. Text in Reuters report 12:56, 07-12-99.

42. *See*, for example, 'Nuclear Risk-Reduction Measures in Kashmir', Brian Cloughley, Stimson Center, Washington DC, November 1998. New edition in Chapter 7 of *Nuclear Risk Reduction in South Asia*, Michael Krepon (ed.) (Palgrave Macmillan 2004).

43. 'Lessons to learn from Kargil', *Dawn*, 17 July 1999.

44. Dr Maleeha Lodhi (former Editor of *The News*, Rawalpindi; former ambassador to the US; appointed High Commissioner in London 2003), 'The Kargil Crisis', *Newsline*, July 1999. A most important analysis, as might be expected from this gifted public figure.

45. A meeting of the DCC on 25 August 1999 delivered, amongst other banalities, the observation that 'It is noted that India's intention to go ahead with the deployment and operationalisation [sic] of its nuclear weapons and delivery systems is fraught with serious risks and dangers not only for the security of the region but the world at large'. Wow.

46. http://www.infopak.gov.pk/writeups/NSC_maiden_session.htm.

47. An Australian major general berated a brigadier for failing to recommend that a particular appointment should be reserved for the army, with the words 'don't forget your loyalty'. It was the general who was being disloyal, of course—but the brigadier was not promoted, in spite of being an outstanding officer.

48. 'Pakistan Islamic head urges 'coward' PM to quit,' Ismail Khan, Reuters 13:16, 08-27-99.

14 The Coup, the Borders, and the Army's Capabilities

The October [1999] coup capped a year of increasing discontent with the Sharif administration, stemming from its crackdown on opposition political activity and increasing encroachments on civil liberties, with the courts providing only occasional relief. Leaders of Pakistan's normally fractious opposition announced on September 14 the formation of the Grand Democratic Alliance (GDA) grouping together nineteen political parties with the avowed aim of dislodging Sharif's government. The government responded with overt attempts to suppress opposition political activity. A GDA call for a protest rally in Karachi led to the arrest from September 24 to 26 of more than 1,000 opposition activists throughout the city, including much of the leadership of the Pakistan People's Party, as well as senior leaders of the Muttahida Qaumi Movement (MQM), the Awami National Party, and the Pakistan Tehrik-e-Insaaf party.[1]

The announcement on 12 October 1999 that Prime Minister Nawaz Sharif had, for the second time, dismissed an Army Chief led to a coup that confused much of the outside world as much as it was approved by most of the citizens of Pakistan. It was essential, by tacit international convention, that the government's dismissal be criticized by foreign countries and institutions, in spite of the fact that they were all well aware that 'democratic' Pakistan was thundering downhill morally, socially and economically. The United States imposed more sanctions, the European Union expressed 'deep concern', the United Nations declared that Pakistan must 'restore civilian rule and the constitutional process', the World Bank and the International Monetary Fund muttered about stopping new development aid, and the Commonwealth suspended Pakistan's membership. The future looked bleak.

One intriguing thing about the dismissal of Musharraf was that only two weeks before Sharif took action to get rid of him, he had appointed him Chairman of the Joint Chiefs of Staff Committee (CJCSC), while continuing to hold his army position. He had been made Acting CJCSC on 8 April 1999, when it was announced he would serve in the position for a year, but in a surprising move Sharif confirmed and extended him in the appointment.

The only other officer to have held both posts was his predecessor, General Karamat, and according to former government figures in office at the time,[2] the reason that Sharif wanted to have one person holding the two appointments was that he thought it essential for his own security to have both in the hands of one pliable individual who would do precisely what he wished. Apparently he considered himself more threatened by the existence of two senior figures than by one who held two appointments. The notion that a Chairman on his own could pose a threat to the government was, and is doubtful. He commands no troops, and although undoubtedly a man of stature and personality— otherwise he wouldn't be in the post—it is troops that matter if any physical move is to be made against those holding political power. And, of more importance, the notion that someone like Musharraf, as either COAS or in both posts, would stand aside limply if an increasingly paranoid prime minister was taking the country through constitutional hoops was also questionable. Z.A. Bhutto had thought Zia would be a supine yes-man, and Nawaz Sharif made the same mistake about Musharraf.[3]

It had been thought that Musharraf would serve only a token period as Acting Chairman, thus allowing the Chief of Naval Staff, Admiral Fasih Bokhari to be appointed at some stage. However, when the Prime Minister extended Musharraf as Chairman until 6 October 2001 he was making it clear that this would not occur. His action resulted in the understandable resignation of Bokhari, who had had only five months left to serve as navy chief, at the end of which time he would be required to retire were he not made Chairman. His public reason for resigning is interesting, however, and was given three years later in an interview with the *South Asia Tribune*.[4] Sharif's decision about the CJCSC was made on 29 September, and Bokhari stated to the *Tribune* that 'I resigned on October 5, 1999, a week before Musharraf's coup of October 12 because I had come to know that he had decided to topple the Sharif government.'

This is an intriguing statement. If the Chief of Naval Staff had evidence that there was about to be a coup against the government of his country it is strange that he did not inform the president of the fact. President Tarar was not the most effective head of state that Pakistan has known, and indeed was a mere puppet of the Sharif family, but Admiral Bokhari owed him allegiance as the nation's highest constitutional authority.[5] Every member of the armed forces swears that he or she will 'uphold the Constitution of the Islamic Republic of Pakistan', and the CNS was hardly doing this by quietly resigning rather than telling the president that it seemed the nation's government was about to be overthrown by the army yet again. Bokhari is quite definite about it: when he was asked 'why, in his view, General Musharraf wanted to topple Nawaz Sharif' the admiral replied 'Because he feared he will have to face a court martial for masterminding the Kargil (debacle)'. But there is the point that if Bokhari had resigned immediately after the coup took place he might have given a rather more effective message to the nation concerning the disapproval he later registered.

Certainly, there were many rumours about a possible coup. At the Saudi Arabian National Day reception in Islamabad on 23 September, General Musharraf answered a question hinting at the possibility of a serious rift with the prime minister by saying 'We enjoy excellent relations with the government', but was also asked about a US statement that 'We [the US] would strongly oppose any attempt to change the government through extraconstitutional means'.[6] His reply that 'It's an old story. I don't want to comment. I am a soldier and don't want to enter into any controversy', was no more nor less than was proper, but it was obvious that something was going on, especially as the PM's spokesman on 29 September referred to 'uncalled for rumours and speculations about change of command in the army' that 'certain vested interests were fanning in pursuance of their political agenda.'

There was a strong element of farce entering the Sharif government's handling of senior appointments, and not just in the armed forces. Over 100 senior civil servants had been moved or reallocated in a large-scale, politically-motivated reshuffle; an unforgivable and completely avoidable disruption of the country's administration, economically and socially, in a critical period when their expertise was essential for effective administration of the country's affairs.[7]

On 9 October 1999, it was announced that the Corps Commander of 12 Corps (in Quetta), Lt.-General Tariq Parvaiz Khan had been 'asked to retire' by GHQ (i.e., the COAS) as from 13 October. The initial notification was terse, and even a later clarification said only that he had been removed 'for service reasons'. In fact, he had met with political figures without informing GHQ. This might not have been unusual in normal times because the general, who attended staff college in Australia and is thoroughly cosmopolitan in addition to being a most likeable person, has a first cousin who was a government minister; but these were not normal times, and anyone in the military who had even fleeting contact with Sharif or his cronies was considered to have ulterior motives. Concurrently, the Commander of 1 Corps (HQ at Mangla), Lt.-General Saleem Haider, was transferred to GHQ, apparently for revealing to persons unknown (but suspected to be in Sharif's circle) the subjects discussed at a recent corps commanders' conference presided over by Musharraf.

These events were strange, to say the least, and created concern throughout the country, as it was obvious that something untoward was afoot. (And it should be noted that it is a thoroughly unhealthy thing for officers to be spied upon. The atmosphere was decidedly rancid.) It appeared that senior officers were becoming at least peripherally involved in politics, which was considered unforgivable. The bizarre series of resignations and dismissals cannot have given neighbouring India much confidence in the way Pakistan was being governed, especially after the Kargil fighting earlier in the year, and it was in this period, according to a highly placed official in Islamabad,[8] that several senior officers decided something was amiss and began to plan for action if Nawaz Sharif decided to move against the COAS/Chairman, which he did on 12 October.

The man chosen by the prime minister to succeed Musharraf was General Khawaja Ziauddin, one of the Sharif family's close associates, who was not well-known for his soldierly qualities.

During the military reshuffle in 1998, when Pervez Musharraf was promoted to become COAS, the PM appointed General Ziauddin as Director General Inter-Services Intelligence, and it soon became apparent that he enjoyed the confidence of Sharif, as he was used in a quasi-governmental fashion to make Pakistan's position on terrorism clear to Washington. This included, and indeed emphasized, Pakistan's commitment to assisting US efforts to kill or capture the infamous Osama bin Laden of the Al-Qaeda organization which was based partly in Afghanistan and was held responsible by Washington for several terrorist attacks on US personnel and facilities well before the 9/11 outrages.

Ziauddin's appointment as COAS was a major turnaround for the Pakistan Army, which had never before had a chief from the Corps of Engineers.[9] All former chiefs have been from a fighting arm, either infantry, armour or artillery, and from what could be gathered from telephone calls by the author to Islamabad at the time, and in later discussions with senior officers, the army was unhappy with him as a person and as a leader. He had been due to retire on 2 February 2000, but received an extension of service when appointed DGISI. He did not enjoy the confidence of his peers or the trust of the army as a whole.

When the prime minister made the announcement of his army chief's dismissal, Musharraf was in Colombo, having attended Sri Lankan army ceremonies marking its fiftieth anniversary, along with several of his international counterparts including those of India and Bangladesh.

The fact that General Musharraf had gone to Sri Lanka at all was an indication that he was not at that time intent on taking action against the prime minister. Indeed, before boarding his scheduled PIA flight to return to Pakistan he played a round of golf in Colombo, which was hardly an indication of a man in the middle of preparations to overthrow a government. He seemed to be completely relaxed.

His attitude changed when PK 805 did not land immediately after arriving in Karachi airspace on time. It circled for almost an hour, with the pilot being ordered by PIA's chairman, Shahid Khakan Abbasi, who was in the control tower, to divert to Dubai. It is presumed the order came from the Prime Minister. The pilot protested that he did not have enough fuel to make the trip safely (that is, to divert to Dubai and still have enough fuel to divert to another airport if for some reason it was not possible to land there), and Abbasi told him to fly to Nawabshah, about 220 km north of Karachi. Musharraf was told of the problem and patched in by telephone from the cockpit to Corps Commander V Corps (Karachi), Lt.-Gen. Usmani, who sent troops to the airport and went there himself as soon as he could. Abbasi and his deputy, Nadir Chaudhry, were apprehended by troops and later arrested. One mistake was to have failed to place obstacles on the runway, or to have otherwise rendered it unusable, but even if the aircraft had flown to Nawabshah, the army would have been there before it landed and would have made sure the COAS came to no harm. It was unbelievably irresponsible of the prime minister and the chairman of PIA to order an aircraft to stand into danger. Had the pilot been forced to divert to Dubai after circling Karachi for fifty minutes he would have been extremely short of fuel, and it is quite conceivable that the aircraft could have crashed. The affair characterized the entire Nawaz Sharif regime: inadequate planning, followed by hasty decisions, resulting in chaos.

After landing at Karachi, Musharraf conferred with Usmani and other officers at Malir barracks and future action was planned. Obviously Nawaz Sharif was behaving erratically to the point of endangering the country as a whole, and something had to be done. The president was entirely in the hands of Sharif and his group of intimates and was powerless to act as a neutral advisor or broker, even if he so wished. Reluctantly, Musharraf concluded that the only course open to him was to dismiss Nawaz Sharif and his associates. He issued orders to that effect and then flew to Islamabad in an air force plane.

In Islamabad/Rawalpindi Commander 10 Corps (HQ at Chaklala, a Rawalpindi suburb), Lt.-Gen. Mehmood, arranged for the SSG detachment at GHQ, and 111 Infantry Brigade, located at Westridge in Rawalpindi, to secure the television and radio stations and to move troops close to government centres in Islamabad. While these deployments were being carried out, Musharraf gave orders to place the prime minister and other prominent figures under house arrest. Throughout the country there were several detentions, including those of the Governor of Punjab, the Chief Minister of NWFP and various provincial ministers known to be Sharif ultra-loyalists. The short-reigning army chief, General Ziauddin, was confined to his house only a few hours after having his new badges of rank pinned on by Sharif (recorded for posterity by government-controlled Pakistan TV). General Tariq Parvaiz and the prime minister's military assistant were also detained. The operation was over quickly.

* * *

Pakistan's army coups have taken place in essence because there was direct confrontation between the most senior government and military figures, fuelled by public dissatisfaction with governmental corruption, warping of the constitution, and gross economic inefficiency. All four seizures of power by the army were without bloodshed and attracted almost total support from a long-suffering citizenry, but the trouble was that military rule went on for too long and made returning to democracy extremely difficult. The inability of politicians to accept probity as a requirement of governance contributed directly to the 1999 takeover, and the country's poor economic situation had been worsened by the Sharif government's terminal corruption. Shady characters made millions from tax-avoidance, strangely-contrived loans from various banks, and favours granted by the Sharif brothers and their immediate advisors, which were a repetition of the sleaze and shameless venality so evident during the two governments of Benazir Bhutto. Sharif was the most powerful prime minister in the country's history but made no attempt to alleviate poverty, provide a decent education or health system, or even run a reasonably efficient administration. The decision to hold nuclear tests, following those by India in May 1998, was internationally disastrous and resulted in painful embargoes by most of the world, and there was no economic plan to cope with the consequences, of which Sharif was warned by President Clinton[10] and many others.

The plight of the average person was pitiful, as they saw their savings decline in value and their quality of life deteriorate week by week, while off-the-cuff price increases penalized only the middle classes and the poor. The exit of the Sharif brothers was welcomed by almost the entire population, and took place on the day that, by coincidence, Mr Moeen Qureshi, a former and most competent interim prime minister, was quoted by *The News* newspaper as saying that there should once again be a caretaker government. This time, he said, 'the caretakers should be given at least two years instead of only three months so that they could introduce reforms with far-reaching effects.'

But there was to be no interim government of carefully chosen, apolitical, incorruptible economic experts with a strong sense of social justice. It was to be the army again, albeit with modifications to the practices of previous military regimes. Although the country benefited as a whole and was relieved to be rid of the squalid soap opera that had been playing for so long, it wasn't democracy by any means. The new management, which was run, appropriately enough, by the 'Chief Executive', as General Musharraf dubbed himself before deciding to assume the presidency, had many problems to resolve, and it is relevant to the story of the army to describe one of them, to indicate where the army fitted in with foreign policy and resolution of domestic problems that were in danger of affecting the stability of the country.

Afghanistan and Pakistan's Border Areas

Allegations have been made that the army was involved in the Taliban take-over of Afghanistan in the mid-1990s and in furthering its members' aims in that savage, unhappy and divided land. So far as can be determined, there was indeed direct military support for the Taliban by the army, although they were already well-supplied with weapons, most of which were left over from the CIA's cornucopia of arms that was showered on the various mujahideen organisations in the 1980s. In 1985, while visiting an Afghan guerrilla group near Dalbandin in Balochistan, I was shown and photographed an enormous arms' kote, with AK rifles, anti-personnel mines and anti-aircraft weapons, all in heavy care and preservation, and hundreds of thousands of rounds of ammunition along with countless boxes of grenades. These, I was told, were being kept for the 'real war' against other bands after the Russians were driven out. Doubtless there were many caches of this nature, but in any event the country was awash with weapons. Pakistan's Inter-Services Intelligence Directorate was deeply involved in Afghanistan, and connived at sending ill-trained fanatics (especially Swatis) to join the Taliban, and according to the excellent *Ghost Wars* by Steve Coll,[11] who drew on a plenitude of impeccable sources, aided them in many other ways. The Taliban are militant religious zealots, but they are not soldiers in the normal sense of the word, being totally unfamiliar with even the low-technology equipment they acquired. In their advance throughout the country they needed artillery support, for example, and while the guns could be manned at least in part by former soldiers of the Afghan army, their technical direction was provided by Pakistanis who, along with most of the many other advisors, were eventually evacuated in night-time Pakistan Air Force C-130 pickups from Afghan airstrips at the time of the Taliban collapse. Some were left to be captured and were either murdered or thrown in jails run by the Northern Alliance leaders who were (and are) every bit as brutal as the Taliban.

Washington was heavily involved in fostering criminal mayhem in Afghanistan in the 1980s through its support of vicious and villainous mujahideen whose human rights awareness was approximately zero, and if the Taliban had existed at the time, it, too, would have been given its share of arms. America washed its hands of Afghanistan once the Cold War was over, and its revitalized concern was based on the Taliban's shielding of the terrorist Osama bin Laden, and thus solely on self-interest. It was in no way the result of benevolent ideals concerning peaceful development of the country. Had this been an imperative, the US would have striven to encourage stable government there many years before, and would have provided the wherewithal for an advance to stability. (Even its de-mining efforts were perfunctory and involved special forces soldiers receiving short-term in-area familiarization and language training, rather than engineer mine specialists.)[12] At a meeting of the UN Security Council on 27 August 1999, Pakistan was castigated by the US and others for 'supporting Afghanistan's Taliban militia and helping fuel its recent offensive with weapons and warriors'.[13] This criticism by the US can be described only as deep humbug, especially as it changed completely when it was realized that Pakistan could once again be useful in implementation of US foreign policy.

A disturbing aspect of Taliban influence (in addition to their appalling human rights abuses and especially their subjection of women to disgusting privation) was their recruitment of hundreds of semi-educated youngsters from *madrassas* (religious schools)[14] in Pakistan and elsewhere. The remnants of the Taliban, and it is alleged, Al-Qaeda, were driven to the borderlands between Afghanistan and Pakistan where troops began searching for them on both sides. Army and para-military operations by Pakistan in the border regions in pursuit of supposed aliens were unpopular, and in March 2005, I wrote in Jane's *Terrorism and Security Monitor*[15] that:

> In September 2004 a news report about Pakistan's military operations in Waziristan, which involved aircraft attacks, stated that 'until now, aerial bombing has never been used to crush an armed insurgency in [Pakistan].' But in 1929 the British bombed exactly the same area. Bombing did not subjugate the tribes then, and will not do so in the future.

In the tribal region of Pakistan, known as the Federally Administered Tribal Areas (FATA) of North West Frontier Province (NWFP), the government in Islamabad is as alien as was the British Raj. South Waziristan is the southernmost of seven Agencies in FATA, and like the others its inhabitants are largely illiterate (the literacy rate for men is 18 per cent; for women, negligible), and as profoundly ignorant of the outside world as it is of them. They are devoutly religious; and can be very aggressive; bound by a code of honour incomprehensible to most westerners; and implacably opposed to any development that might alter their way of life. They are loosely contained by the Frontier Crimes Regulations (1901) which are based on collective responsibility in that the authorities, if they dare, can detain members of a law-breaking fugitive's tribe or quarantine his village should he fail to surrender or if tribal punishment is not administered.

The troubles of 2004–2005 began when Washington insisted that Pakistan take action against tribes sheltering Taliban adherents and possibly (indubitably, in the US assessment) members of Al-Qaeda. The writer was told in December 2003 by a US general in Pakistan that 'the Pakistanis aren't doing enough' to assist America and that the Pakistan government must drive out or kill those to whom the tribes were affording sanctuary.

Concurrently, officials in Islamabad said that increased pressure on President Musharraf to strike in FATA was resisted by the explanation that the area was most sensitive in domestic politics and that NWFP was controlled by the democratically elected Muttahida Majlis-e-Amal (MMA; a group of six political religious parties) whose policies were exceedingly difficult to counter. Military action would result in greater support for the MMA, which was against the interests of Pakistan as a whole. It was observed that attempts were being made to introduce reforms in FATA, and that the process would collapse should there be confrontation. None of these arguments succeeded. Nor did the military operations that followed.

Two operations in South Waziristan in 2002–2003 were intended to eradicate foreign militants. They caused much reaction against the government and the United States, as it was claimed by the tribes that the US military had also participated in the operations. No matter what might be announced by Islamabad or Washington, it is firmly believed in NWFP and the rest of the country that US forces were involved and continue to be involved in operations in Waziristan. This belief was given impetus by a three-hour visit to Wana on 14 January 2005 by five US senators, accompanied by the US defence and air attaché in Islamabad. (She was not wearing uniform, but was recognised.) The official handout stated: 'The elders of the Ahmadzai Wazir tribe profusely praised the Pakistan Army during the meeting [with the senators]... They stressed that military operations against foreign militants enjoyed the support of the tribes.'

The Ahmadzai Wazir and the Mahsud tribes are the most prominent in the Agency. The Zalikhels, a sub-tribe of the Ahmadzai, gave sanctuary to militants fleeing Afghanistan following US bombing and

Northern Alliance massacres in 2001–2002. There are Wazirs on both sides of the Pakistan–Afghanistan border, and kinship bonds are close.

On 14 March 2004, units from the army and the Frontier Corps (FC; a militia force under the Home Ministry but with officers from the army), began an operation in South Waziristan to 'flush out Al Qaeda and Taliban activists and arrest tribesmen who harbour them.' Some 7,000 troops took part, using artillery and mortars. Over 40,000 people were driven from their homes, some hundreds of houses were demolished, cattle were killed, orchards destroyed, and an unknown number of civilian casualties inflicted. The army lost 43 killed and the Frontier Corps 17, eight of whom were murdered after being taken prisoner. The operation was declared a success. (There were Mahsuds among the FC dead, which served to further Wazir–Mahsud enmity. In former days it was unusual to have FC units, which are tribally manned, pitted against tribes in the same general area as tribal members of the unit, as blood feuds are inevitable if there are deaths on either side.) It was stated that 215 'fighters' had been captured, of whom 73 were foreigners. No independent observer has sighted these captives.

At a *jirga* (assembly of prominent tribesmen) at Shakai, near Wana, on 24 April, it was agreed with representatives of the Pakistan government that there would be an amnesty for foreigners handed over. On 3 May, the US commander in Afghanistan, Lt.-General Richard Barno, stated 'Our view is that there are foreign fighters in those tribal areas who will have to be killed or captured.'

Further negotiations resulted in a tribal committee being formed to rid the area of foreigners. It reported in May that there were none. The authorities refused to believe the claim, even when a tribal *lashkar* (army) of some 2000 men was said to have conducted an unproductive search. As a result of perceived non-cooperation, a policy of collective punishment was invoked. On 29 May, hundreds of Ahmadzai Wazirs' shops in and around Wana were closed, as was the hospital. Salaries to state-employed Ahmadzais were stopped, and 70 tribesmen were imprisoned, including a dozen *maliks*, or tribal elders, thus effectively ending negotiations.

From 11 June, military operations began again, involving more air strikes, and a popular local leader, Nek Mohammad, was killed by a heliborne missile. Official loss figures were nine FC and six soldiers killed. In August and September there was further bitter fighting, and it was announced on 14 September that four 'foreigners', suspected members of Al Qaeda, had been killed. They were locals, however, and on 29 September the bodies were handed over to the Pakistani tribes to which they belonged, and their burial was attended by thousands of tribesmen. After further fighting, it was announced in December that 'militants' were no longer capable of 'regrouping and attacking security forces', that 200 soldiers had been killed, and that 'several hundred' fighters had been killed or captured.

For the moment FATA is fairly quiet. A 'peace plan' has been drafted and promises of development 'uplift works' have been made. No foreign fighters have been seen by independent witnesses and none has been put on trial. The tribes are alienated from one another and their suspicion and dislike of the government has turned to distrust and hatred while support for Islamic extremism and militancy has grown.

Military operations confirmed the inhabitants of the North West Frontier Province and much of the rest of the country in their belief that the US was responsible for the decision to invade the tribal areas. As forecast by officials in Islamabad in 2003, the operations worked against national harmony. Further, they did not achieve their aim, and it is unlikely future operations will do so, either. But the hatred will last for a very very long time.

Deployment of the army into the tribal areas was impossible to avoid if Pakistan were to continue to be considered a supporter in President Bush's 'war on terror' and receive economic and political support from Washington for maintaining that stance. US representatives insisted that action be taken and would not agree—could not even begin to understand—that the last resort should be employment of the military on what would be seen by the tribes as a punitive expedition. Anyone familiar with *The Pathans* by Sir Olaf Caroe,[16] and especially his chapter on Waziristan, would realise that little has changed in the Frontier over the last century and that military force, while an attractive solution in the short term, is certain to produce long-lasting resentment.

Use of all the paraphernalia of hi-tech warfare against tribes and their villages, especially armed helicopters firing missiles, looks very good on television and undoubtedly kills many people. Inevitably, some of these are the wrong people, and equally inevitably, the rage and resentment that follow far outweigh any military or social benefit achieved by killing civilians. The fact that over 200 army and Frontier Corps soldiers were killed (and double that number wounded)[17] in operations against the tribes is not surprising, especially as several of the army units had been redeployed from 1 Corps in the east of the country where their training had been almost solely for highly mobile, fully mechanised, 'strike' operations against Indian forces. The lesson is simple: nobody can expect soldiers and their leaders to be instant experts in all types of warfare. Fighting through every defile, every nala—'every rock, every hill',[18]—demands very different skills to those required in an armoured advance. They can be acquired, of course, because that is what soldiering is all about, but not overnight; and it was extremely unwise to commit troops to footslogging, ambush-prone, classic frontier warfare without intensive and lengthy preparation. It takes an ordinary battalion at least eight months of concentrated training to be prepared for operations in terrain and conditions that are utterly different from those with which it is familiar. Little wonder there were problems of morale in some units.

Military operations in FATA have never succeeded in permanently imposing the authority of the central or provincial governments on the region, and never will. The most effective means of capturing or killing dissidents being shielded by the tribes is through a combination of deviousness, patience, and bribery, and to make this work requires a deep knowledge of the region and long familiarity with personalities, dialects and customs. The *maliks* of the Ahmadzai Wazirs (and of other tribes, clans and sub-clans) may say all the right things when US senators drop by on one of their absurdly unproductive junkets, but it is remarkably ingenuous of anyone to believe they mean what they say, especially after their lands, their houses, their people, and their pride have been assaulted so savagely. Kipling summed it up well when he wrote of a fictional but all too believable Afridi outlaw that,

> *'Tis war, red war, I'll give you then,*
> *War till my sinews fail,*
> *For the wrong you have done to a chief of men*
> *And a thief of the Zukka Khel.*

Thieves some may be, when the opportunity arises; but they have their own codes of law and equity with which they are content. The Pakistan army was well aware of what it was taking on when it began its operations in Waziristan, but both it and the government in Islamabad were not only outmanoeuvred by the tribesmen, but also by Washington. It is the goodwill of the United States that is so important for the equipment status of the armed forces—for the navy and air force more than the army, but nevertheless of considerable consequence to the latter in acquiring such items as helicopters, communications systems, ground surveillance radars, air-platform anti-tank missiles, counter-insurgency and riot-control equipment, and night vision devices. The effects of US cooperation and its impact on Pakistan's defence budget and capabilities have been considerable.

* * *

US Weapons' Supplies and the Defence Budget

As a result of their nuclear tests in 1998, the US imposed sanctions on India and Pakistan that adversely affected both countries' military capabilities, but those of Pakistan more than India.[19] Pakistan was even further penalized following the army takeover of 1999, and naturally, sought closer links with China. President Musharraf's declaration of support for the US after the 9/11 attacks spurred the Bush administration to reconsider its stance, when it became apparent that the Pakistan army and US access to Pakistan's military facilities were essential components of what George Bush called the 'war on terror'. United States' laws and principles were subordinated to Washington's focus on Al Qaeda, and the result was re-establishment of defence connections with Pakistan and the opening of an equipment cornucopia. The Federation of American Scientists explains how this was effected:

> The Pakistan-only waiver was put into a separate bill (S. 1465, sponsored by Senator Brownback), which became law on 27 October 2001. This law waives the military coup provision (no arms or aid to countries that have undergone a military coup until democracy is restored) from Foreign Operations Appropriations bills for FY 2002 and 2003; allows for greater flexibility on sanctions related to MTCR [Missile Technology Control Regime] or Export Administration Act violations; and exempts Pakistan from restrictions on aid relating to loan defaults. It also shortens the congressional notification period for transfers of weapons from current US stocks from 15 to 5 days and transfers of excess US weapons from 30 to 15 days for all countries if the transfers would respond to or prevent international acts of terrorism. In June 2003, the State Department formally ended the ban on arms transfers to India and Pakistan, announcing that henceforth all requests would be considered on a standard case-by-case basis.[20]

Pakistan's defence expenditure has historically been opaque and only briefly outlined in annual budget papers. Lack of detail is justified officially by references to the imperatives of national security, but in practice flows from long-term, deeply rooted military influence on the country's governance and an ingrained proclivity for secrecy about almost everything to do with military matters. Even during Pakistan's brief periods of democracy, civilian governments have not provided other than the blandest statements relating to military spending, and there has been no indication that transparency might be favoured, no matter the nature of government in the foreseeable future. Official figures for overall defence expenditure are:

	1998 – 1999	1999 – 2000	2000 – 2001	2001 – 2002	2002 – 2003	2003 – 2004	2004 –2005
US$ billion	3.2	2.9	3.3	2.6	2.9	3.24	3.42

The June 2004 budget increased expenditure by approximately 7 per cent to PRs194 billion (US$3.42 billion) for the FY 2004–2005. The previous year, the allocation was PRs160.3 billion (US$2.88 billion), although final expenditure totalled some PRs181 billion (US$3.24 billion), mainly because of the tribal areas' operations. The budget for 2002–03 had been set initially at PRs146 billion but additional expenditure arising from movement of troops to the India–Pakistan border in 2002 (see below) led to a total of PRs160.1 billion. Defence spending accounts for 20 per cent of the national budget of some PRs903 billion and is about 3.9 per cent of gross domestic product. As is usual, FY2003–04 budget documents provided little information on the division of expenditure other than to state that PRs368 million would be allocated to 'defence administration' and PRs152.772 billion to 'defence services'. It is probable that appropriations for missile programmes and nuclear weapons are disguised in these and other line items.

The figures do not include PRs30 billion allocated for military pensions, or funds spent on procurement made on credit. This last figure is not revealed officially even to economic aid donors such as the International Monetary Fund or the World Bank, although it appears both have been quietly pressuring Islamabad for more transparency. It is probable that as much as US$7 billion of Pakistan's foreign debt is related to defence procurement. Foreign debt relief, although not intended for defence purposes, is likely in some fashion to serve to reduce amounts owing for foreign defence procurement. The military-related debt, including the part funded through foreign loans, is not indicated in the debt figures released as part of the national budget. It is not known if earnings from such diverse enterprises as the Pakistan Ordnance Factories, military farms, land rentals and the National Logistics Cell are accounted for as income or offset against individual outlays.

Defence expenditure statistics are meaningless in the context of military capabilities. On 31 March 2004 the finance ministry informed the National Assembly that Pakistan had received some US$5.776 billion in aid from the US in the past four years, including a US$3 billion package announced while President Musharraf visited Washington in 2003. Of this, the ministry indicated that US$1.38 billion had been granted for 'security and the fight against terror', but function allocations within that amount were not revealed. Provision of defence *matériel* from this military assistance, and generous transfer of spares, systems and equipments under terms of existing regulations and 'major non-Nato ally' status cannot be counted in national budgetary calculations.

US Military Assistance to Pakistan, FY2001–FY2005 (in millions of dollars)

PROGRAM OR ACCOUNT	FY2001 ACTUAL	FY2002 ACTUAL	FY2003 ACTUAL	FY2004 ACTUAL	FY2005 ESTIMATE	FY2006 REQUEST
FMF		75.0	224.5	74.6	148.8	300.0
IMET		0.9	1.0	1.4	2.0	2.0
INCLE	3.5	90.5	31.0	31.5	32.2	40.0
NADR		10.1		4.9	7.0	6.7
PKO		220.0				

Abbreviations:

FMF:	Foreign Military Financing
IMET:	International Military Education and Training
INCLE:	International Narcotics Control and Law Enforcement (includes border security)
NADR:	Non-proliferation, Anti-Terrorism, Demining, and Related [matters]
PKO:	Peacekeeping Operations

Source: Adapted from a paper by the US Congressional Research Service.[21]

It can be appreciated that declared defence outlays are but an unknown fraction of actual expenditure on military equipment and provide no indication of the market or replacement value of equipment obtained from foreign sources. The situation regarding acquisition of weapons and associated systems has been made more complex by declaration of Pakistan as a 'Major Non-Nato Ally' (MNNA) by the US, which was welcomed by Pakistan, although regarded in India as having been handled in a singularly inept fashion.

In March 2004, then Secretary of State Colin Powell visited India and Pakistan. In Islamabad he announced that the US would confer MNNA status on Pakistan, without having hinted at such a major decision to the government in Delhi, and on 19 April, the State Department notified the Senate Committee on Foreign Relations of the president's intention in a letter indicating exactly where the US–Pakistan nexus now hinges:

> We wish to inform you of the President's intention to designate Pakistan as a Major Non-Nato Ally (MNNA) pursuant to 22 USC 232lk (Section 517 of the Foreign Assistance Act of 1961, as amended). Pakistan is one of our most important partners in the Global War on Terrorism. The GOP has stepped up its counter-terrorism activities along the Afghan–Pakistan border and has firmly warned tribesmen in the area that they must stop harbouring foreigners. It has also captured and handed over to the US more than 550 suspected al-Qaeda operatives, including the group's senior commanders Khalid Sheikh Mohammad and Abu Zubaida as well as September 11 conspirator Ramzi bin al-Shibh. Currently [April 2004] there are 70,000 Pakistani troops deployed in the border region, and they have encountered stiff resistance. On March 17 alone, 16 Pakistani paramilitary personnel were slain in an encounter with groups that appear linked to terrorists and Taliban remnants. President Musharraf has accompanied his actions with important efforts to lead the public away from extremism. On February 18, for example, he delivered a nationally televised address calling on foreign extremists in Pakistan to leave, and urging the public to adhere to a moderate course.
>
> The United States has had an important relationship with the Islamic Republic of Pakistan since its creation over 50 years ago. We intend to maintain it in the future and demonstrate our support for the firm actions Pakistan is taking in the Global War on Terror. It is in the US interest to seal our friendship with Pakistan; granting Pakistan MNNA status would signal our continued commitment to strengthened military-to-military ties.[22]

In fact, the status of MNNA does more than signal a commitment: it confers on allies so designated a considerable number of tangible benefits:

- Eligibility to receive US-owned war reserve stockpiles on its territory (22 U.S.C. 2321h) and obtain US foreign assistance to purchase depleted uranium ammunition (22 U.S.C. 2378a); [The latter is judged to be extremely unlikely.]

- US Foreign Military Financing (FMF) may be used by the country for the commercial leasing of certain defence articles (not including Major Defence Equipment, with the exception of helicopters and certain types of aircraft) (Consolidated Appropriations Act, Fiscal Year 2004, Foreign Operations, Sec. 510);

- Entitlement to enter into agreements with the US government for the cooperative furnishing of training, on a bilateral or multilateral basis, provided the agreements are based on financial reciprocity (22 U.S.C. 2761);

- The right to loans, by the secretary of defence, of materials, supplies, or equipment for purposes of cooperative research, development, testing, or evaluation (22 U.S.C. 2796d);

- Expedited US export license approval, as appropriate, for US companies to deliver commercial satellites, their components, and systems (22 U.S.C. 2778); and,

- For those MNNAs located on the southern and south eastern flank of NATO—priority delivery of excess US defence articles (22 U.S.C. 2321j).[23]

After making the announcement, Powell stated that 'in some instances [MNNA status] is more symbolic than practical... I don't know if Pakistan [will] be able to take great advantage of it,' but in fact, Pakistan has thus far benefited greatly from conferral of MNNA status, and will continue to do so. The flow of equipment and especially spares for existing inventories has been considerable, and even before MNNA, included provision (or provision notification) for the army of

40 Bell 407 helicopters, 2000 TOW-2A anti-tank missiles, and 3270 manpack and vehicle-mounted Harris radios (interoperable with US Army and Special Forces' systems). The navy and air force did well, too, with P-3C and Hercules aircraft and Phalanx systems. Then, in March 2005, it was announced in a remarkably clumsy fashion by Washington that Pakistan would receive an unspecified number of F-16 aircraft, probably of the latest type.[24] It appears that for the foreseeable future Pakistan's armed forces will continue to receive quantities of surplus and advanced weapons systems from the US, to complement its inventories of equipment from other foreign suppliers and from its own manufacturing establishments, which have proved remarkably efficient in producing many items.

Defence Production and Procurement for the Army[25]

Defence procurement and production in Pakistan have been affected by the swings and caprices of Washington's policies regarding the sub-continent. Although the overall procurement plan is well-structured and realistic it has been recent practice to accept what is on offer from the US rather than to abide strictly by assessment of sequential requirements as is done in the relationship with the PRC.

Pakistan has a history of corruption in defence acquisition matters, and there has been influence by political figures and service officers on procurement decisions in the past. Former President Farooq Leghari stated in 1998 that the prime minister during his tenure, Benazir Bhutto 'and her husband were involved in efforts to buy Mirage [2000] aircraft from France. This whole deal reeked of corruption from day one, and I insured that [the]deal should not go through because [of this].' (The unit cost had increased markedly and for no apparent technical reason in the course of preliminary negotiations.) Given this and other highly-publicised instances of improbity, particularly the scandalous conduct of Admiral Mansoor-ul Haq,[26] it can be expected that domestic and international media scrutiny of future major contracts will continue to be intense.

The three services are receiving and about to receive large quantities of weapons and ancillary items from the US under various programmes, and Pakistan is in a position in which it may be able to balance US largesse against the financial commitment required to obtain equivalent technology systems elsewhere. Its domestic military equipment programmes are effective, especially in armoured vehicle and ammunition production, and it has cooperation agreements with China, France and Ukraine that are expected to expand.[27]

The views and intentions of weapons-exporting nations other than the US and China as regards supply of weapons and associated systems to Pakistan are regarded as important but subordinate to these two countries' foreign policies. Pakistan wishes to obtain high-technology equipment from almost any source but realises and accepts that some countries cannot or will not engage in cooperation because of Indian commitments or US disapproval. So far as the army is concerned the main technology focus is on mobility, armour and local air defence, which is consistent with doctrine.

* * *

The best tank in the army's inventory is the T-80UD, bought from Ukraine, but the Al Khalid, manufactured by Heavy Industries Taxila (HIT), and developed with much Chinese input, is also an effective fighting vehicle—mainly because it now has a Ukrainian diesel power pack. The story of the Khalid goes back to 1988, when Aslam Beg took over from President Zia as Chief of Army Staff and decided, quite rightly, that the flirtation with the US Abrams tank had gone on too long, and that it was far too expensive and complicated (and, at that time, performed poorly in desert conditions) to justify purchase. This was a remarkably prescient decision for many other reasons, but the outcome was closer cooperation with China and joint development of MBT 2000, otherwise Khalid, from original Russian designs via the PRC's Type-90.

In the early 1990s, I was taken round the factory at Taxila (not then named HIT; it was the Heavy Rebuild Programme) and shown the shop floors (where Chinese personnel kept peeping round pillars) in addition to the entire plan for the future of Pakistan's tank and APC development and production; and most impressive it was. It covered almost all four walls of an office, and the detail, from year to year, of much of what was intended for the future has been kept to schedule as far as practicable. (It is now, of course, entirely computerised.) The delay in the projected M-113 armoured personnel carrier programme was caused by US withdrawal of support because of its sanctions, and Khalid production was delayed in the main by prolonged discussions about the engine—whether to continue with the desert-unfriendly turbine or move to diesel. The results were that the army's programme for mechanisation of infantry battalions came almost to a halt, and it became obvious that in spite of the rebuild and upgrade programmes for existing tanks (shown in great detail in the Taxila production plot) there was a pressing requirement for a modern tank.

The T-80 was first trialled in Pakistan in 1993, and a firm order was placed for 320 tanks in August 1996, with deliveries from Ukrainian army stocks beginning the following year. The initial batches (17 + 18) were unsatisfactory because not all systems could be provided as agreed. Russia, for a combination of reasons,[28] attempted to derail the contract by denying Ukraine access to some components. Ukraine eventually overcame the difficulties and resumed provision of new and fully-updated tanks. Concurrently, the rebuild and upgrade process was expanded to refurbish the Type 59 fleet by a combination of improving its armour and fire-control systems while fitting a more powerful engine and a 125mm smooth bore gun whose ammunition would be interoperable with the T-80 and Al-Khalid (and of considerable importance, manufactured by Pakistan Ordnance Factories). Al-Zarrar, as the rebuilt machine is named, is practically a new tank altogether, and from accounts of two non-partisan sources, is impressive not only in firepower but in mobility. The Kharkiv Morozov Machine Building Design Bureau (KMDB) of Ukraine is a major contributor to its development, and it appears that defence association with Ukraine will continue. The Zarrar programme modifications include:

- Up-gun to 125 mm;
- Upgraded engine;
- Improved suspension;
- Improved Bottom Plate armour (anti-mine);
- New Fire Control System;
- Autoloader;
- Explosive Reactive Armour;
- Fire/explosion suppression; and
- Electronic Tracking System.

Standardization on the 125mm smoothbore gun was essential, but older tanks in the inventory cannot be modified, so retain the 105 mm gun which is of little use in modern armoured operations. Phased-out M-48s, non-modifiable T-59s and all T-69s have been and continue to be replaced by a combination of the NORINCO T-85 II-AP (manufactured at HIT under licence with some components from other suppliers), Khalid, Zarrar and T-80, for a probable total of about 1500, which should maintain a balanced force structure.

HIT manufactures and refurbishes M-113 (*Talha*) armoured personnel carriers which, although not infantry fighting vehicles (IFV) as such, give infantry greatly increased mobility and thus, among other advantages, contribute to flexibility of armoured operations. The temptation to use lightly-armoured M-113s as IFVs instead of fast and fairly well-protected battle taxis appears to have been resisted, as it is recognized that they could not survive in an armoured battle in spite of some being TOW-equipped, but in the HIT model there have been some major design improvements that include, of great importance, better troop comfort.[29] Consistent with the gradualist approach to improved capabilities, manufacture and rebuild/upgrade will continue until at least until the end of this decade, during which time the army will continue to have many responsibilities, including major UN commitments.

Although HIT has the capability to rebuild 155 mm self-propelled (SP) artillery pieces (M-109s) there is a requirement to replace these because of age. There do not appear to be reliable 155 mm SP suppliers other than United Defence LP of Arlington, owned by BAE since March 2005. It is possible they could offer the new International Howitzer which is based on the M109 A6 Paladin, or they could suggest the A5 version (still in production) or Paladin itself, but all would involve large sums. The International Howitzer can probably be ruled out by reason of cost and complexity, and it is more likely the A-5 would be the solution, especially if it could be provided under favourable financial terms.

In general the army's equipment and other systems are adequate for its tasks, although there continues to be a requirement for modernizing tactical command links and for more surface-to-air missiles, which are inadequate in both quantity and quality. Given its present capabilities, however, it is apparent that it could not only withstand an Indian attack but probably take and hold ground in Punjab and Rajasthan. Fortunately it is becoming less and less likely that it will be put to the test, as the process of rapprochement with India continues.

Peacekeeping

In August 2005 Pakistan had 10,063 people serving in UN peacekeeping missions, of whom 9,359 were soldiers, 89 military observers, and 435 policemen. The breakdown of contributions is shown below, and it is of note that of the 103 countries contributing to 14 peacekeeping missions, world-wide, Pakistan ranks first, with Bangladesh and India not far behind. (Western nations are more modestly represented, with the United Kingdom, for example, fielding only 394 personnel (282 in the former colony of Cyprus), and the US, which for national reasons does not place military personnel under foreign command, having 10 soldiers and 18 military observers in five missions, with 274 contract police in Kosovo.)

Pakistan's UN Contributions—August 2005

OPERATION	OBSERVERS	TROOPS	CIVILIAN POLICE
UNOCI/ONUCI Cote d'Ivoire	10	374	0
MINURSO Western Sahara	7	0	0
MINUSTAH Haiti	0	0	248
MONUC DR Congo	25	3770	0
ONUB Burundi	5	1190	0
UNAMSIL Sierra Leone	8	1267	2
UNMIK Kosovo	1	0	161
UNMIL Liberia	16	2749	21
UNMISET/UNOTIL East Timor	9	9	3
UNOMIG Georgia	8	0	0
TOTALS	89	9359	435

Almost all the peacekeeping missions to which Pakistan has contributed troops have been successful in contributing to stability in countries riven by internal conflict, but the exception was Somalia in 1992–1995, from which lessons were learned concerning command, control and cooperation. It was unfortunate that the lessons were learned in circumstances involving the slaughter of Pakistani soldiers.

The Somali operations were a humiliating failure for all concerned—except the Somali warlords who drove out the peacekeepers—and their ineffectiveness was due almost entirely to a convoluted and gravely inadequate international command structure. Pakistan's forces were at the bottom of the chain of confusion, and suffered accordingly. In consequence, the main lesson learned was more political than tactical: do not commit troops to a mission in which their safety is placed at hazard equally by armed opposition and structural deficiencies.

Pakistan was involved in contributing troops from the beginning of the debacle, and it is appropriate to examine just how and why it was placed in a situation that cascaded into chaos.

In 1991, Somalia was ungoverned and ungovernable. (It still is.) Food aid was being provided, but was looted by gangs of criminals who roamed round the country in 'Technicals', pick-up trucks with machine guns mounted on the back, killing each other, menacing aid officials, and as UN Secretary-General Boutros Boutros-Ghali put it, engaging in 'a war of all against all'. Eventually, in 1992 the Security Council was shamed into approving 'United Nations Operation Somalia', or UNOSOM 1, which involved deployment of a security force of 500 troops to protect delivery of food and other assistance in the country. The trouble was the troops were not permitted to use force and that their entry was dependent on permission of the strongest warlord, who at the time was Mohammad Farah Aideed. Although authorized by the UN to arrive in April 1992, they were not accepted by Aideed until September. The UN official description of developments is banal:

On 23 June, the Secretary-General informed the Security Council that both principal factions in Mogadishu had agreed to the immediate deployment of the unarmed observers. The Chief Military Observer, Brigadier-General Imtíaz Shaheen of Pakistan, and the advance party of UNOSOM observers arrived in Mogadishu in early July 1992. On 12 August, the Secretary-General informed the Security Council that, after considerable delays and difficulties, agreement had been reached with the principal faction leaders

in Mogadishu to deploy 500 United Nations security personnel in the capital
as part of UNOSOM. The Government of Pakistan had agreed to contribute
a unit for the purpose. The first group of security personnel arrived in
Mogadishu on 14 September 1992.[30]

Pakistan's soldiers were confined to the airport (where the aid
material and food arrived) because UN rules of engagement forbade
them to take physical action to carry out their mandate to protect its
distribution. The Security Council authorized a further 3000 Belgian
and Canadian troops for the mission but they did not arrive, which was
extremely unfortunate as both country's armies were experienced in
peacekeeping missions. Lawlessness and extreme violence continued,
and foreigners were harassed and humiliated. In December, the Security
Council accepted a US proposal to contribute to and command a force
to establish order. The Unified Task Force (UNITAF), was a mission
of 'armed humanitarianism' and was referred to by the US as Operation
Restore Hope. The US contingent was authorized to participate until 4
May 1993, when the task would be handed back to the UN. When the
first Marines waded ashore in the full moonlight of 9 December 2002,
apparently expecting an opposed landing, they were met by reporters
and cameramen, at least one of whom they arrested.[31] The operation,
involving 28,000 US troops and 9,000 from 23 other nations was
initially successful in terms of providing starving people with
sustenance. Much aid was distributed, but the country remained
chaotic, with no semblance of government emerging. The changeover
to UNISOM II was when the real trouble began.

There were three quite separate military chains of command in
UNISOM II: one in the hands of the UN and two of the US. The UN
Force Commander had no power over US forces, which operated
entirely separately (apart from a logistics element), and although the
UN Deputy Force Commander was an American (Major General
Thomas M. Montgomery), he was also Commander US Forces,
Somalia. He, however, had no control over Task Force Ranger, which
consisted of Rangers and Delta Force personnel and was responsible
solely to the Commander of US Special Operations Command in the
US. The operation's command arrangements would be regarded with
derision by a first-year military cadet. The overall commander of
UNOSOM II, 'the Special Representative of the Secretary-General',
was retired US Admiral Jonathan Howe and the military commander
was Turkish Lieutenant General Cevic Bir. Howe, in the words of

William J. Durch[32] of the Stimson Center, 'might have been an ideal *Deputy* [emphasis added] Special Representative....'

The major problem for the Pakistani contingent began on 4 June 1993 when another US/UN representative, April Glaspie, authorized two US officers to undertake weapons inspections of installations controlled by the Somali National Alliance (SNA), headed by Aideed. The SNA asked for time to consider the matter, and when this was refused, informed the UN that if the inspections went ahead it would mean 'war'. Next day, Friday, the Muslim day of rest, a singularly inappropriate choice for operations by any troops, inspections went ahead, with the two officers being accompanied by a contingent of Pakistani troops who had not been informed of the SNA's unmistakable threat, and were in soft-skinned vehicles. Immediately after the inspection the lightly-armed Pakistanis were menaced by an angry crowd of about 200, but were able to withdraw.[33] Groups of Pakistani soldiers at humanitarian feeding stations and other posts were less fortunate and suffered full-scale attacks by SNA forces amid large mobs of civilians, many of whom were also armed. They requested support from the Italian contingent, but the Italian helicopters that responded strafed the Pakistani positions and wounded three soldiers, and the armoured vehicles that had been requested at 11 a.m. did not arrive until 4.30 p.m., when they found only dead soldiers at the food distribution area. That day the Pakistan army suffered 24 dead and 57 wounded.

These attacks led to aggressive operations, and on 12 June US AC-130 Spectre gunships and attack helicopters strafed the headquarters of Radio Mogadishu and other sites suspected of being Aideed stockades, following which the overall situation deteriorated alarmingly. The US placed a price on the head of Aideed and increased strikes by gunships, and his supporters became even more violent. There were many more attacks on all contingents that involved the killing of soldiers from Malaysia, Italy, Morocco, India, Nepal and Nigeria, and the shooting-down of US helicopters. On 3 October US Special Forces launched an air-landing assault on a suspected Aideed stronghold. The operation had been authorized by Special Forces Command in Florida, and neither Admiral Howe nor General Bir was informed of it until immediately before the attack, which was a disaster. It resulted in the killing of 18 American troops and the well-publicized dragging of a US soldier's body through the streets of Mogadishu. Several hundred Somalis were killed by the Americans. Two days later the US president announced that the US would withdraw its forces, and in the end the Pakistani contingent was last to leave, in February 1995. The entire mission was a failure.

The lesson for Pakistan (and others) is that UN peacekeeping operations should not be supported unless there is a clear task and a well-defined chain of command. Neither applied in Somalia, and the Secretary-General said there were important lessons to be learned about the 'theory and practice of multifunctional peacekeeping operations in conditions of civil war and chaos and especially about the clear line that needs to be drawn between peacekeeping and enforcement action'.[34]

UN operations since that time have been conducted under UN command, and have been successful in subcontinent terms as well as in a wider context, to the point of involving close cooperation between Indian and Pakistani forces. The Pakistan army continues to provide troops for UN Missions, and both it and the missions benefit.

Problems in the Army

The report by Pakistan's Auditor General for 2002–2003 (released in March 2005),[35] showed that there was gross mismanagement of defence funds by almost everyone who had any control over them. There was incontrovertible evidence of inappropriate letting of contracts, cost overruns of absurd proportions, and general inefficiency in management of public monies. Worse, from the point of view of the army's standing and honour, were the cases of hanky panky over construction of married quarters and guest houses, and such grubby antics as ripping-off rickshaw drivers. *The Nation* newspaper's editorial of 10 March 2005 summed things up very well:

> The army remains outside the ambit of the National Accountability Bureau because the military hierarchy believes their internal justice system is better suited and more efficient. The question presents itself then: If their internal mechanism is so strong, why did it fail to detect these financial discrepancies? The army's continuous interference in the political process has definitely played a part in inducing indiscipline within their ranks. As the army became politicised, it resorted to increasingly undesirable practices to prolong [and] cement its position in the power circles of Islamabad. With such political considerations, it is difficult to understand how the military can focus on its primary objective to defend the motherland. That the

military machinery has become corrupt is therefore not incomprehensible. Any process of reformation must commence with its quitting politics and sticking to the job it was created for.

These are strong words, but increasingly reflect the public's gradual swing to considering that it is time the army became less prominent in the country's management. Involvement of the army (any army) in financial matters of any sort is the way to perdition. As a rule, soldiers do not relish professional involvement in economics. Little as many soldiers (including myself) revere those who are pejoratively referred to as 'defence civilians' or 'bean-counters' (and much worse), there is no doubt that civilian bureaucrats have an important role to play in financial management, acting not only as advisors but as brakes, checks and balances, and if necessary, whistle-blowers. The image of the services as a whole suffered badly from the Mansoor-ul Haq revelations. Who would have thought that a Chief of Naval Staff could have behaved in this way? It was all very well for the armed forces to look down their noses at Benazir Bhutto and her allegedly corrupt gang, and to express equal revulsion and contempt for what Nawaz Sharif did in his flamboyant and alleged amoral looting of the country's coffers, but what answer can there be to the sheeting home of undeniable financial chicanery to some of the most senior citizens in uniform?

There are even worse instances of the army using its influence in the country to obtain financial gain. The scandal of dispossession of poor peasant farmers from lands near the border with India in the Okara region of Punjab is a blot that cannot be expunged by claiming it is the responsibility of the Pakistan Rangers. The Rangers are a para-military force, certainly; but its officers come from the army and its persecution of the peasants could not take place without army approval. The report by Human Rights Watch—*Soiled Hands: the Pakistan Army's Repression of the Punjab Farmers*[36] makes sad reading. The facts are readily available to anyone with a computer that can access the internet, but I never imagined I would read anything like this about an officer in the modern army of Pakistan:

We were arrested at six in the morning. We were blindfolded and kept in a vehicle for about forty-five minutes while twenty-five others were arrested. We were brought to Rangers Headquarters. We were made to sit at a cold and dusty place in freezing temperature. Major Tahir Malik ordered us to start doing push-ups. We carried on like that for one hour. Major Tahir then made us stand with our arms raised for hours. If anyone's arms fell, they were beaten. He asked us to sign up and pay the contract money to secure our release. We were also forced to pressure our families to pay contract money. We were kept at Rangers' Headquarters for seven days. During this time, we were whipped and beaten with sticks as well.

Human Rights Watch states that Major-General Shaukat Sultan, the Director General of Inter-Services Public Relations (ISPR, the public relations wing of the Pakistan Armed Forces), succinctly summarized the views of the Army: 'The needs of the Army will be decided by the Army itself, and/or the government will decide this. Nobody has the right to say what the Army can do with 5,000 acres or 17,000 acres. The needs of the Army will be determined by the Army itself.' This is indeed a novel approach to democracy.

* * *

After I drafted the above section I sent it to several friends in Pakistan and to some foreigners who know Pakistan well. The reaction from almost every one of them was words to the effect that 'I thought you were a friend of Pakistan and admired the army very much, so why are you so critical?'

Quite so: I am a friend of Pakistan and admire the army greatly. Which is exactly why I wrote what appears above. There is a virus attacking the army, and it is time it was dealt with. As with most viruses, the cure is a large dose of antibiotics, and in this case the best antibiotic would be a stiff dose of democracy mixed with an injection of accountability.

* * *

International Complications

Cessation of overseas individual training arrangements by western countries as a result of their disapproval of Pakistan's nuclear tests and ejection of the corrupt Nawaz Sharif did not affect professional knowledge or standards seriously, but an entire generation of officers was denied exposure to the wider horizons offered by such nations. Western influence was reduced to the point of creating significant resentment, especially among junior officers. Increased anti-western feelings were then manipulated by a small number of zealots within and outside the armed forces in an attempt to attract adherents to more rigid forms of Islam. The US IMETS military training co-operation agreement was resurrected when Pakistan once again became a valuable consort, as have Commonwealth and European programmes, and it seems that new generations of Pakistani officers will be permitted to experience other social environments—and it is this, more than purely military knowledge, that is so important for Pakistan's overall development.

Australia, many of whose foreign service and civilian defence officials had long wished to break the connection with the Staff College at Quetta that has existed since its foundation a century ago, relished the opportunity to confound and diminish the ties, and Britain, ever intent on the Thatcher era dogma (happily embraced by Blair) that foreign students' countries must pay full-fare for their admission to British instructional institutions (including, ironically, Australia), gave an old ally the message that its citizens were not welcome.

If it was the purpose of those imposing sanctions to drive Pakistan to rely more on Islamic partners, with attendant consequences of alienating a generation of students (military and civilian) from the western world, it has not wholly succeeded, but much work has to be done to correct what damage has been effected. The western world's short-sighted and even spiteful reaction to the coup will be remembered, and although those responsible for damaging their country's relations with Pakistan may rejoice, they have not served their countries well.

Force Structure

The basic structure of Pakistan's army is sound and its equipment is adequate, but GHQ should be transformed to a 'raise, train and provide' organization, with operational functions being the responsibility of a Joint Headquarters which perforce would be army-heavy. Following restructure at the higher level, there should be two main subordinate air-land HQ formed: north and south, and a tri-service HQ should be based in Karachi. If this 'jointery' does not eventuate, the army and the air force (not so much the navy) will not be capable of conducting operations to best effect. (See Chapter 13.)

The Nuclear Factor

The challenges presented by nuclear developments in India and Pakistan are immense and the services are cooperating to the extent that joint doctrine is being considered within a military if not, yet, a national context. Examination of training has shown that it is adequate for conventional war, and indeed, is more than satisfactory in anti-armour tactics, but that the nuclear factor is yet to be fully appreciated.

The North Atlantic Treaty Organization and the Warsaw Pact evolved finely-tuned systems for the command and control of nuclear weapons over several decades—and even then they were far from foolproof. India and Pakistan are in the nascent stages of such development. Moreover, in Europe, confidence building measures (CBMs) and command and control systems grew together (the OK word for this is 'symbiotically'). In the subcontinent, India and Pakistan cannot assess with confidence how far their neighbour can go before there may be pressing or even irresistible internal demands to threaten the use of nuclear weapons. Furthermore, it is not clear whether, as one commentator muses, Indian and Pakistani leaders 'can avoid using Kashmir as a bargaining chip in domestic politics—and nuclear threats as a lever in Kashmir.'[37] A paper published in May 2002 by the Center for the Advanced Study of India, written by Bruce Riedel, drawing on recollections of his period as special assistant to President Clinton,[38] describes possible nuclear preparations at the time of the Kargil crisis. Mr Riedel provides insight to US perceptions of the nuclear threat at the time, and states that the president asked the prime minister of Pakistan, Nawaz Sharif, if he knew 'his military was preparing their nuclear-tipped missiles?' This is an intriguing revelation, although the nuclear expert George Perkovitch and the Indian army chief of the time, General V.P. Malik, stated they doubted Pakistan had gone so far.[39] Nevertheless, opacity concerning nuclear intentions continues, exacerbating regional and international disquiet about the possible direction of nuclear developments in the subcontinent.

The Terrorism Factor

President Musharraf (and thus the army, as he continues to be its professional head) stands accused of failing to do enough to rid his country of terrorism and even of complicity in harbouring some of the West's most violent enemies. Although hundreds of al Qaeda suspects were arrested and handed over to the United States in 2004–2005, and scores of home-grown religio-political activists imprisoned, some commentators are convinced that Musharraf is reluctant to take on the terrorists.

It would be strange if a man who has survived several assassination attempts were not anxious to counter those who seek to kill him, but the purpose of domestic and foreign terrorists in Pakistan is not focused solely on murdering its president, and there are other reasons for Musharraf to want to counter them. They loathe the West, which they consider the root of all evil, and within Pakistan, Musharraf represents all that they are determined to destroy. His western critics may think he is not acting fast or hard enough to combat terrorism, but the terrorists don't agree, and nor do the religious extremists who support them.

In July 2005, Musharraf ordered deportation of foreigners attending religious colleges because these can be 'misused for extremism.' But he was promptly criticized internationally for doing too little, too late to counter the spread of militant Islam, and within Pakistan he was attacked for appearing to follow western dictates and betraying his country's religion. He is in one corner of a boxing ring. Leaping out of the others are the terrorists, their theocratic supporters, and foreign critics, all trying to land a killer punch.

In September 2005, Musharraf was trying to achieve balance between his personal preference for non-confrontational, democratic Islam (which the theocrats consider a non-sequitur), and pragmatic sufferance of religious extremists who promote their highly selective interpretation of Islam as the sole arbiter of all aspects of social and political life. Pakistan's Islamic zealots use their faith as both tool and justification for their assaults on laws and customs based on western jurisprudence. Forceful movement against them is presented as anti-Islamic, while their own violence is portrayed as the inevitable consequence of persecution by *kafirs*, or non-believers.

In spite of limitations on Musharraf's choices for action, hard-line Islam was being contained through a combination of reluctance on the part of the educated classes, especially the business community, to embrace extremism, and the government's measured, if sometimes hesitant responses to extremists' provocation.

The leader of Pakistan's group of politico-religious parties (the Muttahida Majlis-e-Amal [MMA], the United Action Front), is Qazi Hussain Ahmed, a preacher-cum-politician and head of the Jamaat-e-Islami party who has courted arrest by increasing the intensity of his rhetoric. He endorses the Taliban's militant resurgence in Afghanistan and attacks western and especially US influence (although two of his sons are US-educated and one an American citizen), and is implacably opposed to Musharraf's agenda. Hypocrite or not, he is a dangerous rabble-rouser. The government ordered the arrest of some 800 suspected Islamic militants in July 2005 but the subsequent call by Qazi Hussain for civil disobedience to protest a 'global conspiracy' against Islam was unsuccessful, which was an encouraging sign, as were the August 2005 local elections because, although they were in theory non-political, many of the more rabid of the MMA's supporters failed to win votes. It still held 67 of the National Assembly's 342 seats, from the 2002 national elections, but it seemed that Qazi and his ilk might be losing popular appeal.

The test for Musharraf will come if he orders the arrest of 'Qazi Sahib' or other prominent religious leaders who openly support terrorism. The MMA has sought confrontation, and although it appears Musharraf might be in a position to accept the challenge, he has to weight up the possible consequences of action against them.

Unfortunately Musharraf, as Byron had it, 'nursed the pinion that impelled the steel', in that in 2002 he endorsed the election efforts of the religious groups in the interests of sidelining the two mainstream political parties. The results were not wholly catastrophic for the country, but they gave Qazi and his supporters confidence that they could flex the religious muscle that was first given them by Zulfikar Ali Bhutto who cultivated them to the extent of forbidding alcohol described in Chapter 10), and Ziaul Haq who cultivated them because he was himself of similar persuasion. But Musharraf engineered himself into a peculiar position of quasi-alliance with the sort of people who are entirely opposed to his agenda for the country.

Musharraf has a pressing personal interest in destroying terrorists, lest they get him first, but his domestic considerations, not least his own political survival, make it inadvisable for him to move as fast as his western detractors demand in his campaign against religious extremism. Widely-publicized foreign criticism of his efforts has assisted his adversaries while not contributing to their neutralization.

The unknown factor is the army itself. Just how far has it gone in endorsing extremist Islam?

The Pakistan army, like all institutions of state in the country, is religiously-based. It has some religious extremists, but the promotion and selection process is closely overseen by Musharraf, who rarely vetoes an appointment but prefers his subordinates to agree that officers whose priorities centre on religious extremism rather than professional competence should not be posted to positions in which they might influence others. In 2003, there were instances of outstanding candidates for the Pakistan Military Academy being rejected by members of a selection board because of alleged secular tendencies within their westernised families. It appears this policy was emplaced at a low level and has been discontinued, but there is a tendency, as in western armies, for better-educated youth to refrain from seeking to join the armed forces as officers, even when family tradition applies. The result has been a shortage of high grade junior officers, concurrent with some emphasis on religion at the expense of military skills, a tendency that Musharraf is attempting to overcome by more judicious officer recruitment and career management.

* * *

I do not advocate a secular army, any more than I would be so presumptuous as to propose a secular Pakistan. I do, however, suggest that the army of Pakistan should have no religious influence on society, and that it should have no casting vote in governance of the country. It has half a million voters in its ranks. Let them be its contribution to democracy.

NOTES

1. Human Rights Watch—http://www.hrw.org/wr2k/Asia-07.htm.
2. In conversation with the author, November 2002, April 2003.
3. It is interesting to speculate on what might have—or might not have—taken place had Ali Kuli Khan been appointed COAS, as he deserved. There is no doubt Musharraf was a well above average officer, even a brilliant one, but Ali Kuli had star quality and a great deal of influence outside the military, which is probably why Sharif was frightened to appoint him. One thing is certain: had Ali Kuli been COAS there would have been no Kargil operation. He told the author on 29 May 2005 that the Kargil affair was an appalling mistake by the army.

4. Mohammed Shehzad, *South Asia Tribune*, 7-13 October 2002. http://www.satribune. com/archives/oct7_13_02/P1_fasihbokhari.htm.

5. Article 42 of the Constitution states *inter alia* that the President '... will preserve, protect and defend the Constitution of the Islamic Republic of Pakistan.'

6. Reuters 14:39 09-23-99.

7. Benazir Bhutto joined in condemnation by saying 'He has sought to dismantle democracy, he has been sacking everyone—the chief justice, the president—attacked the press, the foreign investors, the opposition'. See http://www.rediff.com/ news/1999/oct/13pak1.htm.

8. In several meetings with the author.

9. This is not in any way to denigrate that Corps. The best army chief and Chief of Defence Force that Australia ever had was the redoubtable, wise and highly intellectual General Peter Gration, late Royal Australian Engineers, who had never heard a shot fired in anger or commanded a fighting formation.

10. Dennis Kux describes the period admirably in *The United States and Pakistan 1947-2000*. The US Senate was forced by the powerful farmers' lobby, however, to 'water down' sanctions to avoid loss of grain sales to Pakistan.

11. *Ghost Wars*, by Steve Coll, The Penguin Press 2004. An outstanding account of Afghanistan's vicissitudes up to 10 September 2001 by an author with deep knowledge of the subcontinent.

12. Official despatch written by the author following five visits to the demining instruction camp at Risalpur.

13. 'Pakistan blamed for Afghan fighting', Nicole Winfield, Associated Press AP-NY-08-27-99 2145EDT.

14. See Cloughley, *Pakistan's Religion and Madrassas* in Jane's *Islamic Affairs Analyst*, January 2005.

15. My thanks to Jane's for permission to reproduce the piece.

16. Macmillan and Company 1958; now available in the Oxford Historical Reprints series, 1983, with a new Foreword and Epilogue by the author.

17. Private sources indicate that 254 army and Frontier Corps troops were killed in calendar 2004.

18. An apt phrase used by Winston Churchill, and the title of a superb book on the area by Victoria Schofield (Tauris Parke Paperbacks, 2003).

19. The Pakistan army's mechanization process was almost halted because the M-113 programme could not continue, and the PAF's F-16s were running out of spares. The army's helicopters, too, suffered from lack of parts and no upgrades were possible, while the navy's frigates had inadquate close-in protection. It was fortunate for Pakistan that it had not chosen the Abrams tank.

20. http://www.fas.org/terrorism/at/.

21. With thanks to the CRS, and especially to Alan Kronstadt whose personal assistance is much appreciated.

22. See the Federation of American Scientists' site at http://www.fas.org/terrorism/at/ docs/2004/PakMNNAdesignation.pdf.

23. See the Center for Defense Information: 'US Arms Transfers to America's Newest 'Major non-NATO Ally',' at http://www.cdi.org/program/document.cfm?document id=2443&programID=73&from_page=../friendlyversion/printversion.cfm.

24. The Secretary of State, Dr Condoleezza Rice, visited India, Pakistan and Afghanistan from 16-18 March 2005, and was asked repeatedly about possible provision of

F-16s, with India reiterating its considerable concerns. The announcement was made a week later, prompting official criticism in New Delhi.

25. For a well-researched and comprehensive history of Pakistan's defence procurement see *Pakistan's Arms Procurement and Military Build-up 1979-99* by Ayesha Siddiqa-Agha (Palgrave 2003, and Sang-e-Meel (Pakistan) 2003).

26. Convicted of corruption associated with acquisition of container ships and Agosta submarines.

27. The United Kingdom has almost lost Pakistan as a partner in defence and other matters because the 'New Labour' government demonstrably favours India. The diplomatic skills of individuals and their rapport with senior figures in Pakistan cannot counter what is perceived in Islamabad to be British government policy. The result has been diminution of British influence to the point of nullity.

28. Russia is the main supplier of armaments to India, and the T-80 is operated only by Russia, Ukraine and Pakistan. Commercial loyalty to India and a general desire to disoblige Ukraine whenever practicable resulted in the Moscow government denying some components made only in Russia, forcing Ukraine to agree to penal terms for their supply and then to manufacture as many as it could.

29. There is no point in being able to speed around the battlefield if all that happens is fast delivery of disoriented and travel-sick soldiers. The old M-113 and its international equivalents were excruciatingly uncomfortable. Much practice is required if APC-borne soldiers are to be properly trained for operations, but exercises use up a great deal of fuel and few armies can afford to conduct prolonged realistic training. One problem with APCs is that during exercises their young commanders sometimes imagine themselves to be latter-day Guderians and try to take on AFVs, which tendency is to be deprecated.

30. See http://www.un.org/Depts/dpko/dpko/co_mission/unosomi.htm which is 'Not an official document of the United Nations. Prepared for the Internet by the Information Technology section/Department of Public Information (DPI). Maintained by the Peace and Security Section of DPI in cooperation with the Department of Peacekeeping Operations.' It should be noted that in the Pakistan Army the correct rank description is 'brigadier' and not 'brigadier general'.

31. Description by reporter Richard Dowden http://www.somaliawatch.org/archivedec/01/011218201.htm) in which he states the Marines made a considerable mistake when they ordered the arrested people to separate, with 'Whites over here; Somalis over there'.

32. See William J. Durch, *UN Peacekeeping, American Politics and the Uncivil Wars of the 1990s*, (Macmillan 1997), an admirable collection of essays, edited by Durch who himself wrote the chapter on Somalia, titled 'Introduction to Anarchy: Humanitarian Intervention and "State-Building' in Somalia", a penetrating analysis which should be required reading on every course of instruction concerned with peacekeeping. Another valuable reference is William Shawcross, *Deliver us from Evil, Warlords and Peacekeepers in a World of Endless Conflict*, Bloomsbury 2000, especially Chapter 4.

33. Information from a Pakistani officer.

34. The US State Department account is somewhat different. 'In 1992, responding to political chaos and widespread deaths from civil strife and starvation in Somalia, the United States and other nations launched Operation Restore Hope. Led by the Unified Task Force (UNITAF), the operation was designed to create an environment

in which assistance could be delivered to Somalia suffering from the effects of two catastrophes—one manmade and one natural. UNITAF was followed by the United Nations Operation in Somalia (UNOSOM). The United States played a major role in both operations until 1994, when US forces withdrew.' See http://www.state. gov/r/pa/ei/bgn/2863.htm.

35. See *The Nation* 9 & 10 March 2005 for a news item at http://nation.com.pk/daily/ mar-2005/9/index12.php and an editorial at http://nation.com.pk/daily/mar-2005/10/ editorials3.php.

36. Human Rights Watch HRW Vol 16, No 10 C, July 2004. At http://hrw.org/ reports2004/pakistan0704/

37. 'India and Pakistan: Can They Arrange a Cold War?'

38. Bruce Riedel, 'American Diplomacy and the 1999 Kargil Summit at Blair House,' Policy Paper Series 2002 (Philadelphia: Center for the Advanced Study of India, University of Pennsylvania, May 2002), Internet: http://www.sas.upenn.edu/casi.

39. Howard W. French and Celia W. Dugger, 'US India-Pakistan Mission Fails to Ease the Standoff,' *The New York Times*, 16 May 2002: http://www.nytimes. com/2002/05/16/international/asia/16STAN.html. George Perkovitch is a Senior Associate at the Carnegie Endowment for International Peace and author of, *inter alia*, the magisterial *India's Nuclear Bomb*, (California: University of California Press, 1999).

Afterword

In October 2005, at the time this third edition was being prepared, there was a horrendous earthquake in Kashmir and northern Pakistan. The casualty figures are meaningless, because it is impossible for most of us to imagine 60,000 dead (and the final figure may be even higher). What is possible, however, is to imagine the despair of those left alive, who have lost their nearest and dearest and are bereft of even the basic necessities for survival. They deserve our long-term sympathy and help.

The army suffered several hundred casualties in the forward areas in Kashmir because trench systems caved in during the massive jolting. Nevertheless, it came quickly to the aid of the civilian population in areas it could reach. There were complaints, of course, that it was not fast enough and did not have enough equipment to properly carry out relief. Quite true: it did not have enough equipment; but it was as speedy as it could be in the circumstances. Its loss of a helicopter and crew was tragic evidence of that.

Out of the quake, however, came some positive signs for Pakistan. First was the attitude of terrorist groups, as noted by Associated Press on 23 October when it reported that 'al-Qaeda's deputy leader Ayman al-Zawahri called on Muslims to send aid to quake victims, despite Pakistani President Pervez Musharraf's cooperation with the United States...' And even some terrorist groups based in Kashmir came to the aid of the population as a whole.

Next was President Musharraf's offer to open the Line of Control for relief efforts. No matter how difficult it is for India to accept such an initiative in practical terms, because there are obvious problems caused by both countries over almost sixty years, the reaction in Delhi was positive. It was part of the growing movement towards establishment of the trust that is so badly needed in the subcontinent.

The main positive outcome within Pakistan was the heartening response to the disaster of Pakistan as a whole. The nation showed itself to be united, although it is sad that it took a calamity to illustrate it.

A major aspect of the earthquake that is worth examining is the comparison of natural destruction with the aftermath of a nuclear weapon explosion. Nature in its fury can cause mayhem, but the result of a man-made nuclear exchange would be even more catastrophic. When the time comes for analysis of the disaster in Delhi and Islamabad, it is hoped that this point will not be disregarded.

Annexure A

Class Composition of Selected Units

	Rajputs	Jats	Gurkhas	Sikhs	Muslims	Madrasis
6 Rajputana Rifles	25%	50%			25%	
2/6 Gurkha Rifles			100%			
1 Sikh				100%		
3/15 Punjab		33%		33%	33%	
2 Madras						100%

Arms Units Allocated to Pakistan in 1947

Cavalry (armoured units):

Probyn's Horse (5th King Edward VII's Own Horse)
6th Duke of Connaught's Own Lancers
Guides Cavalry (10th Queen Victoria's Own Cavalry) (Frontier Force)
11th Prince Albert Victor's Own Cavalry (Frontier Force)
13th Duke of Connaught's Own Lancers

Artillery (former British Indian Army titles are shown in brackets):

1st Mountain Regiment (21 Mtn. Regt.)
2nd Field Régiment (3 Fd. Regt.)
3rd (Self-propelled) Field Regiment (4 [SP] Fd. Regt.)
4th Field Regiment (5 Fd. Regt.)
5th Heavy Anti-aircraft Regiment (18 HAA)
6th Light Anti-aircraft Regiment (25 LAA)

7th Field Regiment (33 Atk. Regt.)
8th Medium Regiment (38 Mdm. Regt.)
13th Survey Battery (2 Indian Svy. Bty.)
1 Air Observation Post Flight (659 AOP Flt.)
HQ 1 Army Group, Royal Pakistan Artillery (HQ Arty. 7 Div.)
HQ 2 Army Group, Royal Pakistan Artillery (HQ 2 Army Gp. RIA)

Infantry (all units had several battalions, many of which shed companies and individuals to the Indian Army):

1st Punjab Regiment
8th Punjab Regiment
Baluch Regiment
Frontier Force Regiment
Frontier Force Rifles
14th Punjab Regiment
15th Punjab Regiment
16th Punjab Regiment

Annexure B

Rank Structure of the Pakistan Army

Non-commissioned Officers (NCOs)			
RANK/ APPOINTMENT	ARMOUR	ARTILLERY	REMARKS
Lance Naik	Acting Lance Dafadar	Lance Naik	An appointment, not a rank
Naik	Lance Dafadar	Naik	Corporal
Havildar	Dafadar	Havildar	Sergeant
Company Quartermaster Havildar	Squadron Quartermaster Dafadar	Battery Quartermaster Havildar	
Company Havildar Major	Squadron Dafadar Major	Battery Havildar Major	
Battalion Quartermaster Havildar	Regimental Quartermaster Dafadar	Regimental Quartermaster Havildar	
Battalion Havildar Major	Regimental Dafadar Major	Regimental Havildar Major	

Junior Commissioned Officers (JCOs)

Equivalents in the Indian Army but in no western armed forces. All wear coloured braid (scarlet-green-scarlet) between the shoulder and the badge of rank on the epaulette. They are highly respected figures who command appropriate fighting elements and perform other duties consistent with their rank and experience in administration and technical matters.

Cavalry	Other Arms and Services	Remarks
Naib Risaldar	Naib Subedar	Wears one star
Risaldar	Subedar	Two stars
Risaldar Major	Subedar Major	Crescent

Honorary lieutenants and captains wear two and three stars respectively, but without braid. Their status is that of Subedar Major.

Commissioned ranks are conventional, from second lieutenant to general (four star rank). The rank of field marshal has not been abolished but is not in use.

Operational Gallantry Awards

1. *Nishan-i-Haider* [NH]
   The highest gallantry medal, awarded to all ranks for acts of conspicuous courage in circumstances of extreme danger.

2. *Hilal-i-Juraat* [HJ]
   Awarded to officers for acts of valour, courage, or devotion to duty.

3. *Sitara-i-Juraat* [SJ]
   Awarded to all ranks for gallant and distinguished service in combat.
   (Usually awarded to officers/JCOs)

4. *Tamgha-i-Juraat* [TJ]
   Awarded to all ranks for gallantry/distinguished services in combat.

5. *Imtiazi Sanad*
   Mention in Despatches—oak leaf on appropriate campaign ribbon.

Annexure C
Glossary of Acronyms and Military Terms

AK Azad Kashmir, or 'Free' Kashmir, as Pakistan-administered Kashmir is known in Pakistan. In India it is referred to as POK, 'Pakistan-occupied Kashmir'. (The converse applies in the acronym IAK.) There is an 'AK' infantry Regiment in the Pakistan Army, and brigades along the Line of Control are known as 'AK' Brigades, as in '5 AK Brigade'.

AMX *Atelier de Construction d'Issy-les-Moulineux*, the French maker of tanks and other armoured vehicles. 'AMX-13' is, for example, a French medium tank.

Armd. Armoured; usually pertaining to tanks. Armd. Bde.: Armoured Brigade (Armd. Bde., q.v.).

Armd. Bde. Armoured brigade; usually of two tank regiments, an infantry battalion (generally in armoured personnel carriers), and an artillery regiment.

Armd. Div. Armoured division; usually of two armoured (tank) brigades, and one each of infantry and artillery. The infantry would desirably (but not always) be mounted in armoured personnel carriers, and the artillery would be self-propelled; that is, the gun barrels mounted on tracked chassis rather than on wheels and towed by a truck.

Bde. Brigade; a subordinate formation of a division.

BRBD Bambanwala-Ravi-Bedian-Dibalpur Canal in Punjab. Sometimes referred to as the BRB canal.

Brig. Brigadier. Commander of a brigade or a senior staff officer. US usage refers to this rank as one star (for the insignia worn). The holder is regarded as a general in the US army (and air force), a practice that was discarded by the British in the 1920s. The Bangladesh army has copied US nomenclature, but India and Pakistan, as yet, have not. Equivalents in the navy and air force are commodore and air commodore.

Cav. Cavalry; usually a tank regiment, as in '6 Cav. Regt.', but can be a reconnaissance regiment with light armoured vehicles.

CFL The Cease-fire Line in Kashmir established under UN supervision in 1949. Replaced by the Line of Control (LoC, q.v.).

CGS Chief of the General Staff. In the Pakistan Army, the senior staff officer of all. In some other former British Commonwealth armies it formerly signified the commander of the army but is now considered an old-fashioned term.

C.-in-C. Commander-in-Chief

CO Commanding officer of a unit, i.e. an infantry battalion, artillery regiment, armoured regiment. Usually a Lt.-Col., q.v.. Unit commanders in the Indian army are full colonels.

COAS Chief of the Army Staff. A misnomer, as he is not just chief of the staff officers, but commander of the army.

COS Chief of Staff. In a division, a colonel, the senior staff officer. In a corps, a brigadier or major-general. At GHQ, it used to signify the army commander himself, before that title was altered to COAS (q.v.).

DGMO Director-General Military Operations, *see*, DMO.

Div. Division. A formation of, usually, three brigades (Bdes., q.v.). The smallest military organization capable of sustained independent action, because it has extensive integral logistic support. An infantry division has only one tank regiment allocated but will have two or more infantry brigades; an armoured division will usually have two armoured brigades and one infantry brigade, usually mounted in armoured personnel carriers.

DMO Director of Military Operations. A brigadier. When it was considered necessary to have a higher-ranking officer as the senior officer involved in day-to-day operational matters, he was titled DGMO.

EME Electrical and Mechanical Engineers. A supporting service of the fighting (combat) arms of the army. It is responsible for the technical maintenance of all equipment, which it undertakes in barracks and in the field, for which it receives too little praise. Its technicians repair tanks (for example) in just as dangerous conditions as the forward troops.

FF Regt. Frontier Force Regiment; a multi-battalion infantry regiment.

GHQ General Headquarters. The main headquarters of the Pakistan Army, in Rawalpindi.

GOC General Officer Commanding. In the Pakistan Army, a major-general commanding a division. In some armies he is known simply as 'the commander', and 'GOC' refers to the officer commanding, oddly enough, a Command, which might, for example, be Training Command, or Logistics Command. You really have to be military to understand all these things, and I'm not convinced, even then, that we know what we're talking about.

Gp. Group; as in '71 Mountain Brigade Group', which was a brigade allocated more than the normal amount of combat and logistic units. It could operate outside divisional command, reporting directly to the next higher HQ, if so ordered.

HMG His Majesty's Government

IAF Indian Air Force

Indep. Independent; usually of a brigade that is capable of operating independently of a division because of extra integral combat and logistic support.

Inf. Infantry. Inf. Bde.: a brigade (Bde., q.v.) of infantry. Similarly Inf. Div(ision) (q.v.).

LoC Line of Control in Kashmir, established in 1972.

Lt.-Col. Lieutenant-Colonel: the commander of a battalion or similar-sized unit, or middle-ranking staff officer.

Lt.-Gen. Lieutenant-General: commander of a corps, or a principal staff officer—i.e., the most senior staff officer there is. US convention is to refer to this rank as a three-star general; this has caught on in other countries.

Maj.-Gen. Major-General: Commander of a division (*see*, GOC), or senior staff officer. A two-star general; *see above*.

Mtn. Mountain. A term referring to brigades and divisions specially trained to operate in their eponymous terrain. They have only light artillery, and no tanks.

O Gp. Orders Group: the gathering of officers by a commander for the purpose of issuing orders. An infantry brigade commander would have the COs of his infantry battalions and artillery regiment, together with officers from armoured element(s), if allocated, and other arms and services.

ORBAT Order of Battle: the listing of troops available for operations, usually in the form of the numbers of units, brigades, divisions, corps. It is rarely a reliable indicator of true comparative strengths because units might not be up to strength; brigades might consist of any number of units—even up to seven on occasions; and divisions the same, with varying numbers of brigades. Training standards, equipment, and other variables are not addressed.

PSO Personal Staff Officer. A senior officer (brigadier or above) appointed as adviser, confidant, filter, and organizer to a very senior officer, usually a commander-in-chief, army chief—or military president.

QMG Quartermaster-General. The senior logistician. Usually a lieutenant-general.

Regt. Regiment. Units of armour and artillery are regiments; so, confusingly, are agglomerations of infantry battalions, e.g., the Frontier Force Regiment, the Punjab Regiment, and so on.

UNMOGIP United Nations Military Observer Group in India and Pakistan.

Bibliography

Abid, Ali (ed.) (1986), *The Secret Documents Recovered from the US Embassy Tehran*, Karachi: Fore-runners Publications.

Ahmed, G. (1986), *Pakistan Meets Indian Challenge*, Lahore: Islamic Book Foundation.

Ahmed, S. (1973), *The Indo-Pak Clash in the Rann of Kutch*, Rawalpindi: Army Education Press.

Akhund, Iqbal (2000), *Trial and Error*, Karachi: OUP.

Andrew, C., (1995), *For the President's Eyes Only*, London: HarperCollins.

Anwar, R. (1998), *The Terrorist Prince: the Life and Death of Murtaza Bhutto*, Lahore: Vanguard Books.

Arif, K.M. (1995), *Working with Zia: Pakistan's Power Politics 1977–1988*, Karachi: Oxford University Press.

Bammi, Y.M. (2002), *Kargil, the Impregnable Conquered*, Delhi: Gorkha Publishers.

Baxter, Craig, and Kennedy, Charles (eds.) (2001), *Pakistan 2000*, London: Oxford University Press.

Baweja, Harinder (2000), *A Soldier's Diary*, New Delhi: Books Today.

Bhutto, Z.A. (1971), *The Great Tragedy*, Karachi: Pakistan People's Party.

Brecher, M. (1959), *Nehru: A Political Biography*, London: Oxford University Press.

Brines, R. (1968), *The Indo-Pakistani Conflict*, London: Pall Mall Press.

Brown, W.N. (1963), *The United States and India and Pakistan*, Cambridge, Mass: Harvard University Press.

Burke, S.M., and Ziring, L. (1990), *Pakistan's Foreign Policy, An Historical Analysis*, Minneapolis: University of Minnesota Press.

Chari, P.R., Cheema, P.I., Iftekharuzzaman (eds.) (1996), *Nuclear Non-proliferation in India and Pakistan: South Asian Perspectives*, Lahore: Vanguard Books.

Chenevix-Trench, Charles, (1988), *The Indian Army and the King's Enemies*, London: Thames and Hudson.

Chishti, F.A. (1996), *Betrayals of Another Kind: Islam, Democracy and the Army in Pakistan*, Lahore: Jang Publishers.

Singh, Sukhwant (1981), *The Liberation of Bangladesh*, Vol. 1, New Delhi: Vikas Publishing House.

Sisson, R., and Rose, L.E. (1992), *War and Secession: Pakistan, India and the Creation of Bangladesh*, Karachi: Oxford University Press.

Smith, C. (1994), *India's Ad Hoc Arsenal: Direction or Drift in Defence Policy?*, New York, NY: Oxford University Press.

Syed, A.M. (1992), *The Twin Era of Pakistan: Democracy and Dictatorship*, New York, NY: Vantage Press.

Tahir-Kheli, S.R. (1998), *India, Pakistan and the United States: Breaking with the Past*, Lahore: Vanguard Books.

Verghese, B.G. (1966), *India Answers Pakistan*, Bombay.

Verma, Ashok (2000), *Kargil: Blood on the Snow*, New Delhi: Manohar.

Viceroy's Personal Reports. In the series *India, the Transfer of Power*, HMSO, London, 1980, 1981, 1983.

Vorys, K.V. (1965), *Political Development in Pakistan*, Princeton, NJ: Princeton University Press.

Wirsing, R.G. (1991), *Pakistan's Security Under Zia, 1977–1988: The Policy Imperatives of a Peripheral Asian State*, London: Macmillan Academic and Professional Ltd.

Wolpert, Stanley (1993), *Zulfi Bhutto of Pakistan: His Life and Times*, New York, NY: Oxford University Press.

Wright, A. (1972), *The Indo-Pakistani War 1965*, Unpublished Thesis.

Ziring, L. (1971), *The Ayub Khan Era: Politics in Pakistan, 1958–1969*, Syracuse, NY: Syracuse University Press.

Ziring, L. (1997), *Pakistan in the Twentieth Century*, Karachi: Oxford University Press.

Index